D1190225

REMEMBER

—when Jerry Lee shook
—Little Richard rattled
—Haley rolled
—and Elvis was King?

REMEMBER

—when school was out
—and there was a Whole Lotta Shakin' Goin' On?

WELL

—put on your high heel sneakers
and relive the Golden Age of Rock,
the days of the Big Bopper and
Conway Twitty, of Buddy Holly and
Gene Vincent, in Ian Whitcomb's
glorious tribute to the music that
shook the world.

*Ian Whitcomb was part of the British invasion
of the American charts with his record 'You
Turn Me On'. He is now a disc jockey, writer,
film-maker, record producer and blues
pianist – and, of course, a rock'n'roll fanatic.
He lives in Los Angeles.*

WHOLE LOTTA' SHAKIN'

A Rock 'n' Roll Scrapbook

IAN WHITCOMB

ARROW BOOKS

in association with

ACKNOWLEDGEMENTS

This book has been a long time coming. It began as a lunch-time idea thrown at EMI publishers Ron White and Pat Howgill, expanded into an EMI picture-songbook, went through the hands of various book publishers and finally emerged as a definite future project at Arrow Books. Meanwhile, I had assembled a half dozen scrapbooks full of clippings and pictures from the pop music press circa 1954–65 (together with my own scrawled notes which needed a code to break) and by the time these books reached their final publisher, Arrow, several years had gone by and two chapters were missing. So were all the photographs, carefully culled from the wondrous archives of Camera Press.

I am not the easiest person in the world to do business with as I have a tendency to fly off to California whenever a deal is solidifying in London, and to fly back whenever I have a chance of joining the great brotherhood of Hollywood stars. I'm good at throwing out ideas and phrases and then letting the professionals cement down those ideas and correct the grammar. But I want here and now to thank all those who have sweated to put this book of celebration together: Richard Evans, my editor at Arrow, Leslie Gardner, my literary agent at London Management, Pat Howgill and Ron White of EMI Music, Michael Ochs of the Michael Ochs Archives, all those who helped at Camera Press, the staff and workers at the British Museum Newspaper Library at Colindale, the editors of *New Musical Express*, *Record Mirror*, *Disc* and *Melody Maker*, and, finally, my mother, who has yet again allowed me to use her very fine dining room table on which to assemble a book, while she has been reduced to eating off an unsteady bridge table in the drawing room.

Rock on!

Ian Whitcomb
Box 451, Altadena, California 91001
USA

WHO'LL STOP THE RAIN?
SETTING THE SCENE

This is a book about heroes of rock'n'roll. It is unashamedly partisan, and nostalgic. It looks back fondly to a golden age and marks that age's end. It regards the British Invasion of the sixties as the Eve of Destruction. It is thoroughly reactionary, but it is honest.

The heroes, fully-armed and belching beat, struck a grey Britain suddenly in its sleep. Where had it come from? America, of course – the land of dreams where comic-strip life happened and there was never any powdered egg, kirby grips, cinema queues, liberty bodices, tea cosies or school caps. The heroes – Bill Haley, Elvis Presley, Gene Vincent, Jerry Lee Lewis, Eddie Cochran, Buddy Holly & Co. – helped millions of teenagers through a bleak era. They allowed us to say a temporary 'goodbye to all that': to the agonies and embarassments of growing up. They delayed the journey into adulthood with its drudgeries such as responsibility, getting a job, settling down, raising a family, changing nappies. Like a good thriller the rocker heroes were bursting with the prurience of arrested adolescence.

For it was truly wonderful to see a grown man like Jerry Lee Lewis stalking the top of his grand piano declaring that there was a whole lotta shakin' going on, and challenging all comers to contest that statement. And to see Little Richard, with those jingly hypnotic eyes, scream on stage at a wandering spotlight to get right back and focus on HIM because he was the STAAAAAR!!

Anything could happen when these wild, natural men were around. They were our alter egos. They did things on stage that off-stage would put them in the nearest jail.

At the start, from 1955, the effect of the heroes had

Elvis Presley at school. Third row, eighth from the left.

to be seized from gramophone records (backed by pix and stories in pop newspapers and annuals). These were purchased on nice, safe, thick 78s from a High Street record shop, just near the sweet shop. So we got a music shorn of its stormy historical background: rockabilly without rednecks; rhythm & blues without racism. What a wonderful way to escape the gloom of Fifties Britain by shutting yourself in your bedroom, flopping onto the bed and spinning a disc on the Dansette that took you straight to Saturday night and you just got paid, you're fool about your money, don't try to save, your heart says go! go! have a time! Well it's Saturday night and baby you feel fine! You're gonna: RIP IT UP!!

And so, while the western world lost its strong and morally certain heroes (like Douglas MacArthur and Winston Churchill) and while Britain, in particular, messed about in a shambles like Suez and quickly shed its Empire and greatness, these wild rock'n'roll heroes took the place of that vanished supremacy. They were musical Bulldog Drummonds, Tarzans, John Waynes and James Deans. They were the new heroes.

For me, the Britain before rock'n'roll struck had been a prison. A cosy and comfy one, with plenty of hot tea and toast – but a prison just the same. A green, pleasant and *boring* land, full of soft refreshing rain. In 1954, on the eve of the heroes' attack, we'd had the worst summer in 100 years. Was it due to Atom Bomb Tests? Or Russians? The newspapers revelled in tales of the fall of those who strayed from the normal path: Lord Montagu and Peter Wildeblood were on trial for getting pleasure from young men. Turn another page and you find details of Roberta Cowell, the chap who'd changed sex and was now a freak. Gilbert Harding, pundit and a star of 'What's My Line', wrote about the British and their Saturday pleasures. At the dog races he found a 'depressed and depressing crowd . . . refreshing themselves with repulsive mineral waters or sloshy tea in cracked mugs. Or else they stand in an interminable queue to go to the lavatory.' Everybody was slouching or sitting, watching others doing things – on the screen, or on the soccer field. 'Strapping young men are letting their muscles get flabby, frightened lest they muss up their greasy hair.'

The Teddy Boys, of course, were trying to stir up some kind of action, mostly by blind brutality to helpless objects like lamp-posts and letter boxes. As yet they had no music to accompany their violence – except for pea-soup dance bands reeking of pre-war, and seedy revivalist jazz bands. Editorials wailed on about 'teenage layabouts, floppers, lumps of human flotsam washed up by the jazz tide. These youngsters should be athletes, footballers, swimmers or mountain climbers'. Tom Finney, soccer star, told them to 'get their hair cut and put hair grease on old football boots'. Jim Peters, marathon runner, was quoted: 'Youngsters are buying one-way tickets to nowhere. Leaders of men never came out of rhythm clubs.'

Even the Public School men who had provided the leaders in Empire days were a sorry bunch. The papers reported high jinks at the exclusive Hurlingham Club: eggs, buns and salads were hurled one riotous Saturday night. Swans were chased by wild-eyed young bloods, some of whom dived into the pond in black tie kit, encouraged by shrieking debutantes.

What were the alternatives, the escapes? The papers showed big-busted glamour girls for us to drool over, and trilby-hatted punters gave us sure winners at the races. And there was always the Pools as the ultimate jackpot to paradise.

Winter came and it was just like summer. I retreated more and more into Kid Colt comics and tough tales of U.S. marines at Iwo Jima. I turned up my pyjamas to look like blue jeans. I prayed for something to happen . . . The Heroes were coming!

1955
HALEY BOOGIES IN
BUT BOONE'S FOOTSTEPS ARE FAMILIAR

'Mister Sandman, I'm so alone,
Ain't got nobody to call my own . . .'

As the car bowled up the never-ending drive, deep in the heart of Dorset, far from Hopalong Cassidy, Desperate Dan and Tennessee Ernie Ford, I murmured and muttered snatches of pop, bearing in mind that a Scout whistles or hums under all difficulties.

'The naughty lady of Shady Lane
Has hit the town like a bomb . . .'

I was shielding myself from impending doom: first term at Public School, end of childhood. Would they allow comics, would they allow pop?

'Hey Mambo, Mambo Italiano!' A final incantation as we rounded a bend and there waiting solidly but without open arms was the huge stone pile called Bryanston. There was absolutely nothing wrong with it, very sensibly designed, every stone fitting with sweet reason, every window placed with taste. Nothing to moan about.

I had been a pop follower since the Forties, had been up Mockingbird Hill, danced to the Tennessee Waltz, and Wigwalk, and watched the lightning stalking around 'This Ole House', as told to me by Rosemary Clooney (Billie Anthony had a British version, but I preferred Clooney). She was bright and cheerful and tingly as toothpaste when she asked 'Where Will The Dimple Be?' and then jolly Guy Mitchell, taking time off from his nautical songs, entered the house to sing, 'Knees up, pat him on the bo-po'. But then – whoosh! – you could be up and away with Jo Stafford flying the ocean in a silver plane, seeing the jungle when it's wet with rain, always remembering that 'You Belong To Me'. That last lovey-dovey stuff I could do without. I just ignored it and went with the melody and general thrust.

Other boys had their passions, collecting stamps or cheese labels, charting international batting averages. But I was following the record star steeplechase in the weekly pop music papers. The *New Musical Express* was cunningly laid out like a real newspaper with columns and headlines and its size and feel was so authentic that you could sit in the library scanning it whilst surrounded by more serious boys who were ploughing through dreary acres of news about the imminence of push-button nuclear wars which might end the human race in thirty minutes or the rail strike and the steel strike, or Winston Churchill's retirement and Anthony Eden's illnesses and Eisenhower's heart attack. A world of grey-suited men with serious expressions and no music in their lives. A world of magistrates and judges whose judgements came down to us weekly in the *News Of The World*.

I pick up the *Dorset Express* and here we are again: George Blizzard, kitchen assistant at Bryanston School, charged with grievous bodily harm, namely breaking a beer bottle over the head of a dance band vocalist, ripping off a sax player's dickey, and slitting a drum skin with a razor. And all this at the Blandford Corn Exchange Dance.

I'd seen this George in all his finery on Saturday afternoons, hanging around the Paradise Cafe off Blandford High Street. I used to cycle from Bryanston and arrive hot and sticky and self-conscious in baggy grey shorts, neither long shorts nor short longs. I'd buy my pop paper and then stagger down to this Paradise Cafe to spy on George and his gang as they mooched and milled, smoking hard, looking for action through hooded eyes, jerking their necks and shoulders in order to re-arrange their Edwardian gentleman outfits. They were rustic Teddy Boys complete with long drape jackets with velvet lapels, drainpipe trousers, pointed black shoes, and above their ruddy faces rolled a wave of greased hair. But just as I'd begun to think how native they seemed, with their echoes of the Edwardian toff or roué (as in 'Gilbert The Filbert') they'd speak – in a cowboy B-picture drawl. That drew my attention to their Mississippi gambler ties, the 'bolos'. Then George turned on his high Mexican-style heel and swaggered into the 'Paradise' calling for egg and chips and 'Shake, Rattle & Roll' on the juke box. And I staggered off, shorts riding up the side of my thighs, face downcast, envying their toughness, beefiness and style.

Of course, I'd heard about the Teds the year before. It was all over the newspapers. They broke this and they smashed that – for no particular reason. They were the 'rough element', the 'common types', the 'vulgar boys' you were supposed to stay clear of, and the school gates certainly emphasised the gap between us. When George worked in the school kitchen he was very 'Gaffer Garge', very quiet and forelock-tugging. Something of the school ethos, saturated into the walls, steamed off and affected this rough-hewn brick of a bloke as he stirred the porridge. He was meek but in the street the dangerous side showed.

Up until the end of 1954 the Teds had no rallying music, no rollicking call-to-arms battle hymn for their new republic. Every so often a real rhythm number got into the Hit Parade – like Tennessee Ernie's 'Shotgun Boogie' with its thrillingly incoherent lyrics about having a 'sixteen-gauge choked down lak a raffle'; or his 'Kiss Me Big' which commanded the girl, 'Don't turn me loose till it curls mah toes'. Both these records rolled along to a masturbatory boogie beat, whipped by precision revolver shots from the snare drum. But such songs were few and far between. The restless ones would have to wait until Rock 'n' Roll sprang upon us in 1955 via renegade music master Bill Haley.

Meanwhile, lie low till the holidays when you can go up to London and *buy* some Bill Haley. Read the pop press, the record star annuals. Even here, in the glossy, creamy printed page, times are changing, times are a-movin': 'And in view of the fantastic caprices of this crazy business, where the record is now king and the stars flood across to us on hot wax from America, there may be three or four new names on the scene between the time this is written and the time it appears in print!'

At the moment, here in early 1955, the vocalists, both ballad singers and belters, are out in front. *Melody Maker*, viewing the pop scene from a jazz slant, rues the absence of true jazz heroes from the best selling lists, complains about the tired sound of the average British dance band. Same old number of brass and saxes and rhythm section, same old voicings, same old burbling vocals, same old sandwiching of soppy vocals mooing about unrequited love between stodgy chunks of instrumental brass stabs and piano tinkles. Same old dance hall, too, with drab shopgirls and clerks all trying to look older than they really were, all shuffling like commuter crowds at Waterloo, one-way round the hall and no bumping please. Were they dancing or merely walking with a shuffle? Every now and then somebody would skip like a soldier changing step. Yes, they were dancing just as they had done since 1939, and through the war and all through the Age of Austerity.

But lately, from out of the moribund dance band scene, these unattached vocalists have appeared and have set the girls screaming and crying and carrying on. But *Melody Maker* can't stand these new vocalists. What has all this got to do with music? With jazz? More of these mooing drips hanging onto the mike for dear life . . .

New Musical Express and the Christmas pop annuals don't share this view on the whole. Like good journalists they reflect what their market wants to know: 'I like pickles', says Johnnie Ray wearing a sensational houndstooth jacket and sports shirt. He used to be a bell-hop, and that was before he graduated to garage hand. Frankie Laine used to be a shipping clerk, and that was when he was Frankie Lo Vecchio. Guy Mitchell grew up amongst the coal miners of Colorado and he was Al Cernik. Dickie Valentine a page-boy, David Whitfield a concrete loader . . . All humble origins and then big break by way of a gimmick and a name change and *abracadabra* they're one of the great brotherhood of stars. And from record stardom they will try hard to enter all-round show business – variety, cabaret, movies.

Nor are these new record stars mere mooers or moaners. They're not like Crosby, casual and easygoing with a pipe in his mouth, one hand in one pocket and the other wielding a golf club. No, this new breed are story tellers who really get into their songs. Like Frankie Laine, the working stiff in the smart Italian shiny suits, who sings of the devil Jezebel and of himself as the Rock of Gibraltar having to deal with temptation and jealousy – which he does, in a voice like a hurricane whipping across steel tonsils. 'I have a voice like a horn because I want the folks to hear me. I'm no crooner – I give out!'

He did, and the girls screamed and cried at this Clark Kent. They didn't mind him wearing his glasses on stage. Just as they didn't mind Johnnie Ray wearing his deaf aid. This made the singers appear vulnerable – they had been visibly affected by life's stresses and strains. But Laine looked like he could take care of himself in a scrap. Johnnie Ray, skinny and gangly and lost, looked like he had just come out of a scrap – and come out badly.

Instead of being content with making the girls cry Ray had a good cry himself. He'd started in 1952 with 'Cry', a real smasheroo hit. Soon he was 'The Cry Guy', 'The Nabob of Sob', 'The Prince of Wails' and he was over here playing the Palladium, wandering across that big stage (where Danny Kaye and Judy Garland had seemed *so* certain) like a puppet whose puppeteer wants desperately to go to the lavatory. Then he'd suddenly stop dead, quivering with emotion, and stamp his foot like a child demanding candy. And he'd punch his hand – maybe he'd punch himself next. So what if he hit a wrong note or two? It was the *emotional content* that counted.

The emotional content – that's what Mitch Miller, his A&R man, said in the papers. He ought to know because he'd steered most of the fifties balladeers and belters towards the Hit Parade: Rosemary Clooney, Doris Day, Tony Bennett, Frankie Laine, Jo Stafford – and Johnnie Ray.

I liked Ray. But I didn't go as far as some silly cows who wore bits of cinema carpet (upon which Ray had trod) round their necks. No, I was content to note his progress in a school exercise book.

We had our British record stars too, but no one to match the likes of Laine or Ray or Tennessee Ernie Ford. I think the big test is whether or not you can praise the Lord and not be excruciating or embarrassing. Laine, Ray and Ford could talk and sing about God a mere breath after they'd sung of salty sex because in America you could meet Good and Evil on the same barstool. The Frontier may have gone but the spirit was everywhere. But we knew the school chaplain would never kill a fly. He praised in that limp flat psalm chant. When we left a big brown turd (made of plastic and bought at Ellisdon's London Joke Shop) in the Divinity Room he didn't explode, he merely covered it up with a neat heap of sand.

The Big Belters were in the same league as Billy Graham. He came to Britain on a crusade in 1955, and 70,000 went to hear him at Wembley Stadium. Girls who had sung along to 'I Believe' now repeated 'I am the way, the truth and the life' after the glowing evangelist. 'Come on!' he said, 'Let's hear it again and louder!' The rain was thundering down on Greater London (not soft and refreshing and gently English) as Graham boomed out, like a singer *a cappella*, 'You have to be BORN AGAIN!' And suddenly, as he pointed to the West, rain ceased and the sun came streaming through the salmon storm clouds. 'BORN AGAIN! It is as certain as that sun which shines upon us now.'

I liked Dickie Valentine just as I liked Vera Lynn. I also liked my cousins and all my family. I felt safe with them. But neither Dickie Valentine nor Dennis Lotis could make the rain cease or the sun shine. They were not into raising the dead.

Ruby Murray, a big British star of 1955, was of the earth, the good earth, the earth of the turf fire in the evening as the sun goes down on Galway Bay. There she was, this simple Irish lass with a face like a rural Queen Elizabeth and a simple, generous homespun figure not like those Sunday paper pin-ups whose tight-sweatered bosoms seemed likely to fire away at any moment, there she was right up in the Hit Parade with the Americans. Five records in the Parade in one week.

Ruby told an annual that she kept her fan mail in rows on her dressing table. 'I like to pretend they really are my boy friends,' she said. Many of these fans were service men rotting out in the Middle East waiting for trouble, dreaming of marrying a girl like Ruby. Oh so many times did she go into print to thank all those who

Bryanston's first rock'n'roll band. Ian Whitcomb on his first electrified guitar.

had helped her to stardom, 'especially the ladies and gentlemen of the Press who have been so kind to me, and not forgetting you who have bought my records and who watched my last television show and who spoke to me last night at the stage door'.

From rip-snorting bellowers and foot-stomping cry guys to the simple 'Softly, Softly' girl, all those lucky ones who had entered this crazy record business put away their backgrounds, whether they be rough or smooth and set out to be responsible royalty in the Industry of Human Happiness, (as Thomas Edison once described the disc trade).

'Lights out and no talking now, Dorchester House!'

So the *New Musical Express* is folded and put inside *The Record Stars Annual* and put away. The others in the dorm put away their POW escape books and their Wisdens. In my cold coffin bed I pull up the alien thin sheet and the alien hairy blanket so that they cover my head. Then with face buried in skinny pillow I cast myself into a twilight dream of life 'Somewhere At The End Of The Rainbow' (as sung by Dick James and the Stargazers, with Malcolm Lockyer and the Barn-stormers, on Decca). Meanwhile voices, some piping and some croaking, start up the inevitable nightly discussion. From sports and current affairs through what's life all about anyway, to rudimentary sex.

Then suddenly Smythe-Crotchford lights upon it! His huge, hissing shortwave radio, sticking up like a tent in the dorm gloaming, has found Radio Luxembourg clearly. And out roars a honking, rattling train of sound clicketty-clacking across the sky, escorted by those apocalyptic riders, firing rim shots at any music teachers nearby, dropping molten rock 'n' roll on the whispering, spinsterish, history-laden trees of Hardy's Dorset! Bill Haley & His Comets telling everyone to –

'Shake, Rattle & Roll'!!

'Turn it off!'

'Turn it up!'

'Shut up, Smith-Crotchford!'

'QUIET IN THIS DORMITORY!'

There's no stopping this Rock 'n' Roll train, certainly not the House Captain. There's no jazzmen, no blues-men, no slums, no lynch victims, no roots, no complica-tions at all, on this train. This train is bringing the good simple news that ROCK 'N' ROLL IS HERE TO STAY.

That midnight, 16 March, 1955, I wrote in the snow on the front lawn: 'ROCK 'N' ROLL IS HERE TO STAY'.

'There will be severe repercussions for whoever did that'.

If ever I got out again into the Other World I would buy some Bill Haley & His Comets. There was something deliciously harsh and metallic about this name, even without the whizzing music attached to it. When you coupled it with the words 'Rock 'n' Roll' the whole thing

was irresistible, and so when the Easter holidays came I rushed to London to see what I could buy.

Up west, and especially down around Charing Cross Road, clustered the trading outposts of American magic. The record shops, music shops, film companies, formed part of a multi-decker sandwich that also in-cluded marital aid centres, strip clubs and tobacconists displaying physique magazines. The streets were nar-row, the buildings disapprovingly Victorian, and the whole area seemed to be smothering in a blanket of soot. Black was the colour but brightness was on sale. Ameri-can-style casual wear – jackets you didn't have to wear with a tie and check shirts, tight trousers and blue jeans. There was the smell of fried onions coming from a hamburger place next door. There were the shops with glinting instruments hanging up like best cuts of meat – saxes, brass, and drum kits, amongst the accordions and ukuleles. There was Dobell's Jazz Record shop.

In here I was full of fright. These men knew their music and it was jazz all the way. Stern of feature, often pointing inflammable beards, they challenged you to know such passwords as Getz, Mulligan (Gerry), Stitt, Monk. Trembling and pink I asked for Haley and was given the freeze. My man returned to his interrupted discussion about the use of parallel fifth riffs, and I quickly retreated from this intellectual G-clipping.

Instead I slunk into cinema's darkness to see *Black-board Jungle* and here I got satisfaction from seeing a class of juvenile delinquents smashing up the jazz record collection of their teacher. But more important was the theme song: 'Rock Around The Clock' played by Haley & The Comets. I had read about the effect of this new Haley release. In America the fans were adopting 'Clock' as their rallying cry, their call to arms. Biffing out of the cinema speakers the song sound linked the new music with bad boys, punch-ups, all kinds of misbe-haviour. So down Oxford Street I raced to buy the record at the HMV shop.

You could audition your prospective purchase in record shops then. You took your time because records were expensive and breakable. You valued them the more. To be a record act seemed as lofty as being a film star. The record company headquarters were guarded by old men in uniforms covered with medals and ribbons and there was no way in for the likes of me, but once I saw an American lady singer coming out of EMI and she was dripping in furs and laden with diamonds. I'm sure she sang of cocktails and moonlight trips to heaven with a sophisticate in a yacht, a scene beyond my ken. Bill Haley had entered the record world with an earthier flavour. HMV had a big poster of him and his Comets, and they looked like big, broad, genial bruisers, with jackets that suggested a circus – dinner jackets in plaid – and a general aura of Western gangsterism. They might be owlhoot hi-jackers of the plains, but on the other hand they could be Hoppy and his pals on Halloween.

I immediately got hold of a photo of Haley & the Comets for use at school. It was sellotaped to the front of my History Assignment folder and it was my gesture towards the Rock 'n' Roll movement. Now, as the summer term began, bringing with it langorous afternoons of cricket and river bathing, I chose to forget the panorama of pop which hitherto I had keenly followed with catholicism. Now I was the local King of Beat, and the scourge of the Jazz Club. I was the first boy at school with a copy of 'Rock Around The Clock' and I treasured it and looked at it and polished it and kept it safe in my tuck box.

Let the others score runs! Let them study Shakespeare and Ovid! Let them frolic fleet-footed up and down the idle slopes of summer. I had found my place in society and Haley was my inspiration.

What will be the next musical era?

WHAT is going to be the next era in popular music? Reader G. Butler, of 37, Hyde Meadows, Bovingdon, Herts, asks for prophecies in an interesting letter in which he says:

Over the past few years we have had different eras in the field of popular music, that is, the "Echo" era, the "Multiple" recording era, the "Mambo" era, the "Cha-Cha" era, and so on. Will they ever run out of these eras? If so, what happens?

I can't figure out what the next one will be, and it will be interesting to see. It will also be interesting to

see what era we shall have in five years hence. Anybody hazard a guess?

Another thing puzzles me. We have had all these eras one after another, but nobody has come up with a new instrument. I firmly believe that the first bandleader to come up with one and use it in his band would find himself a lot richer. Any of our present-day bandleaders got the initiative? How about a new instrument for the latest gimmick?

★　　★　　★

A Ray-ve for Burns is contained in this letter from M. Bloomfield, of Birchfield Road, Birmingham. He writes:

Re your review of "Off The Record" by Frank Harvey, this week's NME, may I say that he omitted just one word. It should have read " Outstanding World Class."

I name Ray Burns without hesitation the outstanding vocalist in Great Britain and had he been allowed to use a background such as Bethe Douglas used and been in evening dress, his rendering of " That's How A Love Song Was Born " would have forced music lovers to rush out next morning to buy this disc.

Having heard him on radio and records and having seen him on the stage (Wolverhampton Hippodrome) and on TV, may I add that his stage presence is terrific in every detail. I do hope to see him billed top at the London Palladium where he so richly deserves to be.

★　　★　　★

John Waterfield, of 55, Avondale Terrace, Devonport, Devon, writes:

It is very pleasing to

of the lack of interest ing of "The Breeze A the BBC and Radio

True, "Family Fav to my knowledge, pla now, but only because realises that it is ver the troops out in Ge far I find to my disg one else is keeping public in the dark ove this recording (and th follow) is a big hit. cause it's not " British

★　　★

Lewis Teasdale, of Grove, High Heator upon-Tyne 7, wants informed person to e: why Sarah Vaughan mercial success in th goes on to say:

Surely for clarity of of tone, flexibility of important, discerning cording material, the

RADIO LUXEMBOURG
208 Metres

BILL HALEY'S COMETS

BILL HALEY AND HIS COMETS
" Dim Dim The Lights "
" Happy Baby "
(Brunswick 05373)

BILL HALEY and his Comets follow up their hit record of " Shake, Rattle And Roll " with two more fine sides and how these boys rock!

I marvel at the wonderful beat, which is something we never seem to get in this country, and the recording engineers have decided not to hide the drummer in the background. As for the gentleman on the guitar, he really can play.

This is more than just a new record release: it is the answer to those who think that groovy records do not sell. The atmosphere on this disc is amazing and when you listen to " Happy Baby " sit back and think when you last heard something as good.

" Dim Dim The Lights " is also in the rave class and when Bill Haley sings " The beat is jumping like a kangaroo " he just about sums up the whole record.

Sorry to say it again but this is a fantastic rhythm section and if you can only afford one record this week, I suggest you make certain it is this one. You won't regret it.

★

WINIFRED ATWELL WITH FRANK CHACKSFIELD AND HIS ORCHESTRA
" Song Of The Sea "
" The Black Mask "
(Decca F.10448)

NOW that Winifred Atwell has moved back to the Decca label, some of you may be expectin

Popular records reviewed by famous Radio Luxembourg disc-jockey GEOFFREY EVERITT

think this piece of music has what again. The orchestra it takes. However, I've eaten so mainly as a backing unit many h
prophecy no diffe

Perso " other show t Winnie to you

FRAN HAYE ROBE IN

her latest sides. You can only have one real voice, Suzi, so why not stick to it?

★　　★　　★

WYNONIE "MR. BLUES" HARRIS AND HIS ORCHESTRA
" Bloodshot Eyes "
" Lollipop Mama "
(Vogue V.2127)

IF you like something that is just that bit different, then you'll go a bundle on " Bloodshot Eyes " and you can take it from me that if only this disc gets a few airings it will find its way into the best sellers.

It has terrific atmosphere and although the lyric may at times be a little doubtful, it is entertaining and highly amusing throughout.

Take my advice and get a copy of " Bloodshot Eyes "; I promise you it's a cracker.

" Lollipop Mama " is in the same vein but not as exciting, although the bass-player sets out with a fine beat and keeps things rocking all the way through.

The style is not far away from that of Bill Haley so you know roughly what to expect. Look out for " Bloodshot Eyes."

★　　★　　★

BOB JAXON
" Ali Baba "
" Why Does A Woman Cry? "
(London HL.8156)

HERE'S a new name with a brand

The day I bought 'Rock Around the Clock' I also bought 'Tiger Rag' by the Original Dixieland Jazz Band in 1918. To me it was all excitement but school jazz buffs said about both bands that they 'didn't swing'.

Wynonie Harris was serving up piping hot R'n'B – but we needed a milder curry in those days.

THE METEORIC RISE OF THE COMETS

REX MORTON tells the success story of BILL HALEY

IT happened with Don Cornell's "Hold My Hand"—and now it has happened again. this time to a rocking. rolling group known to other people. as Bill Haley and his Comets.

You'll remember the wonderful plug that Cornell's best-selling record had in an unimportant movie called "Susan Slept Here." Just having it played on the soundtrack sent an unknown platter soaring to the top of the Hit Parade.

So America Decca (Brunswick) pulled off a very smart stroke by having Haley's "Rock Around The Clock" similarly featured in "The Blackboard Jungle," a far superior movie to "Susan Slept Here" . . . thus giving Bill his third really big seller, on both sides of the Atlantic, in considerably less than twelve months.

R - and - B

The name of Haley became a household word here when " Shake, Rattle And Roll " first hurled itself across the airways last spring. Then came " Mambo Rock "—and now, still on a relentless twelve-bar blues kick, it's " Rock Around The Clock."

" Clock " came into the Best-Selling Lists for a short time last January, but then dropped out. Now, with its big film boost, it is back again.

But Bill, by popularising rhythm-and-blues in areas where it was never heard before, has not been the over-night sensation that some of you might have thought.

He was born twenty-eight years ago in Highland Park, Michigan, and he started playing his first instrument, a home-made pasteboard guitar, while still a schoolboy.

Soon he was the proud possessor of a real guitar, given to him by his father. So it came as a logical step when he started working as market-place entertainer in Booth Corner, Pennsylvania—the district to which his family moved when Bill was still very young.

All kinds of casual employment helped add valuable experience to the Haley career . . . a medicine-show tour through the Middle West, a trip through the New England states with a singing group called the Down Homers.

Two members of this unpretentious outfit decided, with Bill, to form their own unit, but it soon folded . . . though not before the distinctive Haley voice and virile manner of guitar strumming had been heard over thirty-eight different radio stations, and in forty-two of America's forty-eight states!

Saddlemen

Eventually, however, Bill returned home to Pennsylvania, heard that there was a new radio outlet (WPWA) in a township called Chester, got in touch with the owner, telling him that he had a "fine band" for him to hear.

Bill did not really have a band of any description. big. small. good or bad. But in three days he assembled one, made a successful audition, and commenced a series of daily broadcasts with his Four Aces of Western Swing!

The first Haley recording (his band was called The Saddlemen then) was " Rocket 88," made for a small local label which distributed it to the extent of some 10,000 copies. " Rock The Joint " did even better.

Nevertheless, one can confidently state that even **Bill** was surprised when "Crazy, Man, Crazy," cut for the Essex company in America just about two years ago, suddenly began to appear in *Billboard's* best-selling charts throughout America.

He had just changed his band's name to Bill Haley and his Comets at that time, prompted by Philadelphia songwriter Bix Richekner . . . and it was, of course, under this guise that Bill and his boys made their American Decca debut in June, 1954.

" Shake. Rattle and Roll," " Dim, Dim the Lights," " Mambo Rock," " Rock Around The Clock " . . . these and other titles have passed the 5,000,000 total sales mark now.

There are also estimated to be no less than 8,000 Bill Haley fan clubs in America—so, although the Rockets shot upwards towards fame quickly enough, it's a very safe bet indeed that they will stay up there among the stars much, much longer than any other pyrotechnics known to man.

" We decided to try for a new style," explains Haley. " Mostly using stringed instruments, but somehow managing to get the same effect as brass and reeds.

" Frankly, our market is the 'teenagers, and they are the ones whom we constantly try to please. We keep very close to them, listening for their new expressions of speech, and asking them what they want in the way of music."

Excitement

That's how " Crazy, Man, Crazy " —a popular high-school phrase of approval in America—came about. And that's how " Happy Baby," " Live It Up " and " Fractured " (just three of Bill's 150 original songs) originated.

One of the biggest factors in the Comets' success has been the excitement they put across on records. They admit that they model themselves closely on such " authentic " r. and b. attractions as Earl Bostic, the Wynonie Harris group, and blues-shouter Joe Turner (who originated " Shake, Rattle And Roll ").

But to these elements. they have added something of their own. Something, perhaps. drawn from the country-and-western sphere of American music. with the result that no one could ever mistake a Bill Haley performance.

Bill Haley and his Comets are likely to last as long as r. and b. lasts. And as r. and b., in one form or another, has been going on now for approximately thirty years, we can look forward to having Bill and his riotous colleagues around for quite a while yet!

NME MUSIC CHARTS

BEST SELLING POP RECORDS IN BRITAIN

Last Week	This Week		
2	1	MAN FROM LARAMIE	Jimmy Young (Decca)
3	2	COOL WATER	Frankie Laine (Philips)
6	3	BLUE STAR	Cyril Stapleton (Decca)
1	4	ROSE MARIE	Slim Whitman (London)
9	5	YELLOW ROSE OF TEXAS	Mitch Miller (Philips)
5	6	EV'RYWHERE	David Whitfield (Decca)
4	7	LEARNIN' THE BLUES	Frank Sinatra (Capitol)
7	8	THE BREEZE AND I	Caterina Valente (Polydor)
8	9	CLOSE THE DOOR	Stargazers (Decca)
18	10	HEY THERE	Rosemary Clooney (Philips)
11	11	HERNANDO'S HIDEAWAY	Johnston Brothers (Decca)
20	11	HERNANDO'S HIDEAWAY	Johnnie Ray (Philips)
—	13	ROCK AROUND THE CLOCK	Bill Haley Comets (Brunswick)
10	14	INDIAN LOVE CALL	Slim Whitman (London)
12	15	EVERY DAY OF MY LIFE	Malcolm Vaughan (HMV)
—	16	HEY THERE	Johnnie Ray (Philips)
13	17	LOVE ME OR LEAVE ME	Sammy Davis, Jnr. (Brunswick)
14	18	EV'RMORE	Ruby Murray (Columbia)
—	19	I'LL COME WHEN YOU CALL	Ruby Murray (Columbia)
17	20	HEY THERE	Lita Roza (Decca)
—	20	GO ON BY	Alma Cogan (HMV)

BEST SELLING SHEET MUSIC (BRITAIN)

Last Week	This Week		
2	1	BLUE STAR	(Chappells)
1	2	EV'RYWHERE	(Bron)
4	3	THE MAN FROM LARAMIE	(Chappells)
3	4	EVERMORE	(Rogers) 2s.
5	5	EVERY DAY OF MY LIFE	(Robbins) 2s.
11	6	THE YELLOW ROSE OF TEXAS	(Maddox)
20	7	HEY, THERE	(Frank) 2s.
7	8	LEARNIN' THE BLUES	(C. & C.) 2s.
6	9	UNCHAINED MELODY	(Frank) 2s.
9	10	CLOSE THE DOOR	(Duchess) 2s.
10	11	STARS SHINE IN YOUR EYES	(Peter Maurice) 2s.
8	12	I WONDER	(Macmelodies) 2s.
18	13	HERNANDO'S HIDEAWAY	(Frank) 2s.
13	14	COOL WATER	(Feldman) 2s.
12	15	JOHN AND JULIE	(Toff)
18	16	LOVE ME OR LEAVE ME	(Keith Prowse) 2s.
14	17	I'LL COME WHEN YOU CALL	(Michael Reine) 2s.
—	18	STRANGER IN PARADISE	(Frank)
16	19	SOFTLY, SOFTLY	(Cavendish)
23	20	GO ON BY	(Bluebird)
—	21	THE DAM BUSTERS MARCH	(Chappells) 2s. 6d.
21	22	DREAMBOAT	(Leeds)
15	23	YOU, MY LOVE	(Dash)
22	24	WHERE WILL THE DIMPLE BE	(Cinephonic)

★ BEST SELLING POP RECORDS IN THE U.S. ★

Last Week	This Week		
9	7	Seventeen	Fontane Sisters
7	8	Tina Marie	Perry Como
	9	Shifting, Whispering Sands	

Lots of cowboy-ish records hitting, and three versions of 'Hey There' from the 'Pyjama Game' musical.

THE BOONE BOOM!

The story of the new singer whose records are making a big hit— PAT BOONE

A RHYTHM-AND-BLUES song, with a rhythm-and-blues beat, but with country - and - western colorations in the sound of voice and horns, that seems to be today's most potent formula for success (witness the popularity of Bill Haley!)—and a new singer called Pat Boone is the latest to jump aboard the gravy train.

Pat's version of "Ain't That A Shame," an r and b song composed and originated by Fats Domino, reached the British market several weeks back. Nothing much happened at first, but Pat's platter entered the NME Best-Selling Chart just seven days ago, and it has started to climb faster and higher than the proverbial kite.

This is an amazing break for someone who was virtually unknown, even one who was, at the beginning of this year. So we think it's time you became acquainted with the fortunate Pat, whom Stateside columnists, falling for the obvious line, have already described as "A 'Boone' to Music."

Pat Boone, said to be a great-great-great-great-grandson of the legendary pioneer Daniel Boone, was born in Texas twenty years ago. He now attends North Texas State College as a student, but he has three weekly TV shows—and on Sundays he preaches at a Slidell, Texas, church.

A deeply religious man, Pat also finds time to be a cub-master—but it remains to be seen how long such extra-curricular activities will continue, now that the Boone voice is being heard in juke-boxes and over radio networks, not only in America but also practically everywhere the English language is spoken!

Boone began his vocal career at the age of ten, purely as a youth-club entertainer, and he made his broadcasting debut seven years later. He won the East Nashville Talent Contest at the age of eighteen, went to New York to appear on the Ted Mack Amateur Hour (a highly regarded radio programme) and won three times.

Hit debut

Arthur Godfrey also took an interest in the lad's virile stylings, and for a while Pat made the most of each day by playing one "Talent Scout" (Mack) against the other (Godfrey).

Eventually, however, he returned to Texas for further schooling, dabbled in baseball and basketball, won a sizeable number of "A" ratings in his college courses, and commences his TV shows for Texan teenagers.

Approximately six months ago, Randy Wood, of the Dot Record concern (handled by Decca's London subsidiary over here), offered Pat a contract. He cut "Two Hearts, Two Kisses Make One Love," outselling both Frank Sinatra and Doris Day on this, the first number he ever waxed!

His platter sold nearly three-quarters of a million copies throughout the U.S. . . . a fact which pleased the Dot people and Pat himself no end, as you might well imagine.

To follow through convincingly after such an impressive tee-off was, nevertheless, a problem. The song had to be exactly right for Pat, and for the public. "Ain't That A Shame" came along at precisely the right moment.

It had the kind of simplicity which spelt success. Its reputation in the r and b field was already made on the strength of Fats Domino's original version (also available here on the London label).

Pat handled it so persuasively that his rendition stayed at second place —only behind Bill Haley's "Rock Around The Clock" at first, and Mitch Miller's "Yellow Rose Of Texas" afterwards—in the U.S. sales frame for six consecutive weeks.

A Pat Boone audience in full fervour. The contemporary caption said, 'Although the girls have sophisticated hair-do's, like all teen-agers they have a tendency to puppy fat.'

THE CREW CUTS

READERS' questions on the Crew Cuts, the famous American vocal group, who have just ended their first tour of Britain, are answered here by Rudi Maugeri, the quartet's baritone and vocal arranger.

★

Q. "I saw the Crew Cuts when they were at the Finsbury Park Empire, and I liked their act very much. I particularly liked the 'Gum Drop' number, but though I have tried all my local record shops, I can't seem to buy a copy. Could you ask the Crew Cuts if they have recorded this number and where I can buy it?" (L. B., Portsmouth).

A. Yes, we have recorded this, on the Mercury label, and we are now in the top 15 on the record charts in the USA.

At the moment, I am afraid, you can't buy this record in Britain, but as soon as the distribution difficulties are ironed out, you will be able to get your copy of "Gum Drop."

★

Q. "I believe this is the first time the Crew Cuts have toured Britain. Could you ask them if there is any big difference between audiences here and in America?" (James O'Reardon, Carlisle).

A. The main difference we notice is that audiences are more reserved in Britain. In America we have a more flamboyant act, so we ask the audience to clap a lot. Over here, you don't seem to go for that kind of thing so much.

It seems British audiences like to get to know your act, and wait a while before they show their feelings. But they're great audiences, and if they like you, they let you know it.

You really feel that they're listening to you and giving you all their attention. That's not so back home.

Another thing, in the USA, you need to have a big record behind you when you go on tour. On our trip this time, there is no new top record of ours available, but it hasn't made any difference at all. We've still had a great reception everywhere we have been.

★

Q. "I am nearly 17 and want to become a member of the Crew Cuts' fan club. How do you go about it? Also, I have three girl friends at our youth club in Nottingham. We like singing together and would be grateful if you could ask the Crew Cuts for some tips on forming a vocal group." (Veronica Johnson, West Bridgeford, Notts).

A. The girl to contact about our fan club is Miss Dene Harrison, 18, Heron Road, Meols, Hoylake, Cheshire. In the USA we are the only artists to produce a regular monthly magazine for our fans.

In this, we keep all our fans in touch with all our latest news about records, etc. Next year we hope to institute the same thing here.

It is very difficult, you know, to give advice about forming a group, because every one is run differently and each one has started differently. All we can say is that you must give up everything, be prepared to starve for anything from months to years, work hard and have patience.

As it happens, all of us in the group started with a good musical training, but this is not essential. A great number of top singing stars began with no musical or technical knowledge. They just had the urge to sing, and the talent to go with it.

★

Q. "Have the Crew Cuts enjoyed their stay here? Are there any of our artists or bands that they particularly liked, and are they coming back next year?" (Jackie Sharman, London, S.W.3).

A. May we answer the first and last questions together? Yes, we like it here very much and, yes, we are coming back next spring.

We really didn't think we would have such a marvellous reception as the one we received this time. We are thrilled about it, and look forward to coming back. We are hoping to try out an idea we started out back in the States. We recently have been playing one-nighters at ballrooms, and we have had a lot of success with this. In fact, we heard from "Downbeat" that we had been voted "Top Attraction At Ballrooms."

We haven't had much opportunity to hear many of your bands, but one we must mention is that of Johnny Dankworth. This band really knocked us out, and if Johnny toured the

---

Pat Boone had to be gently persuaded to record 'Ain't That A Shame' because he didn't like the grammar lapses in the lyrics. When he came to Britain there were sighs of relief – a well-groomed college boy who crooned ballads as well as smiley beat numbers. He'd done some preaching, too.

Crew-cut hairstyles became so popular at school they had to be banned.

1956
ELVIS!
AND MORE!!

I suppose for thinking people 1956 was a terrible year. There was the Suez crisis and the Soviet crushing of the Hungarian uprising. And Elvis Presley had appeared in all his early glory.

I measured time and events in terms of pop. Elvis was the hero of 1956, the king of the new breed of solo rockers and the man who had snatched Haley's crown. But in January Haley looked like he could do no wrong. He was No. 1 in the charts with 'Rock Around The Clock' and he went on to bombard us with records like 'See You Later, Alligator', 'Razzle, Dazzle', 'The Saints Rock And Roll' and 'Rockin' Through The Rye'. All good locomotive numbers with Bill as train conductor, shovelling on the coal and collecting the tickets.

I wasn't completely alone at school with my liking for the big beat. Gradually a circle of juniors formed around me and my records. We got a gramophone and played Haley at full blast from our junior house room. A record by the Crew Cuts, 'Sh-Boom', had an anarchic effect on the Sea Cadet Corps drilling just outside our house room window: at each 'Sh-Boom' a few cadets would change step and this disruptive action tied us in with the press reports of rock riots in America. Poor Haley had been picketed in Alabama by the White Citizens' Council: 'Ask Your Preacher About Jungle Music' – but I was glad to read that teenage counter-demonstrators had held up a sign saying 'Rock And Roll Is Here To Stay'.

Of course, I had written this in the snow the year before, but I can't claim to be the first. Reports had come in of rock slogans appearing all over the western world. The *Dorset Express* told of a demand in green paint on a wall of the ancient Shire Hall at Taunton, Somerset: 'We Want Bill Haley'. There's nothing like a good slogan to banish life's complexity. Everything should be expressed briefly and without too much thought. Instinct is all. But instincts were in trouble here in the fifties and life was the spicier for that. The White Citizens' Council were on the attack again in February. Member Asa Carter told a disc jockey over the air during a Rhythm & Blues broadcast: 'Rock and Roll is a means of pulling down the white man to the level of the Negro. It is part of a plot to undermine the morals of the youth of our nation. It is sexualistic, un-moralistic and the best way to bring people of both races together.' As far as we rock fans were concerned Negroes didn't really come into the matter – we could take them or leave them. We liked Rock 'n' Roll. But this sort of racial slur incensed the jazz fraternity at school.

The school jazz band, having done quite well in both 'O' levels and 'A' levels, were now allowed to play again, within reason. They guarded their new freedom and weren't about to allow a lowering of standards. They guarded their music, hewn out by Negroes from a mountain of oppression, with great jealousy and they took umbrage at the current debasement of syncopation by us beat merchants. Our music was the deadly nightshade sprung from their jazz garden. Ladey, jazz club secretary issued a statement from his study: 'Shake, Rattle And Roll' was an old traditonal black saying, as in 'Shake, rattle and roll them dice', a crap game call. 'See You Later, Alligator' was equally old, being a typical piece of black 'jive talk', dating back to at least the 1930s. A typical reply might be, 'Be On Time, Porcupine'. We had raided their jazz.

I noticed that most jazz fiends were badly-built, frequently weedy and be-spectacled and spotty. They read too many books, as opposed to magazines and annuals. Not that I was keen on team games and mass exercise – but the running about could produce supermen. I meant a First Eleven rock hero – that would be something!

Meanwhile, news was coming in about an extraordinary film. At least, its *effect* was extraordinary. *Rock Around The Clock*, the film, was out in America and causing disturbances. There was even one on the campus

of Princeton, a high class university. When the film reached Britain journalists had a whale of a time, although they had had to wait till after the film had played 300 cinemas before there was any trouble. 2,000 Teddy Boys had rampaged through the streets of South London, leaving a trail of broken windows and over-turned cars, after a showing of *Rock Around The Clock* at the Trocadero. Said the *Daily Express*; 'A Lewisham mob sang, "Nine little policemen hanging on the wall", before being arrested for rioting. At a Croydon cinema they squirted the protesting manager with a fire exting-uisher, and returned to their jiving in front of the screen. Seats were ripped up and lavatory bowls cracked.' The Reverend Albert Carter of Nottingham was quoted as saying that 'the effect of this music on young people is to turn them into devil worshippers; to stimulate self-expression through sex, to provoke lawlessness, to im-pair nervous stability and to destroy the sanctity of marriage.' The Queen asked to see a print of the offend-ing film and must have at least approved because the

next thing I was reading was about how she and the Duke were seen rocking and rolling till 2 a.m. at the Duke of Kent's twenty-first birthday party.

I went to see the film in the holidays at the Putney Regal and there wasn't much audience noise. A bit of clapping on the off-beat, but it didn't 'evoke a folk response' (to use an American sociologist's expression). I thought it was jolly good though, and the story rang quite true: about how Bill and the boys were found by a talent scout in a small town, where they'd been making the kids dance happy, and put under a national spotlight via coast-to-coast TV in New York, nerve centre of show business. I must say I was a bit put off by the sight of an accordion in the Comets, and also a Hawaiian guitar. I didn't associate that with rock 'n' roll. Nor did I care to see that the sax player wore braces underneath his scotch plaid jacket.

In between the rocking there were some nice lulling moments from a harmony vocal group called 'The Plat-ters'. They sang 'The Great Pretender' and 'Only You' with a fetching accompaniment from a cling-cling-cling-cling-cling piano. They smiled a lot too. So it wasn't all devil's music. Actually Bill Haley had a very avuncular face and as he was an older man he could well have been a liberal schoolmaster.

Elvis Presley was something else. Maybe Head Boy in an ideal school, after a few terms of wild oat sowing and being sent to Coventry. I heard him first in May telling of 'Heartbreak Hotel', a voice crying through the ether wilderness of Europe. Radio Luxembourg was hard to catch clearly for more than a few seconds; your song came at you close and tantalisingly, and then was dragged away screaming as foreign voices in French, German, Dutch and what have you, crowded in with their old-fashioned gibberish. But you knew Elvis would return with more about this weird, sad hotel where the desk clerk's dressed in black and where there's always room for broken-hearted lovers to cry there in the gloom. It took several weeks of hard listening to decipher all the words, but that was half the fun – like those POWs who spun out their crossword puzzles for months.

Elvis Presley. The name was very odd and angular. Bent notes and broken words fell clanging from such a name. Press photos from America showed him twisting and swivelling, with his eyes closed and his upper rose petal lip contorted into a sneer, and overall his look to be that of a comic book hero, a Greek battler from 'Classics Illustrated'. Every line of body and face in the true action comic style, idealised and slick and pared down and shiny. His hair was thick and shiny with grease. I knew he must be good when *Melody Maker* reported his performance to be 'very mannered' and 'dripping with ersatz emotion', nothing more than a 'male burlesque dancer' and musically a 'cross between Johnnie Ray and Billy Daniels with Country & Western overtones and poor diction'. In Los Angeles he was asked to remove the more offensive bumps and grinds from his act, especially the routine where he mimicked a gross act on a model of His Master's Voice dog. Girls screamed and fainted, carrying on as usual, except more so. 'He brings out the beast in women', said Henry Saperstein, the man who ran the Elvis Presley merchandising campaign. Saperstein was in charge of licensing Presley trousers, shirts, caps, hankies, and lipsticks like 'Heartbreak Pink' and 'Blue Suede Red'. 'I'll give him another two years as a top merchandising subject. Will we sell this stuff abroad? Sure – because teens are the same all over the world.'

Melody Maker snorted that 'one of the embarrassments of democracy is that this is the age of the common man'.

I never thought of Presley or Haley as being common men. Gene Vincent, a new rocker pushing through with a steaming, breathless record called 'Be-Bop-A-Lula', could have been a British street corner oik, judging by his looks – but you knew he was from Capitol records of Hollywood, and you read that he was reared in Virginia. Outside of class, as we understood it. Class

soaked everything in Britain, as it still does. 'Toilet' or 'lavatory', dinner at noon or dinner at night, cooked tea or cold tea, sleeping in pyjamas or sleeping in vest . . . It was all quite clear and laid out precisely in the unwritten code.

So when Tommy Steele came chirruping out of the portable radio, as a home-grown rival to Presley, Pelvis Esley, with his 'Rock With The Caveman', the class matter was too apparent not to be mentioned. He was a clear-cut cockney of the ancient pattern, a Sam Weller of the type who had cheerfully kicked footballs through No-Man's Land in World War One, and laughed off Hitler in World War Two, and always went for a burton with a joke trickling from the mouth. What was I doing slumming with such a wotcher-cock, slap on the shoulder, clip on the ear-hole, ketchup-all-over-the-mixed-grill-type? That was what masters and peers, and even I myself, asked. Surely pop music had been the pastime of shop girls during the soppy crooner era, and the riot trigger of yobs during the Haley era?

Truth was, me and my pals didn't get too excited by Tommy Steele. We soon discovered his real name was Hicks, and he went down a treat with mums and dads and debutantes and Royal Variety Shows, just as George Formby and Gracie Fields had done in earlier times. The court jesters. He also lacked sex urge, which was an essential thrust of Presley and Vincent. He defused it with bubbles.

Lonnie Donegan's 'Rock Island Line', a top tenner in February, started a craze for 'Skiffle' and the Skiffle Group. This meant an energy-devouring hobby, deflecting music from the subject of physical love onto folk tales about railways, picking bales of cotton, digging potatoes and exotic places like the Cumberland Gap. The authorities heaved a sigh of relief. The jazz experts shook their heads yet again for they knew that Donegan had once been a decent ensemble banjo player in Ken Colyer's authentic New Orleans jazz band. He had deserted fundamentalism for the Hit Parade. He had pandered to the kids and their thirst for motion.

Such arguments were mere piffle to us. Skiffle was easy to play and easy to sing, a do-it-yourself music. The required kit included washboard, tea-chest bass, banjo, mandolin, kazoo, mouth organ – well anything, really. The point is you didn't have to go out and invest heavily in saxes or brass or electric guitars and amplifiers. The most important instrument was the acoustic guitar. The race for guitars was on. Everyone seemed to be buying them, even at school. Up I went to Selmer's in Charing Cross Road with my father and there he did some tricky negotiation exchanging my accordion for a smart-looking acoustic guitar with steel strings and a golden sunburst finish.

So in the Summer of '56, while Frankie Lymon, a real teenager, was asking a precocious question, 'Why Do Fools Fall In Love' and Elvis was bang on target by linking clothes with rock and warning people not to step on his 'Blue Suede Shoes', me and my pals were practis-

ing the folk songs of long-dead, oppressed Afro-Americans. We also learned 'Green Grow The Rushes, O!' and it was this number more than any other that won our school skiffle group a spot at the Annual Bryanston Fête and an introduction by the school chaplain.

That winter I went up to Soho and took in some skiffle clubs. Everyone and his brother seemed to be skiffling now. In one direction the music was getting a bit heady, a bit intellectual. I mean that some of the skiffle groups actually performed *sitting down*, and I saw many listeners concentrating with head in hands, hunched in their duffle coats, while nut cutlets sizzled in a dingy kitchen whose decor was dominated by a poster for *Look Back In Anger*.

Coming out of this dour gloom and into the refreshing early afternoon rain of the West End I looked into the windows of the leisure wear shops to see what was new. 'Be Gay' Knitwear were pushing 'Initial Cardigans', direct from the USA, bright stripes round the arms and a bold K on the breast. Vince Man's Shop displayed their 'Waterfront Look', an outfit of husky denim jacket with special stitch jeans to match. Jeans were becoming more plentiful and better cut, but still not the real McCoy, the Levi. So much for the clothes side – important, of course, but the music was still No. 1.

At the HMV record shop they were advertising new plastic unbreakable 45 rpm discs. Nothing like as impressive as a solid and fragile 78. The old 78 world was still in evidence, like the music publishers in Denmark Street hanging out their printed wares, proud of being up-to-date and yet within tradition with their 'Rock & Roll Opera' and their 'Rock & Roll Waltz'; like the seven different disc versions of 'Only You', including one by Louis Armstrong, and the five versions of 'Blue Suede Shoes' but only three of 'Rock Island Line', not counting Stan Freberg's rude but funny parody on Capitol. Freberg seemed outraged by the new evangelism in pop – he savaged Johnnie Ray, the Platters, and Elvis – and he said, as a lover of good jazz, he just couldn't accept this wilful distortion of the language: 'You-oo-oo-oo-oo'. The vowel, he said, isn't that many notes long, I'm sorry. Yes, but it was an effervescent sound as was 'Be-Bop-A-Lula' and 'A Wop Bop A Loop Bop A Lop Bam Boom'.

This last phrase is an approximation of the shout in Little Richard's 'Tutti Frutti'. It was getting harder to trap the hot air of rock onto ink and paper. The words looked silly in print and the notes were hiding somewhere in the cracks between the piano keys. The singer *was* the song anyway. Little Richard and 'Long Tall Sally' were intertwined forever and Pat Boone's cover version was a pitiful thing. He just couldn't spill out 'He saw Aunt Mary coming so he ducked back in the alley'

without making it sound awkward. I liked him for his croony, pleasing tone on 'I'll Be Home', especially when he sang it on *Sunday Night At The London Palladium* on TV. But his 'Ain't That A Shame' was too much of a pretty melody and I preferred Fats Domino's original. OK, so he slurred the words, but they were his own words anyway and the slurring was all a part of an overall rolling that got into the bottom of your stomach and felt good like a solid meal should.

Here were we rock fans standing on Land's End looking at a beckoning sea of self-expression. Jump in and splash and gurgle with Elvis and Gene and Richard and Domino! I could see the experienced faces of British pop music stalwarts sternly warning of the danger ahead. I could see Frank Chacksfield, Frank Weir, Mantovani, Jack Payne – all urging one to learn the crochets and quavers, to study breath control for correct intonation, to get a proper musical education before embarking on a career in the music profession. Thus far it had only been skiffling, but with this wave of wild rockers who knows when the opportunity would arise? For a moment I faltered and thought of falling back into the warm maternal embrace of Anne Shelton. From *Melody Maker* screamed a winter headline: ROCK & ROLL SWAMPS 1956 MUSIC SCENE. Inside top jazz writer Steve Race claimed that 'Rock and Roll is one of the most terrifying things to have happened to popular music'. I turned to the *New Musical Express* and there in the readers' letters column was Mavis Purnell describing her Italian holiday where she found village bands playing classical impromptus and where there were Mario Lanzas up and down the lanes and yet from the higher musical spheres of show business 'all we get is smash, battle and bawl'.

And yet already there were signs that R&R might be cooling and settling down. Bill Haley was vowing in a Christmas annual that he would 'clean up rock & roll music' and never use 'questionable numbers'. Elvis came out with the peaceful 'Love Me Tender' song. Pat Boone, speaking as a representative of the teens, said, 'I refuse to offend anybody . . . I try to make sure my children wake up each morning with a good clean taste in their mouths'. He added that he'd had the lyrics of 'Tutti Frutti' changed before he cut the record. 'I am a religious man'.

On December 21 the *New Musical Express* ran a reassuring editorial: 'Christmas comes to a world filled with strain and worry. It is a gratifying thought that the popular music industry which we are proud to represent is playing a tremendous part in keeping people cheerful in these difficult times. Rock & Roll has its critics, but the rhythm helps to relax and revitalise young people so that they are better equipped to face the problems with which they are beset'.

IS TRICK-RECORDING CHEATING THE PUBLIC?

Your Views Wanted On A Topical Subject

JACK PAYNE'S INTERVIEW WITH a recording manager during the TV disc show "Off The Record" last week almost resulted in a challenge of "Swords or Pistols" when the question as to whether engineering tricks on wax were or were not above board was raised. Unfortunately, the time factor prevented lucid argument, so it seemed to me to be of interest to the record-buying public to put the pro's and con's to them so that they may draw their own conclusions.

It may or may not be generally known that in order to attain the best standard possible, all recordings nowadays are first put on tape. As an artiste can make as many recordings as he likes of one title, there are naturally many versions to choose from before the final selection is transfered to wax. If not content with this, however, the engineers in the studio can cut bits of the best of each recording and stick them together to make as near a perfect performance on tape as possible.

By JACK BENTLEY

The gramophone companies defend this policy, using the argument that their job is to produce the best possible records, and, if modern methods are available to attain this, then it's their duty to exploit them.

On the other hand, the opposition declares that although this may be so, it is giving the public a false impression of artistes' talents because a true performer should be consistently good. Further to this, they claim that when a performer, who has made a hit disc via engineering tricks, appears on the stage, TV, or radio, the same standard of performance as was heard on wax is expected. Naturally enough, it isn't forthcoming.

Personally, I feel that on the question of ethics, Jack Payne is right, but, lamentable as it might seem, if the gramophone companies became idealists over-night, I'm sure they would be out of business in almost as short a time.

Again, from rather a selfish point of view, after hearing some discs that have been through the trick treatment, I dread to think what they would have sounded like without it! Anyway, it would be interesting to hear YOUR views on the subject.

Donegan inspired us into buying guitars and doing it ourselves. All you needed was a handful of chords and membership of The Folk. And we were all Urban folk. Few of us belonged to the Show-Biz Club.

THE TRAD MAN IN THE TOP TWENTY

CHARLES GOVEY writes about LONNIE ('Rock Island Line') DONEGAN

THERE'S no accounting for tastes—especially when it comes to the record buying public. And there's no end to the consternation and wonder caused in the music business when these tastes turn the Best-Selling Charts upside down.

Who, for instance, could have foreseen that the current trend in country-and-western music - (with a dash of rhythm-and-blues) would focus attention on the British school of revivalist jazz?

Yet, that is exactly what's happened with one of the recent entrants to the Top Twenty. With frequent airings in the past few weeks, the Decca recording of "Rock Island Line," by Lonnie Donegan's Skiffle Group, has been making rapid strides towards the top.

As a result, the 24-year-old folk music collector and banjoist with Chris Barber's Band finds himself bracketed, in the minds of the public, with top commercial stars like Tennessee Ernie and Bill Haley.

Lonnie, of course, is not a complete unknown. He is already an established name with the staunch musical minority that frequents the traditional clubs and turns up in force for Chris Barber concerts all over the country.

"Rock Island Line" has been a hit with this section of the public for some time. Originally recorded as part of Chris Barber's first LP, "New Orleans Joys," more than a year ago, it was put out on 78 just before Christmas.

Realising its popularity with the traditional fans, Decca began stepping up the exploitation.

The disc had a couple of broadcasts, including one on Eamonn Andrews's "Pied Piper" programme, and, hey presto, it became the rage of thousands of buyers who have never been inside a jazz club in their lives.

Exactly why this happened is one of those eternal mysteries of show business. But one thing seems fairly certain. The disc has quite accidentally cashed in on two very strong trends in the pop record business.

One is the narrative gimmick of "Shifting, Whispering Sands." The other is the "rock an' roll" craze as exemplified by "Rock Around The Clock" and "Sixteen Tons." It has even been suggested that "Rock Island Line" is selling on the strength of its title alone!

And what of Lonnie himself? A native of Scotland—though he has lived most of his life in the suburbs of L o n d o n — he was christened Anthony Donegan. He acquired his professional name following a visit by one of his idols — the great American folk singer, Lonnie Johnson—to this country in 1952.

At that time Lonnie was just finishing his National Service, and making up his mind to learn to play the guitar. After leading his own amateur band for a while, he joined the newly formed Ken Colyer Jazzmen as a semi-pro.

NO SOLO CAREER

An avid collector of folk songs since his childhood, he formed his first Skiffle Group within the band to perform some of the traditional blues and ballads in between the band numbers.

The group quickly established itself with the fans, and when the players eventually walked out to form a breakaway band under trombonist Chris Barber, the Skiffle Group naturally moved over, too.

On the "Rock Island Line" session, Lonnie was supported by Chris Barber on bass and Beryl Bryden on washboard. Since then he has experimented with different instruments—"We even tried Chris on harmonica, but he showed no great aptitude!" — and has now settled for a solid-sounding group featuring two guitars, bass and drums.

As a member of the traditional school, Lonnie has no particular concern for other fields of popular music. He makes no extravagant claims for himself. He is merely attempting to recreate the work of "authentic" folk singers like Lonnie Johnson, "Leadbelly" and Muddy Waters.

How, then, does he regard his success in the Top Twenty? He is amused and, if anything, rather scornful. "I don't think it's a particularly good recording, and even asked to have it withdrawn when I first heard it," he said.

He has no intention of being tempted away from the Barber Band for a precarious career as a solo artist. He has even turned down radio and TV spots to boost the record

NO ROYALTIES!

"For one thing," says Lonnie, "I haven't really got time. We work sometimes as much as seven engagements a week, and as we are a co-operative band, we're all quite well-off financially.

"In any case, I don't want to be swept along on the tide of the latest gimmick and then get left high and dry when it wears off. I've seen that happen to people before."

But he has no objection to being transferred to Nixa's pop label, where he is now under contract. For one thing, he'll be collecting royalties for any future hit records he may make.

For one of the biggest ironies of "Rock Island Line" is that its sales make no difference to Lonnie's bank balance. At the time, Decca presumably thought they were "doing their duty" to a minority public, and simply paid the Barber Band a flat fee for the session. And the boys were glad to take it!

LONNIE DONEGAN'S SECRET

JAMES ASMAN ON

Traditional Jazz

LONNIE DONEGAN HAS BEEN AT IT AGAIN!

On a new Nixa release, this time on the popular series, we are now regaled with "Lost John" and "Stewball" (Nixa N.1536). Since the phenomenal success of "Rock Island Line" (Decca F.10647) both Lonnie and the Nixa people have, reasonably enough, been hoping to provide the rapacious general public with a suitable follow-on. I think that they have only partially found it here.

Not that there is anything subtle or natural about this new effort.

Both sides carefully ape the style of the original hit with Lonnie wailing vigorously throughout to a "skiffle" accompaniment by members of the Barber group.

As a jazz record it can only be described as phoney.

But I suspect that this is really a hardworking attempt to recapture the vast record-buying public which rushed to the shops for the accidental Decca recording. One must, after all, remember that Donegan is now quite a remarkable figure in the popular field. Tin Pan Alley frankly admits its ignorance of the causes which threw an obscure guitar player in what was originally an amateur revivalist jazz band into the Hit Parade. The ones I talked to last week confessed that they were completely baffled about the whole business.

I think I know the secret if a secret exists. And if I am **right the answer is rather ironical, and will certainly set all**

the myriads of Donegan fans back on their heels a-hollering.

GREAT BOOZY DAYS

FOR I KNEW LONNIE years ago when I was running a hit-and-miss kind of jazz club every Monday night down in Abbey Wood in South East London. Bob Brunskill led a rather fervent revivalist group there, and we took the half-crowns at the door, paid the landlord and handed the balance over to the band. Sometimes it amounted to as princely a sum as thirty shillings and sometimes it didn't even reach a pound.

Those were great days, boozy days. I didn't listen to a great deal of music but I certainly had myself a ball most of the time. But, on such meagre income we weren't able to provide much in the way of interval music. We tried gramophone records, and discovered that adherents of "live" jazz clubs didn't usually bother about real jazz on wax discs. So, saddened at heart, we managed to call on the free services of good friends like George Webb, George Melly and Nixa Raphaello.

But, after all, there was a limit to friends who would give us their talents for the love of us. That was when one night I persuaded Lonnie Donegan to sing with his guitar whilst the band clung to the bar and refreshed themselves. Strangely enough, he was by no means a great success. Our club members found his music too much like hillbilly for pleasure. But Lonnie could yodel fine. This was the popular singer the Americans know as the

Irish Hillbilly born.

And that, I believe, is where the secret lies. The comparatively few jazz lovers buy him because they've heard him in the popular "skiffle" sessions which grace the Barber band show. They like him just as they like George Melly, Ottilie Patterson or Ken Colyer.

But, let us be frank. Lonnie didn't reach the Top Ten on the strength of his jazz sales. A new public pushed him there—and it is this new public that will push him up there all over again, providing he gives them what they are looking for. THAT ISN'T SO-CALLED "SKIFFLE" MUSIC, NOR IS IT DONEGAN-ISED VERSIONS OF HUDDIE LEADBETTER ORIGINALS.

For his success equals another record surprise topliner — **Slim Whitman**. It was the yodelling, the hillbilly sound and the bright rhythms that pleased Joe Public so well. To them he was a new cowboy vocalist, and one with enough difference to add variety. That was why they liked "Rock Island Line" and didn't like "Midnight Special" and "When the Sun Goes Down" (Nixa NJS 2006). That is why Lonnie and Nixa will have to select very different material for him to sing if he does really have an itch for the fleshpots and a tidebank balance and who hasn't?

Lonnie might do well to discard his excursions into the dead Leadbetter's library of folk ballads and let the husky Negro folk artiste rest more easy in his grave. Jimmy Rodgers, Hank Williams, Montana Slim, the Carter Family and many of the great hillbilly singers offer songs as well as a style of singing which might pay very healthy dividends.

And don't be worried about your jazz-loving fans, Lonnie. They won't pay the rent of an expensive house or even the fare to

The U.S.A.

again in their own right. Otherwise I can see no future for them.

A KAY 'ROCKER'

KAY STARR
ROCK AND ROLL WALTZ;
I'VE CHANGED MY MIND A THOUSAND TIMES
(HMV. POP. 168)

WHETHER IT CAN BE regarded as a compliment or not, there's no doubt that Kay Starr excels in the "Rock and Roll" idiom. Her rather strident tones and forceful personality fuses admirably with the extrovert themes of such compositions, and here, in the tale of two parents she caught trying to rock and roll in waltz time, the mood is captured intriguingly.

The wordily titled reverse side is noisy, but is a good slow toe-tapper.

ROCK AGE IDOL

THAT'S ELVIS

He's Riding the Crest

of a Teenage Tidal Wave

Hollywood, Sunday.

I HAVE just escaped from a hurricane called Elvis Presley.

A few hints of what this tall, rangy singer is doing to young America with his rock-'n'-roll rhythm had already reached me.

● In Jacksonville, Florida, he had to be rescued from a crowd in a police wagon.

● In Wichita Falls, Texas, the fans broke every window in his car.

● In San Diego, California, a pack of teenage girls had covered his windscreen with phone numbers written in lipstick. . . .

But it was not until I went to the sun-baked desert town of Albuquerque New Mexico, and saw what happened at two shows Elvis gave there that I realised what a frenzy this boy can stir up.

Five Thousand Screamed

I've never seen anything like it.

When Elvis sings it isn't just a case of a few girls sighing and going swoony or stamping and shouting.

I saw him send 5,000 of them into a mass fit of screaming hysterics.

A FEW months ago Elvis was an unheard of youngster driving a lorry round his home town, Memphis, Tennessee, getting about £10 a week.

He made a few records. He did one or two local TV shows. Routine, mildly successful sort of stuff.

He was then spotted by Parker showman Tom R.C.A., who persuaded one of America's biggest recording companies,' to sign him up.

Presley then cut his now famous "Heartbreak Hotel" disc—and, bingo, the teenage tidal wave swept in.

"Heartbreak Hotel" was top

and two wrestlers to pro- tect the singer. "I hope that'll be enough," he said.

A local helper chipped in to say: "It had better be. If these kids run wild it will be like having 10,000 head of cattle coming at you."

The Rush

Hours before the show a queue of teenagers wound completely round the drill hall where it was to be held.

The girls wore suede-check fringed jackets, shirts, jeans held up by leather belts with silver buckles and moccasins.

The boys wore curly-brimmed flat-top Western-style hats, jeans and high-heeled boots.

Directly the doors opened the girls rushed for the table where Presley pictures were being sold at 3s. 6d. 5s. and 7s. each. "Gee, ain't he a living doll,"

greeted with screams; every rhythmic break got a howl. Girls with cameras rushed down to the stage to get a picture of their idol—and then just there, forgetting to press the trigger.

WHEN it was over and a wedge of police had brought Elvis back to the dressing room he felt about this sort of recep- I asked him how he felt tion.

He said: "It makes me want to cry. How does all this happen to me?" He showed me a gold horseshoe ring studded with eleven big diamonds

he was wearing. "Look at all these things I got," he said. "I got three Cadil- lacs. I got forty suits and forty pairs of shoes."

I asked him how he knew it was exactly twenty-seven pairs and he said: "When you ain't had nothing, like me, you keep count when you get things."

No Girl—Yet

What else is he doing with his money?

"I bought Mom and Pop a new house," he said. "I'm saving plenty, too. One day I aim to get married. No, there ain't no girl just now. But she'll come along."

I wonder if it could be a fan like that little girl I saw when I was leaving. She was blonde, about sixteen. She had found a broken string from Elvis' guitar.

"When I left she was roll- ing it reverently round like a lock of hair and tucking it down inside her shirt.

Advertiser's Announcement

Take home it it hot

by **LIONEL CRANE**

ELVIS PRESLEY . . . every move gets a howl

HEY GOONS THIS IS

Just as Elvis Presley arrived (via press and disc) I traded in my accordion for a steel-string guitar at Selmer's in the Charing Cross road where saxes jostled with guitars, and modern jazzmen sleek in satin suits, blew clouds of bent

raised 9th. At school the vice headmaster pointed to an article on Presley and warned: 'Avoid this behaviour.' The school jazz buffs said: 'Presley doesn't swing'.

---

row and has sold the carrying his guitar and wearing a plum-coloured jacket and black trousers, armed police guarding him on each side.

As he walked towards the stage the youngsters let out a scream that I thought would split the roof.

Shakes, Howls

He has the build of a guardsman, an unbeatable D.A. haircut, sleepy eyes like Robert Mitchum and a handsome, olive coloured face.

As he sings he stands with his legs wide apart. His whole body, from his shoulders to his feet, shakes in rhythm and every move draws a new deluge of howls from ecstatic fans.

A few seconds after he started sweat was dripping over his eyebrows and his hair was hanging down his forehead.

Every new number was

And when Elvis goes to Las Vegas soon, a top hotel will pay him £8,000 for two weeks' work.

After that it's Hollywood with a contract for one film a year for seven years.

And all this for a lad of twenty-one who cannot read or write a note of music.

WHY? Albuquerque gave me the answer.

It is a tough town. The people who live there are Westerners, Mexicans and Indians. They drag a living out of the hundreds of miles of desert around their back yards.

Protection...

They are leathery and hard and their children are about as tough as they come.

So Parker, who is now Presley's manager, fixed up ten cops, ten ushers

TWISTWORDS

ELVIS PRESLEY

HERE IT IS — THE FIRST ARTICLE EVER WRITTEN FOR A BRITISH PUBLICATION BY THAT DYNAMIC RECORDING IDOL—

I'M afraid to wake up each morning. I can't believe all this has happened to me. I just hope it lasts.

Thanks to all my faithful teenage fans, I have made a lot of money all of a sudden. Just two years ago I was driving a truck for $35 a week in Memphis, Tennessee, and before that I was knocking down $14 a week (that's less than £5 in your money) as a theatre usher.

Then one day my father gave me a guitar. Although I didn't know a B-flat from C-sharp, I finally learned to play.

My career as a singer started by accident. I went into a record shop to make a record for my mother, just to surprise her. Some man in there heard me sing and said he might call me sometime. He did . . . a year and a half later.

He was Sam Phillips, the owner of Sun Records, and I made a couple of records for him. Mr. Steve Sholes, who is the head of country-western music at RCA Victor, happened to hear one of them and wanted to sign me up with his company.

It was Mr. Sholes who gave me "Heartbreak Hotel" to cut and, as you know, it turned out to be a million seller.

A lot of people ask me where I got my singing style. Well, I didn't copy my style from anybody. I've got nothing in common with Johnnie Ray, except that we both sing—if you want to call it singing.

I jump around because it is the way I feel. In fact, I can't even sing with a beat at all if I stand still.

The kids are really wonderful the way they respond to my style. I get around 10,000 fan letters a week. So many people all over the country are starting fan clubs for me.

I certainly am grateful to them all, and in answer to some of the questions they ask, here are a few statistics about myself.

I was born in Tupelo, Mississippi, on January 8, 1935. I was raised and went to high school in Memphis, Tennessee, which is still my home. I never took any singing lessons, and the only practising I ever did was on a broomstick before my Dad bought me my first guitar.

I'm six feet tall and weigh 195 pounds. I've gained about twenty pounds in the last year. I can't understand that because my appetite isn't as good as it used to be. I don't have much time for regular meals any more, because I'm always travelling around the country, working in a different city every day.

I usually gulp down a quick sandwich in between shows, but when I can, I enjoy having a big dinner with three pork chops and plenty of mashed potatoes and gravy.

I understand there have been a lot of rumours concerning me, I am beginning to think that they have more rumours about me than records. A while ago, they thought I was dead. Well, I'm as alive and kicking as I'll ever be.

I can't seem to relax ever, and I have a terrible time falling to sleep at night. At the most, I usually get two or three hours of broken sleep. There was even a wild rumour that I shot my mother. Well, that is pretty silly. She's my best girl friend, and I bought her and Dad a home in Memphis, where I hope they'll be for a long, long time. I made my father retire a few months ago. There isn't much sense in his working, because I can make more in a day than he can make in a year. There were some rumours, too, about my getting married. Well, I have no plans for that, and I am not engaged. I guess I just haven't found the right girl yet. Besides records and personal appearances, I am looking forward to making a movie. I took a screen test a couple of months ago and Paramount Pictures signed me to a contract. I may make a picture before the end of the year.

In fact, everything is going so fine for me that I can't believe it's not a dream. And, if it is, I hope I never wake up.

THE REEDS

14

I LISTENED WITH HORROR

IT IS, OF COURSE, the era of Rock 'n' Roll and Skiffle, and both of these current crazes are bound to have at least a minor effect upon the material offered by some of the major companies to their faithful jazz customers.

It is my unhappy task this week to have to deal with some of these transgressions, and I would like to remark in passing on the peculiar sleeve-notes to the new 12-inch Elvis Presley album put out by His Master's Voice. These are written by a musical journalist and a well known traditional bandleader named Bob Dawbarn. In fact, Bob used to play in an early group which provided the music week after week at the South-East London Jazz Club where I attempted, once upon a time, to beguile the local fans.

There is even a touch of the hot gospel singers in Elvis — Lawdy, Miss Clawdy, and 'One Sided Love Affair', reminding one strongly of the hot-gospeller Sister Rosetta Tharpe." (Rock 'n' Roll—Elvis Presley—His Master's Voice (CLP 1093.) As a result I have listened to these pieces with an increasing horror. They certainly didn't remind me of the excellent Rosetta Tharpe—but I had in mind one cold night on a friend's farm when one of the cows became entangled in some barbed wire and we had to wade through mud to try and extricate the suffering animal.

So much that has been, and is being, released under the title of Rock 'n' Roll is much more deserving of interest— Bo Diddley, Joe Turner, and Wynonie "Mr. Blues" Harris, for example. But my views on this sort of jive must have become well known by now . . .

But the "Skiffle" is still with us . . .

ELVIS PRESLEY — the new star in the popular music firmament

KEITH GOODWIN tells you all about America's latest singing idol

FROM out of the blue, 21-year-old Elvis Presley has rocketed on to the popular music scene with all the scorching fury of a meteor flashing across the sky. Make no mistake about it. Elvis is the new teenage idol of America. His first long-playing album jumped to the top of the best-selling charts in America's "Billboard" magazine within weeks of its release.

But that's merely the beginning of the story. His "singles"— "Heartbreak Hotel" in particular —have had a similar impact. "Heartbreak Hotel" leaped to the top of the American hit parade and also had the double honour of being the disc "most played in juke boxes," and "most played by disc jockeys." And now, these very same records are finding an eager, excited public in this country.

Magic

What magic does this phenomenon called Presley possess that he is able to mount the very pinnacle of show business in such a short space of time? Certainly, the man who has been dubbed "the hillbilly Johnnie Ray," is already at the top—and present public reaction demands that he should stay there.

He has been acclaimed as the successor to Johnnie Ray, and this has brought forth a spate of fan letters both for and against this claim.

But no matter what the outcome of the argument, one thing is certain —Elvis Presley is here to stay.

Reports in a national newspaper recently have helped back up the claim to mass idolization. Quite definitely, this tall, lanky singer has already received the Johnnie Ray treatment.

He has been rescued from screaming crowds of teenagers in a police wagon. Fans have broken windows of his car while attempting to get near him; girls have written phone numbers in lipstick over his car; and in Jacksonville, Florida, admirers tore the clothes off his back! This in addition to many letters of this nature.

A single note on his guitar can produce howls of admiration from a packed audience of teenagers. A song can turn them into a screaming, almost hysterical crowd. Winning polls has become quite a common occurrence for Elvis. Last year he was voted the "most promising Country and Western artist" by

C. & W. disc jockeys in America. He was also acclaimed the "best new male singer," and the "most promising country male vocalist of the year," during the same year. But Presley is still gaining popularity, and the future holds even more honours.

And how do British fans feel about America's newest singing sensation? Johnnie Ray fans claim he could never replace their hero and, while some agree that "Heartbreak Hotel" is a good disc, they, nevertheless, intend to remain faithful to Johnnie.

From the other side of the fence, Presley fans are adamant that he doesn't copy Ray, and feel that he is already much better than the great "one and only." Elvis certainly has the dark, swarthy, mysterious good looks to get the fans on his side. But the fans have also fallen for the deep emotion, power—and sex appeal—in his voice.

Elvis has an interesting background. Born in Tupelo, Mississippi, on January 8, 1935, throughout his early youth he was always surrounded by the folk music and blues associated with the deep South.

He soon took an active interest in music, and at the tender age of six began singing at folk gatherings and also for his friends. During his youth Elvis worked hard. In the firm belief that one day he might reach the top.

He never had any professional instruction, and his efforts at self tuition were the results of his own ideas. With no money to buy a guitar, he practised "picking" on a broomstick.

A little later he found money enough to buy a cheap instrument and, after more practice and hard work, was able to play tunes. He also sang on street corners to the accompaniment of his guitar.

While still a young boy, he had his first taste of real success when he won a prize in his first public performance at the Tri-State Fair in his home town. And this is where the "show business bug" left its teeth-marks on young Elvis.

Records

Elvis went to high school when his family moved to Memphis, Tennessee and, although his main interest was still with his guitar and his singing, he earned a little extra money by doing odd jobs, including lorry driving.

For the "kicks" and his own amusement, he decided one day to make a private recording—at his own expense. With just this one thought in mind, he walked into the Sun Record Company, Memphis —and, in so doing, walked into stardom!

Sam Phillips, president of Sun Records, heard him sing—and signed him to a contract on the spot. Within a few months, following advice and coaching from Sam, Elvis had his first disc—"That's All Right, Mama"—released on the Sun label. It became an overnight hit—and Elvis has never looked back.

Since then his other discs have caught on with alarming rapidity. Tunes like the aforementioned "Heartbreak Hotel," "Tutti Frutti," "Rag Mop," "I Was The One," "Blue Suede Shoes," and "I Forgot To Remember To Forget," have made him a top recording artist, and an album of words and music to "Elvis Presley Juke Box Favourites" has now been issued in the States.

After graduating from school, Elvis began to make his first personal appearances, and at Shreveport he caused a minor sensation. He won numerous polls, and enlisted the aid of well-known popular c. and w. disc-jockey Bob Neal as his personal manager.

More coast-to-coast personal appearances followed, and as his popularity grew, America's teenagers dubbed him the "King of Western Bop."

smashing box-office records at theatres throughout the South and South-West.

In recent months, his appearances on CBS Television's "Stage Show" have brought him an amazing amount of mail.

Personal details about Elvis prove just why he has become the latest teenage "rave." Standing 6ft. 2ins. in his stockinged feet, and weighing 160 pounds, he has dark wavy hair, blue eyes—and is unmarried.

He has a huge appetite, and is reputed to eat a dozen eggs and either two steaks or a pound of bacon—for breakfast!

Outside of music, Elvis' main interest lies in his two Cadillacs —one in pink and black that carries him all around the country on his personal appearances, the other in canary yellow that he drives in his leisure hours. In addition, he also owns a station wagon and a motorcycle.

He spends a good deal of time buying clothes, and has recently persuaded his 39-year-old father to retire. In his spare time, he has designed some of the furniture for the home he has refurnished for his mother. And—yes, there's more—he now owns his own music-publishing company.

Elvis, 21, is one of the few artists who can claim "overnight success," in anything like the true sense of the words. He is, without doubt, one of the most astonishing personalities to break into the field of popular music for many years, and only recently was presented with a gold disc for his million-plus sales of "Heartbreak Hotel" for RCA-Victor, with whom he has signed a contract involving one of the highest sums ever paid to a new artist.

British fans may get the opportunity to see and hear Elvis in this country in the near future, possibly in next year's London Palladium variety season. And, by that time, the "King of Western Bop" should have more than one gold disc to his credit!

Gold disc

Sensation followed sensation! Teenage audiences were drawn to him like metal to a magnet. They screamed louder and louder at each performance, and just one indication of his immense popularity comes with the latest news that he has been

by
KEITH
GOODWIN

GENE VINCENT
—'The Screaming End,' who has made a great beginning with a hit record

Along Comes A New Contender For The 'King Of Din' Title—Gene Vincent. Complete With Gee-Tar . . .

SUPPOSE IT MORE or less HAD to happen: someone is trying to out-Presley Mr. Presley. Someone who, presumably, thinks he has more on the bawl.

From Norfolk (Virginia) comes 21-year-old Gene (as "with the light brown hair") Vincent, complete with gee-tar, and with backing from his "Blue Caps."

Capitol are responsible for this latest assault on our ear-drums. They are about to release a 78 of Mr. Vincent knocking the living daylights out of "Woman Love" and "Be-Bop-a-Lula."

Early this month, in a garish red-and-black advert in American "Billboard," his disc of these numbers was proclaimed under the heading, "Blasting to the top."

Ad also terms it "*the screaming end*." Having heard an advance pressing, I must agree. As I've written before, these current crotchet-clouters are a subject on which my personal views are vocal, but not printable. Yet since the public are masochistic enough to like them, I find a great cynical, clinical interest in what's going to happen next in this world of rodeo rowdiness. For me, the impending "King of Din" contest

'Blue Caps'

The "flutter echo" was used less obviously on Johnny Hodges' "Castle Rock"—a big hit in the States during 1951, and released here on Columbia—and on Winifred Atwell's Decca recording of " March Of The Cards." But on the Vincent sides, the effect is somewhat over-done.

After quite a few spins, you might be able to follow the lyrics, but it's pretty tough going first time out. A lot of people thought Elvis Presley's diction was a little hard to digest, but this is the real test piece.

But, gimmick or no gimmick, if you fell for the Presley sound, then it's safe to assume that sooner or later you're going to find yourself under the spell cast by Gene Vincent.

Already, Gene's record of "Be-Bop-A-Lula" is tenth in the American Best-Selling list, and has occupied spot No. 30 in the NME Charts for the past two weeks.

In many respects, newcomer Vincent and the much-publicised Presley are much alike—musically speaking. Their styles are a mixture of "Country and Western" and "Rock 'n' Roll," and both, apart from playing guitar themselves, depend on that same instrument for the basis of their rhythmic backing.

Gene's stage and record unit—he calls them the Blue Caps—lay down a sledgehammer-style beat, whereas El Presley's group can, and in most cases does, really swing. (If you don't believe me, ask Mike Butcher!) And both are alike again inasmuch as their diction is sometimes—here we go again—unintelligible!

Like his predecessor, Gene has already collected a title. Johnnie Ray, among other things, was christened with " Cry Guy," and " Prince of Wails." Presley is known as " The King of Western Bop," and now Gene, in a recent Press release, is described as " The Screaming End." So much for the Tin Pan Alley Honours List!

New arrival

Gene Vincent is the new arrival. Make a note of the name, because it's going to rate a great deal in the next few weeks. Mike a note of the titles of his first record too— " Be-Bop-A-Lula " and " Woman Love "—on the Capitol Label.

Already, Gene has run into opposition. As the BBC Restricted list. In other words, they have put a broad casting ban on the record. But this could amount to good publicity, for nothing captures the attention of the public more than the banning of a record.

I recently contacted the BBC Press Office to check their decision, and the reason for it. First answer I received was: If you have heard the record you will know why it has been restricted. It's obvious. I added they added that a further reason was that the lyrics were, in part, unintelligible.

In the light of their comments, I played the record a good many times, and came to the conclusion that the lyrics (or to be more precise, what I could understand of them) were slightly suggestive.

'Unintelligible'

Next, I dealt with the question of unintelligible lyrics. Colleague Mike Butcher and I studied the record at some length, and decided that the "fault" was not entirely Gene's.

For a start, Capitol it appears, employed the "flutter echo" gimmick on the recording, and this helped in no small way to distort the resultant sound. This gimmick does exactly as the words imply—it "flutters" both voice and accompaniment to an extent where the sound seems to come and go, or, if you prefer, "fade and die."

But what's this? A new name appears in the " mumbo-gumbo" stakes. Already, he is staking his claim for the right to wear the "Screaming" tag, and the music business is preparing for yet another battle of words and music.

THE Johnnie Ray v. Elvis Presley battle has reached a stalemate. A new readers' letters still litter the battleground, but the panic has died down, and devoted fans are no longer rushing to defend their heroes.

[Boxed text:]

Vincent sounded leaner and meaner than Presley. Also, less girls drooled over him. In reality he was a Southern gent, very deferential towards his elders. 'Sheriff' Tex Davis, his co-writer, was only an 'honorary', like Colonel Parker.

---

21 years old

CAPITOL'S CROTCHET-CLOUTER TRIES TO OUT-PRESLEY ELVIS

★ VOCAL VIEWS
By Dick Tatham

you can understand

between Mr. Presley and Mr. Vincent has a horrific appeal comparable to that of a pre-war film called, I believe, "Frankenstein Meets Dracula."

So Mr. Vincent has, unfortunately, already made one cardinal error: you can understand The incomparably incomprehensible Mr. Presley realises, for example, that "Heartbreak Hotel" called by any other name would sound just as ear-shattering. He is probably aware that his lyrics are so inane, it don't matter whether you hears Presley the Jungle Boy of the Juke Boxes.

So Mr. Vincent, before making further records, should really take some anti-elocution lessons.

FALSE MOVE. The backroomers have been put to work to decide just what it is that has made Mr. Presley, top secret memoranda, headed " Anatomy of Presley ", have probably been passed from department to department.

And this is the outcome. Reckon some of their shrewdness.

Whether, in a few weeks' time, a similar red-and-black advert in "Billboard" will produce claim, " Veni, Vidi, Vinci—Vincent", remains to be seen.

His 'Blue Suede Shoes' have taken him up the ladder of fame

by . . . JIMMY WATSON

The success story of CARL PERKINS

Perkins: Great rockabilly sound, but distinct lack of sex-appeal.

FOR the second time within the space of a few weeks, a country and western artist has made the improbable come true. Seldom, if ever, before has this taken place, but two artists are featured with hit recordings in all three America music fields . . . country and western, rhythm and blues and "pop."

First to achieve this distinction was Elvis Presley, whose "Heartbreak Hotel" leapt to the top of each section rapidly. Now Tennessee-born Carl Perkins follows close on his heels with another "treble"—"Blue Suede Shoes."

What's the reason for these triple successes ? The gentlemen in question—both composers of their respective hits—have combined country and western style singing with a rocking rhythm and blues beat, and the results have come as a three-way appeal.

Baker

Thanks to the efforts of colleague Keith Goodwin, NME readers already know about Elvis Presley, so now it it my turn to perform the introductions in the case of Carl Perkins.

Carl was born twenty-three years ago in Jackson, Tennessee. He is married and has two children, a boy aged three and a little girl not quite two.

Although music has always played a big part in his life, Carl's first job was as a baker with a local firm. His chief hobby is still cooking, and rumour says that he is very unhappy if he doesn't get some opportunity to dabble at the oven while on tour.

However, for the past four years, music has been his full-time occupation, and now that he has finally hit the big jackpot, it looks like staying that way for some time to come.

The group which accompanies Carl on tour and on wax comprises his elder brother "J.B." (27) on rhythm guitar, family "baby" Clayton (19) on bass, and W. S. Holland on drums. Carl himself plays the exciting electric guitar which is heard on his records.

Humility

Their first two records didn't make much impression—according to Carl the first didn't even get out of Memphis—but number three disc was "Blue Suede Shoes," which now needs no introduction.

A contemporary American magazine, "Country Song Roundup," states that Carl stands six feet tall, weighs over 12 stone, has dark brown eyes and dark brown curly hair. It also mentions that Carl is "a sincere down-to-earth fellow who claims he is still just a 'country boy.' His humility at the success that is coming his way is amazing."

Carl is still a little overwhelmed by the recent events, and is still unsure of its reality. Undoubtedly, his bank account will do a lot to convince him, as a big hit like this in America doesn't pay off in peanuts.

American reports say that Carl and his boys get wild receptions whenever they appear in public and have their frenzied audiences dancing in the aisles or "jiving" in front of the bandstand. He is being hailed as "the hottest newcomer in years."

Having played over his recording a couple of times, I find a tremendous excitement is given forth in his music. There is a constant pulsating beat always in evidence and, although this is not my own particular favourite type of music, I don't find his voice hard to listen to. It is strong and vibrant, as melodious as the material allows, and definitely compelling to the listener.

An interesting story lies behind the writing of "Blue Suede Shoes." One night, as Carl was playing at a dance, he chanced to hear a young fellow make a remark to his partner as they passed the rostrum. "Don't you step on my blue suede shoes" he exclaimed.

Somehow, the words stuck in Carl's mind and then when he bought a pair of blue suede shoes for himself, the full meaning of the words hit him—as all owners of blue suede shoes will bear out.

Gradually, Carl built a lyric round the phrase and then a melody began to fit snugly round the lyric in his brain. The melody had a distinctive beat and so a three-way hit parade topper was born.

With his group to help him, he polished up an arrangement of this inspiration and gave a special performance to the Sun Records magnates. Before you could say " country and western," " rhythm and blues," and "pop," it was on wax and being released around the country.

The disc-jockeys pounced on it—and, more important, the public took to it like an avalanche. The local boy had made good with an accent on success.

offers

Before long, offers to book the outfit came pouring in from all parts of the country. Carl and his boys were signed to appear regularly in the 'Big D' Jamboree'—a Saturday night Ed McLemore show from the Sportatorium in Dallas, Texas, which is broadcast over station KRLD and partly on the CBS network.

To commemorate the booking, Carl was presented with a pair of glittering blue suede shoes and now wears them on all the shows.

Record-breaking crowds now appear whenever Carl Perkins visits a town. It is therefore little wonder that he is tempted to wear his "Blue Suede Shoes" even with a dinner suit or pyjamas !

COMMENT: (with apologies to Stanley Holloway) This is definitely the biggest "footwear hit" since "Brown Boots"!

THE PLATTERS are spinning to the top

by DICK AUSTIN

THE Platters owe a great deal to their " Great Pretender." It took them into the gold-disc class, and established them as one of the leading rock-and-roll vocal groups in the States. But for a time it looked as if this record would never be cut!

The song was specially written by their manager Buck Ram for Tony Williams, the group's lead tenor, and was intended as a rush follow-up to their first hit " Only You." The record company was anxious that no time should be lost in bringing out " Pretender," which meant rehearsals between shows for the already over-worked Platters.

The recording session was arranged to take place one Sunday in Los Angeles. And that was the start of a chapter of accidents!

MILLION SALES

For Monday. Since by this time they were en route to Los Angeles, no-one could locate them or find out what was wrong—so everything was cancelled. The Platters arrived next day and Buck, determined that the record should be cut, began frantically to round up a band and get a studio.

Eventually all was set, and then came the final blow. Tony Williams' voice gave out, because of a cold !

The Platters were at that time appearing in Las Vegas. Buck Ram, the technicians in Los Angeles, briefed the already cans and assembled and rehearsed the band in readiness. They had thought the session was

But "Doctor" Buck had his own remedy for that particular ailment—a strong shot of brandy and a high-pressure pep talk. Medically unsound, perhaps, but musically—well, " The Great Pretender " has topped the million mark and is still selling.

With the Platters teamwork is everything. Although each is a talented soloist in his or her own right, the group always comes first. Their individual personalities are merged into one new and exciting personality—that of the Platters.

Lead tenor with the group is Tony Williams. Born in Elizabeth, New Jersey, Tony, the youngest of seven children, always wanted to be a singer. His mother was church soloist for many years, and music was consequently an important part of Tony's home life.

Both he and sister Linda (later to become well-known American r-and-b recording artiste Linda Hayes) studied voice and while still at school had much early training as gospel singers.

Tony went straight from High School into the Air Force, and it was here that he first entered the field of " pop" music, singing with his company band. The experience he gained stood him in good stead when, on his discharge from the service, he decided to make show business his career.

He worked as a semi-professional in and around New York, and later moved to Los Angeles, where he was working as a car-washer by day and a singer by night when he was discovered by Buck Ram, and became associated with the Platters.

David Lynch was a cab-driver before joining the group. Dave is a colourful character. Raised by foster-parents in St. Louis, Missouri, he ran away from home when he was thirteen. Since then he has travelled the world and tried his hand at just about everything.

Now he sings second tenor with the Platters, usually taking the lead for beat numbers.

Until a few years ago Herbert Reed was a tenor, singing at one is a showman to his fingertips.

Less extrovert, but equally talented, is baritone Paul Robi. Born in New Orleans, he studied piano for nine years, and was working as a single in night clubs, singing and playing piano, when Buck Ram gave him the chance of joining the Platters. Paul takes his music seriously and is emerging as a promising writer and arranger.

Zola Taylor, the femme of the group, is another pianist and composer—this in addition to her singing and dancing. After winning an amateur talent contest she turned professional singer, appearing with several small bands around Los Angeles before taking her place with the group.

On stage, Zola is a "natural". She has a poise and elegance which are striking, but give the girl a jump tune or comedy number and she will time with the famous " Wings Over Jordan" Choir. Then, almost overnight his voice changed to fabulously low bass!

Now this little man with the big voice is a member of the Platters. The Platters, whistler and comedian, he really tear it apart.

THE PLATTERS

New Bill Haley film even rock-and-rolls the cha-cha-cha!

"THE little people are taking over," was the apt phrase Alex Macintosh used to describe the new trend in popular music a few weeks ago. The new Bill Haley film, "Rock Around the Clock," which opens at the London Pavilion today (Friday), shows you exactly how they're setting about it.

The "little people" in this case are the Bill Haley Comets, the Platters and Freddie Bell and his Bellboys, who, between them, get through something like a dozen numbers in a picture mainly designed as a showcase for rock-and-roll.

The story, which tells how a group of local boys are discovered entertaining a small-town teenage crowd and are signed up to bring big business back to the dance hall circuits, might have come straight out of "Variety."

It is only when we come to the sequences linking the musical numbers together that we stray out into the realm of fiction. Here we find the band manager and the female booking agent trying to beat each other's percentages down in the middle of a necking session.

Personally, I'd have thought they'd have done better if they'd concentrated on one thing at a time!

ROCK 'N' ROLL JAMBOREE

But to begin at the beginning. The opening scene shows a "conventional" dance band playing to an almost deserted hall. The bass player looks bored to death, and business is obviously very bad.

Steve Hollis, the manager, can stand it no longer. He tells the bandleader: "The only thing in your outfit that's up to date is your wrist-watch," and drives off into the night. He pulls up at a place called Strawberry Hill, where the posteriors of the local youth are wagging happily to the sound of—yes, Bill Haley and his Comets.

Steve at once shows himself up as a complete square by telling Haley his music is "very good." Someone replies, "You mean 'crazy,' man." But Steve quickly picks his way through the rock-and-roll jargon and, before you can say "Cool," he's got the local boys signed up.

The rest of the film describes how the success of the Comets spreads, first to a college for young ladies, then right across the country.

The climax of the film is a huge rock-and-roll jamboree, which is televised from coast to coast. The visual antics of the Comets during the rocking finale make the Eric Delaney Band look as sedate as a string quartet.

The atmosphere gets so heated that the tenorman starts playing with his hands behind his back (work that one out), taking off his jacket meanwhile; the bass player actually climbs aboard his instrument in an attempt to improve the beat; and leader Haley jerks his guitar up and down like some "groovy" mechanical digger.

As you can see, this isn't a film for the square—or for the person with any degree of musical taste.

Let us not kid ourselves, however, you may find "Rock Around the Clock" horrifying. It may even strike you that the moral of the film—"it's the percentage that counts"—is the exact opposite of that expressed in "The Benny Goodman Story."

But, with the Comets performing most of their well-known recorded titles, the Platters doing their hit versions of "Only You" and "The Great Pretender" and Tony Martinez's Band rock-and-rolling the cha-cha-cha, this a film the young fans are going to turn out in their thousands to see.

The "little people" are coming your way. Don't say you haven't been warned!

CHARLES GOVEY.

ROCK 'N' ROLL SUPPLEMENT

HE WRITES ROCK 'N' ROLL AND HE SINGS IT, TOO

QUESTION — What is the connection between "Ain't That A Shame," "Bo Weevil" and "I'm In Love Again"?

Answer—Fats Domino.

Fats wrote "Ain't That A Shame," which was carried to Top Twenty by Pat Boone. He wrote "Bo Weevil," which made the grade with the help of Teresa Brewer.

Now he has done it solo! His record of another Domino original, "I'm In Love Again," has rocketed to the American best-sellers and is repeating its success in the NME charts here.

Although Fats has only just become a nation-wide hit in the States, he was a big regional favourite for years. For example, last year through the south and south-west, he is reported to have covered no less than 30,000 miles in 355 days.

★

Perhaps you do not realise what a hardship this is. Territory artists in America invariably play one-night stands, often travelling 700 miles through the night to their next date; which, in these underdeveloped parts, will often be at a baseball park, or a converted barn, a fairground—anywhere that an enterprising man can erect a stage and pack in an audience.

The performers snatch a few hours' sleep in their coaches, eat at wayside diners, dress in the bus and wash where they can, for there are seldom adequate facilities on the job. Nevertheless, as they tolerate the discomforts, as they tolerate the discomforts, in the tremendous following in the area for the type of entertainment now known as rock 'n' roll provides handsome dividends.

Born Antoine Domino in New Orleans, 25 years ago, Fats comes from a family of six brothers and three sisters. He started playing piano at five, and eventually worked with local groups as vocalist as well as pianist. Finally, a few years ago, he took his own group on the road.

The Imperial Record firm (with which Slim Whitman is also associated), realising Fats' potentialities, snapped him up in 1953 to record such numbers as "You Said You Loved Me," "Rose Mary," "Love Me," and "Don't You Hear Me Calling You," all of which passed almost unnoticed by the general public, though they were grouped together here on London REP.1022.

Except for the obvious standards he has recorded—"My Blue Heaven," etc.—Fats writes almost all his own material in collaboration with Dave Bartholomew. "Ain't That A Shame" and "Bo Weevil" netted him a tidy sum in royalties.

But since he has reached the goal of all recording artists by winning a coveted gold disc for "I'm In Love Again," events like the Wrigley Field Jazz Festival in Los Angeles, where Fats was introduced to a crowd of 25,000 by Louis Armstrong as "a man deserving of Hall of Fame," will become frequent highlights in his career.

★

The current rock 'n' roll craze now sweeping two continents is a cross between the long-established rhythm-and-blues and country-and-western types of music. The former style is that of the Southern Negro, while the latter is of the American Hillbilly. However, Fats can laugh at these idioms, as he has been combining their styles for many years.

His group includes country-styled guitarists—whereas his saxist is very much r. and b. Domino's singing bridges the gap between the two conventions, and his originals range from "Bo Weevil" (typical c. and w.) to "I'm In Love Again" (characteristic r. and b.).

In the States, "My Blue Heaven," the reverse side of "I'm In Love Again," accounted for almost 50 per cent. of the record's outstanding popularity.

FATS DOMINO

"My Blue Heaven," in Fats' c. and w. vein has an obvious sequel in "When My Dreamboat Comes Home," heard on his latest coupling here. The other side, "So Long," is an earthy blues directed at the r. and b. fans.

These titles are both showing vigorous signs of life in the American Charts, so it may well be that Fats will soon have another gold disc to his credit.

Recently, Fats has been signed to appear in a new film, "Shake, Rattle And Roll," being made as a sequel to the controversial "Rock Around The Clock." He is also featured in disc-jockey Alan Freed's current rock 'n' roll package show.

So if Alan's proposed British tour comes off this autumn, we may soon be seeing Fats Domino in person over here.

Guy's R And R!

I'VE BEEN BENDING my ears happily to a new rock 'n' roll disc which will hit the counters in a Philips' sleeve during December.

Titles are "Crazy With Love" and "Singing the Blues". It's a disc which is going to set the fans on fire—a first-rate rocker.

By a new star?

BY GUY MITCHELL!

'Happy Music'
(to replace 'R. & R.')

BUCK RAM, THE SONG-WRITING MANAGER of The Platters, is one of the men behind the rock 'n' roll boom. Buck not only stages tremendous rock 'n' roll shows, not only manages rock 'n' roll artists, he also writes rock 'n' roll hits like "The Great Pretender" and "Only You".

"But now," says he, "I'm getting worried about the bad name this kind of music is attracting. Lots of folk are picking up the unpleasant things connected with the stuff—influenced by off-colour lyrics and riotous demonstrations."

Therefore Buck is trying to change the name of rock 'n' roll to "Happy Music." His future shows will all go out under the heading "Buck Ram Presents Happy Music." The slogan he is trying to popularise is "The Happy Beat For Happy Feet."

"I'm trying to stop people from calling it rock 'n' roll because of the bad connotations the name has in their minds," adds Buck.

I reckon he's got about as much chance of getting people to call rock 'n' roll "Happy Music" as Gene Vincent has of appearing in opera at Covent Garden!

Leaves Decca

Buck Ram had arranged for Big Swing Bands. He groomed the rough coloured boys into Las Vegas material. Most of his songs (e.g. 'Twilight Time') were pre-rock ballads.

Curiously, there were no riots when this film was first shown in Britain. The violence snowballed only *after* we read about minor skirmishes in the Press. 'Clock' is still one of the best R&R films and quite accurate, a real document of its times. The fact is there was no band that sounded like Haley – so if he was copying he was a bloody bad copy cat. No! Haley was an *original*.

Friday, September 21, 1956

DON'T THINK IT ALL BEGAN WITH PRESLEY AND HALEY!

A survey of the 30 years of musical history that lie behind rock 'n' roll

by **MIKE BUTCHER**

IT certainly didn't start with " ROCK Around The Clock " and " Shake, Rattle And ROLL." Or with the record called " Rock And Roll" which the Boswell Sisters made as long ago as 1934!

The mixture of " nerve-jangling piano, neurotic sax and jackhammer rhythms " (to quote *Down Beat's* recent description of rock 'n' roll) got its present name just a few seasons ago, when U.S. discjockey Alan Freed hit upon the three magic words, used in quite a different context by the Boswells.

As a billing tag for his programmes.

Most of the discs that Alan liked to spin came from a thriving but specialised section of the American catalogues headed " Rhythm-And-Blues," devoted almost exclusively to coloured artists without a general pop reputation at the time—Fats Domino, Clyde McPhatter and Earl Bostic, for instance.

However, far from representing a new trend, rhythm-and-blues records have existed in the States in one guise or another since soon after the end of the first world war !

'Fhev were called " race " records then—a tactless reference to the Negro race, for whom they were primarily intended—and our story begins in 1920, when the first coupling by a Negro blues singer appeared on a major American label, Mamie Smith's " Crazy Blues " and " It's Right Here With You " on OKeh.

Legend has it that the important U.S. companies had been reluctant to record coloured talent until then, for fear of antagonising their white customers, and that OKeh decided to take a chance on Mamie because they were desperately in need of an " answer ", to Sophie Tucker whose style Miss Smith approximated.

Race discs

Sales of " Crazy Blues " turned out to be fantastic, nevertheless, so not only OKeh but every firm in the record field began to use Negro entertainers as a regular policy—though a lurking fear of " lily-white " disapproval prompted them to segregate a large proportion of their coloured artists in special, separate lists.

Such now-famous blues, jazz and popular performers as Louis Armstrong, Duke Ellington, Ethel Waters, the late Fats Waller, King Oliver and Jelly Roll Morton made their first discs for the " race " market in the early 'twenties.

Bessie Smith, the unsurpassed " Empress Of The Blues," accounted for American Columbia sales figures totalling more than 6,000,000 (a phenomenal figure then) between 1923 and 1929 with the sides now reissued on four Philips LP's (BBL.7019, 7020, 7042, 7049) . . . and, in time, as prejudice against Negro performers began to break down across large areas of the States, those who showed signs of having interracial appeal were transferred to the main " pop " catalogues.

The economic depression of the early 'thirties which came close to putting the entire U.S. record industry out of business, caused the supply

until it almost stopped. Bessie Smith made no discs at all between a session in 1933 and her tragic death four years later.

But as the financial conditions improved, the " race " record output started rising again. Louis Jordan made his first titles for American Decca's " race " list in 1938—and before long he had won international stardom on the strength of " G.I. Jive," " Choo Choo Ch'Boogie," " There Ain't Nobody Here But Us Chickens," etc. All of which would still have a direct appeal to the current generation of rock 'n' roll fans, incidentally !

Then came a vocal group known as the Cats And The Fiddle, never very well-known in Britain but a Stateside hit during the war with more than 40 fast-selling RCA platters to their credit. Your present writer caught the Cats' act at the Apollo Theatre, New York, in 1944. And everything they did—vocally or physically—is reflected in the sounds and gestures of a typical rock 'n' roll singer today.

In 1946, at the instigation of *Billboard*, American record companies decided to drop the now-resented " race " tag in favour of a fresh term for their indigenously Negro releases—rhythm-and-blues.

The Cats And The Fiddle disappeared from sight, but dozens of other r and b specialists took their place, all giving out with the same rockin', rollin' body gyrations onstage, all favouring the same kind of violent vocal or instrumental projection, the same high-tenor and deepbass singing soloists.

And one by one, the trek of entertainers once categorised as r and b continued without end into the limitless universe of " ordinary" popular music . . . Nat " King " Cole, Billy Eckstine, Nellie Lutcher, Dinah Washington . . . until the inevitable happened.

Rhythm-and-blues *per se* became the latest commercial craze for white and coloured fans alike.

Coverage

Earl Bostic's riproaring alto-sax rendition of "Flamingo" (1953), made to sound as if he were using a razor blade instead of a reed, excited a

Los Angeles to New York, to Paris, London and Stockholm, when King Records released it in America. Vogue in Europe.

Next, before the current period of almost complete integration, a whole series of r and b hits, in coverage versions by " accepted " pop artists swept the world from the early months of 1954.

The white Crew-Cuts (Mercury) covered the coloured Penguins' "Earth Angel" (London) and Chords' "Sh'Boom" (Columbia); Perry Como (HMV) covered Gene and Eunice's "Ko-Ko-Mo" (unreleased here); and Bill Haley's Comets boosted their fast-rising popularity with a commercially momentous remake (Brunswick) of Joe Turner's wailing blues sensation, "Shake, Rattle And Roll" (American Atlantic).

By 1955/56, the r[..] b[..] came near to completing its [...] over in the white-American [...] European public's affections from [...] to r and b à la Perry Como, [...] Berry's "Maybellene" (London [...] P[...]der, "Only You," and [...] Prayer," "Magic Touch" ([...] "Why (Mercury), the Teen[...] [...] mbia) Do Fools Fall in Lo[...] Fats Domino's " I'm In [...] Again" (London); Clyde McP[...] " Trea- sure Of Love" (London) Little Richard's "Long, Tall [...] (unreleased here) and often [...] domin- ated the " Billboard" [...] frame. often the NME's Blue [..]

won complete favour, on [...] cords and in person, in America's [...] s' neigh- bourhoods where the [...] oured per- formers had invariably [...] coloured hitherto. Boyd Be[...] and Carl Perkins (whose "S[...] crashed "Blue Suede Sho[...] America's localised rhythm-and-blues charts) and above all Elvis Presley and Bill Haley (who turned as big a proportion of Negro [...] as white for their discs) are good examples.

So it can fairly [...] d that the rock 'n' roll craze has brought about at least one social b[...] in the vital sphere of racial relations. It has produced—or, rather, de-loped—a form of musical entertainment in which race is no longer mainly Negro-American but, simply, American.

And every white tone-see teen-ager who learns to regard the Dominos and McP[...] of their nation as idols is knocking at least a small nail into the possible coffin of racial hatred.

Literally hundreds of Negro show people had gained a huge white public in the States over 30-odd years before rock 'n' roll hit the headlines, of course, by specialising in Tin Pan Alley ballads (Cole, Eckstine), smart-set sophistication (Lena Horne, Dorothy Dandridge), art music (Paul Robeson Marian Anderson) or jazz (choose your own examples!)

However, the present rage of rhythm-and-blues, rock 'n' roll—call it what you like—a musical pastime once restricted to the vast mass of American Negro people, especially in the south, has grown huge enough to embrace all races and regions.

Benefit

Nor was the traffic [...] a one-way track for several white vocalists

---

Elvis Presley is reported to be entirely fancy free as far as the opposite sex is concerned, but this picture rushed from the States captures the young lady on left as his girl-friend, Judy Spreckles, heiress to some sugar millions. The other glamourette is dancer Liza Haundon, and the picture was taken at a TV rehearsal.

Tony Crombie (at back, centre) rehearsing his new Rock 'n' Roll stage show which opened with great success at Portsmouth last week.

Jazzers and folkies were always ready to find black precedent for R&R originals. Actually, ragtime began it all back in the 1890s – but who says there's no Father Christmas?!

ANOTHER CURRYS BARGAIN!

Best portable radio value ever!

VIDOR PORTABLE RADIO

'MY LADY CATHERINE'

20/- DEPOSIT — BY POST

The new Vidor luxury portable radio complete with batteries for only 20/- deposit—posted to your home! With its attractive handbag size case, high volume 5" speaker, low-consumption valves and Home and Continental tuning MY LADY CATHERINE is the best portable radio value ever!

BUY this easy way. Set and batteries supplied for 20/- deposit. *Refunded if not completely satisfied.* Balance by eight monthly payments of 32 6.

Cash Price 11½ Gns. Batteries 11/6 extra.

FROM YOUR LOCAL BRANCH OF CURRYS OR BY POST: Send 20/- deposit to Currys Ltd., Dept. G.53 Worthy Park, Winchester, Hants.

CURRYS LTD

Why no demand for these baby discs?

TALKING POINTS

Conducted by CHARLES GOVEY

GEOFFREY BIRD, of Tavistock Street, Leamington Spa, Warwickshire, raises an interesting point. He writes:

I recently made the amazing discovery that in my home town of Leamington Spa, only one 7-inch standard play record as sold to every hundred 10-inch 78s.

Do the public realise that standard play discs are (1) unbreakable; (2) have no surface noise; (3) weigh one-ninth as much; (4) are the same price as the 10 in. America. so why not here?

I think insufficient publicity is given to these "babies... They are all the go in America, so why not here?

about the same time as "Shake, Rattle And Roll."

Then, of course, it soared to the top in America and subsequently here as well (Autumn, 1955), and now it

Because he's Elvis

Miss R. HOYLAND, of Huddersfield Road, Elland, Yorkshire, writes:

Does reader "Mac" (Talking Points, Sept. 28) really blame Lonnie Donegan for the style which has made Donegan so famous? Does he think it. Does "Mac" think Donegan would be so popular if he altered his?

With regards to Presley, I have the honesty to admit that he cannot sing, but he has got something! When he does appear in England next year, I shall be one of the first to go and see him—not because he can sing, but because he's Elvis!

Complete loss

Reader K. WOODWARD, of Kenilworth Drive, Rickmansworth, Herts, writes:

I could not agree more with reader A. Vincent about the Tony Crombie show at the Palladium. I watched them on TV, as I was unlucky in getting a ticket—or was I lucky?

The band appeared to be at a complete loss as to what they were playing. If we can't have rock 'n roll bands that come up to the standard of Bill Haley, then why try?

In the open

Reader R. McCALLAM, of Moorclose Estate, Workington, Cumberland, writes:

If 'teenage' reaction to "Rock Around the Clock" is so riotous in

our major cities, I hate to think what will happen when Bill Haley and his Comets eventually appear in this country.

Could the banning of their film put an end to their proposed visit, or are the cities just going to sit back and see what happens when our teenager and Mr. Haley stand face to face?

Perhaps Mr. Haley (and theatre managers) would feel safer if these concerts were held on the outskirts of the cities?

Cradle singers

CHRISTOPHER LOVELL, of Westcroft Road, Carshalton, Surrey, writes:

I like reader Yardley's nerve in saying that Johnnie Ray was a topliner when Presley and Vincent were still in their cradles. The way Ray cries, he sounds as if he's still in his!

The world's coming to something if you have to be born before JR to be a great singer, and anyway, millions of other singers were topliners before the Ray fuss ever started.

Great success

VALERIE BEACH, of Chestnut Road, Tottenham, London, N.17, writes:

I went along to the London Palladium to see Tony Crombie's TV show, and I'm glad to say he was a great success. Everybody was clapping and tapping their feet, and I'm certain it won't put anybody off buying Bill Haley's records.

In fact, I'm sure there'll be quite a few looking for Tony Crombie's records. I say good luck to him, for I'm certain he'll be a success.

Baker butchered !

RALPH JEFFERY, of Hollin Park Road, Leeds, writes:

Something worse than rock 'n' roll has happened to British dance music! What used to be the only high quality programme in a welter of Tin Pan Alley mediocrities — Kenny Baker's Dozen—was foully murdered the other evening.

The best outlet for new R&R was Radio Luxembourg, on the Continent. Hard to obtain good reception; you had to fine twiddle getting a lot of German and French babble in your search. Because of this remoteness the music seemed that much more exciting. From a distant land beyond the blue horizon, or maybe up in the clouds of some Rupert Bear world. Today Rock is too accessible!

Pity 78 rpm discs became obsolete. I liked them *because* of their bulk and fragility. I treasured them more because they might smash. I felt I'd got more for my money – a pop Dresden or Ming. 45s are insignificant midgets by comparison.

SPECIAL BY

NEW BATTERY-OPERATED PORTABLE PLAYER MARKS

End Of The Handle-Turning Machine

DESPITE THE POST-WAR BOOM in gramophone records and gramophone equipment and the fantastic progress made in the realms of Hi-Fi and microgroove discs, one thing has remained an important sales item amid every company's product.

The ordinary, portable, hand-wound gramophone.

Even as late as six months ago an executive of one of the top firms in the business told me that the hand-wound portables were still selling in tremendous quantities.

"There are parts of the world", he said, "where the hand-wound portable is the only possible means of playing gramophone records. Remember that there are still places without electricity, that people buy the handle jobs for picnics and for boating on the river. We have to keep making them".

★

NOW AT LAST, the death knell is sounding for the hand-wound machine. It has hung on grimly, and while it has remained so has one of the strongest arguments for the retention of 78's. The end for both is now in sight.

It is to be brought about by the appearance on the market of the battery-operated portable record players. No winding, no plugging-in needed either.

I have been listening to one of the first of these machines

to reach the counters in quantity in Britain. A neat little job, it stands only eight inches high!

Perfectly portable it plays 45 rpm discs, is powered merely by four torch batteries! Secret of its size and strength, of course, lies in the fact that this is an all-transistor set doing away with old-fashioned valves.

FOR PICNICS IT'S A NATURAL . . . for the teen-ager who wants to use it in another room away from the family; it's a gift that doesn't need a power plug. So compact is the design that you can store 24-45 rpm discs inside the player. And it will play 1,500 sides before the batteries need changing.

The new portable has other teen-age attractions too. It can be used as a morse code trainer for boys. There's a talkback accessory which can make the set useful for a two-way communication, or as a baby alarm.

The set I tested was a Philco, but Pam and other firms are also manufacturing along these lines.

The new portables are not all that expensive, which is another reason why they will be finding their way into teen-age hands.

NEWS OF THEIR development has been somewhat over-shadowed by Hi-Fi talk and the growing battle of the speeds.

But to me the machines are perhaps the most important factor in the battle. They mean that the 78 can die peacefully without any disc fan having to suffer. Throw away that handle!

— GEE NICHOLL

Friday, October 5, 1956

What makes them do this?
A psychologist reports on ROCK 'N' ROLL

(Note: New York disc-jockey Art Ford recently shared his WNEW radio microphone with Dr. Ben Walstein, a psychologist, for the purpose of analysing the appeal of rock 'n' roll. The following interview is taken from a transcript of that programme).

ART FORD: People say—"Why do you play rock 'n' roll?" I say—"Don't ask me, ask the people why they like it, why they want it. Find out why they want it. If you have a complaint, complain to the people, complain to life—don't complain to me. I try to reflect it in playing the music people want, because if I do anything less I am being false to them. It's difficult for me to understand rock 'n' roll sometimes, then it's also my job to do what I am doing today . . . get hold of an expert find out, and study the subject.

So we searched the field of psychology for a brilliant person like Dr. Ben Walstein and I have brought him to our studio here tonight to psycho-analyse some records of rock 'n' roll. He admits he's on new territory, and he admits it's a brand new field for everybody.

First of all, Dr. Walstein, we would like to listen to a song by Elvis Presley. He sings "Blue Suede Shoes."

(Music)

DR. WALSTEIN: Well, the first impression I think that I get from it has to do with this business of "don't step on my blue suede shoes" . . . allow me to have a sense of independence. The interesting thing about this has, I think, to do with the adolescent's desire for some degree of privacy.

Presley

I think also that there is some sexual component in this in that one may say that the blue suede shoes represent something that has not been tried yet by the adolescent. I think, too, that this need for independence that the adolescent has is the thing that he is striving to achieve and he has not yet achieved it, and I think it has a lot to do with an attempt of adolescents to strike some kind of roots in this world.

It has to do, too, with a search for something indigenous and, of course, the theme of the song again has to do with the awkwardness and the lost quality that we find in adolescents. That they realise they are not quite as smart as they thought they were and they really don't know how smart they are.

AF: There is sort of a savage, animal-like quality in his performance, in a way which is lacking in the usual theatrical refinements of show business, sort of a naturalistic school of singing. You think there might be some remarkable connection between this and the popular Marlon Brando, who also works very naturally? He comes from a school of acting which supports and endorses naturalism.

BW: Well, it seems to me that this is a general trend in all of the arts. You will find it in non-objective paintings, as well, where there is an attempt to project a moment of feeling a person has. There is certainly an anti-formalism in Presley's style, and this is due to the fact this is in part what all adolescents do. It's a kind of rebellious mood. Some may idolise their parents, others may feel that their parents failed and they would like to strike out anew, for this anti-formalism. I think, is one of the characteristics . . . One of the things that is necessary for this kind of rebellion.

But I think that the emphasis is on the moment of experience . . . the immediate experience as you call it . . . the return to naturalism, to get away. Well, this is something that all adolescents go for, to get away from the phoniness that the adults are immersed in.

The singer's use of falsetto is significant, because here we have an expression of a kind of problem that all adolescents have, and that is the attempt to struggle through the period where at males, for instance are trying to achieve some kind of masculine identification, and I think that this falsetto expression is it.

There's another point that I would like to make about this record, and that is this business about "having fun tonight", "let's have fun tonight". You know, if you took a poll of a lot of these youngsters and asked them exactly what they mean by fun, I doubt if you would get a very clear picture of what they are talking about.

I don't think they really know . . . but this has to do generally with a kind of aimlessness and at the same time a searching for a meaning in life.

AF: I certainly agree with you after observing a lot of the kids over the years, and I don't think we can blame them for that desire. I, personally, just wish that they find what they are looking for.

Elvis Presley is so important in the popular music picture that our guest psychologist this evening certainly should have a second chance to hear him sing Elvis Presley . . . I particularly choose this record because there is less of the usual overemphasis on the echo chambers, and it's a little bit easier to hear what he's singing about . . . "I'm Left, You're Right."

(Music)

Aimlessness

AF: This next record by Little Richard—"Long Tall Sally"—is rock 'n' roll at its wildest and lustiest. I'll say no more than that.

(Music)

BW: Well, this is a rather interesting record from another standpoint. It continues in the same feeling that the other record has, but at the same time in this record we see much more clearly the fact that the words are not quite as important as the rhythm

BW: There's a definite sort of cowboy, western style to this music. And I think that this has to do with a general tendency that I've noted in people going back to folk music in the last 10 or 15 years and it's . . . the people liking it very much and it's achieved quite a bit of popularity.

AF: A very interesting statement, Dr. Walstein. I think that a lot of the kids sitting there by the radio are saying, "I think he's right . . . he's cool."

Not harmful

Too many large forms of amusement have rejected rock 'n' roll . . . scoffed at it . . . large media, . . . because they cannot understand it . . . won't make the effort to understand it. In general, I just wondered if, in concluding, you had any overall thoughts in just how harmful they are for our youth, or how harmful they are for anybody to be played, using some discretion of course.

BW: I have listened to some of the rock 'n' roll records at home, and I have listened to these records here this evening, and in my opinion I see nothing particularly harmful about the music as such.

I have already suggested that in every generation adolescence finds some style of music that expresses some of the yearning, the frustrations, the loss, and at the same time, the frantic searching quality that adolescents have, and I don't see why—if the kids today have decided that this is the kind of music that expresses their search and their frustration—why we should ban it or interfere with their listening to it.

In fact, it seems to me that it would make a rather interesting study to look into the motivations, perhaps not so much the conscious rationalisation about it, but some of the unconscious motivations of adults who are so concerned about the fact that kids listen to this kind of music.

AF: May I say I know a lot of kids who would be delighted to submit their parents to the test.

An early example of useful employment for psychology in R&R. The Doctor says it's 'anti-formalism', a projection of a 'moment of feeling'. It certainly was a moment, a wild one that soon got tamed by regular show-biz, but it was worth the fleeting sensation of pleasure – like gulping a thick squidgy cream eclair.

'Green Door': one of my favourite novelty songs. All three versions got on the charts, showing that songs could still be more important than singers. Sturdy song vehicles are in even shorter supply today.

THE 'GREEN DOOR' OPENS TO SUCCESS FOR—

No less than six recording artists or acts came up with the same problem a few weeks back. They all wanted to know what was a-cookin' behind the " Green Door"—an oblong piece of wood which, as immortalised in song by tunesmiths Marvin Moore and Bob Davie, apparently acts as a barrier to pleasures as mysterious as "The Thing."

Ray Ellington did it for Columbia, the Maple Leaf Four and Tanner Sisters for Oriole, but if you want to think of the " Door " as an *entrée* to success, it's Jim Lowe (London, the original American version), Frankie Vaughan (Philips) and Glen Mason (Parlophone) who were lucky enough to fling it wide open with their respective efforts.

a lot in the lives of all three vocalists, so let's open the files and remind ourselves what each of them has been doing until now.

Although Jim and Frankie were holding 8th and 9th positions on last week's NME sales chart, strenuously trying to nose each other out of the way while Glen lagged behind at 26th place, the contest for ultimate honours had only just started then. So turn to page 5 of our current issue to see how the various candidates are faring.

Whatever the outcome, however, " Green Door " will certainly mean

mercial artist" when the show-biz bit him good and hard.

Frankie

We thus find Frankie trudging to London after National Service with the RAMC, ostensibly to look for work with his pencil and brush and actually on the look-out for any kind of theatrical audition.

Billy March of the Delfont Office listened to Vaughan—then asked within a split second if Frankie could " do Kingston Empire next week, bottom of the bill, pay your own accompanist."

Needless to say, Frankie could—and did! The bookers liked his act. Which meant that our handsome " hopeful" was set for an instructive year on the road with " The Old And The New " (starring Hetty King) in due course, even if he did suffer a somewhat hungry period in between.

Subsequent dance gigs with both Nat Temple and a Maurice Winnick unit gave Frankie the useful experience of working with name bands, and HMV made him a significant name on wax from 1953 onwards, thanks mostly to " My Sweetie Went Away," " Istanbul," apart from the aforementioned " Help."

He was big enough by 1955 to head the resident London cast in " Wildfire," the profitable ice-extravaganza which gave Frankie at least one ideally fashioned feature number in the shape of " That's How A Love Song Was Born " (recorded after he had left HMV for his present label, Philips).

Variety tours, augmented with summer seasons at the coast, added each week to the host of Vaughan fans when a nation-wide audience, seeing " Mr. Dynamite" in action, revelled in his smoothly confident showmanship. And a long-awaited movie break comes his way in " The Cast Iron Shore" currently before the cameras with Anna Neagle in the lead.

There can be few artists more actively interested than Frankie in donating their talents to charity. It's therefore a happy coincidence that " Green Door" will be of direct benefit to the fund which this warm-hearted star particularly favours.

For Frankie Vaughan volunteered to give the National Association of Boys' Clubs his entire sum of royalties derived from sales of the record in question—a typically generous gesture which he made as soon as plans for him to cut " Green Door" were announced.

He has " sold " the songs to millions via TV as well as in his stage act and on wax, the small screen representing yet another medium in which Frankie excels.

Jim

Jim Lowe is such a newcomer to even comparative stardom that it would be in order, for us to delete " remind ourselves," and insert " find out " in his case. " Door" was his first record for the fast-rising Dot company in America. But Jim showed signs of life in another field when he wrote " Gambler's Guitar" (a Mercury success for Rusty Draper) in 1953.

He's 29 years old, six feet tall, and hails from Springfield, Missouri, where he spent his boyhood years. Lowe studied medicine at the University of Missouri in 1942—and he might have been a doctor today if the army hadn't called him a few months later.

Instead of returning to college, Jim worked as a radio announcer on demob . . . first for a local station, then as staff announcer and disc-jockey for CBS and NBC in Chicago until the sales of " Gambler's Guitar" prompted him to settle in New York a couple of years back so that he could be permanently close to Tin Pan Alley.

Lowe sang a bit in his radio days, and extended his vocal activities to include some in-person dates after publishers had heard him demonstrate his own songs—and were duly impressed.

Nevertheless, the international triumph of " Green Door" (for Jim's waxing has reached and held a coveted position in the U.S.," Top Three" as detailed by *Billboard*) came as an exciting surprise to everyone from Dot Records downwards . . . so the fortunate Mr. Lowe is only beginning to wonder which he should concentrate upon, writing ditties for other artists or singing them himself.

Frankie Vaughan has no such problem, of course. He's already known to the entire British fan public as one of our foremost personality vocalists. And allowing that " Green Door" is his biggest hit to date, some of Frank's earlier platters —notably " No Help Wanted" and " Tweedle Dee"—made quite a positive impression on the market.

Born in Liverpool 28 years ago, Frankie trained as a commercial artist at Leeds College of Art, but in the words of one pun-loving reporter, he became a different kind of " com-

Glen

But perhaps it is our third " Green Door" entrant, Glen Mason, who in 1956 has had particular reason to bless television. ATV to be precise, and those watching it on a Sunday evening.

Glen studied and taught acting techniques in his native Scotland—he's a 25-year-old son of Stirling and ferociously proud of his north o' the border accent—before progressing to Scottish summer shows as a vocal entertainer in 1950.

Three years later he came south " to conquer London," seldom an easy task however gifted you are, and a lack of funds or solid prospects forced him to return home for a while no less than three times in 12 months.

A purposeful Scot will always keep coming back for more, though . . . as, in fact, Glen did.

He landed a cabaret date at Churchill's and recording sessions for

Philips. Nothing happened. Months of occasional jobs, continually fruitless hunts for more work, and a gramophonic switch to the MGM international list. Still nothing in the wind.

Then, suddenly, he clicked. A growing realisation in the trade that Mason was a " natural" for TV prompted Jack Jackson to leap into action.

Jack hired Glen for his ATV series. And after 40 weeks someone added up the score and found that Glen had made no less than 36 appearances on the " Jack Jackson Show " meanwhile!

He's a firmly entrenched television favourite now with all generations of viewers—so much so that he could now easily step into any area of the pop field. Parlophone Records took him from MGM and thus brought him back to the " home" catalogue.

Which brings us to the point where the " Green Door" opened for Glen, as well as for Jim Lowe and Frankie Vaughan.

SIX HIT RECORDS! ON ONE HIT SONG !!

FRANKIE VAUGHAN ★ GLEN MASON (Parlophone)
(Philips)

JIM LOWE
(London)

GREEN DOOR

MAPLE LEAF TANNER SISTERS ★ RAY
FOUR ★ (Oriole) ELLINGTON
(Oriole) (Columbia)

WHAT'S THE SECRET
YOU'RE KEEPIN'? ★

FRANCIS, DAY & HUNTER, LTD.
138-140 Charing Cross Rd., London, W.C.2
Telephone : TEMple Bar 9351/5

NORTHERN NEWS

The **R**... GONE CRAZY MEET ROP

It's Taken Only Eight Weeks For Him To Become A Topliner!

'DON'T CALL ME ANOTHER PRESLEY... I'M JUST A HAPPY SINGER,' Says New R & R Star

'And Don't Associate Me With Any Sexy Stuff'

● INTO MY OFFICE last Saturday afternoon were ushered two sprightly and smiling young men. One I immediately recognised. He was JOHN KENNEDY; he was a photographer for the RECORD MIRROR in its early days. The other looked familiar to me . . . oh, yes. I remembered—he was the guy with the guitar and the rock 'n roll songs on the previous Monday's 'Off the Record' TV show . . . TOMMY STEELE.

John Kennedy had been to see me four or five weeks before to tell me that he was packing up his photography career and going into show business as a manager . . . "I may have some interesting news for you . . . about a sensational English Elvis Presley," he said. rather vaguely I thought at the time. "His name is Tommy Steele and I guarantee that when I call on you next time he'll be big news."

Well, last Saturday was the 'next time' and certainly John's guarantee had been fulfilled.

For, as you must already know, Tommy Steele is big news.

"I've brought Tommy along," said John, "so that any-

from Bermondsey, too, you know," he said. "I want everybody there to be as proud of me as they are of him."

Well, it's up to Tommy.

If I'm any judge of character, I think he'll be a big hit without getting a big

Next? Plenty.

Impresario Harold Fielding got busy. He sent for John Kennedy and Larry Parnes (Kennedy's partner); now the Fielding office will be responsible for Tommy's bookings under the direction of Ian Bevan.

TOMMY STEELE (above) is a ...... but when he's in action he's still ..... Pictures below, taken by RICHI ..... RICHI HOWELL give you some idea of Tommy at ...

Tommy's real surname was Hicks. 'Steele' was the first of a long line of 'abstract' surnames – Marty Wilde, Billy Fury, Johnnie Gentle, Mory Storm – reminiscent of Dickens. As George Melly wrote later, these names were 'descriptive of their properties' sexual potential.' Steele's success led to an incursion of 'rough trade' lads into the G.B. pop scene, not a few of whom were protégés of 'chicken-hawk' queens. But Tommy Steele soon became the darling of the still influential 'Deb' set, wowing them at the chinless wonder Stork & Condor Clubs, and later entertaining mums and dads. I saw him later on Yarmouth Pier and he was superb – in the tradition of Panto and George Formby. He had, and has, a lovely grin and a chirrupy nature. Thumbs up all round. R&R gave him his chance, but he could have been big any time, especially in war-time.

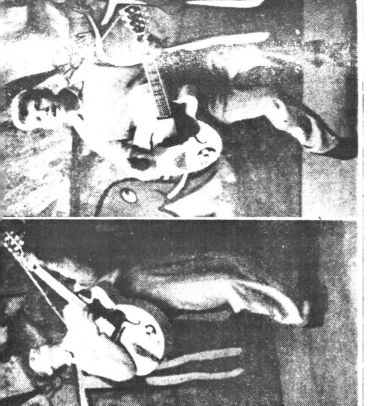

No. 8 in the U.S. hit parade!

JIM LOWE
The Green Door

LONDON RECORDS

HLD 8317 78 or 45 r.p.m.

THE DECCA RECORD CO..

IN TWO MONTHS

TOMMY, A SLIGHTLY-BUILT YOUNGSTER with quite a baby face, his blond hair flowing down his forehead, relaxed into one of the green armchairs (a distinguished visitor's seat) which luxuriously decorate my sanctum — yes I've got TWO of 'em! — and looking first at John Kennedy and them at me, said very quietly:

"**I sure don't know what's hit me. Less than two months ago I was a bell-boy on one of the Cunard Line's ships, at everybody's beck and call and now I'm told I'm going to top bills at variety theatres up and down the country**".

To be quite fair to John who, I think, has done a wonderful publicity job on Tommy, the 19-year-old singer from Frean Street, Bermondsey, London, was permitted to answer all my questions without interruption.

For instance, I asked Tommy: "Are you deliberately imitating Elvis Presley?"

The new rock 'n roll star was emphatic in his reply.

"**Absolutely not. When I was in New York a few months ago on shore leave, I saw Elvis on television. I went crazy about him; but I had developed my own ideas about singing long before I saw him. All my life I've had dreams about singing fast numbers in my own way and everything I do comes naturally, with no thought of anyone else.**"

They say Elvis has cultivated a kind of sexy style and that's how he 'sends' the women. Are you thinking of getting 'em that way, I asked.

"**No sex in my style**," protested Tommy convincingly and vigorously. "**I sing from the heart. I put feeling and power into my numbers. Sex is the last thing in the world I want to suggest when I sing. I want to make everybody happy when I sing. It's because I feel happy when I give out that I want everybody to feel the same way.**"

It was impossible not to mistake the sincerity underlying Tommy's answers. He's a youngster with the zest and zing of youth. He goes all out to spread it.

INTRODUCE HIM

ABOUT EIGHT WEEKS AGO whilst in between leave dates from his ship, Tommy called at the "Two I's" coffee bar in Old Compton Street —the Espresso Street — asked the proprietor, enterprising **Paul Lincoln**, an Australian who has made quite a hit in this country with his novel ideas, if he could play his guitar and sing to the customers. "**I don't want any money for it,**" explained Tommy. "**I just feel like singing and making your customers happy — just for the fun of the thing.**".

Lincoln was impressed by the kid's enthusiasm, and being a man who likes novelty, said okay. And Tommy was in his glory. His local fame spread and soon he was a bigger attraction at the "Two I's" than the excellent coffee served there.

One night Johnny Kennedy happened to look in the cafe, heard Tommy and from that moment on an entirely new career was mapped out for each of them. John packed in his picture-taking agency. Tommy re-signed from the Cunard Line.

An engagement was obtained at the Stork Club in London's West End. Tommy was a sensation with the ritzy customers.

Then quickly followed a gramophone - record test by Decca.

1,100 LETTERS FOLLOW TV SHOW

THEN CAME THE "Off The Record" date. Tommy registered solidly. Up to the time of penning these notes, ELEVEN HUNDRED letters have been received by the singer from viewers who saw and heard him. (Each and every one of them enthusiastically hails him as "England's new wonder singer".)

A return "Off The Record" date has been arranged for December 24; a Jack Jackson ATV engagement is scheduled for Sunday, November 4.

...of November 5. The Empire, Sunderland; week of November 12: The Empire, Nottingham; week of November 19: The Empire, Sheffield; week of November 26, The Hippodrome, Brighton; week of December 3: The Empire, Finsbury Park; week of December 10: The Hippodrome, Birmingham.

Meanwhile, Tommy is filming with Pat O'Brien in "Try Me Tomorrow" at Elstree Studios, and I was told that Paramount Pictures are interested in him, will give him a film test immediately.

Tommy's fame has spread to France, and the other week a leading French impresario made the journey to England to see him in action at the Stork Club.

He was so taken with him that after the show he made him a startling offer to appear in a Parisian cabaret—even though Tommy cannot speak a word of French. But John Kennedy had to turn the offer down. Said John: "**It was a terrific offer. The money was fantastic, but Tommy and I decided we'd prefer, for the time being anyway, a tour round the British music halls**".

Tommy passed without difficulty and rushed on the market by the company was "Rock With the Caveman" — which the youngster himself wrote. It is selling big. Decca has just waxed another Tommy Steele record — "Elevator Rock", backed by "Doomsday Rock". This will be released in a few days.

'BIG TIME, MAYBE BIG HEAD, NEVER'

IT'S A FABULOUS SUCCESS STORY.

Such fame for a young man, barely 20 years of age, and all within two months...

'That's how show business works . . . weird and wonderful. Some artistes I should say, most of them — have to bash away for years and years before cracking into the Big Time; most knock themselves out all their lives without even smelling it.

Here's a mere kid—a top-liner after eight weeks!

Good luck to him. Why not? If some are blessed with good fortune why shouldn't they squeeze every ounce out of it?

I asked Tommy how all this was reacting on him; was he feeling any different today than, say, three months ago?

"**I promise you, Mr. Green, it won't go to my head**," he said sincerely. "**I'm happy, of course I am. It means I can sing like I want to. It means that mum and dad will be able to live more comfortably. It means joy for them and joy for me.**"

Tommy added that Max Bygraves was his idol. "He came ...

WOW! THOSE RIOTOUS ROCK 'N' ROLLERS!

● ROWDY, riotous, rabid, rampaging, roistering rock 'n' rollers — these are the noise-makers who, throughout 1956, have captured the show business spotlight in both Britain and America.

Start of the craze can, of course, be traced back well before this year. Some researchers point to specific records, such as Haley's "Shake, Rattle and Roll," or "Sh . . . boom!" by the Crewcuts. Others argue — and with seeming truth — that there is nothing new in R & R, that it is just a slightly different form of "beat" music to be found at all times in the entertainment of the past half-century or so.

Yet, so far as 1956 is concerned, there seems little argument about the main "rock" practitioners. They are two: Haley and Presley.

Let's take the boisterous Bill first. As this edition of the RECORD MIRROR goes to press, back into the Top Twenty comes his "Rock Around the Clock,"

Britain if its early impact on disc sales is any criterion.

Reports persisted till late 1956 that Presley would visit Britain in person, but (though a Cafe de Paris booking was rumoured) inside opinion suggested he would be too busy filming in Hollywood to make the trip.

　　　★　　　★　　　★

IT WAS TOWARDS the end of June that the Capitol label announced a rival to Presley—Gene Vincent.

This 21-year-old from Norfolk, Virginia, fronts a group called The Blue Caps.

In American advertisement, he was referred to as "the screaming end."

His first release, "Bebop-a-Lula", was said to have passed the 200,000 mark in three weeks in America.

Disc collectors in Britain who bought it heard a high-pitched, stuttering wail, with a nagging, thudding, thumping rhythm accompaniment. While not equalling Presley's eventual successes, Gene quickly established a more than useful British following.

Another American import later in the year were the Teenagers, led by 13-year-old Frankie Lymon. Their ranting "rock" version of "Why Do Fools Fall In Love?" eventually gained a lot of prominence in the Top Ten.

Naturally enough, one early result of the success of these American imports was that Britain started to produce its own home-grown article!

　　　★　　　★　　　★

The Astounding Impact Of An Astounding New Craze:

IT'S MADE MILLIONS FOR ITS INTERPRETERS

popular disc—enjoying spells of popularity extending over many months.

This number is so prominent in the growth of the R & R cult it is worth digressing a little to learn just how it came to be written.

Following pertinent account is quoted from a New York music publisher's release.

★

JAMES E. MYERS, publisher and writer under the pen name of Jimmy DeKnight of "Rock Around the Clock", and many other-hit songs, together with Max C. Freedman writer of "Sioux City Sue" etc., got together in Philadelphia in 1952.

Noting the low ebb of the music industry they decided to try to create something new to stimulate the business. They got the idea of using the big beat in the music world. utilizing the blues progression, the repetitious jazz licks and the **Texas two-four swing beat** — i.e. accenting the second and fourth beats of the measure. This gave it a so-called rocking rhythm.

Naturally the need was for dance music because the big bands were not in vogue and the general public was not dancing. so with the idea of writing about a dance in a party atmosphere the title suggested itself. "Rock Around the Clock", or dance around the clock, which is inferred by the title.

After many hours and days of thought, the final outcome was the finished musical composition, "Rock Around the Clock", which turned out to be the daddy of all rock n roll songs.

It was the theme song in M.G.M.'s ... Blackboard

BRITAIN AND AMERICA WITH THE ROCK N ROLL CRAZE ... BILL HALEY (centre) AND HIS COMETS. THEIR DISCS HAVE SOLD. AND STILL ARE SELLING, BY THE MILLION.

Jungle", Columbia Pictures made a full length film which is currently playing throughout the United States using it as the title of the picture. Today there are over 50 recordings in about fifteen languages, with over thirty five American printed editions.

Over five million records of the number have been sold thus far throughout the world. It has been the number one song in nearly every nation.

Myers selected Bill Haley and his Comets, a billbilly band, to record the song and placed it with Decca Records. At that time Bill Haley's group **was little known but now have become one of America's leading rock 'n roll groups.**

Effect of Haley and "Clock" on Britain has received so many headlines in the national press. it is fairly familiar history.

★

THE "ROCK AROUND THE CLOCK" film. after a fairly quiet opening in London's West End, started causing uproarious behaviour in the suburbs and provinces.

In some towns. indeed. it was banned.

Recordwise, Haley discs came crowding into the Top Twenty. So did those by other

publishers, Hill and Range, signed him as a song writer, and set him up in his own publishing company, Elvis Presley Inc.

★

SOON PRESLEY WAS THE PROUD OWNER of two Cadillacs—one black-and-pink, one yellow. Despite that. reports indicated that he remained quite a natural, unspoiled character.

Cyclonic though his impact on the American public might have been, there was a delayed action effect when his discs were introduced to Britain in the spring of this year.

For weeks after his "Heartbreak Hotel" had been released over here, nothing was seen of it in the sales charts.

★

Those behind the scenes were temporarily. nonplussed. Without the American example to spur them, they might have given up hope. Then things started to happen.

Elvis singing(?) to his own guitar accompaniment. started by calling himself "King of Western bop".

Early in 1956. two deals were signed which pretty well guaranteed him a lucrative future.

First. R.C.A. Victor, one of America's biggest labels. purchased his contract from Sun Records—a minor company which had given him his first chance on disc. Reported

EVENING NEWS—reported:

"Presley appears on stage dressed in a vivid open-necked shirt, two-tone shoes and a light shirt. He stands feet apart. strumming a guitar. his tall. strongly built body held limp. a sleepy-eyed stare on his face. Slowly. above the howls of his fans, Presley works himself into a fever until—hair hanging over his eyes—he resembles a shouting, screaming dervish wracked by St. Vitus dance."

There came reports, too, that "Heartbreak Hotel" had sold two million in one week in America — and an early British "plug" for the disc came on May 13. in Jack Jackson's TV show.

★

Then, at last. "Heartbreak Hotel", started to show in dealers' returns — and from then on, the Pelvis became a big name, and big money. in our record world.

★

"Blue Suede Shoes," "Hound Dog" and "Love Me Tender" are examples of other Presley successes on 78. Also. his first LP to be released over here lost little time in striking high in the Top Five.

IN THE STATES, Elvis the Pelvis (as he had inevitably been dubbed) had really been "whipping things up" in galvanic public appearances," backed by his bassist "Bill," and fellow guitarist, "Scotty."

In recent weeks, press publicity from Elvis's first film, "Love Me Tender", has boosted his appeal greatly. Though reports from the States say. its reception over there was lukewarm, it will be received with enthusiasm in

News of the hysterical behaviour of his fans began to make its way into British news papers. The DAILY MIRROR made headline news of him. and John Gould — New York

his considerable experience of playing before the public, and with no small aptitude for showmanship, he pulled out all stops in his first London variety appearance at Finsbury Park Empire, in North London. and was an immediate success.

He gained a record contract with the Columbia label. and seems set for a profitable future for at least as long as the "rock" craze lasts.

★

ENTIRELY DIFFERENT circumstances surrounded the emergence of **Tommy Steele.** He had only a brief preliminary period playing in comparatively obscure spots in the West End before he was signed to disc for Decca—with strikingly rapid results in the Top Twenty.

Tommy, a likeable youngster from Bermondsey, found himself in a matter of weeks—catapulted into variety bills with top billing performers whose stage experience was. in some cases, longer than his 19 years.

Audiences have definitely taken a liking to him. and the further outlook is decidedly rosy.

★ ★

ART BAXTER, from Canterbury, is probably the greatest explosive fanatic, the most British "rock" pedlars.

He had been known in jazz circles as an eager, demonstrative singer but for long wasn't considered a commercial proposition.

Rock was his big chance. He took it with abundant determination Crowded audiences both in London (Chiswick, Finsbury Park) and the provinces (Bolton, Middlesbrough, etc.) applauded him frantically.

His opportunity to earn big money has come after years of waiting. He's taking it with full energy. H.L.

MITCH MILLER

(The American Columbia recording wizard)

writes—

'HOW I FOUND HIT SONGS FOR FRANKIE LAINE, GUY MITCHELL & JOHNNIE RAY'

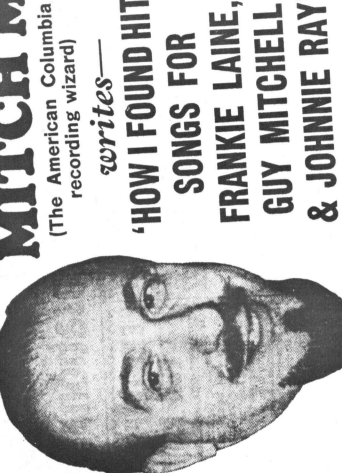

I TOOK up my first artists-and-repertoire management job with a record company some seven years ago. Until then, I'd generally thought of music from a musician's specialised standpoint. Lyrics, I seldom bothered to think about at all, unless they were by a Lorenz Hart or Ira Gershwin.

When Mercury made me the a and r chief of their pop division some seven years ago, however, I was faced with a list of more than a dozen contract artists in the vocal field alone, including the "up-and-coming" Frankie Laine, Patti Page and Vic Damone.

The first thing I realised was that a famous writer's name like Cole Porter, Irving Berlin or Harold Arlen on top of a song copy did not mean an automatic hit. Even the top professionals estimate the number of hits to songs written at about 50 to one!

'Mule Train'

Furthermore, the latest Porter, Berlin or Arlen manuscript might be ideally suited to Nat Cole, Perry Como or Frank Sinatra, yet fail to "ring the bell" for any of the singers under my control in the studios. So I began to approach each new number, whatever its source, with an open mind.

Frankie Laine and I helped each other get firmly established on Mercury when he made "Mule Train" . . . from the score of an unimportant Western movie called "Singing Guns." Then we both moved over to American Columbia in 1950, and a found little opus credited to Wayne Shanklin helped us to continue our run of luck.

"You never heard of Wayne? Probably not . . . but I think you'll recall his song—"Jezebel".

One songwriter whom I began to have faith in during my early Columbia days was Bob Merrill. Bob had penned a couple of hits in collaboration with other writers at the time notably "If I Knew You Were Coming I'd Have Baked A Cake" and I was especially impressed when he brought me some novelties o

which he had composed alone. Right away I assigned "Sparrow In The Treetop" to Guy Mitchell as a follow-up to his first big sides, "The Roving Kind" and "My Heart Cries For You," and before long, almost everything Guy recorded was a Merrill tune.

Successes

"My Truly, Truly Fair," "There's Always Room At Our House," "Feet Up" and "She Wears Red Feathers" spring immediately to mind, as, of course, do the more recent Merrill successes associated with other artists than Guy: "Make Yourself Comfortable," "Mambo Italiano," "Sweet Old-Fashioned Girl," etc.

A somewhat similar story lies behind my encounter with a great songwriting team, Richard Adler and the late Jerry Ross. Like Bob Merrill, they were just starting to become important when I received a lead-sheet of their ballad "Rags To Riches," and decided it would suit Tony Bennett's style.

It promptly became a terrific hit for Tony in the States and David Whitfield in Britain. Therefore, when they turned in that wonderful score for "Pajama Game," I wasn't amazed to find it included at least one song of unusual pop appeal.

In fact "Hey There" impressed me so much that I covered it with two separate recordings by Rosemary

Clooney and Johnnie Ray, both of them best-sellers in several countries including the United Kingdom.

Adler and Ross went on to complete another sensational Broadway show "Damn Yankees," before Jerry's tragic death at an early age last year. Nevertheless, sometimes a writer who conceives one excellent song is unfortunate in his attempts at further hits.

The janitor named Churchill Kohlman has not yet come through with "Cry," a natural, I realised, for the then unknown Johnnie Ray.

Nor were Ross Bagdasarian and playwright William Saroyan able (or should I say willing?!) to repeat the triumph of their Armenian novelty which I persuaded Rosemary Clooney

to tackle—"Come On-A My House."

It's seldom, however, that even a "fluke" hit is written purely by chance. Scratch beneath the surface of a good melody writer, and you'll find a man who is almost always a trained musician—who knows a fine musical line can accomplish in the way of moving and touching and pleasing people.

Advice

In the same way, a good lyric is usually a man who understands people and knows what makes them think, feel and act. Some of the simplest, apparently spontaneous words and themes are actually the results of hard work, sold think, and the burning of much midnight oil.

About 200 songs reach my office each week. Of these only a hundred say five or six are finally recorded. The untrained amateur obviously stands a slim chance in such a market.

But I'd like to end on an encouraging note, so if you honestly feel you have the knack of putting attractive musical or lyrical ideas down on paper, here are a few words of advice before submitting your first "masterpiece" for publication:

Study music. Study people. Learn how to make people laugh. Know how to make people cry

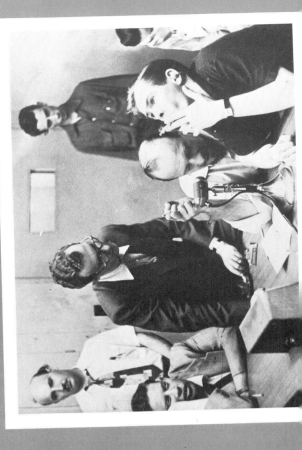

Miller was the first big record producer, the A&R man supreme. He fitted the song to suit the singer, and brought French horns into pop. He had a good classical background – but he came from within the pop establishment.

1957 ROCK 'n' ROLL HEROES

'Just Walking In The Rain' I sang as I sloshed across the hockey field towards a Saxon burial mound. Was Ray a rocker? One might just as well ask whether Frankie Vaughn was a rocker, via his 'Green Door' and 'Garden of Eden'. Both could sell ballads bombastically, could moon in June very well, but they always sang with passion and so I considered them rockers *when* they did a rocking song. But they were both poised to dive into the world of variety forever . . . However, 'Walking In The Rain' was a good idea for this grainy, rainy February day. I'd read that it had been written by black prisoners in a Nashville jail. *Incarcerated* – as I felt now as I trudged up the mound and sheltered under the famous tree where three years ago a new boy had hanged himself dead after being caught stealing a few shillings from the school church collection salver. *Incarcerated* – wearied by interminable talk of games and legs and thighs and jock straps and whether Baring was going with Ridley or with Melford-Carding or both and myself playing no part in all this muddy romance but stuck with trying for popularity through skiffling and yearning to get an electric guitar and start rocking. Thoroughly *incarcerated* – but how was I to find instant fame, recognition in the street, at bus stops, in cinemas? 'This is a time of emotional unbalance and it will take time for you to find your feet', said the school psychiatrist. 'Think of what the Prime Minister has to go through every day, and your adolescent problems will seem but trivial.'

Instead I unwrapped a pacifying pork pie and thought about what Bill Haley must be going through. He had arrived early in February for his first live tour of Britain. We had been promised Elvis every other month but he never came. In retrospect this was probably a wise decision: record stars were for the record. Spinning on the turntable they could whirl up a heaven where the listener drew in the details. Haley the Scotch-plaid cowboy gangster had become Haley the terrified tourist, visibly puffing and ageing as he made his escape from the

fans down at Southampton. 'Cuppy', his wife, had never been on tour with him before and was putting on a brave smile, glad that the five children were safely back home in 'Melody Manor', as a gaggle of fans sat on the top of the Haley limousine beating out a rock rhythm. Her husband turned to the *Melody Maker* man and said, 'There's a time and a place for that beat – but it isn't here!'

There was no need to worry though. The tour was a quiet affair, with a decent sprinkling of young marrieds and middle-agers amidst the young ones in the theatres and luxury cinemas where Haley & The Comets played. Then afterwards in the dressing room the Comets apologised to the press about their stage antics, explaining that this was only a way of making a living, that their guitarist had once played in the Benny Goodman band, that their drummer had done a spell with Glenn Miller. And Haley added that he was going to take time out to visit relatives in Lancashire, his mother's home county.

Yes, Haley got along fine as far as his well-being physically – but his record sales were badly affected. They slumped and stayed slumped. Lonnie Donegan, who had been sent to America under the Musicians' Union exchange agreement, returned bright as a wasp, brimming with success as the first beat act to carry coals to Newcastle and get paid for the shipload. Then he got down to keeping up with the circus of skiffle groups shooting out the hits. His 'Cumberland Gap' was beaten in May by the version by the Vipers, but he had the field to himself with 'Gambling Man' and the hilarious 'Putting On The Style'. He was starting to get laughs, following in the bright and breezy Music Hall tradition. But he still sang of legendary America, of 'Dixie Darlings', as did his skiffling rivals like Chas. McDevitt and Nancy Whiskey on their 'Freight Train'. All were songs by the mysterious folk from the A.N.Other family – though every so often an A.N.Other would materialize from anonymity to claim authorship and royalties (as

happened with 'Freight Train').

In the Easter holidays I went up West again and found that the artsy-folksy skiffle element had settled down to nest in certain coffee bars, while the clean-shaven, more modern guitar boys were to be found hanging around the Two 'I's coffee bar, playing the latest American hits on the juke box. They knew this was where Tommy Steele had been discovered when he was the vocalist with the Vipers, and they knew that though they too were still scrubbing out the skiffle a visiting talent scout could easily pick them up and groom them into stardom. So they listened to the juke box and learned up the songs.

The American rockers were coming in strong now. Apart from Elvis and his stream of grunting, hiccupping love-blues like 'Don't Be Cruel', 'All Shook Up', 'Teddy Bear' we were to get to know the blustering bravado of an even freer personality – Jerry Lee Lewis, the Louisiana wildman with his pumping piano, his weapon-like steel comb, and his liking for stalking the top of a grand piano shouting about having a chicken in the barn – whose barn? MY barn! He was absolutely certain of

who he was and what he could do. He was the greatest. He came leaping off the record and out of the papers and we couldn't wait for him to visit Britain. We were, of course, still waiting for Elvis. But he was coming next month, or next year, or sometime. Then we heard he was going into the army, reporting for duty on 20 January, 1958. He was certainly dutiful and he also sang hymns. Little Richard, another wild and crazy guy, the whirling dervish, had raged far from any cage in 'She's Got It', 'Jenny, Jenny', and 'Keep A Knockin'', but then he suddenly renounced his rocking as devil's work. He said he was going into the church to study evangelism and he made a dramatic first gesture by throwing his rings off a bridge in Sydney. 'To prove my faith in God'. This was something of a shock. The next thing, we'd be learning that the 'Whole Lotta Shakin'' man, Jerry Lee himself, would be taking holy orders. And it wasn't long before a press story told us that he was a keen church goer and had done a bit of preaching in his time. You could accept that Pat Boone was a churchgoer – but all these other rockers! It had to be a different kind of church to the doomy edifices in which we all had to sit po-faced while the chaplain sang in a strangulated mono-tone and then the visiting preacher talked of finding God in a World War One dug-out and then the Latin master said interminable prayers for the world, especially including all members of the Royal Family, interjecting an occasional 'Shut up at the back, Smythe and Farr-Johnson!'

American teenagers seemed to have their problems too but they were 'neath sunny Western skies, roaring in fast cars from school to pick up their girl for a necking party. Chuck Berry talked about 'Another School Day' but he also raved about big, fat cars with grilles like George Formby's smile; the Everly Brothers told about the trouble they got into at a teen party in 'Wake Up Little Suzie'; Paul Anka shocked us by confessing he was having an affair with an old woman called 'Diana'; and Frankie Lymon told the authorities that high spirits was all he fooled with and 'I'm Not A Juvenile Delinquent'.

Teenagers were having their own interests described on record now. Teen life was shown to exist and to be separate from regular adult life. The records could be used to dance to, to annoy older people, and to soften up girls with.

Girls! They no longer looked like dinky toy versions of women. They wore jeans and check shirts, they could be almost one of the gang. Two or three times a term busloads of selected girls from our nearby sister school were brought to us for activities like square dancing, ballroom dancing and plays. Sometimes they came for mixed tennis and we could admire their coltish charms as they dashed about after the ball. We put them on a plinth and wrote them up in poems. One boy screwed a local girl and got expelled. On summer holiday, we played the rock blues under gentle skies, surrounded by a costume picture set. Pat Boone's 'Love Letters In The Sand' was climbing the charts and I had a copy and a portable

sweet little sixteen

Words & Music by

CHUCK BERRY

Recorded + Featured by
CHUCK BERRY

PRICE
50¢
IN U.S.A

ARC MUSIC CORP.
1619 Broadway • New York 19, N. Y.

gramophone. One afternoon I was deep in a punt with Alison, an effervescent girl that everyone was after, and I had Boone singing: 'On a day like today we passed the time away writing love letters in the sand', with those saxes wailing ethereally. Eventually I got a first kiss with Alison and it was terrific! A huge tingle that zoomed around my whole body, more delicious than a gallon of Tizer. Nothing was ever the same after that. Life seemed to have been building up to that first kiss and it seemed to get less romantic afterwards, day by day, experience after experience.

But from the pop angle that kiss was a good thing. I had now entered the girl competition and as I wanted to hold onto Alison, to see her outside during the dance and so forth, and as I was no good at tennis, golf, or cards, I decided to study rock more closely. I wanted to be a rock & roll star.

I studied hit singles to see how they were put together. I played 45s at 33⅓ so that I could catch the licks. I bought long-playing albums so that I could study the work of Little Richard, Jerry Lee Lewis, Larry Williams, etc. And I found that rock & roll lost some of its excitement on an LP. Too many songs sounding too similar. And duff stuff, too. The duff tracks really destroyed the heroic status. So these men made mistakes! Of course, if they were extraordinary free personalities like Jerry Lee Lewis the odd under-par track didn't matter because the singer was bigger than the song. But most rockers were only as good as their latest single. Also, on an LP you lost the wild variety you got when you heard rock on the radio, because for every one 'Great Balls Of Fire' there were several soppy records like 'Tammy' or sophisticated adult records like Frank Sinatra's 'All The Way'. 1957 wasn't as good as 1955 when rock was a lone Haley voice crying in the wilderness of ballads, when it was difficult tuning in to the fresh and wild sounds flying across from Radio Luxembourg and the American Forces Network. But 1957 was choc-full of rock by December and no fan could complain about a shortage – the December chart contained 'Wake Up Little Suzie' by the Everlys, 'I Love You Baby' by Paul Anka, 'Let's Have A Party' by Elvis, 'Ma, He's Making Eyes At Me' by the Johnny Otis Show, 'That'll Be The Day' by the Crickets, 'Great Balls of Fire' by Jerry Lee, and 'Keep A Knockin'' by Little Richard.

Thirteen-year-old Laurie London hit with a rock gospel song called 'He's Got The Whole World In His Hands'. He even scored in America. Slightly older Britons were getting into rock by now, hard on the heels of Tommy Steele. At first the British rockers were very thinly-disguised adult jazz and dance bandmen, simply playing a bit of slack boogie, playing down to the kids: Tony Crombie and his Rockets, Art Baxter and the Sinners. But just as Tommy Steele was heading into show business proper with tuneful songs full of appeal for the mums and dads and the Royal Family (he appeared in the 1957 Royal Command Variety performance, but Lonnie Donegan wasn't asked to appear) so Britain produced her first crop of boy rockers. Terry Dene, with smooth angelic features, hit with 'A White Sports Coat' (anglicised from the American original, 'A White *Sport* Coat') but soon found the strain too much and was forced to retire. His Waterloo was National Service with the Green Jackets. We were to follow his sad story told in detail in the daily tabloids: 'Rock 'n' roll star Terry Dene (19) has been discharged from the army after spending eight weeks in a mental hospital following an "emotional collapse" after only 24 hours with the Green-jackets'. Later he was able to piece himself together through finding God. National Service scared me dreadfully as well. I had decided to go into the catering corps or the Army Kinema corps. Or to become a rock star and live in America. To be an American soldier seemed different, the costumes were much more dashing for a start. I thought of Errol Flynn.

I returned to school for the winter term equipped

with an electrified guitar. The same sunburst acoustic from Selmer's, only now this machine had an electric plug and a pick-up. Plug it through the gramophone and the strumming became amplified. My brother-in-law, an officer in the Royal Electrical and Mechanical Engineers, had performed the trick. The new guitar was the sensation of certain elements at school. The rowing Eights were green with envy. New boy blonds flickered their blue eyes but I wasn't interested after the punt experience with Alison. All that was necessary now was to start a group on the lines of Buddy Holly & The Crickets. This group was a direct inspiration because they were almost our age and they were compact and played our kind of instruments – guitars and drums. Bill Haley's band had saxes and accordions and that funny Hawaiian guitar you played like a table, and anyway they were OUT. The winter term was spent practising. We watched other British boys getting into rock & roll. It might just be possible . . . even before A levels . . .

In the Christmas holidays I used a contact of my father's to get an interview with a real professional music man in Charing Cross road office. This was the first time I'd met anyone in the pop business. I felt like dropping in on Dobell's Jazz Record Shop and telling them. I wanted to tell the uniformed guard outside EMI records, and the queue outside the Dominion Cinema at Tottenham Court Road. I didn't, but I'd *liked* to have done.

Laurie Kline remembered the 'good old days'. He tipped back in his swivel chair, shot his gold cuff links and put his hands behind his head. 'It was beautiful', he said. 'Everybody was on first-name terms and we all lunched at Isow's where they do very good brisket and chopped liver. We had our names embossed on the backs of our chairs'. Laurie Kline was known to my father as a golfer, but in the trade he was a song publisher. His hits were in frames all round the walls of his office. 'We would deliver our song plug list to the BBC each week and they would choose their music from that list. They were very lovely songs. They were like the songs we heard before the war, all moonlight and roses. Classy stuff.' Then he returned his chair to the upright position, pulled out the pen from the presentation pen set in front of him and stabbed at me: 'This beat stuff came in and ruined the scene! Just couldn't put the junk

into print. And I who had worked my fingers to the bone publishing tasteful tunes, I who had come up from the back streets of Stepney, who had pulled myself out of stench and slime and the rotten life in general, I was told that this gutter music was IT!' I began to realise I had come to the wrong man, but I kept nodding and looking solemn. '*You* go to a good school. *You* can understand what I'm saying. This new muck is being purveyed by a new set – amateurs in the music business, young whelps from advertising and journalism and what have you! Wet behind the ears and most of them *nancy boys*. Never bend down in their company. You young boys should be careful – they will pick you up in some milk bar, commit a gross indecency and then give you a stage name based on your performance – Harry Hurry, Billy Bouncy, Charlie Cheeks!' I told Mr Kline that I wanted to get into the business. 'You get your 'A' levels first. Then try publishing because the good songs will come back. I'll give you a tip: this rock-rot is finished as a craze. The next craze will be calypso. Look at Harry Belafonte. Yes, calypso coupled with narrative on the lines of "The Shifting Whispering Sands". You mark my words.'

I did. I wrote them all down. And I wasn't worried. Not for long anyway. Because a new TV show was inspiring us to make our own music and to feel we had a chance in a scene that wasn't going to die. *6.5 Special*, which had started in February of the year on BBC TV as a very camp-fire jollity show, was turning into an exciting showcase for not only hot US rockers but also boys of my own age. It came on every Saturday after children's hour and before adult evening viewing. Exactly at *teen time*, in fact. There was always a lot of noisy enthusiasm from the studio audience. One voice stood out from the rest. A special, urgent, messianic 'Hooray!' I later learnt that this was the voice of producer Jack Good, an Oxford man. An Oxford man in rock 'n' roll! So the new music wasn't just for oiks, yobs, imbeciles, cretins! Then I caught a radio interview one night on Luxembourg. Jack Good said that Elvis would go down as one of the great artists of this century. At last I felt totally secure. The staff, the music teachers, the industry professionals could all stew in their own juice. I was going to follow Jack Good through hell or hot water.

BING ATTACKS SONG 'TRASH'

'Talented Writers Crowded Out Of The Picture'

SINCE WHAT HAPPENS in America musically inevitably happens a short time later over here (though it's rapidly shaping up as a simultaneous operation these days), the current Stateside songwriters' battle is relevant and worthy of comment in this column.

And especially when a gent of **Bing Crosby's** show biz stature feels compelled to sound off publicly about the calibre of current pop music on TV and radio. Bing lays the blame for the low quality of present day offerings directly at the door of the organisation known as BMI (Broadcast Music Incorporated), and says in a statement to a Senate Committee investigating monopolistic practices *"it galls me exceedingly to see so much trash on our airlanes and TV screens while the work of talented, dedicated songwriters is crowded out of the picture . . . people whose unquestionable musicianship has been long established and who take pride in writing something worthwhile".*

Crosby was here referring to the songsmiths who belong to the long-established ASCAP (American Society of Composers, Authors and Publishers). Controversy rages over the issue of whether or not the spate of poor stuff being served up to the public is the result of pressure exerted by BMI with its radio and TV affiliations.

'No Real Reflection Of Merit'

Bing went on to say he didn't believe the character of current music is "attributable to a radical change in public taste, nor due to a sudden unanimous failure of talent among established songwriters," and that while he liked all kinds of songs he thought *"a healthier balance should be maintained for the benefit of youngsters who follow these trends so religiously".*

The disc business' elder statesman added "there is much to be said about the influence of popular music on public tastes, morals and ideals, and what they are hearing these days hardly achieves a salutary result. **It is just not too good.** I honestly don't feel that the choice of the public, as reflected in the most-played list, represents the selection on merit."

'No Pressure On Me'

Crosby admitted that no direct pressure had been tried on him but there had been subtle solicitation of his co-operation and he felt the 4,000 ASCAP writers of proved ability weren't getting much of a shake. Thirty-three of the top ASCAP songwriters are bringing a £50,000,000 antitrust suit against the BMI organisation which countered the Crosby blast by producing statements from 22 top musical performers denying pressure from either organisation.

However, the American equivalent of Britain's Songwriters Guild quickly pointed out that all but seven of these artists had financial interests in music publishing firms subsidised by the BMI set-up.

Whatever the outcome of this struggle, the fact does remain that our ears are being assaulted with an overabundance of inferior crudity and the originators of this teenage pap are associated largely with the BMI outfit. If the influence of prominent folk like Crosby, Como, Sinatra, etc., can help pinpoint and abolish the mainspring of today's baleful balladry we'll all owe them a tremendous vote of thanks. The few fine, listenable tunes in our current Top Ten come from the pens of accredited professional ASCAP writers. Some very decent tunes have come from BMI pens, too, over the years, but in the area of quantity and quality they're no match for the ASCAP brethren.

Let's hope the end of the domination of the mediocre is in sight.

... ONE OF

THE 'MUSICAL EXPRESS' BOARDS THE ROCK 'N' ROLL EXPRESS !

IT seemed that half the population turned out on Tuesday to welcome Bill Haley on his British tour. I know from experience, having been in that welcoming crowd for most of the day . . . on the "Daily Mirror" specially chartered train—on the dockside at Southampton—and in the second "battle" of Waterloo that greeted us on our return (writes **Doug Geddes**).

I know from talking to Bill later in the day that he'd never seen or experienced such a welcome. It will certainly leave a lasting impression on me.

The "Bill Haley Rock 'n' Roll Special"—for which British Railways printed special tickets—left Waterloo around midday packed with 300 colourfully dressed fans, Rory Blackwell and his Blackjacks, a coachload of journalists and photographers, British and American newsreel cameras—and some VERY bewildered Pullman dining-car attendants.

No sooner had we left than Rory Blackwell's boys had set themselves up—and all one could see through the length of the train was a mass of wriggling, gyrating, excited bodies. The seats for which they had paid were left, in the main, unoccupied. Where the music couldn't be heard, handclapping was sufficient.

Sweaters with Haley slogans, skin-tight jeans, badges, banners, and scarves were the dress and order of the day. Several fans wore full-page Haley portraits torn from our companion magazine HIT PARADE, and our new "Rock 'n' Roll Magazine"—pinned to their sweaters.

SOUTHAMPTON WELCOME

At Southampton, the mass left the station led by Rory Blackwell's outfit, which gained in numbers as they proceeded to the dockside. The Pied Piper of Hamelin had nothing on this lot . . .

As we waited, so the rock 'n' rollers passed the time. Rain and muddy pools meant little to them. Ships in the Solent hooted their welcome, trains joined in with their whistles, and the band added to the general cacophony, the like of which Southampton will probably never see again. Irate diners in the nearby hotel waited whilst all the staff suspended themselves in every possible vantage point over the front of the hotel.

The first sight of the Haley limousine was a spontaneous signal for his first British teenage welcome. The car disappeared from view amidst a mass of bodies. Somehow it reached the station. An excited girl shinned straight over the top of the car and almost landed on her head on the exit side of the car ! A host of not-so-pleased policemen got Haley on to the platform and to his compartment. Until he was settled, the fans were kept outside, but this didn't stop them storming another platform, going through the coaches past some bewildered local passengers, down on to the line and clambering up on to the official platform . . .

At last the fans were given the signal to go on to the platform. An ill-advised ticket-collector started to ask for tickets. That was the last I saw of him . . . I think he disappeared underfoot somewhere !

As we left Southampton, the atmosphere was electric. Fever pitch was mounting, especially as we now had valuable cargo aboard.

All along the route, people stared from windows, stood in gardens and on the railway embankments, and hung precariously over bridges. "King" Haley was on his way.

BATTLE OF WATERLOO, 1957 !

After thousands of pictures were taken of Bill as we sped along (mostly by newspapers that were anti-Haley not so long ago !) he came and had a chat with newspaper men before going the length of the train to say "hello" to this train-load of happy, by now delirious fans.

Through eight coaches, swaying and rockin', Bill had a word and an autograph for them all. Such a bunch of excited kids you never saw . . .

If Haley thought Southampton was a welcome of a lifetime, Waterloo station was soon to alter his previous thoughts.

The whole forecourt of Waterloo was crammed with over 4,000 Haley-worshippers making a noise which rapidly reduced Glasgow's famous "Hampden Roar" to a whisper.

Nobody could do much with that crowd, least of all the police. Once in the middle, the car and its driver were powerless—and there it remained for a full 20 minutes before Haley could be taken to his hotel.

Apart from a few words with Bill on the train, I had to wait until the evening press reception before having a chat with him.

I and colleague Keith Goodwin passed on the good wishes of all NME readers, and I can assure you that he is certainly thrilled with your loyalty to him and the Comets—and he is looking forward to seeing you in various parts of the country.

And what do the Comets themselves think of rock 'n' roll ? Let guitarist Billy Williamson sum it up: "Man, it's just music with a beat—for people who WANT music with a beat. That's all !"

Our seniors throw water on our enthusiasm. Don't knock the rock – Let childhood go on and on and on and on . . .

R. 'N' ROLL: THE REAL STUFF!

MAY I INTRODUCE YOU TO PAT, PAULINE AND SHIRLEY?

All three are Rock 'n' Roll fans, and all three are delightfully representative of the youngsters who sport Bill Haley jumpers, wave Elvis Presley banners and tote slogans for Little Richard.

They were, I would guess, a vociferous part of the enormous audiences at the recent Haley shows in London's Dominion theatre in the Tottenham Court Road, and but for the necessary nuisance of work and the unreasoning attitude of such squares as office managers and foremen, would have stamped and screamed with a will at Waterloo when the kiss-curl king arrived.

Every Friday at five o'clock sharp they burst into the Jazz Centre, throw the whole works into a complete and utter turmoil and play Rock 'n' Roll records with what I can only describe as a gay abandon.

And they are so typical of their kind that I would like to address some part of this column to them . . . .

TO THEM . . . THEY'RE 'SMASHING'!

First of all I would like to know why they find the Haleys, the Presleys, the Vincents and the Guy Mitchells of this peculiar recording world of ours so attractive? I can almost hear them answering that these brash gentlemen all rock, that they are hep with the jive, run amok with the rock or are top of the poll with the roll, or something equally odd. And what they might mean would be that Messrs. Haley, Presley, Vincent and Mitchell, to say nothing of Mr. Steele, Don Lang or a hundred others, have the ability to swing sufficient to send them into ecstasies of pleasure.

Apart from that I suspect that they would declare all these lively gentry " smashing ".

Last week they tripped exuberantly into the shop and, in the course of their session, asked Dot if I liked Rock 'n' Roll. Dot, truthful as always, had to admit that I didn't. " Jimmy's no square," denied young Pat, and I had to blush in answer. Such youthful support makes me happy.

Especially when I had already been told, in no uncertain manner, that square I was, four-sided and solid.

THEY BUILT R 'n' R's FUTURE

That was when Dot and I made our enquiring trek to a neighbouring cinema to see and hear " Rock Around the Clock " during the press-inspired demonstrations.

As we trooped out, commenting to one another that the Race records we collected twenty-odd years back were much more exciting, we couldn't for the life of us see what it was caused all the uproar.

" I didn't even think it swung all that much," said I, and two youths next to us in the crowd leaving the foyer nudged each other.

" Listen to that square ! " they said in unison.

Still, despite such admonishments as these, I would like to mention the hallowed names of artists like Tommy McLennan, Washboard Sam and his Washboard Band, Texas Alexander, Huddie Ledbetter, Sonny Terry, Sonny Boy Williamson and Leroy Carr. Singers such as these forged the future path of Rock 'n' Roll. The specialised Race music which was issued in the States on series designed to appeal to the large Negro markets over there rocked and rolled thirty-odd years ago, an awful long time before Pat, Pauline and Shirley were born, well before the youth in the cinema crowd was a twinkle in his father's eye.

The patent simplicity of a current Rock 'n' Roll favourite allows us to dissect it easily. The chord structure is that of the Negro twelve-bar Blues. A million recordings, and more, have been made with this identical sequence. It is, after all, the basis of the Blues, and the very heart of jazz music, modern or traditional.

The " tunes " are made of familiar riffs, every one of which can be found within the early jazz structure. The " lyrics," far removed from the simple beauty of native Negro Blues phrases and verses, have now descended to deliberately monotonous repetitions of injunctions to " rock around the clock," "don't knock the rock" or "rock, rock the rock." It is as if all the traditional richness of simple Blues songs has been exaggerated, twisted out of context and gimmicked to appeal to record buyers who know nothing of the standards laid down by jazz history and natural environment, and care less.

If only one single character out of all the Pats, Paulines and Shirleys would take the trouble to listen to the real stuff. If only one of them felt so strongly about Bessie Smith that she could boast of a Bessie Smith jumper, a Leadbelly banner or a slogan for Big Bill Broonzy . . . . .

I've seen Haley in person and he's great. Like Roy Orbison he stands his ground while beat pulses around him. However, by this time the girls had taken over as bosses of R&R record sales. They always do! They wanted soppy sex, they wanted to lasso a 'rough trade' rocker into a domestic animal – wedding bells ahead! Haley was over the hill. He'd had it.

He's never made a record that wasn't a hit!

"EVERY Little Richard record makes the 'Billboard' and 'Cash Box' hit charts," claim Specialty Records of America in a recent Press hand-out.

by KEITH GOODWIN

An exaggerated boast designed to impress the powerful gentlemen of the Press? Not on your life! Because this was not merely idle boasting, but a statement of cold, hard, unassailable facts.

With a couple of minor exceptions, London Records (who release the Specialty material in Britain) would be justified in making a similar claim, because here, too, Little Richard's records can always be relied upon to make an early entry into the best sellers.

At a time when many of America's top rock 'n' rollers are experiencing a steep and sudden decline in popularity—Bill Haley, Gene Vincent, Freddie Bell, for example—Richard's records are still selling in their thousands.

Three hits

Not so very long ago the pint-sized bundle of bounce had no less than three records in the hit parade—"Long Tall Sally," "She's Got It," and the title song from the technicolour movie, "The Girl Can't Help It."

"Rip It Up" constituted another Little Richard winner, and the pounding "Lucille" was prominently displayed in the hit parade just a few weeks back.

Last week he gate-crashed the Top Twenty with his latest release "Jenny, Jenny, and this week you'll find it placed No. 16. Proof indeed that far from taking a tumble in the popularity stakes, El Richard is gaining more and more staunch fans each week!

But the music world may be losing Little Richard very soon. During his recent successful tour of Canada, he appeared at Vancouver's Exhibition Gardens on June 12 and surprised reporters by announcing his intention of deserting the bright lights of show business in the near future to become an evangelist.

An ardent follower of the Seventh Day Adventist movement, Richard told the Press that he had been preparing himself for this important step for some considerable time.

Richard claims that he has "never read any book but the Bible," and "only went to one movie" in his life. The title he doesn't remember, only that it was "something with Shirley Temple in it," and that he only stayed 20 minutes.

Nobody seems certain of the exact date when the dynamite-packed r & r star will plunge into evangelism, but it's unlikely to be before October 20—projected starting date of Little Richard's forthcoming British tour with Alan Freed's rock 'n' roll package show.

This news has been enthusiastically received all over Britain by teenagers who have followed Little Richard's progress since he first burst on to the pop music scene some years ago.

You'll no doubt recall that his early American hit records were unavailable here for some time, and that two of his biggest successes—"Tutti Frutti" and "Long Tall Sally"—first got off the ground via the Pat Boone versions.

Bill Haley and his Comets made the most of the frantic "Rip It Up" before Richard's version reached the stores. But this position existed only in Britain. Across the Atlantic, all three tunes were Little Richard's hits.

Big draw

The success of his many other records eventually made the piano-playing LR a number one box-office attraction in the States, and his "on the spot" performances really have to be seen to be believed.

According to one report in the American "Rhythm and Blues" magazine, "The fabulous Little Richard doesn't work a show, he exploits it!"

Wildly enthusiastic scenes greeted each and every performance by the 21-year-old five-feet-nothing "rock" star in Canada.

In Victoria, B.C., he was mobbed by crowds of teenagers who rushed on stage. At Nanaimo, fans gathered round his motel and waited all night to catch a glimpse of him, whilst at Vancouver, several girls collapsed as a result of the tremendous crush around the bandstand.

Having played dates in Australia, the Philippines, America and Canada, Richard recently ventured the suggestion that teenagers are "wild" everywhere. He feels that rock 'n' roll is a "rage which is part of teenage life."

For his Canadian dates, Little Richard was backed up by a power-house six-piece unit — comprising guitarists Duncan Conway and Thomas Harwell, tenorists Grady Gaines (Little Richard's step-brother)

and Clifford Burks, pianist Wilbur Smith and drummer Charles Connor. Little Richard (real name: Richard Penniman) was born in Macon, Georgia, in 1935. The son of a labourer (and one of 13 children), Richard was raised in a very religious atmosphere, and after "dabbling" with music during his early childhood, he was "hired" to work as organist, pianist and gospel singer in a Macon Sanctified church.

The emotional hysteria he often caused among the congregation led to his acquisition of the nickname "The War Hawk," but Richard's spirited singing of religious songs resulted in his dismissal from office at the age of 14.

Reason? According to the church, he was confusing religious fervour with "boogie-woogie and "barrelhouse-style" piano playing!

At 15, Richard toured as a singer, dancer, and pianist with a road show and later won an amateur talent contest at the "81" Theatre in Atlanta.

That's the truth about LITTLE RICHARD

His prize — a recording session for RCA-Victor—resulted in a disc that pleased young Mr. Penniman but meant little to the general public.

After winning six further amateur talent competitions, Richard travelled to Nashville, where he met up with three equally ambitious and equally hard-up young vocalists — Jimmy Swann, Bobbie Brooks and Bang Gilmore.

The four joined forces to wax under the collective title "The Tempo Toppers," and after a series of comparatively inconsequential appearances, cut their first sides for Peacock label — "Good News," "Roll At The Wheel." The teenstar did moderately well saleswise but never a contender for hit parade honours.

In Hollywood Richard was spotted by Art Rupe, boss of the Specialty label, who held a lucrative recording contract under his nose. Richard signed on the dotted line, formed out a touring version of himself, cut a few weeks later, and himself one of the most talked-about performers in America when that disc record entered the hit parade.

Hit record followed hit record—"Long Tall Sally," "Rip It Up," "Slippin' and Slidin'," "Ready Teddie," "Heebie Jeebies," and "She Got It," among them.

And when Decca's lawyers didn't subsidiary decided to release Richard's sides in Britain, the records quickly gained favour, an appreciative and excited public. Little Richard had arrived!

Since then, Richard has been seen in two movies—"Don't Knock The Rock" (in which he stole much of the thunder from ex-King Bill Haley) and "The Girl Can't Help It."

The reaction of teenagers in both instances, was little short of unbelievable—a clear sign that Richard will be more than welcome here anytime he cares to make the trip Atlantic crossing.

JAMES BLACKIE writes from

a gateway through which the pub- but all to no avail.

One of the true blue rockers – never trying to be an all-round entertainer. Like the greatest rockers, he was all style – an attitude, a pose. He sang like he spoke, full of fire and brimstone and bragging. Cassius Clay did it in boxing. Very evangelical. Richard, like Jerry Lee & Elvis, was born between body and soul, sin and salvation. They deal in extremes in the Deep South and when they live they roar. And in the morning they have a bath in church.

impersonation, and there is a solo

REG BARLOW.

the same often, they call you to task." DICK TATHAM.

THE 6.5 SPECIALISTS

Some of the famous BBC TV "6.5 Special" artistes who have made the Long Player described on the right by Roy Burden. Group snapped at the EMI studios last Sunday evening, are, from left to right : TONY OSBORNE; GEOFF LOVE; JIMMY JACKSON; JIM DALE; JOHN BARRY; JACK GOOD ('6.5' producer); TERRY WAYNE and DON LANG. Lad in the forefront is LAURIE LONDON, young sensation from the East End.

Printed by Merritt & Hatcher Ltd., High Wycombe and London, for Cardfont Publishers Ltd., 116 Shaftesbury Avenue, London. Sole Distributing Agents for Great Britain, Surridge, Dawson & Co. Ltd. 136-142 New Kent Road.

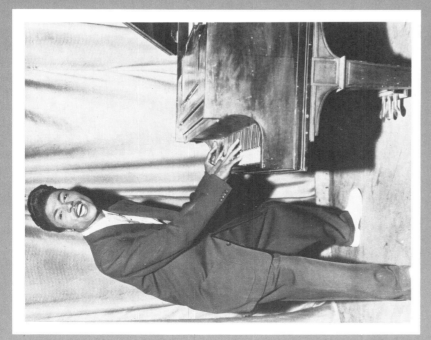

Jack Good, Oxford man and Shakespeare buff, appears on the scene as co-producer of the catch-all children's romp '6.5 Special'. Jack sensed the theatrical potential of R&R and soon became the Headmaster of Rock. Jack was to be the Dr Arnold of R&R. Also in the picture: Laurie London, teen singer of hit song 'He's Got The Whole World in His Hands' (religioso).

Introducing the Sensational
EVERLY BROTHERS

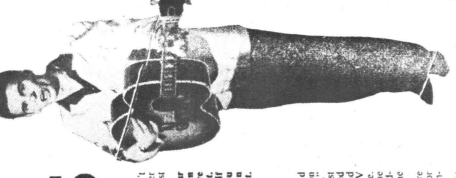

PHIL EVERLY

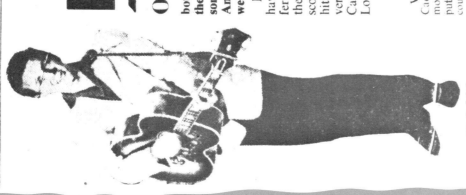

DON EVERLY

By CHARLES GOVEY

ONE of the most potent forces in pop music on both sides of the Atlantic in the past few years has been song and artists from America's country - and - western catalogues.

But few country singers have made a more rapid transfer to the popular market than the Everly Brothers, who scored a nation-wide smash hit in the States with their very first release - on the Cadence label, "Bye Bye. Love."

On roster

When Archie Bleyer, boss of Cadence, recorded the boys a few months ago he was planning to put them in his newly-formed country-and-western roster.

But "Bye Bye. Love" took off so fast that it zoomed into the pop and rock 'n roll fields as well. The disc moved rapidly up the "Billboard" charts and for the past four weeks has been one of the nation's top sellers at No. 2 position.

Now, within a few weeks of its release here on the London label, "Bye Bye, Love" looks all set to repeat its success on this side of the Atlantic.

Although newcomers to recording, the Everly Brothers—Don, 20, and Phil, 18—have been singing country-and-western music from a very early age.

Kentucky

The boys were born in Brownie, Kentucky, and their father and mother, although retired now, have been active in the country music field most of their lives.

Their father, in fact, was brought up with the well-known c-and-w composer, Merle Travis, who wrote "Sixteen Tons," and worked with him for some time.

Don and Phil began in the entertainment world at the age of eight and six respectively, when they appeared on their parents' radio show in Shenandoah, Iowa. From then on they became regular members of the family group, singing on radio stations all over the country.

The family finally wound up in Knoxville, Tennessee, where the boys went to school and the parents retired from show business.

But Mum and Dad still had plenty of friends in musical circles. One day an old colleague of theirs heard the boys sing and put them in touch with a show business agent.

The agent was so impressed that he at once asked Archie Bleyer to come and hear them. The disc that resulted took them from nowhere to top record-sellers within a matter of weeks.

How do the boys react to their overnight success?

Farm folk

"We feel we're country people," they say. "We were raised up on country music. But we're very thankful and glad that 'Bye Bye, Love' caught on with the pop fans too.

And they have quite decided views about the songs they sing. "Music has changed so much that we don't worry about barriers—about whether a song is country or pop. We just like music.

"We're just as young as our audience, and we feel that when we dance to a song, all we care about is whether it has a beat. We don't listen to the lyrics. If you want to listen to a song, you don't want to have to sit down and decipher it and figure it out.

To the point

"It has to be simple, direct and to the point. That's the reason country music is so popular today."

Since the success of their first record, the Everlys have been signed for regular appearances on "Grand Ole Opry," the top c-and-w TV show from Nashville, Tennessee. They have also been busy on the major network programmes, including the Ed Sullivan, Vic Damone and Julius La Rosa shows.

Later on, in the autumn, they are to move over to the East Coast for the first time for a string of in-person appearances.

The boys are hoping hard that their record will be successful enough in Britain to justify a visit to this country. If the disc maintains its present rate of progress, it seems that neither they—nor we—will have very long to want!

Like Buddy Holly, their self-made songs had a tremendous influence on embryonic British groups. Especially their weird, wide-open space harmony voicings. Not a stage act – a sound.

Both acts *wrote* a lot of hits – a fairly novel thing in R&R, but Anka is probably worth more these days: he co-wrote 'My Way' *and* Johnny Carson's TV theme.

PAGE left London for Paris on Tuesday with her husband, Charles O'Curran, the

Unknowns Frankie Lymon and Russ Hamilton composed and recorded their own tunes and shot into the Hit List ... and now JAMES LYNN tells of a 16-year-old Canadian who does it all over again

Paul Anka wins fame with 'Diana'

THE best way to start any story about young Paul Anka is to latch on to the unbelievable pun staring you in the face and say that "Anka's Away." I know it's the acme of corn, but under the present circumstances, such an outrageous pun can surely be forgiven, for Paul really is "away" —with his very first recording.

It's a song about a girl acquaintance by the name of "Diana," and Paul must be feeling mighty happy right now that he chanced to meet her.

The record started to move just a few weeks after its initial release in America, but even before it had reached the coveted top twenty frame there, it began to attract the attention of Britain's record-buying teenagers.

A couple of weeks back, "Diana" was modestly positioned at number 26 in the NME best sellers. A week later, it jumped to number 13, while in the U.S. it entered the sellers for the first time at number 18.

Take a quick glance at this week's ratings and you'll find that it is still selling fantastically well on both sides of the Atlantic. In Britain, it's placed at number 4; in the U.S. at number 15.

Composer

The amazing thing about Anka's success story is that right now he's only 16 years old, and "Diana" was recorded for the ABC-Paramount label shortly before his last birthday.

Ready for another surprise? It's this: Not only did he compose "Diana," but also the flipside, another cute little ditty titled "Don't Gamble With Love."

Judging from the vast fan following which Paul has already amassed, it seems he's going to be around for some considerable time to come, which means that a few facts about his short, but eventful, life won't go astray at this point.

Paul was born in Ottawa, Canada, on July 30, 1941. He is the oldest of three children, and his father operates a restaurant in his home town.

He began singing in public at local affairs at the age of ten, and just two years later, made his first

night club appearance at the Ocean Beach, Massachusetts!

He impersonated Johnnie Ray and some other famous singers. The usually hard-to-please night club audiences were so impressed that they threw money on the floor. This resulted in Paul finishing up his act with something like 35 dollars in his pocket!

At 12, he began his first piano lessons, but after fumbling his way through scales and simple exercises he quit.

A few months later, he was back again at the piano—this time minus the fumbling tactics. "I just don't know how it happened." he says. "It just came naturally to me . . . sudden like!"

Over the past few years, he hung around night clubs in Ottawa, talking to the stars. Advice and encouragement was forthcoming from people like the Four Lads, the Diamonds and the Crew Cuts, and Paul is quick to express his grateful appreciation.

He formed his own vocal group for a while, and named them The Bobbysoxers, but an unquenchable urge to travel led him to disband the group and work as a "single" until he had saved enough money to make the long trip to Hollywood to visit an uncle. He went to California, but nothing happened.

Back in Ottawa he decided the time was ripe to make an all out bid to crash the "big time," and

to that end, he started out on another journey—this time to New York.

One of the first persons he contacted was Don Costa, a & r head of popular music for the ABC-Paramount Recording Company.

Don listened attentively to young Paul, liked what he heard and immediately saw in him a potential new star.

They talked things over—man to man—Paul was still only 15 at the time, you'll remember—and almost immediately, Paul's parents signed a long-term contract for their son to record for the ABC label.

Costa arranged the two songs Paul chose to record ("Diana" and "Don't Gamble With Love") and personally directed the accompanying orchestra. The result? A smash hit record!

Paul, incidentally, has written songs for Johnny Nash, Micki Marlo and Dick Roman, and as his favourite singers, he names Patti Page, Judy Garland, Frank Sinatra and Sammy Davis, jnr.

"I hope to write songs for them some day," he says.

If he can keep up the standard of "Diana," I'm sure he will.

Just as a lot of folk (established singers included) will be naming Paul their favourite singer!

Parents sign

DIG THIS...

THE LIFE OF EVERY PARTY...

THE STAR OF EVERY SESSION...

PHILCO

FROM RAGS TO RICHES

ultimate glory of fame and fortune

CHARLES GOVEY introduces the new singing group sensation from Texas —

IF somebody asks you where the hit records come from these days, you won't be far wrong if you reply : " Deep in the heart of Texas."

For the important Texan township of Lubbock has suddenly become the focus of the record industry through the activities of four young citizens who call themselves The Crickets.

And The Crickets, we need hardly remind you, have just chirped their way to the top of the American hit parade with a home-grown number called " That'll Be The Day."

This, their first release on the Brunswick label in the U.S., has hit the top in four weeks.

American charts for six by making its first entry at No. 7 and climbing to No. 9 in three weeks.

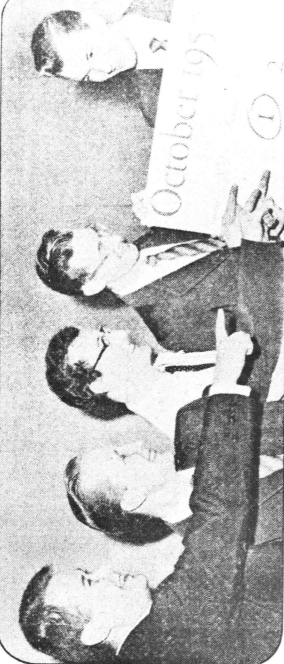

Started young

" That'll Be The Day " is certainly an all-Texan affair. Three members of the group were born in Texas, and the fourth has lived there for the past 17 years.

Back-bone number of the group is 21-year-old BUDDY HOLLY. He started his musical career at the ripe old age of eight, when he began learning the violin.

But a few weeks of scraping and squeaking convinced him that he wasn't going to be another Paganini, and he found himself much more at home on guitar.

At the age of 15, he started singing and playing at various clubs round the south west. Then one day he made a trip to Nashville, the home of country-and-western music.

There he was heard by a talent scout for Decca Records, who wanted him to record some of his own western material. Buddy was signed by Decca, but when his first two releases failed to make any impression his contract was dropped.

He returned home to Lubbock.

Together for the first time

Some other musically-minded young friends convinced him that there must be some other way of breaking into the recording field. It met another budding young musician called JERRY ALLISON.

Jerry, aged 19, is really a farm boy. His first musical interests involved piano lessons at the age of six, but he soon changed his mind and decided upon drums as the source of his enjoyment.

Jerry played drums at various clubs while still at school. But when he was offered a job with a group to tour the southern states, he left study behind in favour of becoming a full-time musician.

Friends

Then he met Buddy Holly. Both boys had a lot of ideas in common, and they quickly became friends.

They decided to form a musical group called The Crickets, and they wrote a song for the group titled . . . " That'll Be The Day."

They started looking around for suitable musicians to join the group, and found two right on their own door-step.

One was a 26-year-old guitarist named NIKI SULLIVAN. Born in California, he has spent the past 17 years of his life in Texas. He has had a variety of odd jobs, but his main ambition was to make a career in music.

One day he was invited to go to the home of Buddy Holly, to watch some home recordings in the making. When he arrived, he was asked to join the group.

THE CRICKETS

'Little fella'

For their bass-player the boys selected 18-year-old JOE MAULDIN, who, like Buddy, was born in Lubbock. Joe is known as the "little fella" of the group, for he is quite a few inches shorter than the rest of The Crickets, who are all six-footers.

The starting-point for the new group was a trip to Clovis in New Mexico. There, the boys knew, was situated the finest recording studio in the entire south west.

The studios were owned by a technician named Norman Petty, a musician who recorded with his own trio and had penned a hit song, "Almost Paradise."

Petty saw the potential talent in the youngsters and took a special interest in them from the start. He became their manager, guided them through many hours of practice, and re-shaped " That'll Be The Day " into likely hit parade style.

At last he judged they were ready to make a test disc. The result of the session was sent to music publisher Murray Deutch, in New York.

Deutch passed the disc on to Bob Thiele, the a & r manager for Coral Records, who at once realised he had potential hit material on his hands.

The next step surpassed the four youngsters' wildest dreams. Not only did Bob Thiele give Buddy a solo recording contract with Coral, he also decided to record The Crickets as a group on his subsidiary label, Brunswick.

This was really ironic. For Coral and Brunswick are both subsidiaries of Decca, who had rejected Buddy's solo efforts some time before. He had got in by the back door after being thrown out at the front !

Anyhow, the boys have little cause to complain. For under their new recording agreement, they not only record as a group for Brunswick, but provide the musical sup-

port for Buddy on his solo Coral discs as well.

" That'll Be The Day " gives The Crickets, as they celebrate October 1, the day on which they expected to pass the millionth sale of their hit record. Helping the Crickets to celebrate this special date (extreme left), the a & r head of Coral and Brunswick.

Composers

This, combined with the fact that they write a lot of their own material, means that these young Texans aren't going to be short of cash for a long time to come.

The boys intend to provide for the future by investing some of their earnings in stocks and bond companies. They also want to open their own music publishing concern, so that they can give fellow songwriters and songwriters a break.

And like all true-blue Texans they are proud to have put their home town of Lubbock on the entertainment map.

They'd certainly be happy if we in Britain began to associate Texas not just with cattle, oil and big buxom girls like Jayne Mansfield, but with the latest line in modern musical groups as well.

Buddy Holly and the Crickets – Much more revered in G.B. than in the U.S.A., had more hits here, too. Sold on sound and not on looks. Pure pop music – meaning equal amount of energy to actual notes. First self-contained guitar group, writing and performing own songs, polished in the studio by producer Norman Petty, Mr Straight. Guess who got inspired by this group? The Beatles, the Hollies, Peter and Gordon. Graham Nash has said they were the most influential group in the World. Ironically, Holly's only number one G.B. hit was posthumous: 'I Guess It Doesn't Matter Anymore', which he didn't write. Paul Anka did.

After JERRY LEWIS, now comes

JERRY *LEE* LEWIS

into the Hit Parade with 'a lotta shaking'

IF I were endeavouring to carve a name for myself in the hall of fame, my first move would be to ensure that that name was sufficiently striking to catch the public's imagination. The one thing I wouldn't do is to take a famous star's name, amend it slightly, and use the outcome. For what degree of success could I expect with a name like Tommy Syd Steele, or Frankie Van Vaughan?

By—
DEREK
JOHNSON

These, at any rate, are my initial thoughts on the subject but, with the world of music being as topsy-turvy and unpredictable as it is at the moment, it is only to be expected that my own considerations should be proved totally unfounded.

This preamble is intended to say that I would have thought Jerry Lee Lewis's name in itself was a considerable drawback, and a hindrance to the progress of his career.

Whether or not it happens to be his real name, it would appear that confusion with the famous Hollywood star. Jerry Lewis, was inevitable and to the detriment of the newcomer! But the very fact of Jerry's flourishing record success, "Whole Lotta Shakin' Going On," sitting snugly in 16th position in this week's NME chart, shows that there is no such thing as an "expert" in the music business these days!

Jerry, a fair-haired, blue-eyed youngster from Farriday, Louisiana, has developed into the latest rock sensation in the States, within the short space of six weeks and largely on the strength of one record.

He is no newcomer to entertainment, however, for he gave his first public performance twelve years ago (at the age of nine), when he appeared at an automobile show in his home town. Inspired by his father's constant encouragement and belief, the boy began devoting his entire spare time to learning about the art of making music.

First record

When he regarded his talented son as ready for launching, Jerry's father took him along to meet the head of the principal record company in Memphis, Sam Phillips of Sun Records. You've heard that name before? I'm not surprised, because it was for Sam that Elvis Presley cut his first record.

Sam has a reputation for knowing a good thing when he hears it, and, as previously, he was not slow to recognise a potential money-spinner here. He persuaded Jerry to organise an accompanying group, and together they cut his first record, "Crazy Arms," which hit with a greater impact than the first Presley disc. Unlike Elvis, Jerry has remained with Sun, and his latest international success still finds him on that label, although the outlet in this country is by way of London Records.

Suddenly, Jerry finds himself in great demand on radio and TV, and in the important clubs across the country. He has recently been seen on the Steve Allen Show, and on Alan Freed's "The Big Beat Programme."

Meanwhile, his niterie engagements have been flowing in thick and fast, and he has just completed a season at the famed Apollo in New York. Billed as The Jerry Lee Lewis Trio, the act features the leader singing at the piano. He uses the keyboard in much the same thumping, pounding way that Presley uses his guitar, though despite all the showmanship and effort, he never seems to miss either the beat or a note.

TV dates

In less than no time, Jerry Lee Lewis has jumped to the top. "Whole Lotta Shakin' Going On" is booming out of America's loudspeakers from coast to coast, and is acknowledged as one of the hottest discs to be heard on the nation's airwaves for many a month.

Jerry has been subjected to a certain amount of criticism in the Press, because of his unnecessary stage antics — combing his hair after each number, for instance. But it seems to go down well with the girls, so the artist naturally retains it in his act.

The accompanying instruments in his current group are drums and electric guitar, but these play a subsidiary role, the spotlight always being upon Lewis.

around for some long time to come.

I understand that he has just completed making a new disc, and I am quite sure that the company will try to cash in on Jerry's tremendous sales of his current hit, by issuing the follow-up as quickly as possible.

When one surveys the musical scene these days, it is a pretty true reflection to say that the word "Whole Lotta Shakin'" is going on.

Shattering

There is no doubt that Jerry Lee Lewis, the youngster who found an extra-stage star's name an advantage rather than an obstacle, is going to shake up show business a whole lot more before he is through.

With his new style rock, this youngster has descended upon the pop music scene with shattering effect. Judging by the cheers with which he is being acclaimed on tour, and the amount of airings his discs are obtaining, it looks as though he has hit upon the right formula and will be

JERRY LEE LEWIS

BILLY ECKSTINE admits—

Jerry Lee Lee Lewis – the greatest live performer I have ever seen. As electric as Al Jolson was – and Lewis has all Jolson's records. When Lewis is on stage it's high melodrama and the audience plays the heavies. In real life the man would be in solitary confinement. Like Boone and Richard he has done a bit of preaching.

THE MEN BEHIND THE DISCS

GEOFF LOVE

NORRIE PARAMOR

RON GOODWIN

They back the stars to win!

MUCH as the success of a hit record depends upon the personality and talent of the artist concerned, seldom would it achieve best-selling proportions, were it not for the novelty, both in conception and arrangement, of the accompaniment.

Listen again to some of the important records of the moment, paying particular attention to the instrumental backing. Maybe you have never noticed before how perfectly tailored and carefully moulded to the singer's style, is the orchestral accompaniment.

And that, of course, is the secret of the ideal backing—it must not be overwhelmingly obtrusive, thus detracting from the performance of the singer; on the other hand, it must not be dull or lacking in imagination, causing an overall loss of appeal and effect. It must carry the singer along smoothly, and with subtlety. It must adorn and embellish, but never submerge.

This is one of the most complicated tasks any musician has to face, especially as he knows that his efforts will make or break a record, and will be perpetually preserved. We have in Britain a select group of musical directors, who specialise in the recording field, and who between them are responsible for almost the entire output of home-produced discs from our five major studios.

It is an old journalistic custom to establish a link between personalities about whom one is writing. To find the link which binds the three recording MD's about whom I am writing today, let us go back ten years, and look in at a ballroom, where the dancers are enjoying the foot-tapping music of Harry Gold and his Pieces of Eight.

Cornermen

On trombone, there's an energetic young man, with quite the broadest smile in the business; he's been around for a few years, starting with Freddie Platt at the Carlton, Rochdale, and subsequently moving to Jan Ralfini and Sid Millward—but now he's just come out of the Army, after serving six years with the King's Royal Rifle Corps, playing with their band, and gaining his first insight into arranging.

Meanwhile, the pianist—a familiar sandy-haired figure with blue-tinted spectacles—is not long out of the RAF, where he has been touring with the Gang Show, and in fact, will tell you that he has played every NAAFI piano in the world. Now he is Harry Gold's pianist-arranger, but has previously had experience with Billy Gerhardi, Jack Harris and Maurice Winnick.

And the trumpeter this evening has

recently joined the band, after fronting his own semi-pro group. His band won many contests, during which time he was arranging for such famous names as Stanley Black, Ambrose and Peter Yorke.

Now he's arranging for the Pieces of Eight, too, and filling in on trumpet when necessary.

In those days, they were three solid cornermen of a bouncy dixieland band. Now they are re-united, but in a far more important capacity, and fulfilling a totally different function. For their names, respectively, are **Geoff Love, Norrie Paramor** and **Ron Goodwin.** And, all acknowledged as brilliant recording MD's, they are responsible for a large percentage of the discs which emerge from EMI's studios in Abbey Road.

These backroom boys came out of the Big Band days, provided competent accompaniment for the GB rockers, and went on to weather everything that came after. Helmsmen all, real professionals. Literate music men with the pop knack for M.O.R. will never die.

I always wanted to be a comedian, but...
I'm a hit singer instead!
moans
JIM DALE

SOMEBODY once gave me a piece of advice: "Just make up your mind what you want to do, Jim boy, and do it! That's the way to get on. If you want it enough, it'll come to you in the end."

Well, I've always tried to follow that piece of advice, and quite early on in life I decided I was going to be a comedian. But did it work out that way? Did it heck!

Ever since I started in show business, I've been trying to persuade people to give me a chance as a comedian. I've never missed a chance of demonstrating that I really could be quite funny, if only they'd let me try.

But people always have said: "I think you'd do better if you tried something else, Jim," and they'd give me a job as a dancer or a tumbler.

Now, with "Be My Girl" suddenly showing up in the Top Ten, everybody has decided that I have to be a singer—and that's something I never made any plans for at all.

It looks as if my last chance of being a comedian has gone down the drain!

BRUCE CHARLTON invites you to meet

JOHNNY OTIS

who made an oldie into a new hit by adding rock, hard drive

AND

MARIE ADAMS

and the

3 TONS OF JOY

LATEST addition to the constantly growing list of revivals, which are continually being taken from the shelf, dusted off and presented in new dress, is the happy-go-lucky, war-time song, "Ma, He's Makin' Eyes At Me."

No longer echoing around the air - raid shelters, or bellowed chorus-style in NAAFI canteens, the tempo has been dropped to a slow, insistent rock—to meet the demands of the day and age—and a fierce, dynamic drive, not apparent beforehand, has been added.

The result? A hit record. And the man responsible for seeing the rock possibilities of the song, and adapting it accordingly? Meet Johnny Otis—enjoying not only his first record release in this country, but his simultaneous entry into the best-sellers, where this week his disc has shot into position number ten.

In this respect, he shares a distinction with Billy Ward, in that his first available record in Britain has appeared in the charts, and that it happens to be his version of a revival.

Although a newcomer to collectors here, Johnny is very well established in the States, where he has been touring with his own package show for eight years.

DRUMMER FIRST

Hailing from a small Californian town, where he was born 36 years ago, Johnny was much impressed by the Goodman and Basie Bands when he was in his teens, as a result of which he decided to be a drummer.

He promptly took it up to good effect, and it says much for his talent and initiative that he now additionally plays vibraphone and piano—and sings, too!

During the forties, Johnny worked

JOHNNY OTIS

with many of the well-known contemporary bands, until in 1948 he formed his own 18-piece group.

"Nat Cole was just starting out then, and we worked the Orpheum Theatre with him." he recalls. "Then I decided to open my own club in Watts, California. It was the first niterie in the world to feature rock 'n roll exclusively. The following year, I assembled a smaller band, but with personality singers and groups, comprising a sort of package show, like I have today."

Since then, the Otis Show has been a successful feature of many American night spots, and is at this moment undertaking a lengthy tour around the West Coast area. Yet, despite these commitments, Johnny still manages to fit in a nightly rock 'n' roll show on station KFOX, and to cut records regularly for Capitol.

It is from his latest batch of eight titles, that two were selected for release in this country. As frequently happens, the newcomer's novelty value has captured the public's imagination and the record has scored heavily.

TEENAGE GIMMICK

No doubt the success of "Ma" can be attributed in part to the gimmick effect of teenagers screaming throughout the singing.

But its principal appeal lies in the robust, belting rhythm singing of "Marie Adams And The Three Tons Of Joy," as they are labelled.

Actually, this vocal group comprises three rather large coloured girls who, although being unable literally to total three tons, can at least amass a combined eight hundredweight! Marie Adams, who is really the star of the record—and the other side, "In The Dark"—is the lead singer of the group.

It is fortunate for these ladies that, of the eight sides cut by Johnny recently, it is their two titles which have been issued here, for they are not featured on the other six.

The Otis unit, being essentially a package, boasts many speciality performers, all of whom are Johnny's own discoveries—and that includes Tons of Joy.

Here are Marie Adams (left) and the Three Tons of Joy.

At the same session, Johnny cut a couple of titles with his vivacious 16-year-old singer, Jeannie Sterling; a pair of ballads, featuring the voice of Mel Williams; and two bouncing rock items, with Johnny himself doing the vocal honours.

It is a safe bet, in view of the success enjoyed by his first release, to assume that one or more of these additional couplings can be expected from Capitol in the near future.

Johnny's entourage consists of eighteen people, ten of whom are vocalists. For the rest, there are two saxes, trumpet, trombone and rhythm section. The majority of the routines are arranged by Johnny himself, who is also no mean composer. Two of his better-known rock originals are "Hound Dog" and "Dance With Me, Henry."

According to the well-known song, "Miss Otis Regrets." Whether or not she is any relation, I don't know. But it's a dead cert that **Mister** Otis has no cause to regret the current turn of events.

Only two hits but what a great belting rock band sound! The claim-rumour here is that he co-wrote 'Hound Dog' – but Leiber and Stoller now get the credits. The world of R&R is indeed a dark one!

THERE IS A STANDING JOKE BETWEEN Paul Lincoln and myself that when we go for a coffee, we don't have one in the Two I's. It's always crowded to bargain basement density. We go to a coffee bar down the road. We

Lots of us came to making up our own rock via skiffle groups. So cheap to form them, so easy to play! Embryonic Beatles formed skiffle groups – so did Marty Wilde, Adam Faith, and Cliff Richard. Our school chaplain gave his blessing to my group. We sang 'This Land is Your Land' and other Leftist songs, unwittingly. The chaplain smiled, told us we were making a 'cheerful noise unto God', and promised a 'skiffle mass' in the near future.

THE TWO I's CAME INTO SHOW BUSINESS JUST AS A SHEER MATTER OF ACCIDENT

did that last week, when—over coffee (1s.) and cheese cake (2s. 6d. a slice, or 2s. 10d. on deferred terms)—Paul told how it all came about.

In the summer of 1956, he and Ray Hunter earned their living via the groan, grapple and grunt of all-in wrestling.

This trade has drawbacks. It calls for some wrestling skill, some ability as an acrobat, a sense of showmanship, and a flair for acting not far short of Old Vic standards. Yet, with a few exceptions, there's not a fantastic amount of money in it.

So Lincoln and Hunter (without wishing to forsake entirely the land of leg-lock) decided to seek a more reliable source of income. Friends told them, "There's gold in them thar coffee bars", so they checked through agents' lists looking for somewhere suitable.

It Didn't Kick Off Too Well

On one such list they found the Two I's. In they went, all set to clean up. They had the coffee bar itself upstairs, meals served downstairs, somewhere to hang your hat, service with a smile, and all the general paraphernalia of the table d'hôte fraternity.

Things moved quickly; but, unfortunately for Lincoln and Hunter, in the wrong direction. They lost money quicker than a drunk in a brag school. Compared with the joint and two veg. lark, all-in wrestling seemed as safe and set as a career in the Civil Service.

On Lincoln's estimate, they started losing thirty to forty quid a week.

Then came a change in their fortunes: they got worse. They had heard the sounds of renovations, reconstructions, refurbishments and what not coming from next door. "What gives?" they asked one of the workmen.

"We're getting things ready for the Heaven and Hell."

"Huh? For crying out loud, what's that?"

"A coffee bar, chum."

So throughout the summer of 1956, business at the Two I's went from the lousy to the non-existent.

Bearded Gents Got On His Nerves

Things then picked up slightly, mainly through a coffee-drinking clientèle who, in Paul's eyes, were a bit more eccentric than somewhat.

One or two sported beards, several brought guitars along, and the resultant strumming and singing fretsawed through Paul's nerves unbearably.

One night, when a session was getting well into gear, he ordered everyone out. The exodus took a minute or two, so—by the time the last few were moving out—Paul's irritation had ebbed considerably. He started talking to one of the guitarists.

The youngster explained he was with a regular group.

"What do you play?"

"Skiffle."

For all that conveyed to Paul, the answer could have been in Hindustani.

However, feeling he might as well have a go, he fixed for the group to come and play at the Two I's. It was called **The Vipers.**

Lincoln will tell you: **"The moment we put a notice up saying 'Skiffle On Fridays,' things started to change in a big way. On skiffle nights, we had queues half-way round the block. So, of course, we soon came to the point of having skiffle every night. Business was certainly looking up."**

Much has been told about **Tommy Steele's** connection with the Two I's, but here's a cute detail which seems to have been left out: **TOMMY FIRST PLAYED DOWN THERE AS A MEMBER OF THE VIPERS SKIFFLE GROUP WHEN ITS LEADER, WALT WHYTON, WENT ABROAD FOR THREE WEEKS ON HOLIDAY.**

When he came back, the vacancy no longer existed, and Paul Lincoln describes coming into the coffee bar one evening, and finding an indignant youngster at the top of the stairs.

"What's up, Tommy?"

"What's up! Here's a blinkin' fine turn-out. I play wiv the group for just three weeks, and now I BIN SACKED!"

Lucky There's No Trombone!

If you've never been to the Two I's, don't get the idea it's some ritzy place occupying a couple of acres or so.

Upstairs, it's just like other snack bar, except for w bedecked with photos of its s biz offspring.

Downstairs (unless the dec tors have moved in since l there last) is a slightly d basement. In it, from long be the performance till some w after it, the kids (as there are seats) stand packed together bearings in a ballrace right top of the group. (Luckily, the no trombone in a skiffle gr otherwise dozens of 'em w get laid out every night).

So, you see, proprietor l Lincoln has landed himself show business quite by accid But, having done so, he's ing the experience.

He's a genial, easy-manne

Continued on page 8

To make the scene was to cram into a dingy Soho frothy coffee bar.

COMPLETE GUIDE TO S-DISCS

(Note: EPs of titles already issued on 78s not included).

LONNIE DONEGAN GROUP
"Rock Island Line"/"John Henry"
"Digging My Potatoes"/"Bury My Body"
"Lost John"/"Stewball"
"Dead Or Alive"/"Bring A Little Water, Sylvie"
"I'm Alabamy Bound"/"Don't You Rock Me, Daddy-O"
"Cumberland Gap"/"Love Is Strange"
"Puttin' On The Style"/"Gambling Man"
Backstairs Session (EP)—"Midnight Special"/"New Burying Ground"
"It Takes A Worried Man"/"When The Sun Goes Down"
(EP) "Railroad Bill"/"Stackalee"/"The Ballad Of Jesse James"/"Ol' Riley"
Lonnie Donegan Showcase (LP)

CHRIS BARBER GROUP with DICKIE BISHOP
"Can't You Like 'Em" / "Gipsy Davy"

CHRIS BARBER GROUP with JOHNNY DUNCAN
"Doin' My Time"/"When Could I Go"

BOB CORT GROUP
"It Takes A Worried Man"/"Don't You Rock Me, Daddy-O"
"Six-Five Special"/"Roll Jen Jenkins"
"Schoolday"/"Ain't It A Shame"
"Maggie May"/"Jessamine"

With LIZ WINTERS
"Love Is Strange"/"Freight Train"

LES HOBEAUX
"Toll The Bell Easy"/"Oh, Mary, Don't You Weep"

JIMMY JACKSON AND HIS ROCKIN' SKIFFLE
"California Zephyr"/"I Shall Not Be Moved"
"Sittin' In The Balcony"/"Good Morning Blues"
"River Line"/"Lonely Road"
"White Silver Sands"/"Build Your Love"

STATION GROUP
"Bagged My Honey"/"Don't You Rock Me, Daddy-O"

KEN COLYER GROUP
"The Grey Goose"/"I Can't Sleep"
"Sportin' Life"/"House Rent Stomp"
"Old Riley"/"Stack-o-lee Blues"
"Down Bound Train"/"Mule Skinner"
"Take This Hammer"/"Down By The Riverside"
"Streamline Train"/"Go Down, Old Hannah"

ALAN LOMAX and THE RAMBLERS
"Dirty Old Town"/"Hard Case"

DICKIE BISHOP AND THE SIDEKICKS
"Cumberland Gap"/"No Other Baby"

BERYL BRYDEN'S BACKROOM SKIFFLE
"Casey Jones"/"Kansas City Blues"

SONNY STEWART AND HIS SKIFFLE KINGS
"The Northern Line"/"Black Jack"

THE VIPERS GROUP
"Ain't You Glad"/"Pick A Bale Of Cotton"
"Don't You Rock Me, Daddy-O"/"Ten Thousand Years Ago"
"Jim Dandy"/"Hey, Liley Liley Lo"
"Cumberland Gap"/"Maggie May"
"Streamline Train"/"Railroad Steamboat"

LORRAE DESMOND and THE REBELS
"Kansas City Special"/"Preacher, Preacher"

DON LANG GROUP
Skiffle Special (LP)

JOHNNY DUNCAN AND HIS BLUE GRASS BOYS
"Kaw-Liga"/"Ella Speed"
"Last Train To San Fernando"/"Rock-A-Billy Baby"
"Jig Along"/"Blue, Blue Heartache"
(EP)—"Freight Train Blues"/"Press On"/"Johnny's Yodel"/"Out Of Business"

2.19 GROUP
"Railroad Bill" / "Freight Train Blues"
"I'm A-Looking For A Home"/"When The Saints Go"
(EP)—"This Little Light Of Mine"/"Union Maid"/"Where Can I Go"/"Roll The Union On"

DELTA GROUP
"Skip To My Lou"/"John Brown's Body"
"Pick A Bale Of Cotton"/"K Moan"

CHAS. McDEVITT GROUP with NANCY WHISKEY
"Freight Train"/"The Cotton Song"
"Green Back Dollar"/"I'm Satisfied"
"It Takes A Worried Man"/"House Of The Rising Sun"
"Face In The Rain"/"Sporting Life"

And on the borders of skiffle are:

TERRY DENE AND HIS DENE-ACES
"Start Movin'"/"Green Corn"
"White Sport Coat"/"The Man In The Phone Booth"

KING BROTHERS
"Cradle Rock"/"Crazy Little Palace"
"Heart"/"Railroad Steamboat"
"Mary"
"White
Ha-Ha
"In Th
"Rock

HYMAN ZAHL and PAUL LINC
THEIR FIRST LONDON (
TROCADERO, ELEPHANT
SUNDAY, SEPTEMBER 22nd

Paul Lincoln – 'President of Soho' – an Aussie who ran the Two 1's Coffee Bar. (1957)

Rhythm with the

VICEROY SKIFFLE BOARD **39/6**

HAVE FUN !

Complete with

DRUM.   WASHBOARD.   COWBELL.

TAPBOX.   RIM-SHOTS.   HOOTER.

Ideal for parties and playing with radio or gramophone
Also the Junior Model available at 23/6

ROSE, MORRIS & CO. LIMITED
79/85 PAUL STREET, LONDON, E.C.2

Friday. November 1. 1957

Bob Cort *tells you how to* Get Skiffling !

LET'S get it quite clear that skiffle is not some mysterious form of intellectual folk music, that must have definite instruments and use a particular type of song. Skiffle is party music. So whatever tunes you use, never forget that it must be music and it must be entertainment.

People at parties like to sing, so your tunes will be most popular if they have simple choruses that people can join in.

Work songs and sea shanties nearly always have these choruses, and are therefore the main source of numbers for skiffle, but folk song is by no means the only place to find tunes. A lot of student or club songs, for instance, make wonderful skiffle material. So don't stop at the tunes in my book*—go ahead and adapt your own from any source. Indeed, go on and make your own skiffle.

NO STRICT RULE

The usual line-up for a skiffle group is from one to three guitars, a washboard or snare drum, and a string or box bass. But there is no strict rule. If you want to include a mouth organ or clarinet, go ahead; but use them to take an odd solo, and don't let them confuse the sound, so that people can't hear what you are singing.

The only essential instrument is the guitar, and if at least two can learn to play good strong chords, the group will have a sound basis for the singing. I prefer the cello-built plectrum guitar, because it gives a crisper, stronger rhythm, but as long as you fit steel strings to them, round hole guitars are very good, and you can get them at a more reasonable price.

Unfortunately, there are a number of so-called "skiffle guitars" for sale today that, to say the least, are not very good. When buying, make sure that the neck is straight, it has a fixed bridge and, in the case of second-hand guitars, there are no cracks which may develop buzzing, and the cogs on the machine-head are not loose.

A word about the washboard. There are a number of metal ones on the market, some from Sweden, but there is one British make of heavier gauge metal, which seems to be the best—the ridges last longer, and the tone is not tinny.

Get hold of a dozen steel thimbles (heavy gauge is kinder to the fingers). Some people use a thimble on each finger, others use only two or three; this is a matter of personal choice.

An important feature of skiffle is its visual effect. It is most important that you all look happy. However worried you are, never let it show; get through as best you can. Some sort of uniform is a great help, though ordinary casual clothes are perhaps the best, as long as you all wear exactly the same.

Skiffle is essentially free and easy, happy, living music, and if you have ideas that conflict with mine, go ahead and use them. There are no rules for skiffle—that's where half the enjoyment lies; in experimenting with ideas.

*Extracted from " Making The Most Of Skiffle " by Bob Cort, published by McGlennons.

WHEN YOU'RE A DISC JOCKEY ... YOU ENTERTAIN

THE PUBLIC— NOT YOURSELF — SO...

IF IT'S PRESLEY THEY WANT, GIVE 'EM PRESLEY !

"*YOU'VE GOT A HOME*, a record player and a lot of records, so you can play the records you like at home. But when you are on the air you play the ones the public likes."

That is probably the finest piece of advice I have ever received since I did my first B.B.C. disc jockey show two years ago and started a career which has so far taken in a "Housewives Choice" session and a couple of series of "Just For The Record."

The advice—from an old and trusted friend—taught me a lesson.

When you are given a disc jockey programme you are supposed to entertain the public, not yourself. If the public likes Elvis Presley and you don't, you still play Elvis Presley.

After all, as my friend so rightly said, you can play the records you like at home.

HOT FROM THE FACTORY !

THAT'S WHY having a disc jockey programme is not quite the simple job some people believe it is. On the contrary, to prepare a good disc show takes a tremendous amount of time. The actual half hour or so you spend on the air represents only a tiny fraction of it.

Each day the postman staggers up to your front door with boxes of records. They are hot from the factory. They are the records which you, the members of the public who make or break an artiste, will buy or ignore in your local shop within the next few weeks.

These records are sent by the record companies and by the music publishers. The D.J.'s first introduction to a new record is through a hastily-despatched, one-sided review copy, which is followed by the finished article.

So when **Tommy Steele** makes a new disc, into my lap fall two one-sided review copies—the main side and the flip side, remember—from the DECCA boys. Then the music publishers will probably see to it that I receive a copy — two songs, two publishers, two discs.

Then when DECCA have their finished copies ready, my weary postman once again rings the front door bell and I stretch a hand over the top of the huge pile of record boxes and take delivery of ... yes, you've guessed it, the new Tommy Steele record !

Yes, it could mean five copies of the one disc, so is it any wonder that I read the recent "78s v. 45s" controversy in the RECORD MIRROR with the greatest of interest ?

And is it any wonder that I made suitable uncomplimentary remarks to each letter I read which supported 78s ? No, give me the 45s any time, thank you. They give my family and me a spot of room to live in our own house ... and they are less likely to be ruined when my 12-year-old daughter goes through them with a critical eye.

NOT A RECORD IS WASTED

THESE DISCS ARE NOT WASTED, for every D.J. spends hours in solitary confinement listening to disc after disc after disc.

It's only coffee and cigarettes which get you through such a session ... and you haven't to forget that disc show which you must listen to on the radio. For after all, it would be a poor disc jockey who didn't listen to other disc jockeys to find out what they are playing and how they are presenting their programmes.

Even Isidore Green, you know, reads other newspapers and magazines!

So please don't think the life of a disc jockey is all feet-up-on-the-mantelpiece leisure ... there isn't any room on the mantelpiece, which is stacked high with new records.

Listening ... sorting ... trying to find the hits of to-morrow ... trying to find a balanced programme so that there will be something for the rock 'n' roll fans (but you mustn't offend the anti-rock 'n' roll fans !) ... making a note of this record which doesn't fit into this week's programme but must get serious consideration for next week.

And when you have it all sorted out and are working out your script, the telephone rings. *Who is it?* Yes, **right first time**. It's one of the record company boys, and he's got news.

His company has just brought out "a wonderful new disc" which is going to sweep the world, and, yes, a copy of it is on the way round to your house at this very moment.

For the record business never stands still. There is always movement, always change, always interest.

So it's hard work, but it is entertaining work, fascinating work, and although we all complain when we are up to our eyes in it, just ask any of the disc jockeys to give it up and get a job in an office ... and then run !

SO WHY SHOULDN'T I LIKE MUSIC ?

MANY PEOPLE, of course, have often asked me how I come to be mixed up in it. After all, sport is supposed to be my life.

When people say that to me I always feel like breaking the 78 I like least over their heads. Okay, so I write about sport, I appear on television covering sport, and I love sport. **But that doesn't mean I don't like anything else.**

Why shouldn't I have an interest in music and records as well?

I'll let you into a secret. I am one of those people who can't work if it is quiet. Perhaps it is that I love doing

football commentar[...] rounded by 100,00[...] cheering fans.

I don't know. B[...] ever I write an articl[...] my record player [...] overtime — and I ha[...] learned how to [...] volume down to the [...] mark.

And my taste in m[...] my taste in sport . [...] the lot. I am thrille[...] ball, by swimming, b[...] and by almost every[...] bull fighting —I cann[...] stand why anyone [...] that under the h[...] sport.

My music ? Well, [...] from **Gigli** to **Garlan[...]** write powerful pro[...] editors don't agree [...] but who cares abou[...] even at Christmastim[...] the record player is [...] **Bing Crosby, Dea[...]** (*anyone got a spare [...] "Pretty Baby" to rep[...] which is almost w[...] ballet music, the [...] parable **Mantovani,** [...] **Sid Phillips, Peggy** [...] *even makes me lik[...]* ... the lot, in fact.

All right, so I do [...] crotchet from a c[...] **that doesn't stop [...] music.** Nor does [...] liking all kinds of [...] I cannot help thi[...] those people who [...] rock 'n' roll, jazz, [...] some other small [...] the vast world of [...] missing an awful l[...] is so much that is g[...] that it is silly to con[...] just one section of m[...]

ALL PART SHOW BUSIN[...]

WHAT ELSE IS [...] like about the [...] dustry besides the [...] Well, records are pa[...] cel of Show Busi[...] Show Business is an [...] part of that wider [...] the Entertainments [...] which also, let's f[...] cludes my bread and [...] sport.

So being a disc jo[...] sports commentator [...] all, a natural alliance [...]

That is why in [...] The Record" I [...] each programme [...] chosen by a sportin[...] They ranged from [...] chosen by **Bert** [...] Manchester City's [...] to the **Louis Armstr[...]** by **Bill Roberts,** [...] swimmer. The spo[...] women who had [...] United States nearly [...] for something they [...] have ... " My Fa[...] To such requests [...] reply, " Just You W.[...]

KENNETH WOLSTENHOLME, The Celebrated BBC TV Commentator, In This Especially Written Article For The RECORD MIRROR Annual, Reveals Some Intensely Interesting Sidelights Of His Career As A Disc Jockey, Introduces Many Famous Folk In The World Of Sport And Entertainment, And Hails Howard Keel As One Of The Finest Artistes He Has Ever Met.

1958
LAST OF THE GOLDEN YEARS

SCHOOL REPORT:
Spring Term, 1958

Maths: He batters at the subject with argumentative fury, impatient with himself, with me, and with the world, when the mystery does not at once unfold.

History: Superbly ingenious, an extraordinary haphazard mind. Nobody can teach him anything if he doesn't choose to be taught.

English: An extraordinary fellow of apparently boundless frivolity. His written style is too conversational. Must improve his reading matter.

Art: Keen on this subject but must begin to realise that there is more to art than speed boats, aeroplanes, guns, soldiers and sudden death. Once he has these action subjects out of his system we can then get down to more serious endeavours.

Music: Could be taught to play quite well if he were prepared to practise – but as he says he has no intention of doing this, the decision to stop piano lessons is a very wise one.

Housemaster's report: Has enough intelligence to grow up to be a useful citizen but won't grow up if he can help it. Loses control of himself at least once a day and ceases to be a rational creature. Must learn self-control and resist the temptation to be an exhibitionist.

How to react to that? Put on a record of 'Bony Moronie', jump into a hot bath and shout, 'Owwwww!' Pull on your jeans, plug in your guitar and sing, 'Oh Boy!' My rock 'n' roll group was coming along well, and pretty soon we'd be ready to give a concert. 'His light relief is in music – of a sort!' wrote my tutor to my parents. The rowing Eight might get more food, but I was kingpin of another world within the school, where there were no score cards, where there was no responsibility, no self-control, no curb on exhibitionism. If you were Jerry Lee Lewis you could be a SHOW-OFF and also *get paid*!

'Society cannot afford such people,' said the senior monitor in my house. Jerry Lee Lewis had suffered like a martyr on his first trip to Britain. Press and public had got all heated up about his life off the stage. What did it matter *what* he did off the stage? 'You talk too much and too loudly', said the head boy. 'You should forget your "self" in your work and just draw', said the art master. But Jerry Lee, like all the best wild men of rock 'n' roll, revelled in being *himself*. He had a tremendous sense of being Jerry Lee Lewis – there was no-one on earth so aware of his own unique qualities. And Chuck Berry felt the same way about *him*self. So did Little Richard. They all knew that there was only one of them in the world and it happened to be them and they were tickled to death!

When the audience at the Hackney Empire booed

Jerry Lee Lewis because they disapproved of his life-style Jerry Lee wasn't phased. He raised an eyebrow superciliously, pulled out his steel comb and slowly combed his long golden aryan locks. He combed and combed until the audience, rockers and all, ran out of venom. Then he gave out with 'Come on over baby – whole lotta shakin' goin' on!' Pretty soon he had the audience right in his demonic power and doing the rock 'n' roll 'call & response':

'We got a chicken in the barn.'
Audience: 'Whose barn?'
Jerry Lee: 'MY BARN!!'

You could trace this sort of word fun back to Africa or back to medieval England and before. Long before *Beowulf*. Back to dim distant times when people naturally 'spoke in tongues' as the spirit moved them: 'whaaatinwillim-goo-goo-boo . . .' They were possessed and knew nothing of syntax. In modern America, between skyscrapers and freeways, were folk like these possessed ancients only now they were shouting 'Rama lama ding dong!' So that you had a country that was the last word in modernity spreading world-wide the babel of first words spoken by men when civilization was still a baby.

I tried to nutshell these historical ramblings into an intellectual argument. I tried to repress my intuition. 'Et Nova Et Vetera' was the school motto: 'Both New And Old'. Right! At the Debating Club I argued that most rock 'n' roll was a direct descendant of our own British Folk Music Heritage. Rockabilly music was from Country & Western sources – most of the singers we liked in Britain were white Anglo-Saxon Protestants bringing us an electrified transmogrification of the jigs, reels, laments and Morris dances of Great Britain, see Vaughan Williams and Cecil Sharp. British folk song with a new beat. The rockers I cited were Bill Haley (he'd started as a hillbilly bandleader), Elvis Presley (once dubbed 'King of Western Bop'), Jerry Lee Lewis (his first records were country tunes). Then there were the Everlys and the Crickets . . . Eventually I was told I had successfully 'made my point' and that there was 'room in a progressive school for a society dedicated to creative contemporary folk music'. So I didn't get on to rock 'n' roll's power of causing 'instantaneous energy' – which was just as well because this might be seen as a justification for self-abuse and only recently we'd had a sex lecture by a travelling sex doctor who had said about our consuming hobby: 'Don't Do It!'

History and Music having been dealt with, I now turned to English. 'Must improve his reading matter'. So I gave up Kid Colt Action comics and started reading a current best-seller, *On The Road* by Jack Kerouac. It was a hard-backed but it jumped like crazy, splashing the fireball grain alcohol of a rocking life all over the neo-Georgian floor of the dormitory. There was a lot about jazz but I knew it wasn't the jazz of Britain. It was *something else*. Here was Sal Paradise chronicling the frenzied rush-travels of Dean Moriarty and his pals as

they criss-crossed America in fast cars, always pressed for time but always with enough time to dig a wild tenorman bawling horn with an 'EE-YAH! EE-YAH! EE-YAH!'; to dig a big coloured guy in coat, hat, and scarf, with veins popping out of his forehead, as he heaves back and blows a big foghorn blues out of every muscle of his soul; to eye the thighs of the sexy waitress as she pours you your thick milkshake in a truck-stop somewhere in the Mid-west prairie; to get back in that beat-up car and take off with a 'whooo!' and the radio pounding out mad coloured records jockeyed by a bull-voiced daddy advising, 'Don't worry 'bout *nothing*!' Dean Moriaty's advice was 'Go!' Where? Anywhere – but fast. Why? For kicks. 'Everybody's for kicks, man!' cackled Dean. They pass an old Negro. 'Yes!' yells Dean. 'Yes! Dig him! Now consider his soul'. And they stop and look at the old jazzbo moaning along. 'Oh yes, dig him sweet; now there's thought in that mind that I would give my last arm to know.'

So would I, figuratively. I was determined to study Negroes and to find out how their inner souls ticked and then to maybe emerge a honking, rocking bundle of beat – like they all were. I was heading towards the real rhythm & blues.

But what about the literature in *On The Road*? Was it better reading matter? Was it 'great art'? I never found out what great art was or is, but I do know that Kerouac's way of looking at life was like mine. He walked along a dusty California road, and likened it to all the roads you see in Western B movies; he likened a dawn to the dawn when Joel McCrea met Veronica Lake in *Sullivan's Travels*. That was how I saw nature, rather than asking, 'Shall I compare thee to a summer's day'.

Dorset was beautiful, granted. England was beautiful and peaceful, I suppose. A good place to get married into and settle down and let the grass grow under your feet. But America was a kid on the move, travelling light, beyond the blue horizon, following up the promise.

And now I had a chance of being a Deputy House Monitor and taking responsibility. Slow down! Luckily we had Connie Francis.

In April she sneaked into the charts with 'Who's Sorry Now?', by June she was at No. 1. She stayed there a long time, and by year's end she had been 22 weeks in the charts. Photos showed her to be glamorous like a big sister, well-built but well under control. Bio sheets told us she liked foreign accents, steaks and roller skating. *Hates*: boastful men. *Ambition*: To get to the top in the acting field. *Favourite Companion*: Her father. It was her father who had suggested she record the old and much recorded standard 'Who's Sorry Now?' I had always liked the tune and its heart-churning chords, chords that slid snugly along from home to home as they had done for years. Her voice leapt and dived like a wounded bird; she sounded like she had suffered (or was about to suffer) broken love affairs; she was best appreciated coming out of a loudspeaker system at a fun

fair dodgem stand. That was how I first heard her and there was something thrilling about such a bruised sisterly voice amidst the clang and bash of the bumper cars.

Connie Francis went on to revive lots more old standards (just like Fats Domino, the Platters, Elvis, Pat Boone) but she also dealt with teen problems, complaining about 'Stupid Cupid' and telling us about how she overcame hypertension and skin trouble. But we didn't try to imitate her musically. The Everlys sang about teen life, of course, with 'Wake Up Little Susie' and 'Bird Dog', and The Crickets celebrated it in 'Oh Boy!' and 'Peggy Sue'. But more than that – both groups had a sound that was worth copying. The Everlys had a wonderful open prairie harmony vocal sound, and The Crickets had a quintessential rock guitar group sound. Both groups were accessible: they were what we could be, with a little work. The same do-it-yourself appeal as skiffle.

But what about the look? Ricky Nelson had that ideal All-American face, fed by milk, burgers and sun. I wanted to look like him, and therefore I'd have to join a team or diet. Most others wanted to be like Elvis. And at this time British boys, out of school, were being trained to act like real American rockers by one man – Jack Good.

Everybody involved watched *6.5 Special* for action

tips. And then in 1958 Jack moved over to ITV to give us *Oh Boy!*, *the fastest show on television*. Now he presented us with the 'teenage face', clean-cut but wild, the good boy gone bad. Circled by spotlight in inky darkness. Then pow! The lights went up, the camera pulled back and up smoothly, and we saw a symmetrically-arranged stage – band, singers, dancers in well-drilled but wild routines. Precision. Costumes were glamorous but not scruffy, there was no back alley oik-scrubber feeling. Zap, zap, zap! – song followed song in musical montage. The band, Lord Rockingham's XI, rocked away like the Little Richard or Fats Domino bands. The singers, like Cliff Richard and Marty Wilde, performed precisely, distilling the essentials of Elvis. Jack Good had realized the theatrical potential of rock 'n' roll and applied the training he had learned while doing Shakespeare and Greek classic tragedy at Oxford. The result, *Oh Boy!*, made the American beat movies look very tatty and third-rate – B pictures slung together by a Hollywood that regarded rock 'n' roll as the lowest form of musical.

So we watched *Oh Boy!* religiously. We watched and learned and inwardly digested as more and more quite ordinary local boys were sent through the Good academy and emerged as stars.

At the same time 'A' levels loomed. And the future. A career and so forth . . .

HOUSEMASTER'S REPORT,
Autumn, 1958:

I am a little concerned lest he should treat his work as Just Another Activity. He has plenty of absorbing interests, among them creative music of a contemporary kind, but he must scotch the suggestion of a playboy attitude to his 'A' level work. Does this stem from a feeling that 'A' level passes are not absolutely vital to his career?

FOCUS ON 'Six-Five Special'

BRUCE CHARLTON VISITS BBC TV STUDIO AND SUGGESTS:

COMEDY NOT REQUIRED • MORE REHEARSAL TIME • STOP OVERCROWDING SHOWS

IS the BBC-TV " 6.5 Special " defeating its own ends ? Is the series (which set out to be totally uninhibited), being a little too spontaneous ? Is the tendency to cram in as much as possible causing it to become overloaded ?

These thoughts occurred to me last Saturday when, in a programme of fifty-five minutes, none of the artists participating (apart from the resident Don Lang and Frantic Five) performed more than one number. Four of the groups concerned had originally been scheduled to do a second spot, but lack of time and overrunning resulted in encores having to be cut out—whilst the show was actually being transmitted — even though they had rehearsed.

The idea of an informal TV session, with enthusiastic youngsters clustered around the artists, is basically a good one. With such a casual approach, mistakes are bound to occur—people wandering in front of cameras, microphone booms swinging in view, youngsters who are determined to be seen at all costs. Is the audience at these sessions getting out of hand ? Fundamentally,

the visitors are well-behaved, but these days during a " 6.5 " transmission it's almost impossible to move in the studio. Last Saturday one of the cameras went out of action—causing engineers a difficult task in clearing a path through the audience, before a replacement could be installed.

Studio space

To have scores of teenagers standing around is all very well, providing there is room to operate. There was, when the show was regularly televised from the BBC's spacious Riverside Studios, but recently, it has been emanating from Lime Grove's Studio G—barely half the size of the previous location. This, of course, is no fault of the producers, who would doubtless declare they must retain audiences of the same size, in order to maintain atmosphere. Another complication evident at

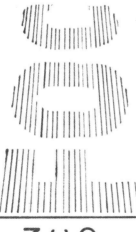
JACK GOOD

FREDDIE MILLS

Saturday's final run-through (to which the audience is admitted), was the difficulty of keeping a group of inquisitive youngsters quiet, when trying to work out technicalities of sets and camera angles. Much valuable time was lost in beseeching silence: in fact there was no time for a complete run-through before transmission.

What, then, is the solution — to reduce or abandon the audience ? No, that may ruin the show. A greater length of time could be given prior to rehearsals, before the day of each programme, actually in the studio—so that all major complications would have been ironed out by the time of transmission.

Preparation

It is incredible that one of the BBC's topline shows should be allotted only a Friday morning band-call and the day of transmission, for its rehearsal: many programmes of similar length and importance have days of advance rehearsals. With so many people taking part, plus working to such a fine schedule, surely the " 6.5 " needs longer preparation.

Even if present difficulties cannot be overcome, what can be done to improve the " 6.5 " ? For my part, I believe in the principle that viewers can take an hour of virtually un-

interrupted music, without the need of " comedy relief." It may be argued that the show set out to be a teenagers' programme, and has never claimed to be essentially an all-music show.

But it is my belief that a majority of viewers are interested solely for its music content, and all else is just so much ballast. By all means, have the occasional relevant interview, but some of the comedy is a little trying.

The present tendency seems to be trying to squeeze a quart into a pint pot,

In expressing this viewpoint as an outside observer, probably it fails to take into account many unknown

obstacles. A producer whilst presenting a programme based on his own taste (and rightly so!), is always prepared to bow to public opinion.

Probably you, dear reader, have thoughts on the " 6.5 Special "—maybe you like it exactly as it is now, or perhaps would prefer to see some changes.

We will be interested in receiving your comments; furthermore, they will be placed before the producers of the show.

Praise

The very fact that we can devote so much space to a critical analysis of this series is proof of its success and importance. Not only is it just about the most outstanding of all BBC-TV's shows today but, as any pop music artist will tell you, it is considered the most desirable showcase on television at the moment. The possible exception is the Palladium

This action shot from a recent edition of " Six-Five Special " shows two of the regulars—Josephine Douglas (extreme left) and Pete Murray (extreme right). Guests in the centre are Tony Brent, Edna Savage and Ronnie Carroll.

show, which in any event is limited to a select few.

" 6.5 Special," originally a six-week stop-gap programme, now looks like continuing indefinitely. To Jack Good goes my award as the TV Producer of 1957. He conceived the show, and nursed it along from a hesitant opening to its present high standing.

A special word of praise, too, for to Douglas, who co-produced with Jack for many months and in conjunction with Pete Murray and Freddie Mills, still lends his own brand of charm to the compering of the show.

THE GUITAR BROOCH.

All-metal with beautiful untarnishable gold finish, with Blue, Red or Green filigree safety catch pin fastening with back that opens and contains 11 different photos of your favourite stars, or you can insert your own personal photo.

4/6 inc. P. & P.

Your Initials or Name Stylishly engraved on any Article Add 2/- Extra.

● Items are posted to you within 24 hours.

The 6-Star Identity Bracelet

(Not illustrated) contains 6 photos of your favourite stars. Gold finish untarnishable link chain.

5/- each, inc. P & P.

THE HOLLYWOOD

HOLLY BRANCHES OUT ON TOP 20 TREE

AS a well-known recording executive was heard to comment when an unknown singer won a gold disc with his first release: "Surprise? Not at all! Anything can happen in the music business, and it does—all the time!" The point, of course, is that he was so right. The music game, especially in more recent times, has developed into a completely unpredictable, topsy-turvey business where surprises and absurdities are relatively commonplace (writes Keith Goodwin).

Consider, for example, the success story of young Buddy Holly—the tall Texan who's currently singing his way higher and higher up the hit parade with a song all about a girl named "Peggy Sue."

BUDDY HOLLY

Composer

The manner in which Buddy eventually crashed the "big time" can only be described as "somewhat absurd." Take note of the facts that follow and you'll see exactly why. Some time back, he was signed to record for American Decca, but his initial releases failed to get off the ground. The contract was dropped. But Dame Fortune smiled kindly upon lanky Mr. Holly and very soon, he had yet another recording agreement in his hands. The company? Coral Records—a subsidiary of Decca in the States! Buddy had been kicked out the front door only to return triumphantly through the back, so to speak. And this time, he made the grade in a really big way.

"Peggy Sue" quickly made headway in America where it's currently resting among the nation's top ten best sellers at position No. 6. In Britain it hovered around the lower regions of the hit lists for some time, but this week made a remarkable jump—by nine places from 21 to 12.

Although this record marks Buddy's first hit here as a "single," he has already figured in the best sellers for some considerable time with a record that wasn't under his own name. To clarify the position, we'll explain right away that he is leader of the vocal group, the chirping Crickets—but rocking quartet who topped the hit lists on both sides of the Atlantic with their million-selling "That'll Be The Day." The group. "That'll Be The Day" is hitting the high-spots incidentally, are hitting the high-spots right now with their latest Coral release, "Oh Boy."

Aside of playing guitar, Buddy is making great strides in the composing field. It was with colleague-drummer Jerry Allison that he penned the high-flying "That'll Be The Day."

Buddy was born in Lubbock, Texas, on September 7, 1936, and began his musical career as a violinist, attending his first lessons at the age of eight. The sound of this instrument, however, somehow didn't appeal to him, so after bowing and scraping away for several years (getting nowhere fast) he switched to guitar where (and) he reached its

He was completely at home on the instrument from the word go, and his early musical training enabled him to master the guitar within an exceptionally short space of time. While practising, he often sang to his own accompaniment. It wasn't long before he had acquired a deep and lasting interest in folk songs and country-and-western style music.

After singing and playing in numerous clubs in the Southwest, Buddy made a trip to Nashville (Tennessee), where a talent scout heard him and urged him to make some recordings. This ultimately led to Buddy's first discs on American Decca—four of his own Western-style compositions, that evaded the attention of Stateside buyers.

'Crickets'

Disappointed, but still eager to make good, Buddy returned to Lubbock, where he met up with Jerry Allison. After working on "That'll Be The Day," and other compositions, the pair decided to form their own vocal group. After enlisting the aid of guitarist Niki Sullivan and bassist Joe Mauldin, The Crickets came into being.

Brown-eyed Mr. Holly rehearsed the quartet diligently, then decided upon a visit to Norman Petty's recording studios in Clovis (New Mexico). The purpose of the trip, of course, was for Buddy and The Crickets to wax further audition discs they could submit to record companies.

Petty, who wrote and also recorded the top selling U.S. version of "Almost Paradise," quickly realised that Buddy had an extremely talented foursome on his hands. He consequently offered advice and encouragement at each and every rehearsal. The boys eventually cut "That'll Be The Day." Petty was so impressed that he immediately offered to submit the test disc to a key figure in the music publishing business on behalf of the group. That person was Murray Deutch, of the Southern Music Publishing Company in New York—another man equipped with a good eye and ear for talent.

In turn, Deutch passed on the good news about the "potential new stars" to Bob Thiele, a & r manager of the Coral group, who, to use a well-worn but very apt cliché, "flipped"! Thiele's first reaction was to offer Buddy a solo contract with Coral and at the same time, he decided to place The Crickets group on the U.S. Brunswick label which he controlled.

Under this set-up, The Crickets struck an extremely profitable bargain. In addition to their own Brunswick sides, it was decided they should accompany Buddy musically on his solo Coral discs. So it's The Crickets you hear supplying the musical background on "Peggy Sue."

Jackpot

Holly the has black curly hair; stands five feet, eleven inches tall; and weighs 145 pounds, by the way) had reasonable returns with "Words Of Love," and "Mailman, Bring Me No More Blues," before "Peggy Sue" hit the jackpot; now his popularity in the States is so high that his immediate future releases can be relied upon to start with a heavy advance order.

Despite the fact that he is fast gaining recognition as a solo artist, Buddy is still working with The Crickets on recording and innumerable TV, radio, club and concert dates. He and the group feel they owe much of their success to people like Norman Petty, Murray Deutch, and Bob Thiele, the "backroom boys" of the music industry.

With the hope that one day they may be able to help newcomers in a similar fashion, one of their ambitions for the future is to set up a music publishing house—surely a commendable and praiseworthy method of expressing their heartfelt gratitude.

January 10, 1958

ELVIS PRESLEY

may have to curtail his singing activities—but he won't starve in the Forces

Says DEREK JOHNSON

IN pursuance of the policy of being able to bargain from a position of strength, America inducts an extremely powerful and explosive weapon into her Forces in March. Its name—Elvis Presley. Yes, in exactly ten weeks time, the idol of the world's teenagers exchanges his guitar for a rifle, trades his sideburns for a crew-cut, and embarks upon an enforced retirement from show business for two years.

Just what effect will this drafting have upon his popularity and his career? Can he take this set-back in his stride, and emerge once again to shatter our equilibrium, leaping back to the phenomenal success he is now enjoying?

Or will the public, usually so quick to forget, allow their interests to steer into new, and more hysterical directions in his absence?

A great deal will depend upon the attitude of the Army authorities in deciding whether he will be permitted to undertake other activities in his off-duty moments. An official spokesman has said that Presley's performances will be restricted to troop concerts and defence-bond rallies.

No time

It has also been suggested that he will not be allowed to make records in his spare time, on the grounds that in the Army there IS no spare time—a soldier for 24 hours every day.

But more recently, indications are that the rigidity of this axiom will be relaxed, as happened in the case of Eddie Fisher, to enable him to make records—if the vicinity of a studio. Obviously, he will not be retained in a specific area, or even in America itself, solely to enable him to do this.

However, even if Elvis is not in a position to record for the next two years, his company—RCA—will not be unduly worried, for they have been busy stock-piling Presley recordings over the past weeks.

They now have sufficient to ensure that a new Presley record can be issued to the public every two months, while he is in the Forces.

It is true, of course, that he will not be in a position personally to exploit the records — on TV, radio and concert appearances—as he has done in the past. With any other artist, this may rank as a major obstacle.

But with Presley, knowing as we do his potential as a record seller—not to mention the fact that vast quantities of his discs are always ordered long before they have actually been issued to the public—I cannot see this being more than a slight set-back.

Presley is quoted as saying that he is proud to go into the Forces. I regard it as absolutely essential that he should. For so many teenagers look up to him as the symbol, the essence of American youth, even to the extent of modelling themselves upon him, that it could do immense harm were he not to be conscripted.

From his point of view, it may well come as a relief, or respite, from the breathless whirl of activity and frenzy, in which he has been caught up, over these past months.

What will he miss most in the Forces? Doubtless the hero worship. Frankly, I would not like to be in his shoes for the first few weeks during his basic training at Camp Chaffee, Arkansas, for he is bound to come in for a tremendous amount of ragging.

him substantial returns. In two years, Presley has become the highest paid entertainer the world has ever known; he has accomplished more in that brief span than many other artists of international fame have been able to do in a lifetime.

It is difficult to estimate his earnings during those two years, with money pouring in from every conceivable source. But they must be in the region of five million dollars—and that's a conservative estimate.

Yet in the next two years, assuming that he remains a private, he will have an earning capacity of approximately 2,000 dollars!

This may not be as great a hardship as it may appear on the surface. Quite apart from the fact that he must, by now, have sufficient cash in his own private vaults to equal that at Fort Knox, other handsome dividends will be coming in throughout his service.

There will be royalties from his records—from previous issues and from those which RCA will regularly be releasing.

A shrewd move on his part produced a special arrangement, whereby his RCA record royalties will be spread over a period of 20 years. So even if he did not earn another penny from show business, he would still be guaranteed a steady income until 1980!

Sales of Presley discs are, in fact, one of the most remarkable and startling developments in the history of the record business.

Consider the fact that, in America, he had the best-selling record for 19 of last year's 52 weeks—an unprecedented achievement.

What is even more shattering is that, in this age of fantastic record sales, very nearly one-half of the entire sales of pop music in America in 1957 were Presley records!

Here in Britain, a check with RCA (and his former label, HMV) revealed that Presley sales have reached an all-time peak. A glance at the best-sellers lists proves his extreme popularity here — if proof were needed.

Millions

According to my calculations, Presley must have sold, during the past two years and on a world-wide basis, something in the region of 100 million records. On each and every one of these discs, he collects a royalty—and a larger cut than that given to most artists, too!

And beyond that, Presley has now formed his own music publishing company, with most of the numbers he records emanating from that source.

Even with these securities, Elvis will not starve in the Forces. But there's more to come. For, during the months ahead, he will be collecting on the box-office receipts from his films.

Presley's latest film, "Jailhouse Rock," which is being premiered in London next week, is certain to bring

Elvis with his sideburns clipped—one of the scenes from his new film, "Jailhouse Rock."

At the top

It is evident, then, that the world will not be allowed to forget Presley in the coming two years. The situation really resolves itself into another problem—would Presley have maintained his status in any event? At the moment, he has climbed to such heights that he is, as it were, sitting astride Mount Everest.

He can't go any higher, and, as we know, there's only one direction to travel from the top. But I believe that he will remain there at the top for a long time to come.

When he comes out of the Army, his character and outlook will have changed. So, possibly, will that of the screaming millions who now worship him.

But remember—Sinatra was once surrounded by screaming bobbysoxers, swooning in the aisles. Now that phase has passed, but Sinatra is more solidly established at the top than ever.

There is no reason why, being possessed of limitless personality and star quality, Elvis should not pass out of the gimmick-conscious teenage period into a more mature and durable phase.

It could well be that the Army will prove the dividing line between these two stages in the fabulous career of Elvis Presley.

Will the Army harm his career?

THE GUITAR BROOCH. All-metal with beautifully coloured gold finish, with Blue, Red or

Income

Another enormous contrast will be

Terry Dene has a 'hangover'

By JERRY DAWSON

IT was a very contrite Terry Dene who arrived at Oldham Empire on Monday evening—only an hour or so before he and his Dene-Aces were due on-stage—after a hurried rail journey from London.

Earlier — in London — Terry had been fined 40s. for being drunk and disorderly.

To his relief, the fans at Oldham gave him a big welcome.

'Stupid thing'

"The one thing that has worried me ever since I did this stupid thing was how the fans would take it," Terry told the MM. Tonight's reception meant everything to me. It will certainly be a long time before I have another drink, because, far from not remembering what happened, it has gradually come back to me all too clearly during the past two weeks ... I couldn't feel more ashamed."

Keeping fit

As he spoke, he adjusted a set of chest expanders and proceeded to exercise his muscles.

"I have always prided myself on keeping fit," he said, and added ruefully, "Drink won't help that—will it?

"I was very foolish. In future it is soft drinks for me," was his final remark.

What an ace chart! Vintage rock and roll with a pleasant decoration of ballads. 'Jailhouse Rock' is from the film (Elvis's best in my opinion) and was written by Leiber and Stoller, the Beaumont and Fletcher of R&R. They always saw the humour of the whole situation, but they also totally understood the new pop art form, that moment of explosion. 'All The Way' is a well-carpentered tune with a message in the tradition of middle-class Alley eroticism – and a nod is as good as a wink and my room number's 507. Nice to see the soul-suave Jackie Wilson in the chart. Frankie Vaughan 'covering' Jimmie Rodgers (not to be confused with his long-dead namesake, The Singing Brakeman) on an old folk song. Jim Dale, the reluctant pop star, in with two hits; Eydie Gorme with a 'good music' record; and Little Laurie London, just into his teens, singing a spiritual with 'hands' coming out pleasingly colloquial as 'hunds'.

But look at the classic rockers! Again – what a chart!

DENE: 'I'M NOT FINISHED'

TERRY DENE, the 19-year-old rock-'n'-roll singer who hit the headlines following his court appearance last Friday, told the MELODY MAKER this week that he intends to "pick up the threads" after a rest.

"I'm not washed up," he said. "I want to get back to show business just as soon as I feel fit again. And the one place I would like to go back to is Gloucester."

"As a gesture of good will I am prepared to offer my services to the Gloucester Police Fund."

'Breakdown'

It was at the Regal, Gloucester, that Terry Dene—in his own words—had a "nervous breakdown." Colin Hicks and his Cabin Boys took over from Terry at short notice.

This week, Terry's place on the bill at the Gaumont, Norwich, has been filled by Marty Wilde and his Wildcats. Meanwhile.

Spotlight

...been added to the bill which will start... 23-day British tour which starts... Other stars billed include Reg... Peter Groves Trio, comedian Reg...

Record date for Dave Brubeck

Terry has been ordered by his specialist to take at least two months' rest.

'Golden Disc'

"The Golden Disc," the film marking Terry's screen debut, is scheduled for general release on April 21. The West End premiere takes place at the Rialto, Coventry Street on March 20.

*Terry was fined a total of £155 at Gloucester on three charges of malicious damage.

Dave Brubeck created a record at St. George's Hall, Bradford, last Thursday.

His group was the first jazz unit to fill the house before the day of the concert.

Over 2,200 people (extra seats had to be brought in) were there to cheer him.

NME MUSIC CHARTS

BEST SELLING POP RECORDS IN BRITAIN

(Week ending Wednesday, Jan. 22nd, 1958)

This Week	Last Week		
1	1	JAILHOUSE ROCK	Elvis Presley (RCA)
2	2	MA, HE'S MAKING EYES AT ME	Johnny Otis Show/Marie Adams (Capitol)
3	3	ALL THE WAY	Frank Sinatra (Capitol)
4	4	OH BOY!	Crickets (Coral)
5	1	GREAT BALLS OF FIRE	Jerry Lee Lewis (London)
6	5	MY SPECIAL ANGEL	Malcolm Vaughan (HMV)
6	6	PEGGY SUE	Buddy Holly (Coral)
8	9	REET PETITE	Jackie Wilson (Coral)
8	15	THE STORY OF MY LIFE	Michael Holliday (Columbia)
10	7	KISSES SWEETER THAN WINE	Jimmie Rodgers (Columbia)
11	8	KISSES SWEETER THAN WINE	Frankie Vaughan (Philips)
12	12	APRIL LOVE	Pat Boone (London)
13	10	I LOVE YOU, BABY	Paul Anka (Columbia)
14	11	WAKE UP, LITTLE SUSIE	Everly Brothers (London)
15	23	BONY MORONIE	Larry Williams (London)
16	16	AT THE HOP	Danny & the Juniors (HMV)
18	16	THE STORY OF MY LIFE	Gary Miller (Pye-Nixa)
—	18	LOVE ME FOREVER	Marion Ryan (Pye-Nixa)
14	19	JACK O' DIAMONDS	Lonnie Donegan (Pye-Nixa)
—	20	THE STORY OF MY LIFE	Dave King (Decca)
13	21	ALONE	Petula Clark (Pye-Nixa)
22	21	BYE BYE BABY	Johnnie Otis Show (Capitol)
26	23	BE MY GIRL	Jim Dale (Parlophone)
30	24	CRAZY DREAM	Jim Dale (Parlophone)
21	25	I'M LEFT, YOU'RE RIGHT, SHE'S GONE	Elvis Presley (HMV)
—	26	LOVE ME FOREVER	Eydie Gorme (HMV)
27	27	REMEMBER YOU'RE MINE	Pat Boone (London)
20	28	ALONE	Southlanders (Decca)
17	29	HE'S GOT THE WHOLE WORLD IN HIS HANDS	Laurie London (Parlophone)
19	30	DIANA	Paul Anka (Columbia)

BEST SELLING SHEET MUSIC IN BRITAIN

This Week		
1	MY SPECIAL ANGEL	(Yale) 2s.
2	KISSES SWEETER THAN WINE	(E.D. & H.) 2s.
3	MA, HE'S MAKING EYES AT ME	(Feldman) 2s.
4	APRIL LOVE	(Robbins) 2s.
5	ALONE	(Duchess) 2s.
6	ALL THE WAY	(Barton) 2s.
7	THE STORY OF MY LIFE	(Sterling) 2s.
8	FORGOTTEN DREAMS	(Mills Music) 2s. 6d.
8	TAMMY	(Macmelodies) 2s.
10	WAKE UP, LITTLE SUSIE	(Acuff-Rose) 2s.
11	DIANA	(Robert Mellin) 2s.
12	I LOVE YOU, BABY	(Sherwin) 2s.
15	MARY'S BOY CHILD	(Bourne) 2s. 6d.
14	AN AFFAIR TO REMEMBER	(Feist) 2s.
15	LET ME BE LOVED	(Sterling) 2s.
16	PEGGY SUE	(Southern) 2s.
17	HE'S GOT THE WHOLE WORLD IN HIS HANDS	(Sterling) 2s.
17	REMEMBER YOU'RE MINE	(Belinda) 2s.
19	LOVE ME FOREVER	(Kassner) 2s.
20	LONG BEFORE I KNEW YOU	(Chappell) 2s.
21	OH BOY!	(Southern) 2s.
22	BE MY GIRL	(Sheldon) 2s.
23	PUTTIN' ON THE STYLE	(Essex) 2s.
—	GOTTA HAVE SOMETHING IN THE BANK, FRANK	(Campbell Connelly) 2s.

BEST SELLING POP RECORDS IN U.S.

This Week	Last Week		
1	1	AT THE HOP	Danny and the Juniors
2	2	STOOD UP	Ricky Nelson / Waitin' In School
3	3	GREAT BALLS OF FIRE	Jerry Lee Lewis
4	4	APRIL LOVE	Pat Boone
5	5	PEGGY SUE	Buddy Holly
6	6	JAILHOUSE ROCK	Elvis Presley
9	7	JINGLE BELL ROCK	Bobby Helms
10	8	YOU SEND ME	Sam Cooke / Summertime
8	9	KISSES SWEETER THAN WINE	Jimmie Rodgers
6	10	RAUNCHY	Bill Justis
11	11	SILHOUETTES	The Rays
16	12	OH, BOY!	Crickets
13	13	MY SPECIAL ANGEL	Bobby Helms
12	14	WAKE UP, LITTLE SUSIE	Everly Brothers
13	15	ROCK AND ROLL MUSIC	Chuck Berry
19	16	CHANCES ARE	Johnny Mathis / The Twelfth Of Never
18	17	BONY MORONIE	Larry Williams / You Bug Me, Baby
17	18	RAUNCHY	Ernie Freeman
15	19	BE-BOP BABY	Ricky Nelson / Have I Told You Lately That I Love You
22	20	ALL THE WAY	Frank Sinatra / Chicago

The American chart is published by courtesy of "Billboard"

FROM TIMBER YARD TO TELEVISION

MARTY WILDE

IT was ambition that took Marty Wilde out of a South London timber yard—to his envied place in show business.

A car caught his eye in a local showroom and made him realise that if he ever wanted to possess such a thing it would take him over seven years at his current rate of pay to purchase it.

Also the thought of spending a lifetime amongst timber was too much for the ambitious Marty.

So this six-foot-three 19-year-old made up his mind, drew out his savings, walked into a music shop and speculated on a second-hand guitar.

By sheer determination, he mastered the instrument in three months, and then set out to conquer Soho's coffee-bar territory. He soon made an impression, and was spotted by Larry Parnes,, co-manager of Tommy Steele.

A chance came to appear in " Six-Five " and he was invited by Johnny Franz of Philips records to put his voice on wax.

His first record established him, and he enjoyed considerable success with his " Honeycomb " and " Wildcat " (his own composition).

Since those first chances, Marty Wilde has chalked up successes in every sphere of entertainment. He is a frequent visitor to television screens, and during the month of February he made eight appearances.

Marty also had the unique experience last month of appearing on the Jack Jackson show on ITV, then appearing on " Six-Five " within half an hour on BBC.

Marty, whose father is a London bus driver, has two passions apart from his singing—sports cars, and Italian food.

The guitar seen with him on his shows is somewhat different from the first one he possessed. This one cost over £200.

Life-lines of MARTY WILDE

Real name: Reginald Smith.
Birth place: Blackheath.
Birth date: April 15, 1939.
Hair: Dark brown.
Eyes: Ice blue.
Height: 6 ft. 3¼ ins.
Weight: 13 st. 8 lb.
Present home: Greenwich.
Parents: Reginald Smith (a bus driver) and his wife, Jessie, who retired from working in a Laundrette a few weeks ago.
Education: Halstow Road Primary School; Charlton Central Secondary School.
Jobs before entering show business: Working in a timber yard for £4 a week, and doing odd jobs as an office boy for the same wage.
First "local" appearances: With the Hound Dogs Skiffle Group in Blackheath.
First cabaret engagement: At London's Blue Angel Club in July, 1957.
Lucky break: While appearing in cabaret later at the Condor Club in the West End, he was "discovered" by artists manager Larry Parnes.
First public appearance: In a package show at London's Trocadero Theatre, Elephant and Castle, in October, 1957.
First variety engagement: At Sunderland Empire on November 4, 1957.
First radio appearance: A broadcast over Radio Luxembourg in December, 1957.
TV debut: In the BBC's "6.5 Special" during October, 1957.
Other major TV appearances: In "Oh Boy," "The Jack Jackson Show," "Cool For Cats," "Off The Record" and Hughie Green Show.
Recording company: Philips

Recording manager: Johnny Franz.
Personal manager: Larry Parnes.
Selection panel for disc titles: Marty, Johnny and Larry.
Turning point in career: When TV producer Jack Good encouraged him to listen to and learn a new American song "Endless Sleep".
First major disc hit: "Endless Sleep", which enjoyed a lengthy run of popularity in the Top Ten and also completely outsold the original American hit version by Jody Reynolds. It is No. 16 in this week's hit parade.
Other disc titles: "Love Bug Crawl", "Afraid Of Love", "Honeycomb", "Wildcat" (his own composition),

"Sing, Boy, Sing", "Oh, Oh, I'm Falling In Love Again", "Her Hair Was Yellow", and his latest coupling—"Misery's Child" and "My Lucky Love". He is currently recording his first LP, comprised of standards, beat numbers and pop songs.
Instruments played: Guitar, banjo, harmonica and drums.
Forthcoming pantomime debut: Portraying Will Scarlet in "Babes In The Wood" at Stockton Hippodrome, opening on December 24.
Hobbies: Taking out girls, studying photographic technique: collecting discs.
Favourite food: Spaghetti.
Favourite drink: Lager and lime; he never drinks spirits!
Favourite clothes: Casual wear, just a little on the "flashy" side; smart Italian style suits.
Favourite sports: Swimming and motor racing; although Marty does not race, he owns an MG red sports coupé.
Favourite variety theatre: Liverpool Empire.
Favourite singers: Jerry Lee Lewis, Elvis Presley, Johnny Mathis, Peggy Lee and Ella Fitzgerald.
Favourite bands: Count Basie, Duke Ellington and Lord Rockingham's Eleven.
Favourite pin-up: Brigitte Bardot!
Age at which he'll think of marriage: Between 24—26.
Personal ambitions: To be happily married, and to be respected by everybody in show business.
Private ambitions: To be a film director; to see every one of his records enter the hit parade, and to become the biggest star in Britain.

BUDDY HOLLY and the CRICKETS

BRITISH disc spinners get double value for their money with the current visit of the American group, Buddy Holly and the Crickets. These three barnstorming youngsters have two hits in the charts at the moment—"Peggy Sue," under Buddy Holly's label, and "Oh, Boy!" under the banner of the Crickets.

But there is really only one act—singer Buddy Holly, with his two side men Joe Mauldin (bass) and Jerry Allison (drums) to put the kick into beat numbers.

They add up to one of the breeziest packages to be imported into Britain. The million-plus teenagers who have bought their discs will not have any illusions dented.

Off stage they are a very cautious trio.

"We've been going a year," Buddy Holly told me, "and one always wonders how long it's going to last. But so far the public seems to like us and we hope that as long as we don't make any mistakes we shall be all right."

Gold dust

At the moment they are certainly all right; they estimate they got $2,000 a night during their recent American coast to coast tour. And even with two managers and a booking agent to pay, that's still gold dust.

I went to hear them at the

4,500 disc fans pack Troc — despite Elvis

Trocadero, Elephant and Castle, on Saturday where, despite a Presley film across the road, they drew 1,500 into the first house and 3,000 to the second.

And I might as well say now that, though it's an excellent show, I was disappointed that Buddy Holly and the Crickets were on stage little more than 20 minutes. With tickets up to 10s. 6d. shortweight is hardly forgiveable. Still this was the first show.

Breaking the ice

Strangely enough, they unload all their disc hits with feverish speed. Perhaps they wanted to break the ice a bit. It wasn't really necessary.

In Britain the custom is for the best sellers to come as the punch line at the end. By having them at the beginning, the act seems to end on an anti-climax.

They are fortunate in being able to sit both sides of the fence. Country and western fans need to look no further than the best selling "Peggy Sue"—and Buddy Holly is every bit as good as on the disc. And for the rock-'n'-rollers "That'll Be The Day," "Oh, Boy," "Rip It Up" and so on are given plenty of punch.

I didn't feel quite at home with Buddy Holly when he added the Presley movements. He seems so obviously out of his depth.

Screams

But—though I did detect a few scornful laughs—it produced the usual screams from the usual bevy of teenagers.

There's no doubt about it, the outdated Variety halls could learn a lot from these teenage coast-to-coast tours.

Supporting the Crickets, Gary Miller, bronzed from his visit to the troops at Cyprus, was in good form and went down well. Both he and the Tanner Sisters kept the atmosphere up to date with hits from the best-selling charts. And they were well rewarded

HOLLY-CRICKETS give us loudest rock show yet!

By KEITH GOODWIN

IF enthusiasm, drive and down-to-earth abandon are the ingredients necessary for success in the rock 'n' roll field, then Buddy Holly and The Crickets are all set for a long and eventful run of popularity!

They rocked their way through a tremendous, belting 25-minute act without letting up for one moment at Kilburn's Gaumont State Cinema on Sunday, and the audience showed their approval in no uncertain terms, via handclaps, whistles, shouts and long bursts of sustained applause.

Much of the trio's success can be attributed to the fact that their "in person" sound is almost identical to the sound they produce on record. They generate a brand of contagious excitement that is irresistible.

Without doubt, The Crickets are the loudest, noisiest trio I've ever heard in my life! On Sunday, they completely overpowered the 13-piece Ronnie Keene Orchestra in relation to the volume of sound produced and, at times, I felt that leader Holly's guitar was badly over-amplified.

But as far as the audience was concerned, everything was just fine. They loved the group's spirited, lusty rock 'n' roll style, and they went for Buddy's easy-going, natural stage personality in an equally big way.

The tall Texan cavorts around stage quite a bit, but his gyrations are not nearly as wild as the Elvis Presley type. Drummer Jerry Allison attacks his kit with murderous intent, but bassist Joe Mauldin remains relatively calm, and looks rather miserable most of the time!

But how these boys manage to make such a big, big sound with their limited instrumentation still baffles me!

Buddy is extensively featured with the group and he's the only one who sings, incidentally. His announcements (few and far between) are relaxed almost to the point of being apologetic.

That he enjoys his music is immediately obvious, and his personal mannerisms—grinning broadly at his colleagues, strumming his guitar while announcing, jerking his head around like a chicken, making his long legs almost do the splits, breaking into a run across the stage—all add to the showmanship of the act.

Shattering

The group opened up with "Every Day," then shattered the first 20 or so rows with ear-splitting, vigorous versions of "That'll Be The Day," "Peggy Sue," "Oh, Boy!" and their latest release "Maybe, Baby" (which is clearly stamped "Hit Parade Material"!).

Two Little Richard epics—"Keep A-Knockin'" and "Rip It Up"—were thrown in for good measure, together with a revival of the early Gene Vincent hit "Be-Bop-A-Lula."

Then The Crickets hopped away from the footlights as applause drowned the final bars of "Ready Teddy."

Take my word for it—this was rock 'n' roll like we're never heard it before in Britain!

Heading the strong supporting bill is Gary Miller, a pleasing personality with an adaptable, powerful voice. I liked his non-exaggerated movements, and he impressed the audience with palatable versions of "Toot, Toot Tootsie," "Put A Light In The Window," "Garden Of Eden," "That's What A Rainy Day Is For," and "The Story Of My Life."

Although I personally enjoyed his short "Carousel" selection—"My Little Girl" and "You'll Never Walk Alone"—I nevertheless felt that it was perhaps too sentimental and possibly over-dramatic for a "big beat" show such as this. Nice songs, good singing—but out of place!

Columbia recording artist Des O'Connor, who compered the show, was phenomenally good. He divided his time between singing (a likable, relaxed voice) and clowning, and his constant stream of slick patter was one of the highspots of the show.

The effervescent Tanner Sisters went down extremely well with a fast-moving, well-balanced act. Light-hearted yet dynamic in an extrovert manner, the girls' performance included rousing versions of tunes like "Puttin' On The Style" and "At The Hop," and appealing interpretations of several slower tunes—"Handful Of Songs," "My Special Angel," and "Love Me Forever."

Pianist Ronnie Keene's rocking band completed the bill, and they impressed with "Woodchopper's Ball," "C Jive," and "The Saints" (which included an amusing Wee Willie Harris skit by Frank Gillespie). They have a useful little singer in pretty Eunice Adams, a 22-year-old blonde newcomer who shows distinct promise as a bright, rhythmic songstress.

NOW WE'RE AT

"**W**HAT in heaven's name is happening to popular music? Do none of the old standards still hold good? Are you a square if you try to sing in tune; if you like relaxed, well-scored accompaniments; if you can read or write?"

With those words I introduced the subject last week. Now let's get to grips with it.

It is not a pleasant subject.

It is not pleasant to watch a whole generation of British teenagers associate themselves with the cheapest music even America has yet produced.

It is not pleasant to take a more specific case, to hear a bunch of *sub-teenagers* (The Imps) taught lyrics about the sexual attractions of a "Dim Dumb Blonde" for a recording session.

Infantile

By "pop music" in this context I don't mean the records of Ella Fitzgerald, Perry Como, Dickie Valentine, Johnny Mathis or a hundred other artists whose work still preserves a high standard of taste and musicianship.

I mean that particular kind of infantile and often suggestive chanting known by such names as "rock-'n'-roll," "rockabilly" and—yes, let's include it—"skiffle."

As I suspected would happen, the thin dividing line between rock-'n'-roll and skiffle-for-profit has just about vanished. Though I still welcome genuine amateur skiffle as a revival of home music-making, the

AND EVERYONE IN THE POP MUSIC BUSINESS THESE DAYS KNOWS IT, SAYS

STEVE RACE

professional cash-register version of skiffle is glued just as firmly to the Bottom of the Barrel as the rock repertoire itself.

Boom

The Bottom of the Barrel . . . Everyone in the music business these days knows that we have reached the bottom at last.

Coincidental with our arrival there, however, is the biggest boom in record sales ever known, and the consequent appalling fact that the people with the power to improve matters are the ones with the least incentive to do so.

Will the leaders of the British

"Rock" industry somehow find the courage to take matters in hand? We can only wait and hope.

Meanwhile the stars which they build cannot even do the job which they are so overpaid to do. Unprofessional professionals, their lack of ability is carefully screened from an adoring public.

A voice?

What are the minimum requirements for success as a pop singer, anyway? A singing voice? The subject just does not arise any more. Stagecraft? As showmen some of the top-of-the-bill vocalists and skiffle

bandleaders have not yet reached the chapel-conce stage.

The ability to sing in tun Listen to those American voc quartets. A feeling for bars a beats? Try working with som of the top Palladium acts.

Good looks? See those we corseted gentlemen with oblo faces, who stare at us from t record-shop windows.

Experience? You can be record star at 14 these day Personality? Many of the lea ing singers couldn't hold intelligent conversation with bookie's runner.

Business acumen? Some them have more managers th guitar strings.

And consider the way th work. Take just three exa ples:

By ear

1 *The Record*: A British tee age favourite sings a n skiffle number.

The story behind it: Nat ally he can't read music, before recording he has to taught the tune by ear.

A secret record of the n song is therefore made in key by an established vocali Our young friend then takes home and learns it, note note, phrase by phrase, infle tion by inflection.

A week later he reproduc that performance for t delight of his fans.

Abortive hours

2 *The Record*: A No. 1 H sung by a No. 1 British roc 'n'-roller.

The story behind it: On again a sneak recording is ma behind locked doors by a prop singer, and the young star pla it to himself for a week or s

Comes the record session, b he still hasn't got the hang it. After several abortive hou the company sends the orche tra home, having made accompaniment disc.

The following day young st comes back, listens to h accompaniment through ea phones, and tries to add h own voice to it. Still he car keep his place in the song.

Desperate to complete a j that any decent profession could do in one hour, the con pany records his voice four ba at a time, and then sews up th

They're willing to take a chance on jazz

visit to the United States is bound to read like a catalogue of the

ng my recent visit with my quartet, I heard so much jazz that it rasp it all.

ul start when Ben Webster invited me to the **CBS TV** studio to watch a show called "The Seven Lively Arts," which turned out to be sixty minutes based on the twelve bar blues. In the band were Basie, Ed Jones,

about whether he was known here.

The only two clarinettists I saw were Sol Yaged, who is a Goodman carbon copy, and Jimmy Giuffre, who is something quite different.

He is bringing the clarinet back into some repute in the modern jazz world and

ROCK BOTTOM

... into what sounds like a
...mal performance.
...t sells like hot cakes.

Only three

The Record: An LP by a
...young rock-style vocal group.
...he story behind it: The
...ord includes quite a lot of
... numbers, which the lead
...elody) singer picks up well

But Ella is still at the top

...ugh. But the others (non-
...ders, naturally) cannot sort
... the harmony parts.

...ather than abandon an ex-
...sive recording session, the
...mpany brings in an older,
...re experienced group, which
...ceeds to supply — anony-
...usly — four-fifths of the
...es.

...esult: the public *buys* an
... of the ABCs, but what it
...rs is Mr. ABC, supported by
... XYZ Vocal Group. The
...Cs adorn the label and col-
... all the royalties.

...nly three of many possible
...mples. Do you wonder that
... profession looks on such
...ctices with a mixture of
...r anger and helpless amuse-
...nt?

Laughter

...o you wonder that, in a
...nt TV rehearsal when the
...dio manager suggested a
...k-'n'-roll star should "save
... voice," the whole orchestra
...red with laughter.

...What is there left when a
...ger has to learn a song from
...neak recording, can't sing it
...n then, and—as in Example
... has to be replaced by some
...onymous professional?

...'ll tell you what's left—the
...al, terrifyingly successful
...ord, and the effect of that
...cess on the singer, the pur-
...aser, and the assorted
...gers-on.

...ext week we'll take a look
... that sordid subject.

...SSON
PARIS
...M SYSTEM

On the air
FLUFFS AND
FEELING

Portable Electric
REED ORGAN

Artistic suicide

that's what sexy songs will lead to, says...
Dr. DONALD SOPER
in an interview with Tony Brown

"If people foisting rubbish on the public get their hands dirty they mustn't complain if we notice it," says Dr. Donald Soper. "It may seem that they do no real harm. I say they do."

THE music business today is thick with men who agree that, artistically, we have hit bottom. Charge them with their responsibility in this state of affairs and they look injured.

"I'm in this business to make money," they say. "I have to give the public what it wants."

Suggest that they also have an artistic responsibility and they are stung into irony. "I'll laugh all the way to the bank," they sneer.

This answer, screamingly funny though it may be, doesn't satisfy everybody. It doesn't satisfy Dr. Donald Soper, for one.

"If people foisting rubbish on the public get their hands dirty," he says, "then they mustn't complain if we notice it."

Dr. Donald Soper—famous Methodist preacher and a man respected by all religious denominations—doesn't speak as a bigot. He was a jazz enthusiast and still takes a keen interest in popular music. It is as a family man and spiritual leader that he makes this forthright attack on bad songs in general—and on sexy songs in particular.

DISTASTE

"It may seem that they do no real harm. I say they do—the distribution of popular music in the form of records has become so wide. The objectionable nature of much of it is bound to be regarded with distaste by parents who take their responsibilities seriously.

"What I object to in particular is the undue emphasis on sex in so many songs.

"Of course, there are rarely direct references. But there is so often a combination of ambiguous or suggestive words with the gestures and significant phrasing from the singer. Together they can produce a distinctly erotic impact."

Dr. Soper points out that the fact that this material reaches beyond teenagers may be the more serious. Some of the poorer items in the vast pop output find avid listeners in schoolchildren. Age group for trash extends from the bright 10-year-old to the retarded adult.

"Let's be frank about this. Impressionable youngsters are being bombarded with the 'Love me, possess me' type of song. When they see some of the performers on stage, they may be treated to highly suggestive pelvic contortions.

"The implication is that the physical expression of love is as right as it is inevitable. This is not only morally dubious. It is practically dangerous.

"Don't misunderstand this. I am not against any reference to sex in songs. What is wrong is that one aspect of life is being exploited out of all proportion—and solely for financial gain.

"It seems that the writers of lyrics have only two approaches: sickly and unrealistic sentiment on the moon and June level, and plain smut."

Sex, contends Dr. Soper, plays a leading rôle in the experience of young people. It is the "spinal approach" that is wrong. He believes that the interests of youngsters should be acknowledged and catered for in an adult way. Songs, he says, have a psychological power. A catchy melody serves to impress words of doubtful taste on the mind. Repetition dins them into the subconscious.

CONTROL

Dr. Soper feels, too, that we are being overwhelmed by those aspects of the American musical scene that many right-thinking Americans deplore. Other nations seem to draw on American material without cramping their own musical traditions.

"We all know that the Americans produce pop music of the highest quality. I've heard so much that I've liked since the days when I was an enthusiast and fancied that I was something of a jazz pianist.

"Nevertheless, it was found necessary to control the import of horror comics which were being sold freely to children. It may be just as necessary to curb trashy songs.

"Not that the Americans are the only offenders. We often hear sneers about the sentimental ballads beloved by the late-Victorians — themes like where - is - my - wondering-boy-tonight. But at least they were sentimental about morality. We're sentimental about sentiment.

"There's a remarkable complacency abroad, too. The other evening I saw one songwriter on television.

"He apparently thought his song said as much as a Shakespeare sonnet. That is what I call invincible ignorance.

"I watch '6.5 Special' sometimes—as a penance. I'm perplexed. I can't understand how intelligent people can derive any sort of satisfaction from something which is emotionally embarrassing and intellectually ridiculous."

What to do about the situation? Dr. Soper is equally definite that some kind of censorship is necessary. No sane person denies the need for a police force to protect our physical welfare. The preservation of artistic and moral standards is just as important.

"Perhaps what is needed is something on the lines of the very efficient film censorship which is operated by the trade itself.

SHOCKING

"We need courageous disc-jockeys who will refuse all blandishments and reject trash of all types.

"But everybody who is in the business of writing, publishing, recording, publicising and selling popular songs is involved in this.

"To set out to deprave young people and to plead prosperity as a justification is shocking. Nothing worth while was built on the gold-standard alone.

"To try to do so is, to be blunt, immoral. From an artistic point of view, it is suicidal."

STARS ROW OVER ROCK-'N'-ROLL

While Jack Good stood up for R&R in 'Disc', the 'Melody Maker' editors, shot off banner headlines against the Big Beat. Jack felt R&R and the kids could be disciplined into a theatrical 'happening', while the old M.M. editors hoped that they might grow up and back into jazz. Whatever the rights and wrongs the controversy helped sell papers.

NEW YORK, Wednesday.— Mitch Miller, the "genial Svengali" A and R man behind so many Columbia disc stars, made a slashing attack on rock-'n'-roll and other "teenage music" at an assemblage of the nation's dee-jays in Kansas City, Missouri.

Already his speech has brought a sharp reaction from rock promoter and dee-jay Alan Freed, who says: "As my per-

From REN GREVATT

sonal protest against Mr. Miller's speech, I'm hereby banning all Columbia records from my show."

Adds Freed: "It sounds like sour grapes to me, since Mitch can no longer be the dictator of pop music. He's always been classical minded and my feeling is that he's a musical snob. Let's face it: rock-'n'-roll is bigger than all of us."

Nothing adult

Miller said that on American radio today it is difficult to find a "grown-up" hour before midnight. "Adults everywhere are longing for a break in the day's cacophony," he said. "It's all right to give the kids some of what they want, but how about some music for the rest of us?"

The speech produced a rash of comment. One writer called it "the Gettysburg address of the music business."

ALAN FREED

Still hoping . .

ALAN FREED also told me that he still hopes to do a British tour.

"If we can possibly make it next October we will do it," he said, "with the talent to be drawn at least partly from the group we have lined up for our tour of this country starting next week."

The tour, which starts its 0-day-plus trek Friday (28th) includes Jerry Lee Lewis ("We may be bringing him back to England with us," said Freed), Buddy Holly and the Crickets, Chuck Berry, the Diamonds, Danny and the Juniors, Billy and Lillie, Frankie Lymon, the Chantels, Billy Williams, Dicky Doo and the Don'ts, Screamin' Jay Hawkins, Jo Ann Campbell, Sam (the Man) Taylor and Ed Townsend.

LAURIE LONDON

New trend ?

"HE'S Got The Whole World In His Hands" may have started a new religioso trend here in the record scene.

The Laurie London record is heading for a million sale, and it has been covered by Jo March on Kapp, Barbara McNair on Coral, and this week by the one and only Mahalia Jackson on Columbia.

MARVIN RAINWATER

TWO MORE NEWCOMERS TO THE

Starvin' Marvin is well-fed now !

JUST as a book can sell by its cover, so can an artist overcome the first obstacle in show business if he possesses a sufficiently colourful and distinctive name. Our latest newcomer to the best-sellers' list — Marvin Rainwater—must surely have one of the most distinctive and fascinating monikers in the profession.

You might even be tempted to think that his surname is reminiscent of a Red Indian chief!

And you wouldn't be so far wrong at that—for it so happens that Marvin is a full-blooded Cherokee Indian by birth.

Yet only just over ten years ago, when the rugged six-footer decided to leave the Oregon logging camp where he was working to try his luck at show business, his friends were calling him "Starvin' Marvin"—for the breaks just wouldn't come his way.

But finally he managed to impress the veteran country singer, Red Foley sufficiently to be invited to guest on his popular "Ozark Jubilee" show.

Foley was inundated with requests for further appearances by "the new singer with the Indian name," following Marvin's success. Other country shows were quick to latch on to this new entertainer and he began to receive offers from outside the c & w stronghold as his fame grew.

He intrigued the Eastern States by appearing in cabaret, dressed in buckskin and moccasins—and singing with that simple sincerity now reflected in all his recordings.

Marvin next undertook a tour with a "Grand Old Opry" troupe (which in rock 'n' roll circles would be known as a "package show"), but his nation-wide acclaim was really clinched with a succession of appearances on The Arthur Godfrey Show.

These prompted Coral Records to sign him up. He cut two titles, "I Gotta Go Get My Baby" and "Daddy's Glad You Came Home," writing them both himself (as he does all his recording material).

Competition

The former title was covered by five other singers. The Coral label did achieve a million seller, but not with the composer's version. It was Teresa Brewer's more commercial treatment which won the Gold Disc.

But Marvin was quite happy— it's seldom that a pure, out-and-out country singer tops the quarter-million mark, as he did.

In January last year, he transferred to the MGM label. Without much advance ballyhoo, they released a Rainwater disc entitled "Gonna Find Me A Bluebird." Only fifty thousand copies were pressed (the standard pre-release order).

Dealers were flooded with repeat orders. This was unprecedented for a disc in the strict country idiom, but the company kept pace with demand, and the final tally resulted in a million sales for Marvin.

Now he is doing extremely well with his latest disc, "Whole Lotta Woman," which not only provides him with his first British hit parade entry (this week standing at 18th place), but also turns the spotlight onto MGM, the "Cinderella" label of the recording industry over here.

Recently, Marvin has cut an LP for MGM in the States, and in view of his current success and his impending visit, it is not unreasonable to suppose that we may soon expect its issue over here.

There's also a Rainwater duet coming up — with that delightful MGM songstress, Connie Francis, who appeared in the "Disc Jockey Jamboree" film.

His hit record could not have come at a more appropriate time, for next month Marvin arrives in Britain to undertake a tour of one-nighters with Johnny Duncan, and appear in a couple of television shows.

Rainwater had one of the all-time great rockers in 'Whole Lotta Woman'. I'm surprised it's not revived more.

Connie Francis wins fame from a song twice her age!

PERT and provocative Connie Francis has never been one to sit back and let a good chance slip by. She has proved herself scholastically and now she's set to become one of the big stars of tomorrow.

Frantically busy today, she's clutching at a success that has caught her perhaps a little sooner than she had anticipated.

For Connie, at 19 the youngest female hit parader for quite a long time, is almost certain to add a Gold Disc to her sideboard collection of trophies. She's in the top sellers in both Britain and America with "Who's Sorry Now?"

She has been trying in show business for 15 years. The long wait for fame has suddenly ended; stardom is around the corner.

by MALCOLM JOHNS

Now?" is a song nearly twice as old as Connie, but she's made it as fresh as this morning's milk.

In Britain she was previously best known as the ghosted voice of Freda Holloway, the leading actress in "Disc Jockey Jamboree." Earlier, she had been a unseen voice in "Rock, Rock, Rock," a film featuring Alan Freed.

In America, she has a much wider reputation. Max J. Rosenberg, producer of both films, was very surprised she was unknown here.

Well she might have been, because in America she has figured in many leading roles.

Her real name is Connie Franconero and she was born in 1939, in Newark, New Jersey, just across the river-border from New York City.

When she made her first attempt at being an entertainer, she was just four! It was in a radio show featuring amateurs.

room. Connie found time to be assistant editor of the students' own paper, and write and produce a musical comedy.

Though show business was not far from her mind all the time, she never neglected her studies. She provided positive proof of this when gaining a scholarship to New York University.

During vacations, and occasionally in term-time, too, Connie shot off to the TV studios.

Her appearances were not only in minor shows. Comedian Milton Berle, Dean Martin and Jerry Lewis (then still teamed), and Eddie Fisher thought enough of this singing student to invite her to guest in their shows.

She has a natural flair for hard work. A day that would tire a veteran leaves her fresh and ready to prepare for something else. She has learnt to play an accordion and to write songs good enough to be published.

Between her so important studies, Connie's career has gradually and

surely developed. Selected stage dates have taken her to some most important locations—the Steel Pier in Atlantic City (the Blackpool of Eastern America) and to Grossinger's, the mountain resort in the Catskill's, among them.

With a hit record, everything has taken a tremendous leap forward, for Connie. The number that brought her so rapidly to the top is a surprising and notable one.

A joke

Surprising because oldies rarely get a second lease of life. Notable because "Who's Sorry Now?" was never intended to be published at all. The plain truth of it is that it was written—in 1923—as a joke!

One of the composers has just told the story. He is Harry Ruby. The other writers were Ted Snyder and Bert Kalmer. The whole thing was a private joke—until a publisher heard it.

If you fellows think this a joke, then you better go right ahead and write some more gags, he told them.

Ruby and Kalmar were writing a Broadway show called "Helen of Troy, New York," at the time. They didn't want to bother plugging "Who's Sorry Now?" The musical was a flop. But the song was a big hit. Now 35 years later it's an even bigger one.

Regrets?

Who's sorry now? Well it could be Miss Francis. A studious type, she let her university chances slide a little to cope with her hit parade success. Not wanting to ignore education completely, in February she enrolled as a part-timer at Ruiger's University in her home State.

She reads such subjects as philosophy, psychology and logic. Her life is torn between the two paths of study and stardom.

This hit parade success must increase the chances of her devoting more energy to the latter. Her background shows that she should be ready for all the opportunities coming her way.

MARVIN RAINWATER says about CONNIE . . .

MARVIN RAINWATER, in London this week, said about Connie Francis: "It's a great pleasure to be able to tell you about her. She's 19, maybe 20, small, vivacious, sincere, with a great voice.

"She had a record out in the States some months ago called 'Eighteen.' Soon as I heard it I was her fan.

"I thought it was tremendous and was sorry when it didn't get away, but that's the disc business.

"I was her champion. Then out of a clear blue sky she said to me one day : 'Could we do a record together ?' She played me the song she had in mind and I enjoyed it tremendously. (Mind you, I'd have made a record with her even if I hadn't liked the song.)

"It was 'Majesty Of Love' and the lyric spoke for itself. I never regretted making it with Connie.

"She's overwhelmed with her success, right now. 'Who's Sorry Now?' is a hit both sides of the Atlantic and it couldn't happen to a nicer Miss."

JERRY HAS SURPRISED SONGLAND

WHENEVER famous show business partnerships break up, the question is which one will survive? Who was the real brains of the double act?

In the case of Dean Martin and Jerry Lewis, both have made a success of their "single" lives, but whereas Dean has not tried to be a comedian (he was always the singing straight man, of course), Jerry Lewis has surprised everyone by becoming a serious, straight singer—and a successful one, too!

He shook the disc world with his soft crooning style in "Rock-A-Bye Your Baby," which caught the imagination of both American and British pop music fans, resulting in a place in the top twenty in America for some time, and also getting into the Sellers in this country.

An LP also sold well, featuring not the sharp, falsetto voice we know

TV shows

A little later she was to get a lot of television experience with Arthur Godfrey. He put her on his daily morning and weekly evening programmes, noted for spotting future stars. Connie was still in her early teens.

She combined this activity with a very comprehensive school schedule.

She collected a sackful of honours and trophies to match. They ranged from debating to an inquisitive study of psychology. She even won a typing championship!

Still at school, but out of the class-

made his first professional appearance.

This was at Swan Lake, in the Catskill Mountains, the vacation resort near New York City. Jerry sang "Brother, Can You Spare A Dime?" His age? Five!

Since then, Jerry has been a performer. Is it any wonder that he can turn his hand to anything in the way of entertaining? He's been brought up the hard way. He's no one-record star. He learned to be a star before he even made a record.

And one can't help wondering what a surprise it must have been to his former partner, Dean Martin, when he found Jerry had become his rival—in the pop music stakes!

LONDON COLISEUM

First London Appearance of Famous American T.V. and Recording Star

MARVIN RAINWATER

JOHN SMITH presents

THIS SUNDAY, 20th APRIL, at 7.30 p.m.

JERRY LEE LEWIS told the principal (of institute) that's the way and I would play that long as I did live. music teacher the same when I was nine and in two weeks of the on lessons I ever did take

CHUCK JUMPS TO SWEET 16 IN CHARTS

2

READERS who study the weekly best selling pop records in the States charts will have noticed that quite frequently names crop up which mean precisely nothing to the fans over here. And they disappear without ever achieving any sort of reputation in this country.

An exception to this state of affairs has occurred with the advent of Chuck Berry who, over the past years, has established a firm foothold in the best-sellers, in which he continually appears with the regularity of a season-ticket holder.

He hit the Stateside headlines with such recordings as "Maybellene," this first really big seller, "School Day," "Rock 'n' Roll Music" and "Roll Over Beethoven," all of which enjoyed enormous sales across the Atlantic.

Although issued in this country, they didn't achieve any great degree of popularity, with the slight exception of "School Day," which did make a very fleeting appearance in the British charts.

But it had difficulty in competing against the big British version by Don Lang and his Frantic Five. And the principal reason for the failure of "Maybellene" was that the lyric contained a certain amount of advertising, making it unsuitable for broadcasting here.

Recently Chuck has enjoyed his biggest success so far in America, when his "Sweet Little Sixteen" shot into second position in the U.S. charts. This nearly all the numbers he sings, this is one of his own compositions.

But there's something different

about this Berry recording . . . for once it's beginning to create a stir in Britain, where this week it stands at "Sweet Sixteen" in the NME chart.

It looks, in fact, as though Mr. Berry has really arrived, so far as British record enthusiasts are concerned.

A comparative newcomer to the big-time, Chuck is not without show business experience. He was working as a little-known singer-guitarist around the Chicago area for several years before the break came. This was an offer from a rhythm-and-blues record label called Chess, one of whose representatives spotted him in the club where he was appearing.

Rock specialist Alan Freed enthused wildly about this new discovery, and began playing Chuck's records on his disc-jockey sessions. He then signed the youngster to appear in several of his touring package shows and concerts, and also signed him to appear on the coast-to-coast "Alan Freed Show" on television.

Chuck's reputation increased rapidly, and the next development saw him signing to appear in a film, "Rock, Rock, Rock," with which Freed was associated.

Moviegoers may recall his dynamic presentation of "You Can't Catch Me" in this picture.

Before he became a nation-wide favourite in America, Chuck was already recognised as one of that country's most outstanding r-&-b exponents, and his name had appeared on many occasions in the charts devoted to this specialised idiom.

Now he is in demand in all the most exclusive spots in the States and has performed in the majority of their most celebrated niteries and supper-clubs, in addition to guesting on various important TV shows.

Chuck Berry is an artist whose emotional exuberance and pulsating rhythm have rocketed him to fame in America, and are now having a similar effect in this country.

He is living proof of the contention that, even though rock 'n' roll may not be as strong as it used to be, the idiom has produced its own crop of international stars, who will remain in the limelight for many years to come.

It's my belief that Chuck's magnetic singing still will be a feature of the hit parade, when the expression "rock 'n' roll" is as outdated as "jitterbug."

At this very moment, Chuck is sitting back and smiling at the thought of his latest recording hovering on the verge of the best-sellers lists in the States. This week, Billboard shows his "Johnny B. Goode" "Around And Around" at position No. 22, having arrived there literally from nowhere. Chances are it will be in the American Top Twenty next week.

DEREK JOHNSON

Chuck Berry – now revered as the poet of early rock, the man who wrote about teen topics like cars and school and teeny boppers. Surprisingly few hits in Britain. He came into his own in the later rock revival period. Personally I don't rate his songs that high – samey-samey tunes, with good words, but not a patch on Leiber and Stoller. A very spikey personality.

Lyric too American?

ONE of America's top r 'n' r stars is Chuck Berry, but so far he hasn't made the slightest impression over here. He is currently riding way up the U.S. hit parade with "Sweet Little Sixteen."

Apart from the title, the words seem to be specially directed to American kids, which will prove to be a handicap to sales on this side of the water.

Aside from that, it's a very ordinary rock number with nothing specially exciting or catchy about it. I don't think London-American can place too much faith in this platter.

Connie Francis – at one time I thought her the world's greatest girl singer. Now I let her share that position with Ruth Etting. Both have voices like angelic dive-bombers. Both sound easily-bruised. But Francis has a rougher edge – a real bleacher-reacher, perfect for fairground bumper-car stand loudspeakers. Can cut through the bumps and bangs. She also gave sensible advice to mixed-up teens (as did Pat Boone).

SAM COOKE—MAN TO WATCH!

From REN GREVATT

NEW YORK, Wednesday.—England has heard little about Sam Cooke so far. But mark it down, Cooke will be a name to conjure with.

Since his first disc, "You Send Me," Cooke has risen to the dizzy heights of success and now enjoys three discs on American best-selling record charts.

Cooke is 22, but he's a veteran of six years' standing with the Soul Stirrers, one of the top American spiritual singing groups.

Currently he's on the charts not only with the initial disc, but also with " (I Love You) For Sentimental Reasons," and " Desire Me," his second for the same Keen label, and " I'll Come Running Back To You " and " Forever," on the Specialty label, his original company with the Soul Stirrers and the firm that made a star of Little Richard.

British fans should watch all three.

velop some activity, which it may well do. Donegan will be in a still better position for his appearances here in March, now being projected by the William Morris office.

LIBERACE

Plans for England

LIBERACE has succumbed to the lure of the "down under" territory. He leaves for a tour of Australia on February 24.

When he arrives, he'll no doubt point up to the Australians the diversity of talent in the States—since he'll be following by only three weeks the appearance there of Jerry Lee Lewis, the Crickets, Paul Anka and Jodie Sands.

Meanwhile, MCA officials said a deal is in the works for Liberace to return to England

but no firm dates could be disclosed.

JOHNNY DANKWORTH

Sparks off talks

TAKING note of the statements in the MELODY MAKER by bandleader Johnny Dankworth about the farcical aspects of the U.S. band exchange system and other statements indicating a tightening on the part of the British MU on further exchanges this year, a spokesman here told me that the International Executive Board of the AFM would be meeting with James C. Petrillo in New York on February 6.

" It is quite possible that the matter of U.S.-British band exchanges may come up for discussion and review, in the light of current developments," I was told.

JAZZ NOTES . . . . from BURT KORALL

CHARGE OF THE ROCK BRIGADE

MEET THE STARS with REN GREVATT

NEW YORK, Wednesday —Disc jockey Alan Freed, who popularised the modern concept of the term "rock and roll," via his radio shows on WINS here, is in plenty of hot water.

The trouble started after a Boston performance of Freed's touring rock-'n'-roll troupe.

According to newspaper accounts, a wild melee of riot proportions ensued outside the hall following the performance.

During the disturbance 15 people were injured, others were mugged and robbed, and one sailor was stabbed in the chest. During the week, the stories seemed to grow and grow.

The upshot was that performances scheduled for New Haven, Conn; Troy, N.Y.; and Newark, New Jersey, were all cancelled by local city authorities.

Freed indicted

Freed has been indicted by the Suffolk County Grand Jury in Boston on charges of "Inciting to Riot," and has been ordered to surrender himself to the authorities there to answer the charges.

Principles

Freed has also submitted his resignation to station WINS, for "having failed to stand behind my policies and principles" in this matter.

A spokesman for Freed said that discussions were already being held with various other stations regarding the jockey's services. It appeared, however, that the Boston matter would have to come first in any planning by Freed.

ROCK-'N'-ROLL

On the way out ?

IS rock-'n'-roll on the way out? Comments are flying fast this week, with extra impetus occasioned by the unfortunate events involving Alan Freed in Boston.

A trend towards a less savage type of rock-'n'-roll has already been noted. The pop charts carry ballads, many of them revivals of standards, with only a suggestion of a rock-'n'-roll rhythm backing.

On the other hand, Freed says this will help make it bigger than ever. "You can't tell people what they can hear and what they can't hear," he asserted. "In fact, the more you try to suppress it from the kids, the more they will want it."

Song successes

Two numbers written by Australian jazz violinist Don Harper have now been published by Southern Music. They are "Easy Goin'" and "Hi Diddle Fiddle."

Another composition, "Birdcage Walk," has been accepted by the music publishing firm of Peter Maurice.

World Fair debut for World Band

THE International Youth Band assembled for this year's Newport Jazz Festival will also play at the Brussels World Fair.

American impresario George Wein has fixed the band, and singer Sarah Vaughan, for a jazz week at the Fair's U.S. Pavilion towards the end of July.

The band, which includes Britain's Ronnie Ross on baritone, assembles in Brussels on June 17 before leaving for pre-Festival rehearsals in New York.

In all, 15 European countries are represented in the band, for

DISC BID BY

TWO VIEWS OF . . .

JERRY LEE LEWIS

He is the wildest of them all !

TODAY, more than at any time since he became a big-time record star, Jerry Lee Lewis belongs in the category labelled " controversial." They used to say Elvis was controversial. So he was. But he's gone now. He is tucked away in the army and is reported to be an excellent soldier.

The story is different with Jerry Lee Lewis, who will soon explode his talent on his growing army of British fans. Lewis, along with Presley and the famous Little Richard—now safely in Divinity School—might be said to represent the extremist wing of the rock-'n'-roll world.

2 by REN GREVATT

Shouting

Britons may have already seen Lewis perform in films, but they haven't really seen anything yet. When he takes over the stage the standard routine calls for a pounded chorus of piano and shouted, breathless vocalising, punctuated with a series of side shouts, hoots, wheezes and runs up and down the complete length of the keyboard.

As a second chorus, he'll get up from the piano and prance around the stage throwing his head around in such a manner that his long, slightly waving sandy hair flaps up and down on his head in time to the beat.

Then he'll strut back to the piano and pound it with hands in an up and down motion from a standing position, all the while continuing the wild, down-to-earth style of incantations.

Fine art

Between numbers, he'll sit at his piano and calmly, slowly, deliberately comb his hair back into position, while the feminine contingent in the audience squeals with delight. Lewis has made a fine art out of hair-combing.

It's this exaggerated type of performance that has separated Lewis from many of his contemporaries. With fans and critics, there is no real middle ground. They either love him or can't stand him.

Lewis, at the peak of his popularity right now, stands

as a beacon in the gathering storms that surround rock-'n'-roll here. He's a storm centre himself and the attendant publicity has helped keep him right on top.

The man who makes his records, Sam Phillips, has called Lewis " the greatest performer of them all." Others have called him everything from a downright disgrace to a man with no talent.

Twice recently I have seen Lewis work. I have no reason to think there is anything insincere in his performance. He sings what he feels and the feelings come from his long exposure as a youngster to the great Negro spiritual and blues artists in the south. Much of their style is in his own delivery.

Irritant

More recently, some affectations have crept into his act, which many feel could be left out with no ill effects. The hair-combing routine is rough on a troupe, because it holds up the show. It's no secret that it was an irritant on a recent Alan Freed tour of which Lewis was a member.

Those who look frantically for a scapegoat for all the juvenile ills of our day point to Lewis and others of his school of rock-'n'-roll.

Calmer heads know this cannot be so. But just as Lewis is a rallying point for those who love the wildest performance and sound, he is also a focal point for the wrath and indignation of those who hope to destroy the rock and the beat for good.

Lewis is on the spot and in the middle. Britons can soon judge him for themselves. For better or for worse, they will find that he is truly the wildest of them all on the current scene.

I SUFFERED Jerry Lee Lewis—a stoic endurance in four acts.

Act One: Jerry Lee leapt on stage and attacked the Steinway like an enraged buffalo. He took a deep breath. Then, with a battery of amplifiers at full blast, he let forth a yell that has me quivering yet.

In a maelstrom of deafening distortion he launched into his "Great Balls," "Whole Lotta Shakin'" and other masterpieces.

Little girls screamed like stuck pigs as Lewis roared on and the drummer's off-beats gathered both volume and momentum. One cute little lass, in a frenzy of excitement, grabbed me, screeching:

1 by HOWARD LUCRAFT

"What a *beat!*" as she clapped ecstatically on one and three.

The quantity of "beat," as defined by youthful rock-'n'-roll fans, seems in direct proportion to the loudness of the off-beat. (The forthcoming Lucraft rock-'n'-roll snare drum, with built-in 50 watt amplifier, will be the biggest thing since Elvis!)

After a short succession of his sound-alike numbers, Jerry Lee finished his first set in a surge of sweat and saliva, with his blond hair hanging all over his face and his feet on the piano keys.

For the technically-minded, Jerry Lee Lewis carries his own

electric (Fender) guitar-bass (a Mr. J. W. Brown) and his own drummer—Mr. Russell Smith. Mr. Smith plays only rim shots and cymbal on two and four. He may lack technique, taste and tempo but dig that beat!? Man it's the loudest!

Act Two: Came the second set and Jerry Lee Lewis proved, like most of these teenage wonders, that he didn't have the real talent, material or experience to sustain himself. The initial excitement was gone—just some mild girlish squeals now and less enthusiastic applause.

Adjourned

Act Three: Jerry Lee protested strongly and at length against a third set but the promoter insisted. Nothing was left. Now, just a few staunch supporters stood around the stand. The rest of the customers either tried to dance or adjourned to the coffee bar. The Lewis Trio left the stage to polite applause.

Act Four: I went backstage to talk with the taciturn Mr. Lewis. Joe somebody, the promoter's assistant had told me: "He seems a real big shot kid."

Joe was wrong. Jerry Lee and his two boys are an incongruous mixture of brashness and shyness. This is due, I believe, to an adolescent realisation that their musical talent does not match their acclaim.

With much coaxing and questioning, Jerry Lee told me: "Nobody really influenced me. I taught myself.

Favourites

"I like the old guys like Gene Austin and the old Jimmy Rogers. I've no special favourites today except Little Richard and Fats Domino. I like Dixieland mostly."

All the members of the very capable Charlie Aldrich house band were extremely surprised to hear, from me, that Jerry Lee Lewis records were popular in England.

The Aldrich alto man said to me: "Surely British teenagers don't go for this. We always thought that kids over there had so much taste and intelligence. This is music for morons."

The Saga of Jerry Lee Lewis in Britain – how we put him through 'Trial By Press' – (we have the nastiest press in the World, being essentially a nation of critics, of watchers and imitators rather than creators or wild men) – and now we are his staunchest fans . . . well, some of us are.

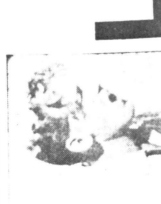

LEW & LESLIE GRADE LTD. Presents TWO AMERICAN HEADLINERS IN ONE GREAT PACKAGE SHOW

DYNAMIC

★ JERRY ★
LEE LEWIS
THE FABULOUS
TRENIERS
and
THE HEDLEY WARD TRIO
In a great all-star concert tour

★ Two shows nightly ★

SAT. 24 May, Regal, EDMONTON
SUN. 25 May, State, KILBURN
MON. 26 May, Granada, TOOTING
TUES. 27 May, Odeon, BIRMINGHAM
WED. 28 May, Public Hall, PRESTON
THURS. 29 May, Odeon, GLASGOW
FRI. 30 May, New Victoria, EDINBURGH
SAT. 31 May, Odeon, NEWCASTLE
SUN. 1 June, Odeon, LIVERPOOL
MON. 2 June, Odeon, MANCHESTER

TUES. 3 June, Gaumont, COVENTRY
WED. 4 June, Gaumont, WORCESTER
THURS. 5 June, Capitol, CARDIFF
FRI. 6 June, Gaumont, CHELTENHAM
SAT. 7 June, Gaumont, WOLVERHAMPTON
SUN. 8 June, Gaumont, BRADFORD
MON. 9 June, Odeon, NOTTINGHAM
TUES. 10 June, Odeon, LEEDS
WED. 11 June, City Hall, SHEFFIELD
THURS. 12 June, Carlton, NORWICH

FRI. 13 June, Gaumont, IPSWICH
SAT. 14 June, Granada, WOOLWICH
SUN. 15 June, Granada, EAST HAM
MON. 16 June, De Montfort Hall, LEICESTER
TUES. 17 June, Gaumont, DONCASTER
WED. 18 June, Gaumont, HANLEY
THURS. 19 June, Gaumont, CHESTER
FRI. 20 June, Adelphi, SLOUGH
SAT. 21 June, Gaumont, SALISBURY
SUN. 22 June, Odeon, PLYMOUTH
MON. 23 June, Gaumont, TAUNTON
TUES. 24 June, Gaumont, SOUTHAMPTON
WED. 25 June, Gaumont, BOURNEMOUTH
THURS. 26 June, Gaumont, ROCHESTER
FRI. 27 June, Odeon, SOUTHEND
SAT. 28 June, Trocadero, ELEPHANT & CASTLE
SUN. 29 June, Odeon, GUILDFORD

— *BOOK NOW!*

● *Tickets now available at the above Theatres*

JOHN ROLLS

||||||||||| LIFE IN THE MIRROR |||||||||||

MEET MYRA FROM MEMPHIS—WIFE AT 15!

A SHINY-FACED girl of fifteen in tight black jeans and striped sweater sat in room 127 at the Westbury Hotel, London, yesterday watching children's TV.

She wore no make-up. Her hair was in an untidy ponytail. Her feet were bare

This was MYRA LEWIS, the third wife of twenty-two-year-old rock 'n' roll singer JERRY LEE LEWIS.

Raven-haired Jerry—who came to fame with "A Whole

Lotta Shakin' Goin' On" and "Great Balls of Fire"—was holding a Press conference to launch his six-week British tour.

He said in that Louisiana drawl: "Mah wife is cute. She might look young and be young, but she is grown."

'Let's Go!'

UPSTAIRS, Myra, from Memphis, Tennessee, sipped a soft drink. She had a bottle of milk on ice in a champagne bucket waiting for Jerry.

She told me: "We've been married about two months. The girls at college were real envious when Jerry was driving me to school. Lots of his at Mom's place when he said I said dearie. Let's get married. It was a bit of a surprise when he said 'Let's go' but I said 'Let's go.'"

"It was all secret. She added. "I didn't tell my parents for a fortnight."

When they knew they had a fit daddy partout Early.

"I was daddy's little girl Momma was furious. She tried to get daddy to settle down.

"He was getting hasty as you would call it. But everything is all right now."

"Children? I want two kids and a boy. Jerry wants three boys."

'Gosh, No'

I ASKED this perky, five ft three ins. sip of a girl whether she thought that fifteen was young to be a wife.

"Gosh, no." she gasped. "Back home you can marry at ten. One girl got wed at nine."

I noticed she was not wearing a wedding ring. "We've been so busy. She said. "we haven't had time to pick one yet. Jerry says he'll get round to it soon.

"But he bought me a red Cadillac car for a wedding present."

Downstairs, Jerry was talking about his other two marriages.

"I married first when I was fifteen, married again at seventeen. This time I've found the right girl.

She's a splendid cook even helps choose man clothes.

He added: "I don't know whether Myra will go on tour with me. She may want to stay in London. But Myra will have company. Over here with Jerry is his fourteen-year-old sister Frankie and Myra's brother Rusty.

He is hair

He needs
more than love

Love to a child is all important. But children need more than love. To grow up happy and healthy, children need all a mother's care and wisdom too. Wise mothers learn from the example of doctors and nurses. They use Dettol to guard against the infections that threaten even a spotlessly clean home.

The Doctors' Choice ... germs but so gentle

VITAL STATISTICS

● Princess Margaret saw the hit musical "My Fair Lady" at the Theatre Royal, Drury-lane, last night. Afterwards she met the cast. Here she is chatting with Rex Harrison, as Julie Andrews and Stanley Holloway look on.

next book will be about Australia.

After that? "I don't know." he said. "You see I've run out of continents."

SUNNY JOB

LUCKY chap George Inspector GEORGE PAT MILLIN. He is in charge of Scotland Yard's Flying Squad office. Millins flew 5,000 miles to Trinidad last year to arrest safe-breaker DENNIS STAFFORD.

Now he has been appointed head of the CID in Jamaica. When Stafford escaped from Wormwood Scrubs jail last year Millin hopped out and that Stafford was in a gaol named TITUS COOK in Jamaica. He had matched One day he sent a cable to Millin.

The cable was crammed with it asking for an increase in a money.

BEER!!

A YEAR ago there was GRANT GORDON

SOME figures are from. For example

38 23 36

These figures are not MONROE

Other ... theless, they are ... exam pies

2

The ... point... to bring

ly.
MON
MAY 26
1958
ror
D WITH THE PEOPLE
No. 16,934

POLICE CHECK UP ON CHILD BRIDE

tery of
French
t

Mediterranean Fleet
ed to sail from Malta
secret destination.

ment followed a week-
the revolt against the
nment spread with
ed.

a spokesman said the
onsists of seven ships—
ake part in manoeuvres.
A a rebel spokesman
ships were heading for

Atlantic Treaty Organi-
Paris that manoeuvres
the ships were return-

yneau, C in-C of the
rranean Fleet, is in
ined the rebels two
giers revolt.

ee General Norstadt,
Commander.

Back Page.

Yesterday's picture . . . Jerry Lee Lewis and thirteen-year-old Myra hold hands at their hotel.

'TECHNICAL HITCH'—JERRY

By IAIN SMITH

THE passports of American rock 'n' roll singer Jerry Lee Lewis and his thirteen-year-old "bride" Myra were examined by a hotel security officer yesterday —AT THE REQUEST OF THE POLICE.

The under-manager at the hotel—the Westbury, in London's Mayfair—said afterwards: "We told the police the passports were in order."

Jerry, 22, admitted yesterday that he "married" Myra, without her parents' consent, in December last year—five months before he was granted a divorce from his second wife.

A Home Office spokesman said last night that the situation was being investigated.

"Reports are being collected," he said. "But we cannot make any comment until the couple's

landing papers arrive from London Airport on Tuesday."

Jerry, who has been hailed as the successor of Elvis ("the Pelvis") Presley, is on a six-week variety tour of Britain.

"It is true I married Myra before my divorce was through," he said yesterday, "and we have not been remarried since.

"But I consider that Myra is my wife morally. She will stay with me in my room at this hotel.

"I guess you could call the mix-up a technical hitch. My manager is straightening it out."

Asked if he thought he had

committed bigamy, Jerry said: "I cannot discuss it."

Myra, a tiny, snub-nosed honey blonde, who wore no make-up and no wedding ring, clutched his hand.

"I love Jerry dearly," she said. "I would marry him again, a million times, no matter what has happened. I love married life."

The couple said they were both members of the Pentecostal Church, which frowns on make-up, drink, tobacco—and divorce.

"But I think my divorce is a

matter for God," said Jerry. "I used to preach at one time, but I don't now. I believe a preacher is a preacher and a rock 'n' roll singer is a rock 'n' roll singer.

During Jerry's show at the State Cinema, Kilburn, last night a man in the audience shouted: "Go home, go home." From the stage Jerry shouted back: "Somebody put a lid on that garbage can."

After the show Myra said that she and Jerry had decided to move into separate rooms if it was found that their marriage was illegal.

serve it !

Outlook: Bright, breezy

By the MIRROR WEATHERCOCK

HERE is a bit of advice from the weather experts for today. . . . GET UP EARLY AND GET GOING.

For they say that thunder clouds over Northern France may be arriving over Britain by late afternoon.

But apart from the odd shower now and then it is likely to be a bright and breezy Whit Monday.

Yesterday thousands of folk made it a stay-at-home holiday and traffic on main coast roads out of London was light for a Bank Holiday week end. But on some coast roads there were

traffic jams. Worst hold-up was outside Colchester, Essex, where a queue stretched for five miles.

People who went to the sea found sunshine and blue skies.

Today's official weather forecast: Sunny intervals, showers.
What the Mirror Says—See Page 2

Jerry Lee Lewis was the 'wildest'

says **CHARLES GOVEY**

SO Jerry Lee Lewis has come and gone! One of the biggest rock 'n' roll stars ever to appear in this country has been killed by adverse publicity, and this article must read more like an inquest than an ordinary review.

After seeing his second performance at the Gaumont State, Kilburn, on Whit Sunday, I'm convinced that the cancellation of his tour here had nothing to do with his ability as a performer.

It's true that he played to less than capacity. It's true there was the usual rowdy element in the back rows trying to get in the act—and perhaps Jerry was unwise in letting himself be rattled by them.

There's no denying, either, that the reactions of the fans were slightly less loud and hysterical than a lot of people expected.

But these facts have been over-played by the national press. The same things are true of half a dozen other American acts that have played long and successful tours here in the past.

Stiff wrists

But, if Jerry Lee wasn't the greatest musical entertainer to hit these shores, he was certainly the wildest.

The first glimpse of those hands prancing stiff-wristed over the keyboard and that blond hair flying in all directions was certainly one of the most electrifying things I've ever seen on the stage.

Jerry's initial entry — a lank, shambling figure, with his hair more brilliantly blond than anyone expected — brought loud "oohs" from the audience.

The comb

He went straight into two fast rockers — "Lawdie Miss Claudie" and "Golly Miss Molly" — before getting down to business. Then he peeled off his jacket—a black, red-lined affair with ocelet trimmings—and combed his ten-inch locks into place.

This won him a round of applause! Warming to the job in "I've Been Looking For You," he stood up, danced around, knelt at the piano, then sat down again and dug treble notes out of the keyboard with the heel of his shoe.

He slackened the pace for "The News Is Out," then whipped it up again for "Down The Line," by which time he was kicking the piano-stool about.

This was an unfortunate gimmick, because he had to pick it up before kicking it down again during the next number!

The tempo varied quite a bit after this as he introduced the titles from his latest recording. The slow number was "Fools Like Me," a ballad with real "bluesy" piano and easily the most musicianly thing in the act.

The fast one was the title-song from his new film, "High School Confidential," for which he had three shots at finding the right key.

He put everything he'd got into "Whole Lotta Shakin'," coming down to the front of the stage and lying down to describe the "shake" in intimate detail. After "Great Balls Of Fire," he staggered off the stage looking completely worn out.

How about "Breathless"? He didn't seem to have enough breath left to sing it!

The chief supporting act was The Treniers, and they alone were worth anyone's money, even for those who had already seen them at the London Palladium.

They had extended their act to fill the whole of the first hour, and what a rollicking, entertainment-packed hour it turned out to be!

I lost track of the numbers they performed, but I remember the relaxed rock beat, the fantastic drum break with bare hands, the stylish "All The Way" of Milt Trenier, and the unflagging zest of the two leaders.

The only British artists on the bill, the Hedley Ward Trio, held their own with a slick combination of comedy and music.

HUMPHREY LYTTELTON CLUB
100 OXFORD STREET

RADIO LUXEMBOURG

My God! If they think Jerry Lee's infant bride is immorality just think what they are in store for – when the Rolling Stones and that lot arrive!

Crescent, Middleton, Leeds.
JOYCE JONES, South Road, Marks.

season at the **Regal, Great Yarmouth,** on June 30.

DISC

Hulton House, Fleet Street, LONDON, E.C.4 FLEet Street 5011.

They MUST be blameless

WE make no apology in returning to the unfortunate subject of the arrival and departure of Jerry Lee Lewis. Indeed, it is you, the readers, who bring about its return.

In the last week, many of you have written, emphatically pointing out that Jerry Lee Lewis, the man, is very different from Jerry Lee Lewis, the performer.

Whatever one thinks of his personal life, you say, it was Lewis the performer you wanted to see and hear.

The publicised reaction to his introduction of a 13-year-old wife which brought about a cancellation of his tour and an early return to America, also brought considerable disappointment to many people. This is what many writers claim.

A fair and reasonable point. Britain always welcomes American top-liners to her shores and to her music-halls, thus giving all a chance to see someone who has given pleasure on wax.

But, as we have stressed in the past, an entertainer—or, for that matter, anyone in the public eye—has a duty to maintain an unassailable standard of private living.

There are many people who welcome each opportunity to denigrate the younger generation—the generation we believe in and seek to serve. Many people and quite a number of newspapers, leap at each occasion and a high-spirited, harmless display of enthusiasm can be transformed into "a teenage riot."

An entertainer, particularly a young entertainer, must know, too, that his likes, his dislikes, his habits, his clothes, his hairstyle, will be copied by many of his fans.

We do not mean, of course, that any will go to the length of selecting an infant bride.

BUT THE MORAL IS THERE. ENTERTAINERS ARE YOUTH'S LEADERS TODAY. IT MUST BE A GOOD, BLAMELESS LEAD. OTHERWISE, SOMETHING MORE THAN DISAPPOINTMENT AND BAD PUBLICITY WILL RESULT.

SIDETRACKS

by JACK GOOD

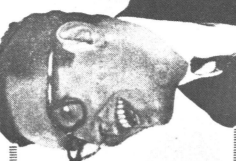

Everything was fine—until he did this

Jerry Lee Lewis was dynamic, sensational, then he combed his hair, someone yelled, "Sissy", and it was open war

I WAS at the first performance given in this country by Jerry Lee Lewis. It was an experience that I think I shall never forget. As I suppose we shall now never have another chance of seeing him in the flesh, perhaps you may

again. The curtain opened and there, cool as a cucumber, was Jerry Lee Lewis. Three more numbers were reeled off. But, of course, any excitement that had been built up was lost. Many of the audience filed out as Jerry Lee carried on. Again the curtain closed. This time finally

one and the same time.

Still, he's coping very well. He should — this boy knows more about pop music than most other Scotsmen have had hot haggis.

He began to be well known as an arranger whilst he was working for Jim Dale—during Jim's would rise

Problems

the orchestrations for Jackie Dennis's records.

That reminds me. H— and Jackie will be working together on our second "Oh Boy" show on June 29.

MEANWHILE, yours truly has had truck-loads of problems tipped over his big head—scenery, lighting, cameras, and not the least of all, costumes. On the jolly old "Six-Five" we didn't have to bother much about costumes.

All the regulars—like Shaw —were allowed to wear what they liked. So you'd have thought you would get quite a motley bunch, wouldn't you? Not at all.

One day, quite by accident. Pete, Freddy, Don and I—just Peacock turned up in practically identical light-blue sweaters.

So next week I determined to be different. I put on—but with massive check of black, brown, yellow and white. I looked a proper Alfred Blow one of that Pete Murray didn't turn up in exactly the same—that the whole studio went into its usual most embarrassing.

A pity?

I AM both glad and sorry that Don Lang has taken over Tommy Steele's disc programme. Sorry because of Tommy's indisposition, glad because I like Don immensely and think he makes a great D.J.

In fact Don's personality could be so good for many sides of the entertainment business. He does some very funny impersonations, for instance, and as a comic he would be a knock-out.

But in another way I am sorry that Don is doing this jockey spot. You see, it will be on the same night and at the same time as "Oh Boy", and Oh boy, we're going to miss him !

Contempt

I CAN'T help feeling that it is a very great pity that there had to be all this trouble, on stage and off, about Jerry Lee Lewis. Here was one of the really exciting, really dynamic witch-doctors of rock 'n' roll, whose personal appearances more than live up to the excitement of his records.

Like all top line artistes, Lewis has authority and stature, and knows he is capable of holding his audience in the palm of his hand. But great artistes must also have humility.

It was here, it seemed, that Jerry Lee Lewis fell short. His attitude, on the occasion I saw him at least, was marked by indifference and contempt.

As for the enquiries into Jerry Lee Lewis' private life, I hate any interference in a man's personal affairs.

But, unfortunately, whether you like it or not the modern teenage-idol is subject to the closest scrutiny, and if he sets a bad example in private life the whole world of pop music is branded as vicious.

So these great figures of the disc world owe it to the profession that gave them their success to lead blameless lives—or at least not to be found out.

Versatile John

WHO said people who play rock 'n' roll are not good musicians? John Barry, generally known as a rocker, has recently arranged and composed music for the great Johnny Dankworth. And that's not all. His latest composition and recording, "Rodeo," has now been re-corded by Frank Chacksfield and is to be released in the States.

'Oh Boy'

PREPARATIONS for the "Oh Boy" show on Sunday, June 15, are forging ahead famously. The cast are all working like slaves on their individual numbers, working up some stunning performances that you really can't afford to miss.

The boy who is hardest worked at the moment is young Harry Robinson—the musical director. He has the job of arranging the 17 numbers in the show—no easy task, when you consider that this means writing for two bands, two vocal groups, a choir and the solo-ists—sometimes all performing at

air to keep it off the ground. He finished the number flapping furiously with his right hand and playing only with his left.

The Lewis-haters made the most of the situation, yelling and jeering. Quite firmly and calmly Jerry Lee marched off the stage and that was that. There was a sudden, dazed silence in the audience. The curtain closed. People stared at one another in wonder and muttered "What's happening."

Abruptly the National Anthem boomed out—and they knew what was happening. Programmes were thrown up in disgust. Some jumped up and yelled "fiddle"—for Jerry Lee hadn't finished half his act.

Then, just as abruptly as the programme had finished, it began

---

guitarist.

Both of them were wearing perfectly ordinary dark suits and looked very dull. Unlike Jerry Lee Lewis. He dashed on to the stage in a bright pillar-box red suit with black velvet collar, cuffs and pockets, and diamanté trimmings.

Lewis was certainly dynamic. He stood the mike between his legs and thumped the keys with his hands on either side of it.

When he got the coat off, except for one sleeve, he obviously changed his mind and didn't think it worth throwing it on the dirty floor, so he swung it round in the

He withdrew a long, black comb from his pocket and carefully combed back his flowing locks. And then, as if he had all the time in the world, he examined his socks. Somebody bawled out "Sissy"—and that did it. Jerry Lee curtly replied "thank you." WE KNEW WHERE WE WERE. IT WAS OPEN WAR.

Lewis knew he could, by his shattering performance, thrill his

---

not. So did the audience, and for that they hated him even more.

He pounded and bawled his way through about four more sensa-tional numbers. Each one was greeted with a mixture of cheers and jeers. Finally he let rip on "Great Balls Of Fire." During this number it was part of his act to kick away his piano stool and then, whilst still attacking the piano, take off his coat.

Jerry was doing fine by the end of his first offering. "Lawdy, Lawdy, Miss Claudy." At long last the audience was getting the message. At the end of his second number Jerry Lee Lewis could have clinched it. His hair was hanging all over his face. If he had brushed it back with a gag, all would have been well. He didn't.

Onslaught

THEN Derek Franklin of the Hedley Ward Trio introduced Jerry. The curtains parted and there on the stage was a large and battered grand piano, waiting for the onslaught.

Next to it was a small, weasel-faced gentleman in dark glasses, bashing out a frantic beat on the

Outside it was a sunny afternoon. Inside the vast Regal Cinema, Edmonton was about two-thirds full. It's a funny thing, but right from the beginning I felt there was going to be a battle. Perhaps it was that the audience at 6.15 on a bright White Saturday was just not in the mood. Or maybe it was just one of those things no one can explain. Anyway hostility was in the air.

At the end of the Treniers the hubbub was still stone cold, but they certainly couldn't complain that they weren't getting value for money.

They were followed by the Hed-ley Ward Trio. Again a very professional act. These boys did a great job warming the audience up —they even got a few big laughs.

"FRIED ONIONS" AND "THE SQUELCH"

JACK GOOD PRESENTS

A FABULOUS NEW SOUND BY

LORD ROCKINGHAM'S XI

Watch this Record climb into the Hit Parade !!

SOUTHERN MUSIC PUBLISHING CO., LTD.

— St. London W.C.2   Telephone Temple Bar 4524

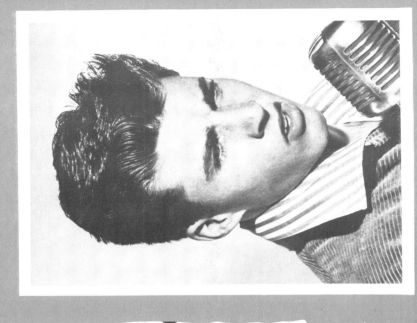

A PERSONALLY WRITTEN LETTER by CONNIE FRANCIS

HELLO, EVERYONE! It's a real thrill to be able to write to so many of you, through the medium of the NME. For nearly two years, since MGM first started issuing my records in Britain, I have been corresponding with several staunch supporters over there. But this is the first chance I have had of addressing a " thank you " note to all of you.

And my personal and very sincere " thank you " is because of your kindness in elevating my recording of " Who's Sorry Now? " into the enviable position of top-selling disc in the country

This is just about the biggest thrill of my life, and I hardly know how to express myself adequately in words.

I can't tell you just how excited I was when I realised, soon after the beginning of this year, that my record was beginning to get away and stood a chance of figuring in the best-sellers.

The tension and suspense of waiting from week to week to see what improvement there was in its position was almost unbearable. I suppose when you've had several smash hits, you get used to it.

But for me, with the prospect of my first break into the disc big-time, it was quite an ordeal, but, at the same time, a tremendous thrill.

As a result of the record scoring this success, I have had very little time to myself just recently. They say that success breeds success, and certainly in the past weeks I have been kept frantically busy on an extensive tour of major cities.

And GAC have booked me into several important coast-to-coast TV shows.

Why, until this week, I haven't even had time to write to my Dad for two or three months!

It's all rather overwhelming suddenly to find myself in demand like this. I've been singing for some years now. In fact, it's true to say that most of my 19 years have been spent in association with show business

Very shy

I had made some sort of reputation, especially on the East Coast—making out reasonably well, without actually hitting the jackpot. And now at last my dreams have come true, and I have got that big record hit for which I have been praying.

I used to be very shy about meeting people, but, fortunately, I have overcome that reticence now. It's just as well, in view of what is expected of me these days.

And do you know how I helped cure myself of shyness? I read and digested that famous book by Dale Carnegie, "How to Win Friends and Influence People."

I know that this book is the subject of many comedians' gags in vaudeville, but I can honestly say that I have formed an entirely new way of looking at life since reading it.

The fact is, I just love living! Don't imagine that I spend all my time in night clubs, and painting the town. No, sir!

My tastes are very simple, and nothing gives me greater pleasure than being at home. Life is so full of wonderful things—this may sound corny, but it's oh, so true.

Say, how about all that for preaching? Guess I'd better climb down off my soap-box now. That's what comes of taking philosophy at college!

Talking of music, as we were just now, I am often asked what kind I like best. Well, the truth is that I like all kinds, so long as it's good. And by " good " I mean just this —that if I derive enjoyment from it, then it's good for me. See what I mean?

Idols

Of course, I have several favourite singers. Of the men, I prefer Frank Sinatra and Nat Cole—but then, who doesn't? And the girls I go for, happy to follow, are Ella Fitzgerald, Doris Day, Kay Starr, Chris Connor and Jeri Southern—plus one of your own delightful British singers, Vera Lynn.

And when it comes to vocal groups, just leave me The The Hi-Lo's.

Until "Who's Sorry Now?" started moving, my biggest thrill had been my association with two motion pictures. About 18 months ago, I was asked to sing "I Never Had A Sweetheart" for the soundtrack of the movie, "Rock, Rock, Rock."

But an even greater experience was being called upon for four songs for the "Disc-Jockey Jamboree" picture, which proved so popular.

Incidentally, last July I remember attending a cocktail party at the Park Sheraton in New York, in connection with the launching of this film.

And it was there that I had the pleasure of meeting one of your leading disc-jockeys, Jack Payne, who was in the States to take part in the picture.

I remember at the time when we were talking, someone mentioned the name of Frankie Vaughan. I had

never heard of him then, but my, he really means something over here now.

A fan wrote to me from Middlesex recently and asked : "Tell me about yourself, what you like and dislike in life." Well, gee, that's a tough one! Because one of the things I detest most is writing about myself.

their innumerable conquests, insects, hypocrites, giggly girls, elevators and rigid conformists. Hey, it sounds like that record of the ". What Is A Girl ? " monologue, doesn't it ?

Well, I guess I must get back to work again now. It's been really well writing to all of you wonderful people, and it is my sincere hope that I shall have the chance of meeting you all in person before long. Nothing would give me greater pleasure.

Thank you again for all your invaluable support, which I am pretty young in my outlook, that I am fairly modern in my tastes.

Likes

But basically, I like to think that I like speed, yellow convertibles, empty churches, sunset, daybreak, animals, food, occasional parties and dancing (particularly the cha-cha).

And I detest men who boast of

hope I can continue to justify. With warm regards to all my friends, everywhere.

Sincerely.

Connie Francis

VERSATILE DAVID SEVILLE

What a relief! On the rails again!

He had a ready-made public for his discs in America, but now he's

WITH Elvis temporarily out of the "in-person" running, one of the hottest pieces of entertainment property in the *in the British Charts, which leads* States right now is young Ricky Nelson.

BRUCE CHARLTON

to declare . . .

RICKY NELSON IS HERE TO STAY

He has just collected his fourth Golden Disc in a matter of just over a year! And with his latest million-seller, "Poor Little Fool", which has entered the NME Charts with a bang this week, he has attained the ultimate in record sales—his first number-one U.S. best-seller.

Doesn't it strike you as rather odd that this young man, obviously not so very far behind Presley in the affections of America's teenagers, should have created so little stir over here until now? Why should this be?

The fact is that both artists arrived in recording circles in vastly contrasting circumstances. Presley's advent came with such a sudden and irresistible impact that he had beaten the youngsters throughout the world into submission in less than no time. This was at the peak of the rock 'n' roll upsurge, and the fans were ready to accept a champion of this exciting new music.

But Ricky, you see, is essentially an American institution. He is virtually "the boy next door," someone with whom the nation's youngsters have grown up for the past ten years. I'll tell you why . . .

Ricky's parents have one of the most successful weekly radio and TV shows in the States. Called "The Adventure of Ozzie and Harriet", it's been going strong for fifteen years, and their intimate family escapades are enjoyed just as much over there as, say, "Life With the Lyons" in this country.

Ozzie used to be a bandleader and Harriet was the singer with the band.

Maybe you remember this show when the BBC used to broadcast edited versions during the war, soon after the series started. Or perhaps more recently you've listened to it on AFN, Germany.

Catch-phrase

At any rate, ten years ago, when Ricky was eight years old, he was introduced into the show for the first time. He immediately endeared himself to countless numbers of families with his boyish charm and impish devilment. His infectious grin quickly became an established part of the show, and he soon developed his own catch-phrase—"I don't mess around, boy

As Ricky grew up his versatility became more apparent. He became an expert dancer, drummer and guitarist. His parents soon began to find excuses for introducing these various attributes into their programme. It was only to be expected that sooner or later Ricky would burst into song!

It was just about 17 months ago that this gifted young man branched out as a singer in his own right and was persuaded into the Imperial Records studios by their enterprising boss, Lew Chudd.

He was far-sighted enough to realise that, since millions had been following Ricky's antics every week on television, it was reasonable to suppose that those same millions would buy his records. And, in fact, Ricky's acceptance as a recording artist was both instantaneous and overwhelming.

Far from a gentle initiation, Ricky had just about the toughest grooming of all. For when his first record— "I'm Walkin'"—was issued, Fats Domino was already in the best-

sellers with his version of the same song.

Yet Ricky not only caught up with Domino, but actually over-hauled him, zooming into second place.

While not detracting from the boy's ability, it is obvious that sentimentality has played a large part in Ricky's initial disc success. We here had absolutely no opportunity of getting to know the youngest member of the famous Nelson family (apart from in a Hollywood film, "Here Come the Nelsons", and a small role in the MGM production, "A Story Of Three Loves") and therefore he had no "ready market" in Britain.

But it was only natural in America

that when a member of one of the best-loved families in the States made a record, people should flock to buy it. Even if only for the novelty value.

As it happened, he consolidated his position with further hits, fulfilling all the requirements...

possess the necessary talent and personality on wax, his recording career would have been as short as it was sweet.

This, however, would not be sufficient to ensure the lasting disc success of any artist. If Ricky did not

He was the handsomest of all the teen faves – and he had terrific back-up musicians – including James Burton, lead guitar, who went on to be on regular call for Elvis Presley and who backed him on numerous records. When he changed his name to RICK and took it all seriously I went off him.

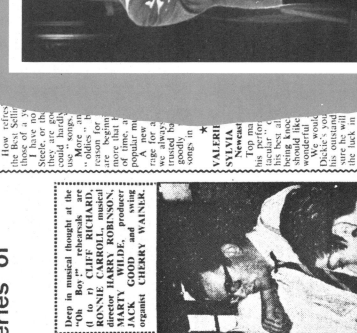

☆ **MARTY WILDE** ☆ **RONNIE CARROLL** ☆ **JACK GOOD**
☆ **CLIFF RICHARD** ☆ **NEVILLE TAYLOR** . . . . . these
are some of the names **KEITH GOODWIN** met at a
rehearsal for the first of the new series of

OH BOY!

THE peaceful tranquillity of the shops and houses adjoining the Four Provinces Club in Islington was shattered beyond repair this week. Suddenly the area has become **a hive of seething activity, though few people yet seem to know exactly what is going on.**

Workmen cart large pieces of scenery into the club and glamorous showgirls periodically invade the quiet little restaurant around the corner in search of coffee; office girls peer out of windows, shoppers are startled by the waves of sound that waft out from the club, and schoolboys run the perimeter of the building frantically clutching autograph books.

The secret of the Four Provinces Club leaked out on a major scale on Tuesday—the second day of rehearsals for producer Jack Good's new "brainchild" series, "Oh Boy."

Inside the hall, chaotic disorder reigns supreme. Sheet music litters every available chair, and instrument cases are strewn all over the floor; artists and musicians mingle with perspiring workmen as scenery is hurriedly set up; the producer tries to make himself heard above the din of 70 or so voices, and a stray dog beats a hurried retreat between the legs of jiving chorus girls as the powerhouse, Lord Rockingham's Eleven explode into action!

Slick show

Out of all this confusion will arise a slick, colourful show—the first of a new ABC-TV series that takes the air at 6 p.m. tomorrow (Saturday).

Chaos will give way to a smooth, precision-timed show that promises to be one of the most exciting ever seen in this country.

In between sips of coffee and a goon-style cross-talk routine with musical director Harry Robinson, Jack Good outlined to me the basic aims of the show. "We intend to make this the most organised show on TV," he began, "and also one of the fastest and most exciting.

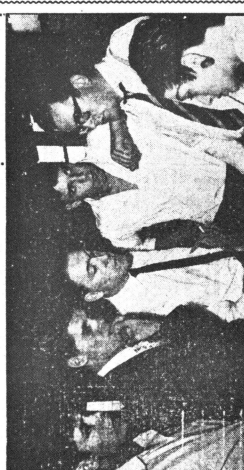

Deep in musical thought at the "Oh Boy!" rehearsals are (l to r) CLIFF RICHARD, RONNIE CARROLL, musical director HARRY ROBINSON, MARTY WILDE, producer JACK GOOD and swing organist CHERRY WAINER.

Richard propped up against a wall listening to the Dallas Boys rehearsing. Introductions completed, we sought sanctuary in a quiet anteroom, where I managed to render Cliff speechless with the news that his first Columbia recording "Move I", had entered the hit parade.

His jaw dropped, and he groped unsuccessfully for words. He spoke in short, monosyllabic phrases: "Already ? . . . well . . . I mean . . . what can I say ? . . Everything is happening all at once."

His composure regained, Cheshunt-born Cliff, 17, set about telling me of his sudden attack of nerves. "It's wonderful to be going on TV for the first time, but I feel so nervous that I don't know what to do.

"I mean, I only turned professional five weeks ago, and before that I was working as a clerk and only playing at local dances and things in my spare time. I wore

BILL BOWEN
How refres the Best Sellin those of a y I have no Steele, or the they are go could hardl use " songs. More an "oldies". b are beginn more that t of time, a popular mu A new rage for a we always trusted ba goodly songs in

★
VALERI
SYLVIA
Newcast
Top ma his perform tacular." C his best al being knoc should like wonderful " We woul Dickie's you his outstand sure he will the luck in

★
BERYL B
Epsom, Su
Last evenin where a big showing and Yet three or f same cinema, Duke Wore Je out.
What has ha film industry a suitable scr office draw i

★
MISS J. MA ham, write
I read w Presley may ances in Bri understand n Elvis.
But surely seen the wo other rock 'n have appeared

by a blistering stage show that never let up for one moment. They'd simply have to sit up, and take notice, and that's what I'm looking for," Jack explained.

"We aim to startle viewers with quick, lively presentation, and because I'm convinced that comedy, no matter how good, tends to slow down a show of this kind, we won't be featuring any comedians. Teamwork is going to count more than anything else, and I'm happy to say that everybody in the show is dead keen," he continued.

"Oh Boy!" will be in direct opposition to BBC-TV's "6.5 Special"—formerly produced by Jack. How does he feel about it? "Frankly, I'm thrilled at the prospect, and the essence of competition must obviously encourage us to work doubly hard," he confided.

Finally, what style of music will we hear on "Oh Boy!"? For a start, there'll be a preponderance of Big Beat material from the cream of Britain's "rockers." But that doesn't mean that ballads are out of favour.

"Right now, the trend in pop music generally, is veering towards a more melodic conception, and we will follow that trend," Jack emphasised.

Now let's meet some of the artists we'll be appearing in tomorrow's show. I found newcomer Cliff original, I think he's right," he said.

John Foster, Cliff's burly, 19-year-old manager, broke in to tell me how tea London agents had given the thumbs down sign after hearing a tape recording by Cliff. "Seems like those fellows can be wrong after all," he grinned!

Coffee for two

Though his first year in show business is still not yet complete, Marty Wilde takes the hectic whirl of rehearsals in his stride. After singing his way through "Think It Over" and "Baby, I Don't Care," he greeted me with a smile and a handshake, and guided me to the nearest coffee bar.

Two steaming cups were placed on the table by an inquisitive waitress, and Marty requested extra sugar with a firm "got one heck of a sweet tooth." The sugar arrived together with a grubby piece of paper which Marty dutifully signed for a devoted fan.

To the accompaniment of Peggy Lee's "Fever" from a nearby juke box, we chatted about Marty's rôle in the show.

"I'm very proud to be associated with the series, because I know it's going to be a great show. That's because we have such a fine producer. You know, I predict that one day Jack will be the world's greatest producer," he confided.

"Rehearsals," he echoed, in answer to my question. "They're fun. I enjoy them because I learn so much watching other people work. I like learning because it helps to broaden my scope. You know, pretty soon I want to have a crack at all kinds of songs—ballads, rock, everything."

In panto

About his future, Marty was very frank. Towards Christmas, he'll be temporarily leaving "Oh Boy!" to make his début in pantomime at Stockton. "I'll be my first and last pantomime," he declared. "I'm not awfully keen on the idea, but I realise that the experience will be good. Anyway, I've always fancied myself as a comedian, so maybe this'll be a good opportunity to try out some gag lines."

Marty is his own severest critic, but I feel he was being hyper-critical when we discussed his latest record, "Misery's Child."

"It's a bad record," he stressed. "And if it gets into the hit parade, it doesn't deserve to." And with that, Marty strode off to the juke box to drop another coin in the slot. The tune? "Fever":

Back in the Provinces Club, Lord Rockingham's Eleven were blowing up a storm on Harry Robinson's new composition, "Hoots, Mon." Girls in sweaters and shorts—the Vernon Girls—were running through dance steps, and Jack Good was frantically waving a piece of music in front of organist Cherry Wainer.

Grouped around a piano were Neville Taylor and The Cutters—the "Oh Boy!" resident vocal quartet—and the group who supplied the high-pitched scat lyrics on the Rockingham outfit's Decca recording of "Fried Onions".

A drum roll brought "Hoots, Mon," to a close, and The Cutters broke into a pounding version of "Yakety Yak." A couple of choruses later, Jack Good nodded his approval, and the group dispersed to various corners of the room. "Like it?" Neville asked. "I want to record with the group soon, because I think we've got a good sound. Anyway, the audiences seemed to like us when we did those two 'Oh Boy!' trial shows a while back."

"You know the boys?" I shook my head, and Neville pointed out Wilf Todd, Basil Short and Sonny McKenzie. "Funny thing, but they all play bass," he beamed. "All good musicians—couldn't work with a better bunch," he beamed again.

Further conversation with Neville was cut short by the arrival of a harassed-looking Jack Good, requesting Neville's presence on the bandstand. We turned around, and I succeeded in treading on Ronnie Carroll's toe!

Finding a relatively quiet spot to talk, Ronnie proceeded to eulogise about Jack. "Great producer," he said. "Jack knows what he wants, and he always gets results. That's why I'm very pleased to be working with him on this series."

TV rehearsals hold no worries for Ronnie, and he was even looking forward to the 45 minutes ahead of him. But I don't think he'll be so keen in a couple of months time, for within the next 12 weeks, he is set to make 20 major TV appearances on shows like the "Jack Jackson," "Cool For Cats," and "Rainbow Room" programmes.

"I'll be the contrast in 'Oh Boy!,' because whereas most of the other artists will be singing beaty stuff, I'll concentrate mainly on ballads. It'll add a touch of variety to the show," Ronnie told me.

Variety dates have no place in Ronnie's work schedule these days. "In the first place, I don't get the time and, apart from that, I never was very keen on variety. But I'm looking forward to doing pantomime for the first time at Sheffield this Christmas," he added, before dashing off to sing the opening bars of "Seven Steps To Love."

In the studio, everything seemed to be happening at once.

Bertice Reading and John Berry—two further stars of tomorrow's début show—weren't scheduled to arrive for at least another two hours, and I suspected that by the time they got there, I wouldn't be able to get a word in edgeways. So I left!

★ NAME BAND DIRECTORY ★

KEN MACKINTOSH
HIS SAXOPHONE & ORCHESTRA
Sole Representation: RABIN AGENCY
30 GLOUCESTER MANSIONS, CAMBRIDGE CIRCUS, LONDON, W.C.2   TEM 2816

LOU PREAGER'S
AMBASSADORS BAND
Specially Chosen Combinations
One-Night Stands Anywhere
LOU PREAGER'S Presentations
69, GLENWOOD GDNS., ILFORD
Valentine 4043

HOWARD BAKER
AND HIS BAND
Available for one-night stands
especially Fridays. Cabaret also
supplied.
69, GLENWOOD GARDENS,
ILFORD, ESSEX.   Valentine 4043

Intellectuals, toughs, or religious fanatics?

STEELE

"**FANOLOGY**"—this is my name for a fascinating new study—the study of how groups of fans vary according to the artistes they support. The sort of question Fanology investigates is : "How do Frankie Vaughan fans differ from Marion Ryan fans?" (Answer: **One lot are girls and the other, boys.**)

Well, I know that's an easy one, but then you're only just beginning aren't you?

What started me off on this interesting hobby was the reaction I got from my rather harsh, and slightly unfair, attack on our Jim the other week. The letters I got from Dale fans were unlike any I had previously received. Jim should be proud of them. They were all spelt right for a start—the thing that rarely happens with the Presley fans and never, never happens with the Steele fans.

More than that, they were intelligent, argumentative and slightly aloof. Most impressive. I can only think that Dale fans are the intellectuals of the fan world.

No illusions

The Dale fans don't have any illusions. They don't imagine him to be their boy friend, father or lover. They don't say "Jim Dale is the world's greatest," as do the firmly state "Jim Dale is **one of England's** (get that) best singers." The reserve of it is amazing.

The Steele fans are, when roused, a violent lot. They feel Tommy is a weak little boy who needs protecting and mothering. If I had written what I did about Tommy instead of Jim the letters would have been of a totally different nature.

Instead of (I quote) "Dear Sir, I read your article on Jim Dale in this week's DISC with annoyance, but not without considerable amusement" it would have been "Dear Slobb (that's to show you what you are). You stinkin idyot, why dont you tak a running jump into the neerist river, you fool, you leeve Tommy alone or you will get very unpopuler and very likely get the sack so watch out my gang is waiting for you if you don't print this I will no you are a coward."

No offence !

The approach of the Presley crowd is different again. Being a Presley fan is like belonging to a persecuted religious sect. They know how much they are hated and so have become very public-relations conscious, trying not to offend and yet not budging an inch from their worship of the martyr **Presley.**

The Elvis faith is liable to possess the most unlikely people, from debutantes to middle-aged office workers. They have a persecution complex about Presley and take offence very easily.

For instance, if I were to mention "... the dark eyes and side-boards of Presley." I would get dozens of letters saying "Why criticise Presley for his dark eyes? He can't help them. And anyway they look smashing, so do his sideboards, so why do you object?"

To his fans, Presley is a father figure. What El says goes. El says to be nice to the Press and Frank Sinatra, whatever they may say, and the fans meekly obey. Just the same, underneath the

---

whenever they can all make it at one time. And that presents some problems.

For instance, for our rehearsal today (Thursday), Marty Wilde flies in from Edinburgh (where he is currently appearing), rehearses for a couple of hours, and then flies back. For this rehearsal John Barry's Seven and Jackie Dennis are coming to London from Bournemouth.

Altogether we do about four days of rehearsal—but only on the day of transmission itself are we able to rehearse at Wood Green

said, in one simple sentence. "You should know, having produced 'Six-Five Special,' that Jim only, says what the script-writer writes. To this there is only one reply : "She knows, y'know."

Jeremy Lloyd—you're an old square !

Good's TV shows realized on the screen what R&R's excitement *should* look like – a vision gleaned almost solely off records and press photos. Much of this vision was Good's own personal apocalypse. He is a man who understands the reality of Good and Evil.

COVER PERSONALITY

GENE VINCENT

DISC cover spot this week is devoted to an artiste very much underrated — Gene Vincent. Our mailbag consistently shows what a strong following he maintains with Britain's pop fraternity.

Why he should have been missing from the popularity charts is one of those indeterminable puzzles of the record business that it is always impossible to answer.

Gene has turned out many exciting records; all having the qualities that the public seemed to demand yet, apart from near-hits, he has never really rung the bell continuously in this country.

His debut on wax in Britain, at a time when worse recordings were reaping rewards, made a considerable impact but the promised interest has not been sustained.

We first heard of this vibrant singer through his distinctive treatment on "Be-Bop-A-Lulu," a fast-moving composition which was coupled with an unusual echo chamber effect.

The repeated echo was enough to bring this record to the attention of many, for it was certainly novel and stimulating.

It sold in vast quantities and, in the States, the disc reaped a good harvest for the Capitol organisation.

The search which the company had made to find a rival to Presley then looked like paying off with big dividends.

Twenty-year-old Gene was the successful competitor from the 200 would-be record singers auditioned by Capitol.

As soon as he could be whipped into the studios he was cutting his first disc, " Be-Bop-A-Lula " coupled with " Woman Love."

From the beginning it appeared that Gene Vincent was destined to be a formidable entrant into the rock field. Many more disc issues followed, each one improving with experience, yet the real hit target seemed to elude him.

Gene Vincent was born in Norfolk, Virginia, and, like many youngsters, Gene found that he was able to put his youthful voice to good use in church choirs.

Additionally, he was constantly surrounded by country and folk music and, not unnaturally, he acquired an interest in this class of singing,

HE STILL WAITS FOR A UK HIT

A visit to Virginia in his early teens was to make a considerable impression on Gene Vincent. He heard, for the first time, a group of negroes singing their kind of music and, such was the effect on him he started transposing all his pop song favourites into their style.

But he was also to realise that his efforts were but an imitation and that he wasn't singing in his own true style. Gradually he developed his own presentation—one which he felt, and knew, was just right.

Meanwhile, though money was scarce, he saved hard and long so that he might possess a guitar. Once it was bought, Gene then had to teach himself to play it.

His guitar was also soon to make him a popular shipmate for, at the age of 17, Gene Vincent joined the U.S. Navy.

Throughout his service days he not only amused himself in his off-duty moments, but he was a regular favourite with the ship's company whenever they had musical evenings.

On his release from the navy, Gene returned to his home town in Norfolk, where he soon fixed himself up with a radio series on the local station.

His fame, apart from a few local concerts, went little farther and it was not until the record audition presented itself that Gene suddenly found himself quickly propelled up the star ladder.

Apart from the string of excellent waxings to his credit on singles, Gene Vincent has three dynamite - packed LPs which have become big favourites with his followers. They are " Bluejean Bop," " Gene Vincent Rocks and the Blue-Caps Roll," and " Gene Vincent and the Blue Caps." The Blue Caps, of course, are a strong feature on all the Gene Vincent waxings.

Friday (August 15) Gene Vincent has a new disc issued— " Yes I Love You Baby " coupled with " Rocky Road Blues" It is another excellent recording by the young American singing star who so much deserves that elusive big hit.

Seen here with the Blue Caps, Gene Vincent has another try this week for that elusive hit.

Doug Geddes

It was Jack Good who first dressed Vincent in black leather, put him on a set full of steps, stood by the camera and ordered 'Limp you bugger, limp!' – thus making this hitherto polite gentleman (who called his elders 'sir') into the Richard III of Rock.

SIDETRACKS

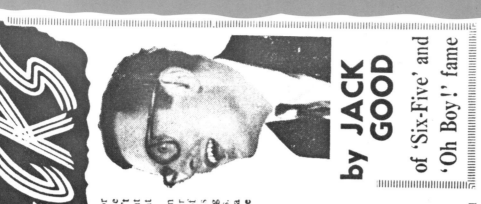

TERRY DENE, Marty Wilde, Jim Dale, Terry Wayne, Wee Willie Harris, Laurie London—again and again my mind has been running over the very first auditions given to all these " sensational teenage discoveries " before they made their first appearances on " Six - Five Special," picturing them, some very nervous and very raw, as they were before their names became household words. The other day I could have sworn that the era of these dramatic discoveries and overnight successes had passed.

Not any more. **Just yesterday I heard the most amazing first recording made by any teenage artiste in Great Britain. Even as I play it over again for the hundred and first time, I still can't believe it. That this disc comes from Britain and not the States is fantastic—absurd. If this is not a hit, I have never heard one.**

This whole startling affair began very quietly. Franklyn Boyd phoned me. Franklyn, a burly winger of the Show-Biz XI and vocalist on radio's "Sing It Again" programme, is a representative of Aberbach Music Publishing Company. He wanted to know if I had a moment to hear the first recording of a new discovery. I said "Yes," but thought nothing much about it—just another promising teenager, I supposed. Round comes Franklyn with a curiously triumphant smile puts on the first side.

It is a goodish commercial number, well recorded and fairly well sung—but nothing outstanding. Then he spins what he laughingly refers to as the " flip-side." Wham! This disc could sell 50,000 on its first eight bars alone.

It kicks off with a forceful, dramatic guitar phrase that runs an electric shock down the spine. In comes the drum, driving a vicious beat right through the heart of the number. Then the voice rides confidently over this glorious backing —a voice with an amazingly "non-imitative" style, considering that this kind of music ought by rights to be foreign to anyone who is not a native of the Southern States. The diction is clear: the phrasing authentic, professional — there is a

real feeling for this country-and-western style. If this disc had been a product of Sun Records of Memphis, Tennesee — the original recording company of Elvis Presley and Jerry Lee Lewis—I should not have been surprised, but would still have rated it as important and good enough to be compared,

he would be the raw material for production. For even if he had the sound and the looks, if he didn't have the intelligence and the right approach, there was nothing that could be done for him.

The time came for the audition in a block of studios near Leicester Square. Running up the flight of stairs I could just catch the strains of the number I had been spinning on disc for the last couple of days. It was good. That much wasn't a fluke at least. As I opened the

Just another beginner?

NO—this boy is really terrific!

by JACK GOOD

of 'Six-Five' and 'Oh Boy!' fame

door of the tiny studio the sound boomed out and there were these three boys whipping up a storm.

They all looked so very young. Especially the singer. He was of average height, very slim, with finely drawn features. His half-Indian descent explained the dark hair, the big dark eyes, as well as the slightly olive colour of his complexion. As he ran through five or six numbers it became clear that he did have a natural feel for this kind of music.

But there was nothing like the polish and presence and punch of a Marty Wilde. This is something

if you didn't know,

you'd think Cliff

Richard was straight

from America, he's

so good

though not, of course, on equal terms, with those two giants of the beat.

But when one considers that this is the product of a 17-year-old boy from Cheshunt, Hertfordshire, the mind just boggles. This, however, is by no means the end of the whole fantastic story. The backing of the drums and guitar, to which

that can only come with experience and serious rehearsal — plus, of course, a star personality. Whether he will make this grade remains to be seen. There was no doubt, however, that these boys could make a very big impact on television with their first number, " Move It."

So it was arranged that they should make their television debut on the first " Oh Boy!" show, September 13. The name to remember is **Cliff Richard** and the **Drifters.** You could be hearing quite a lot more from them.

Fame from first disc opens door to Richard!

THE new British hit parader, Cliff Richard showed an interest in music at an early age —but many miles from a London recording studio.

Born in Lucknow, India, on October 14, 1940, he started playing records at the age of three on an old-fashioned gramophone. Five years later he came to Britain to live with his grandparents—but there was no gramophone, and his musical interest started to fade.

In the meantime, he became something of a schoolboy athlete, playing in the Hertfordshire junior football league, and making a record throw with the javelin at school.

His musical interest returned when he started singing in school shows and he moved with his parents to Cheshunt, where he could listen to records once more.

Soon Cliff was appearing at local dances and clubs with a vocal group, and he did so well that he was encouraged to form his own accompanying group, which he called The Drifters.

Lucky drift

It wasn't long before The Drifters drifted to that new mecca of the entertainment world—the 2 I's coffee bar in Soho, which brought them further bookings in and around London.

A recent appearance at Shepherd's Bush Gaumont brought them an introduction to Columbia recording chief Norrie Paramor.

From there it was just a short step to a successful test recording, their first session and, this week, the first appearance of " Move It", in the NME list of best-selling records.

You can see Cliff and The Drifters, by the way, in the opening edition of Jack Good's "Oh Boy!" TV show this Saturday.

---

will find it as hard to believe as I did. There is more yet. This great number, titled "Move It", was written by the young guitarist of the trio, a quiet red-headed boy named Sammy. All of what I just knows me out.

So I wanted to audition the group that very day. Not a chance. They're all out at work. The vocalist, Cliff Richard, is employed at Ferguson's —the radio firm at Enfield. I had to wait until the following evening. To tell the truth I expected that somehow the record would turn out to be a fluke. Maybe this was just a lucky attempt which would never be repeated. Or perhaps A. and R. man Norrie Paramor had done a very crafty bit of tape surgery and made one excellent track out of a number of indifferent takes.

NO FLUKE

But in any case, however good the boy was sound-wise, it would be too much to expect that he would have anything visually. He would probably look ghastly. I reflected, in which case, as far as television was concerned, there would be no deal.

I spent the following day wondering what this boy would really be like, hoping against hope that

---

When I saw Cliff Richard on 'Oh Boy!' I was stunned and shocked. Stunned by his glowering, dusky, brute looks; and shocked by his aping of Elvis. Bloody copy cat! I said. But he was all that I wanted to be and couldn't. Then, back then, he oozed crude sex! Nowadays he has lost his sting. Deliberately.

" I think Cliff Richard . . . has a personality that shines through the grooves. He could succeed in disc-land "

PAT DONCASTER
'Daily Mirror' July 31st

CLIFF RICHARD

singing

Schoolboy Crush

and MOVE IT!

DB4178 (45 & 78)

COLUMBIA 🎵 RECORDS

so Ker Robertson assured Lonnie Donegan in print last … rage, once … tired of running round in circles after the hula-hoop. Yet … able hotch-potch of tastes, proving nothing other than … in recent rise of … (Capitol … which c… qualities proved H… and by qualifies series.

Unlike the curren… cracy, 38… has a so… Original… Goodma… been pr… men's …

As a Academ… Kelly's … she H… several… toire … perform… pecially… the Ke… —was …

Primitive? Not me! says 18-year-old Cliff Richard

by MARION LEVINSON

WHERE lies the basic appeal of rock-'n'-roll? In elementary, uninhibited sex, of course! And the purveyors of the Big Beat often tend to exploit that fact as far as the code of moral decency allows.

Mention THAT word to the latest of the 12-bar beat idols, 18-year-old Cliff ("Move It") Richard—and he'll react with a blank, uncomprehending stare.

"Arouse primitive instincts?" he asks, genuinely astonished. "Sorry, but I don't see how."

The Mother Grundies—loud in their condemnations of the tremble-and-twitch brigade—are already demanding that master Richard should leave the gyrations to his American counterparts. But he refuses to be intimidated.

"My 'gyrations' are conducive to the type of songs I sing. They express the rhythm and drive of the beat number," he says.

"Sexy? I'm not consciously trying to be. Anyway, audiences seem to enjoy my act—and they're the best judges."

Currently high in the sellers' list is Richard's first disc, "Move It." This number, penned by a member of Richard's group, "The Drifters," is that regrettable rarity—a British hit song.

His latest recording, "High Class Baby," is being widely tipped as a potential hit.

Exults Richard: "They're both British songs. I intend to feature British numbers as much as possible. The Americans tend to sneer at our songwriters—so we're gonna try and beat them at their own game!"

Hopes for the future?

Eyes shining in awe, Richard states in hushed tones: "I may fly to Germany this February to meet Elvis."

The immediate future looks bright for this lad. He's heavily booked for Variety and he's on ATV's "Oh Boy." Secure in his jeans pocket is a Columbia recording contract.

Boosted by the powerful EMI Organisation and music publisher/manager, Franklyn Boyd, this new star will probably remain in orbit for a long time yet.

Wildest ever

I MET Cliff Richard at Newcastle immediately after seeing him given THE wildest reception I have ever seen given to a recording star (*writes MM correspondent John Stuart*).

Screaming girls blocked his way at both stage exits. Two girls rushed up to the foot of the stage to try to touch him as he corkscrewed his hips.

When he eventually got offstage, compere Tony Marsh could not announce the top-of-the-bill Kalin Twins because of "We Want Cliff" chanting and stamping. Cliff had to return to calm them.

And promoter Arthur Howes told me: "This is not peculiar to Newcastle. He has gone like dynamite throughout the tour.

"I don't think there is any other artist in the field who has had the same reaction—not even Tommy Steele."

Howes is already staging Richard with the rocking Most Brothers at Sunday night concerts and is now considering sending Richard out on tour—as top of the bill.

FREE!

WHEN YOU BUY VOCALTONE REEDS

This handsome leather-grained reed wallet with streamlined heat-sealed seams is supplied FREE when you buy 6 Vocaltone reeds. Dries and keep reeds flat and dustproof. For clarinet, alto and tenor. Three baritone reeds supplied in polythene reed holder.

PRICES

Clarinet	packed 6 per wallet	-	7/6
Alto	" 6 " "	-	10/6
Tenor	" 6 " "	-	13/-
Baritone	" 3 per holder	-	7/6

Selmer

114 CHARING CROSS ROAD, W.C.2

Jack Hylton is reported ... Reed to arrange a Russian tour ...

"Oh Boy!" attacked by The Alley Cat

THIS columnist has always high praise for the "Oh Boy!" TV series. But producer Jack Good must be held responsible for permitting the most crude exhibitionism ever seen on British TV—by Cliff Richard last Saturday

His violent hip-swinging during an obvious attempt to copy Elvis Presley was revolting—hardly the kind of performance any parent could wish their children to witness.

Remember, Tommy Steele became Britain's teenage idol without resorting to this form of indecency.

If we are expected to believe Cliff Richard was acting " naturally," then consideration for medical treatment before it's too late may be advisable.

While firmly believing Cliff Richard can emerge into a top star and enjoy a lengthy musical career, it will only be accomplished by dispensing with short-sighted, vulgar tactics.

Finally, ABC-TV has a reputation to uphold and an obligation to viewers. Its first duty is an order to producer Jack Good to forbid any repeat of last Saturday's disgraceful antics.

l Express, Ltd., 5 Denmark Street, London, W.C.2, by The Walthamstow Press Ltd. ... de Agents: Horace Marshall & Son Ltd., Temple House, Tallis Street, London, E.

Is Cliff too sexy?

RICHARD HIMSELF COMMENTS AND READERS REPLY TO OUR ALLEY CAT'S CHARGE

THE cat's certainly amongst the pigeons this week! And the feline in question is none other than the NME's own house-trained Alley Cat, who bristled his whiskers and dug his claws into teenage entertainer Cliff Richard in our last issue.

"The most crude exhibitionism ever seen on British TV," was how he described Cliff's appearance on "Oh Boy!" just over a week ago. But if Cliff himself is unable to overcome the fury of our contributor's attacks, at least he can console himself by the news that readers are flocking to his support by the score.

Mind you, the Cat has a healthy contingent of supporters—though it's significant that they are all male! Alan Steele, of London, E.11, is typical of the anti-Richard brigade.

"Richard has no talent," he writes. "His performance didn't disgust me—it just bored me."

But it's Alan Moore, of Solihull, who really sets the sparks flying when he says: "The people really to blame are the teenagers, who ruin the programme for all those viewing with their screaming, and bring the show and its music into disrepute with adults."

It is only fair to say, however, that Cliff's supporters outnumber those who oppose him—the vast majority being members of the fair sex! Ten girls, comprising a "bunch of thoroughly disgusted teenagers" from South London, declare their intention of not reading the NME any more, until we stop publishing such "trash."

Several readers have theorised that the Alley Cat must be advanced in years, to be unable to appreciate Cliff's work. "Two Cliff Fans" from Watford, say that they consider him to be an artist in his own right, and do not regard him as an Elvis copyist. Another states that her parents are school-teachers and can see nothing revolting or vulgar in his act.

While the enthusiasts seethe over this Cliff Richard controversy (now whipped to fever pitch by a national newspaper, the "Daily Sketch," splashing the Alley Cat's condemnation), there has been an immediate result. ABC-TV officials have decreed that Cliff's antics should be toned down to some extent.

Producer Jack Good has written to the NME claiming that the Alley Cat has raised a lone voice in protest. "Not one of the defenceless Mums and Dads he so touchingly mentioned bothered to write to us, or even pick up the telephone receiver," states Jack. "Perhaps they were too engrossed in their weekly doses of violence and sudden death in our harmless Western serials!"

What does Cliff himself think? Well, when I met him at a party last week-end, I asked him to comment on the Cat's charges.

"Oh, I don't mind," he told me. "It doesn't worry me when someone writes his opinion. But why did he have to choose that one show as being different from any other? After all, I'm always sexy!"

DEREK JOHNSON.

Big Bopper – only one hit (tho' he wrote a lot for other people) but 'Chantilly' is what real R&R is all about. Pure joy!

BIG BOPPER

Chantilly Lace: Purple People Eater Meets Witch Doctor (Mercury AMT1002)

JAPE RICHARDSON, the American disc jockey who hides behind the Big Bopper nom-de-plume, has written both the beat novelties which he sings on this, his first disc to reach Britain.

And, it looks as if Big Bopper will reach our hit parade, too. "Chantilly Lace," with its phone-call gimmick, slides smartly along and Richardson's edgy voice takes the lyric with plenty of variety. Watch this one move. It has a good instrumental backing, too.

"Purple People Eater Meets Witch Doctor" makes use of the same kind of voices we heard on the original number R i c h a r d s o n "marries" here. Amusing and with the right sort of beat.

THE TEDDY BEARS' PICNIC

THE TEDDY BEARS

MEET The Teddy Bears—a recording trio that any royalty conscious A. and R. man would love to cuddle. For these three high school kids have turned in their own song with their own arrangement and the disc has soared to the top of the American hit parade. The title? "To Know Him Is To Love Him."

Who are The Teddy Bears? There is baby bear—she is six-teen-year-old Annette Kleinbard. Then there is the elder bear—an old man of nineteen named Marshall Leib. And finally there's middle bear, eighteen-year-old Phil Spector.

It is Mr. Spector who has the composing and arranging genius. A regular hoard of talent is this young man. Having rehearsed him-self and his companions, he went about getting an audition with an American independent label.

They hadn't even played a club date, they were as raw as uncut celery. But this was no deterrent to Phil. He arranged the date, and landed the contract.

First attempt success. Second attempt . . . . IV . . . . So I think you are going to hear a lot about these youngsters in the near future. They started at the top, and I don't think they will plummet. In fact, watch them send their London release towards the top spot in the charts.

Ralph's 'Gang' raise £1½m.

MR. Ralph Reader the other ha...

This is the second week of his Scout's "Gang Show" at the ... G... po...

I asked him for his most amusing incident.

pro...
day...
eve...
Sho...

I...
set...
hav...
for...

AN...
PO...
cut...

in...
his...
Sho...
18t...
mo...
Th...
ho...

wa...
rel...

First appearance of Phil Spector – legend says he got the song title from the epitaph on his father's grave.

WELCOME TO ANOTHER CHART NEWCOMER

Conway Twitty is a name to remember

BY DEREK JOHNSON

I'M an appellationist! Now, before the comedians come back at me with cracks like "Don't be filthy," let me explain that this is no worse than being a philatelist or an entomologist. The only difference is that I don't collect stamps or insects—I collect names!

There have been several prize specimens to add to my fast-growing collection recently. Why, only this month I have added the choice names of new recording artists Seth Acre and The Big Bopper!

But the gentleman who first fired my interest in this fascinating hobby and who, to my mind, has yet to be beaten when it comes to distinctive and slightly peculiar names is Conway Twitty.

Frankly, I just didn't believe it when I saw the name staring at me from the pages of a Mercury catalogue some months ago. So I dashed into my fellow-collector Keith Goodwin's and confronted him with it.

We both agreed that anyone inflicting a name like Conway Twitty upon the public deserved to get to the top!

Little did we realise that before the year was out our contention would become a reality. For this week, Mr. Twitty finds himself sitting at the very top of the American best-sellers with his recording of "It's Only Make Believe"—and at the same time has shot into the NME top table at 20th position, and with every prospect of rising considerably higher.

Basically a country-and-western singer, Conway is one of those artists who was practically born with a guitar in his hand. Maybe that's a slight exaggeration, but certainly he was playing it very competently at the age of four.

Within a few years, he had been invited to sing on one of the local radio stations in his home state of Mississippi, and at the ripe old age of 12 had formed his own group, known as "The Phillips County Ramblers." This proved so successful that he soon found himself starring in his own radio show.

He continued singing his country music around the mid-West districts until he was drafted into the Army.

But he didn't let his military service interrupt his career, for he formed a group known as "The Cimmerons," and entertained American GI's throughout the Far East. He even undertook his own radio programme on the Tokyo equivalent of the American Forces Network!

By the time Conway returned to his home district, television had established a stranglehold. But he had no difficulty in picking up where he left off—he simply moved over from radio to TV! However, things really started moving for him when a friend suggested that he should send some trial recordings of his work to a leading New York agency.

Speedy Signing

Not only did they sign him up right away, but literally within a matter of hours they had clinched a recording contract for their new artist. This was with the Mercury company, for whom Conway started waxing mostly country material—and, because of their fairly specialised nature, only one of his Mercury releases was issued in this country. The titles were "Shake It Up" and "Maybe Baby," and you'll find it's still available, if you care to ask for it.

Conway has now moved to the MGM concern, and—along with this move seems to have achieved a change of luck.

For his very first release on the one-time "Cinderella" label has absolutely rocketed to the top, and there's no doubt that this tall, dark and handsome 23-year-old artist is really here to stay.

They say that a book often sells by its cover. Probably artists feel

You can take the boy out of the country but you can't take the country out of the boy. Twitty went back to C&W and has had hit after hit. Today he is a country super-star. So what does he need R&R for?

the same way about their names, which is doubtless the reason why Harold Jenkins decided to adopt a name that would not easily be forgotten. Personally, I think he deserves a medal for even thinking of Conway Twitty, let alone using it. But then, as he so rightly says, "It's Only Make Believe.

EPs by Allen Evans

ELVIS SINGS CHRISTMAS SONGS

Elvis Presley, with The Jordanaires, rocks Santa Clause Is Back In Town and Santa Bring My Baby Back To Me. The much slower I'll Be Home For Christmas and Blue Christmas present the sentimental Elvis. On RCA label.

EXCITING EYDIE

Here's Eydie Gorme singing May Bygrave's You Need Hands (a forthright, tuneful version) plus Donna, Kiss In Your Eyes and Your Kisses Kill Me. And Eydie's vocalising will slay you, too. On HMV label.

HEARTACHES

Connie Francis sings her hit, Carolina Moon, alongside tenderly sung You Always Hurt The One You Love, I'm Sorry I

Made You Cry and Heartaches. Connie has just the right amount of sob-throb in her pleasant voice, and Joe Lipman's beaty background adds to a good EP. MGM label.

INK SPOTS IN HI-FI

Here are Charlie Fuqa's Ink Spots on HMV. Dramatic, sentimental songs, sung by high tenor and narrated by deep bass. Tunes are Until The Right Thing Comes Along, Maybe, To Each His Own and Into Each Life Rain Must Fall.

KICK OFF

The almost frantic jazz of Jack Parnell and his musicians is emphasised here in Kick Off, Topaz, Fuller Bounce and Knock Out. Staccato phrases, lots of drumming, fast tempo—all add to excitement on this Parlophone EP.

FLASH!!

MIKE PRESTON, flown to America for T.V. and Radio appearances to promote his Record for DECCA & LONDON Labels:

A HOUSE, A CAR & A WEDDING RING

IN THE USA CHARTS AFTER ONLY 2 WEEKS!

An ALL-BRITISH SONG!) Piano Copies available 2/-

PAN MUSIK LTD., Evelyn House, 62 Oxford St., London, W.1 MUS 0597/8

A sensation in musical world!

Illustrated is the Black Rose Model PS/72 at 43 Gns.

FREE!
Booklet illustrating in Guitars, Pickups and other fretted
JOHN E. DALL

SPOTLIGHT

On Saturday mornings there's a

Free wash and brush-up

(from their fans— but it's 'cars only')

THIS week I'm switching a whole barrage of spotlights on to Lord Rockingham's XI, those rip-roaring hit paraders who must be making those hundred pipers rock in their Scottish graves.

"It's no good doing biographies on us," said the "Hoots Mon" boys. "We lead such dull, blameless lives."

So here are eleven facts about Lord Rockingham's eleven which

ming his guitar and singing at Quaglino's Restaurant.

And Ronnie Black has plucked his double bass at the Astor Club for the past two years.

Reg Weller, percussionist and drummer, performs Greek folk dance music on his spare evenings.

"It's very strange music when you first hear it, more Eastern than Western, but it makes a change from jazz sessions and the Eleven."

He's a well-known figure at

ing around, laughing and stuffing themselves with pies."

Cyril Reuben, who plays saxophone and clarinet, says he's a fraud!

The reason? Every evening he plays in the Saville Theatre Orchestra for the musical "Expresso Bongo," which pokes fun at rock and roll, teenage singing phenomena . . . in fact, everything "Oh Boy!" stands for.

"Then I come along here and

LORD ROCKINGHAM'S XI

HARRY ROBINSON FOUND A NEW SOUND FOR 'OH BOY!'—AND IT PUT 'HOOTS MON' TO THE TOP OF THE CHARTS

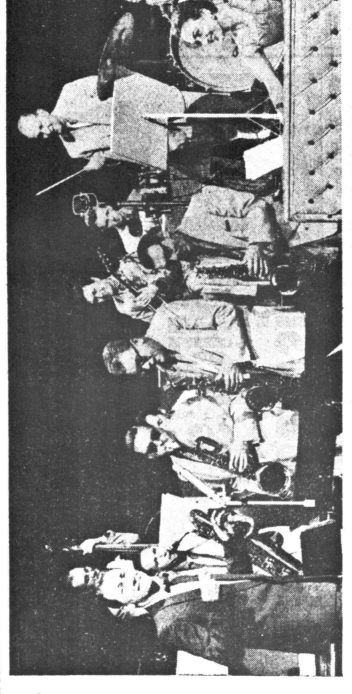

invented their special kind of music in a caravan in the middle of a muddy field last Easter.

Says Jack, "The Chimps, The Champs, The Chumps: I'd considered all those names for this new outfit specially collected together for 'Oh Boy!' But I thought the title I eventually decided on would lend tone!"

Says Harry, "Jack comes up to me with a pile of records; sheets of music and says, 'I want a new sound for this outfit; go off and find one for me.'

"I shut myself away in a caravan for a whole week-end.

"Everyone thinks the buzzing sound of the saxes in the group is something new.

"Really, it's the oldest saxophone gimmick there is, with a few of my own trade secrets thrown in.

Already the Lord Rockingham Eleven has many imitators; and you know the old saying about imitation and flattery.

But it takes more than skiffle arranging, and experienced musicians, to attain the instantaneous success the group have found.

It takes team spirit; and you couldn't find it bettered anywhere than with this friendly, enthusiastic bunch of boys.

And when they play it certainly starts rocking 'em.

Sorry!

Joan Davis

TOP TWENTY

Week ending, November 8th

Last Week	This Week	Title	Artist
5	1	Hoots Mon	Lord Rockingham's XI
1	2	Bird Dog	Everly Brothers
7	3	Come Prima / Volare	Marino Marini
4	4	Stupid Cupid / Carolina Moon	Connie Francis
2	5	A Certain Smile	Johnny Mathis
6	6	It's All In The Game	Tommy Edwards
3	7	Move It	Cliff Richard
8	8	King Creole	Elvis Presley
10	9	My True Love	Jack Scott
11	10	More Than Ever	Malcolm Vaughan
13	11	Tea For Two Cha-Cha	Tommy Dorsey
—	12	It's Only Make Believe	Conway Twitty
—	13	Love Makes The World Go Round	Perry Como
9	14	Born Too Late	Poni-Tails
14	15	Volare	Dean Martin
15	16	Poor Little Fool	Ricky Nelson
18	17	Someday	Ricky Nelson
—	18	C'mon, Let's Go	Tommy Steele
16	19	Summertime Blues	Eddie Cochrane
12	20	Western Movies	The Olympics

ONES TO WATCH

Rockin' Robin	Bobby Day
Susie Darlin'	Robin Luke

...to his Lordship's rock team at all.

The number fluctuates between nine and 13 according to the tune they are performing. Nine of the boys waxed **Hoots Mon**, but usually the whole 13 appear in the "Oh Boy!" show.

Anyway, the group's co-creators, Jack Good and Harry Robinson, admit they are not good at mathematics and cannot count beyond 10 without removing their shoes and socks!

The job the boys in the group hate most of all is car cleaning:

But those who own vehicles—and a motley collection they are, too, ranging from saloons to bubble cars and scooters—have found a crafty way to get the job done—for free.

They park them outside the stage door of the old Hackney Empire, from where the show is transmitted on Saturday mornings.

Miss Mops

While they are rehearsing, armies of teenage girl fans set to with buckets of water, dusters and handkerchiefs and scrub 'em till you could see your face in the bonnets.

Cherry Wainer found her pretty pink saloon shining like new one day last week and when she looked inside she discovered three initialled hankies from fans, lying on the seat.

Some of the boys spend all their evenings in West End night clubs.

Quite harmless, though; they are ... employees, not patrons...

...clarinet player, is writing a book. It's a specialist work on jazz called "The Reluctant Art."

What are Benny's literary qualifications? He's jazz critic of "The Observer" and spends as much time writing as he does playing. He writes disc sleeve notes and anthologies.

The youngest

Baby of the Group is Kenny Packwood.

Kenny is 17 and left school only last Christmas. He plays the guitar, and toured with Marty Wilde as one of the Wildcats.

"This is a great chance for me," he says, "playing with the Eleven. All the boys are experienced musicians and I'm learning a lot. I spend all my spare time practising to keep up."

The boys regard their Saturday afternoon sessions as relaxation.

Most of them are employed by big name bands, and meet together only for the "Oh Boy!" programmes and for recording sessions.

All agree that they have never enjoyed themselves so much before.

No one could have been more surprised than they were when **Hoots Mon** soared to the top of the hit parade. Most agree that in their opinion, their first number together, **Fried Onions**, was better and that they have an even bigger hit in one of their forthcoming discs, **Wee Tom.**

Harry Robinson, who fronts the group, told me: "On the day we recorded **Hoots Mon** we weren't even trying. The boys...

...ham's Eleven':

"Seriously though," says Cyril, "the Saville orchestra's unlike most theatre outfits. They're all topline jazz musicians."

Rex Morris, clarinet and sax, was trained to be a Rabbi.

He was born in Roumania, where his father was a Rabbi.

"I was sent to a theological college, but I was more interested in music.

"My father had been a singer and finally he agreed to let me study music."

Don Storer and Cherry Wainer, both from South Africa, are surprised at the meekness of British fans.

"Call them hysterical?" says Drummer Don. "They're lambs compared with the South African kids. Now they really are vicious.

"They'll fight each other like tigers to get to the front of a queue to see one of their favourites. I've even seen one pull a knife on another...

Saved up

Don and Cherry came to England to do concerts and U.S. Army base shows; found themselves mixed up with the Eleven.

Cherry studied to be a classical concert pianist, but when the first Hammond organ arrived in Johannesburg Cherry decided she wanted it.

It took her 12 months to save enough money to buy it.

Jack Good dreamed up the title Lord Rockingham's XI in bed...

Jack's band reaches the top (with Benny Green on sax, in shades).

Fleming . . . It's reported that rhythm, flute and Laurindo
Nat "King" Cole's pay for Almeida on guitar.

'Tom Dooley' is right on target

From REN GREVATT

NEW YORK, Wednesday.—The hottest record in America today is "Tom Dooley" by the Kingston Trio, on Capitol.

In roughly three weeks, the disc has come from nowhere to the top of the charts. And it's different too.

The three 21-year-olds who comprise the group have spent much time in Hawaii and the disc has a catchy Polynesian flavour, plus a feeling of calypso.

The group's first release was an album. In answer to pressure from disc jockeys and juke box men, the label released "Tom Dooley" as a single. It is now headed for the million mark.

Duo for Colony

CINDY and Lindy, a duo which clicked here a few months ago with "Language of Love," have been signed to appear soon at the Colony Restaurant in London. Deal is being set by the William Morris Office.

Hit-disc barrage

ONE of the heaviest barrages of hit potential discs in many months broke this week, led by such artists as Elvis Presley, the Everly Brothers, Chuck Berry and Fats Domino.

Watch Presley's "One Night" and "I Got Stung" and the Everlys' "Problems" and "Love Of My Life."

Chuck Berry has "Sweet Little Rock And Roll"—very much like his hit "Sweet Little Sixteen" while Domino's "Whole Lotta Loving" and the standard "Coquette" are his strongest in a year.

Other hot ones are the Four Preps' "Cinderella" and "Gidget" and Roger Williams's big arrangement of "The World Outside," which is Addinsell's "Warsaw Concerto" theme with lyrics.

Add to the list Marty Robbins who packs a great punch with "Ain't I The Lucky One" and "The Last Time I Saw My Heart" and Little Anthony and the Imperials with "So Much" and "Oh Yeah."

Tommy Steele

BUY YOUR RECORDS
the MODERN WAY
at NO EXTRA COST!
45 R.P.M.
7-inch · Capitol RECORDS · 45 R.P.M.
LIGHTWEIGHT · SILENT SURFACE · MICROGROOVE · RECORDINGS

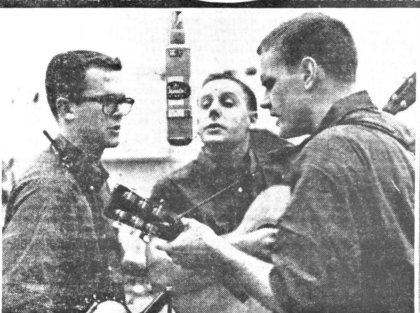

THE KINGSTON TRIO 'TOM DOOLEY'

45-CL14951 b/w 'RUBY RED'

FRANK

The sound of things to come: Folk (still in cropped-hair college state – but presaging didacticism)!

1959-62 MARKING TIME

ROCK 'n' ROLL STARTS GOING SOFT, STRAIGHT AND POP!

I was glad to see Jack Good's band, Lord Rockingham's XI at the top of the charts with 'Hoots Mon!' Firstly, the tune was from our island, showing that we too had folk roots to be re-marketed. Next, Jack had shown that he wasn't only a presenter of beat but also a creator. The XI looked splendidly sartorial as they honked and hooted in big band lines, bolstered by the organ of perky Cherry Wainer. They sounded *good*. Finally, the whole exercise was shot through with humour: 'It's a broad, bricht, moon-licht nicht!' I was beginning to think that having a laugh was an important part of the pop scene. Take it seriously and the whole thing became elephantine. I'd hate to see 'The Decline And Fall of the Roman Empire' on a 45. But on the other hand rock 'n' roll was already beginning to run out of steam and the chart was filling up again with 'industry artifacts', like 'Tea For Two Cha Cha', 'Sing Little Birdie' and classy ballads like 'A Certain Smile' and 'Come Prima'.

The problem was that R&R had originally sprung on us fully-armed and we had been instantly converted, we had been *born again*. Once a rocker, always a rocker. Hooked for life. There was no going back to Doris Day and Dickie Valentine.

The original R&R of Haley, Domino, Richard, Berry Jerry Lee and early Elvis had been meaty beat with a special appeal for active males. 'When the music starts I gotta move,' said Elvis. But gradually the twittery girls had been horning in, calling the tune, and fashioning earthy, mobile R&R into lovey-dovey couch-bound slop. Elvis had sex appeal, of course, whereas the other classic rockers only had R&R. Elvis had started the rot by looking like he did and bringing out the beast in women. But they soon changed into pussy cats as he sang them soothing love songs. And, of course, from there it was only a short step to the altar and the life of an invalid: wife and kids and settle down.

However, there was still a little rocking left. Some new heroes appeared: Lloyd Price with 'Stagger Lee',

Duane Eddy and his gutsy twang guitar, Johnny & The Hurricanes with their sax boogie instrumentals, Sandy Nelson's tribal drumming, and Eddie Cochran's classic teen call: 'C'mon Everybody'.

I admired Neil Sedaka and Bobby Darin. Their musicianship was beyond doubt – almost *too* good. Sedaka had studied piano at the famous Juilliard School of Music and Johnny Mathis was his favourite singer. No question he wrote clever songs, like 'Stupid Cupid', and was a smart cracker. Same with Bobby Darin – 'Splish Splash' was smart, clever and slight. The backing really rocked solid. Who could fault 'Mack The Knife' in terms of mainline show business technique? Darin was so right for the London Palladium. And yet . . . where was the downhome spontaneity? Where was the unexpected? Where was the danger? Where the mistakes that showed humanity? It was all so New York swank hustle. It was all so split-second routined.

I was getting to be a critic, getting to wield the long words. Too much contact with the 'A' level English set and the *Sunday Times* arts section! I concentrated on getting the school R&R band into shape: 'Zane Whitcomb's Rockets'. We had two guitars and drums and we were tolerated by the staff and applauded by certain sections of the boys, the same who'd liked the skiffle. The jazz club abhorred us, but largely ignored us because they now had internecine strife to deal with: the traditional jazz appreciators were warring with the modernists (who gravely dug Dave Brubeck and The Modern Jazz Quartet). Only the master who taught Philosophy and ground his own coffee appreciated us, from the grown-up side. 'One finds a certain farouche quality', he told me after we'd performed Cliff Richard's 'High Class Baby' in the History Room one free afternoon.

I have to admit, though, that towards the end of my last term, a beautiful English summer, I gave in to peer pressure. I was too old to be playing music for juniors. I wanted to keep my own age-group friends – and they

were reading T. S. Eliot's *The Wasteland* (with its attack on junky pop music), listening to Mahler and The Modern Jazz Quartet and generally burning with a hard gem-like flame in the Walter Pater manner. I joined the books 'n' art set and renounced rock 'n' roll, together with all childish things. I studied the set books for 'A' level and tried, in those last days of term, to be one of the team.

And when at the end we stood as one school singing 'God Be With You Till We Meet Again' I felt stabs of regret. Why hadn't I mucked in more and pulled with the crew? Joined in the scrum? Why had I let the side down by going for this outlaw noise that now was turning out to be merely the old pop pap for shopgirls? My peers were ready for the City, for the Civil Service, for advertising, for commerce – while I was ready for nothing. Gone were the dreams of becoming a rock 'n' roll star. The fire was out.

I gave my guitar and record collection to a junior. He was bewildered, but it was a symbolic gesture I had to make. Then I shook hands with the Headmaster and said farewell by the old gate.

I got a job in Harrods, in the record department. The thick pile carpets gave me foot trouble, the semi-tropical heating made me dizzy, and selling lots of silly records put me off pop for ages. 'What Do You Want?' by Adam Faith, 'Seven Little Girls Sitting In The Back Seat' by the Avons, 'Little White Bull' by Tommy Steele, 'Little Donkey' by The Beverley Sisters, 'More and More and More and More and More Party Pops' by Russ Conway, or was it Joe Henderson, or was it Winifred Atwell? Are you being served, madam? No, we have no records by Fat Swallow. She means Fats Waller. I'd rather hear Champion Jack Dupree, the black man who plays blues from the gutter. Oh here comes Princess Margaret. Will she buy 'Jingle Bell Rock' by Max Bygraves? No, she's buying 'Livin' Doll' by Cliff. I'm definitely getting into the blues . . .

In December 1962 The Beatles were in the Top Thirty with 'Love Me Do'. Frank Ifield was at the top with a twenties number called 'Lovesick Blues', but Dell Shannon, a husky bullhorn rocker was close on his heels with 'Swiss Maid'.

None of this chart action interested me because I was into *rhythm & blues*. At least, that's what we called it in Britain. R&B was 'parent rock' and some of the more astute pop paper journalists reckoned it could catch on if the fans didn't see it as just way-out jazz. We R&B lovers didn't want that. A great deal of the music's attractiveness derived from its obscurity. Rare American 45 imports were prized: Jimmy Reed, James Brown, John Lee Hooker, Muddy Waters. The word 'soul' was bandied about, as fingers clicked and pills popped and scotch and coke was ordered. American R&B was the music of the Mods, not the nub of their life but an accompaniment to their special walk – shoulders

swaying, feet turned slightly out, thumbs sticking out from pockets – which modelled their special peacock clothes. In their short box bum-freezer jackets, narrow trousers with no turn ups, winklepicker shoes and Fred Perry tennis shirts, they looked really narcisstic, really tight-assed, ice-cold. Some of them wore make-up. But few of them were queer, even though they'd started a run on the queer leisure clothes shops lying around Carnaby Street.

They despised the motor cycle leather boys and any echo of the golden age of R&R. They saw the Rockin' 50s as coarse and brutish, and were glad that the R&R flame-keepers were confined to rural Britain, mostly in the remoter parts of the West of England.

The mods were from working class backgrounds but they had no truck with cloth cappery, beer-and-

fag satisfaction, belch-and-fart-and-proud-to-know-no better' philosophy. They were a new group, cut off from lower class wallowing by the fact that they had steady jobs and money to spend at weekends. No National Service threatened their future, and their present was supported by hire purchase families: cars, TVs, washing machines, anything on the never-never, an endless vista of shining products pushed by ITV in the new age of Affluence. 'You never had it so good', said Prime Minister Macmillan, falling into the fashionable New Working Class style. The New Common-ness was to become 'trendy'. Smart cheekiness was In.

The golden age of R&R was gone because the age had been made by free personalities, wild men who belonged to no organizations. The Sixties was to be the age of organization, of pressure groups. From Civil

Rights groups to rock groups. And I hated clubs because I'd never been able to join them, whether they be schools or yacht clubs.

By the end of 1962 things looked bleak: Elvis was permanently in Hollywoodland, a good steady showbiz citizen; Bill Haley was in Mexico; Little Richard was in the church; Chuck Berry had been silenced by The Law; Jerry Lee had declared himself broke; and Buddy Holly, The Big Bopper, and Eddie Cochran were dead. Jack Good declared the whole scene to be 'stagnant'. The Establishment had taken over and tamed the original hard rock, he said. Hits were uninspired and turned out like sausages, technical standards were up alright but the noise excitement level was down. Too much unity. In July 1962 Good up and left Britain. 'I am fascinated by America as a way of life, not as a place', he wrote in *Disc*. He went off to Hollywood to see if he could orchestrate some of the musical high energy still left in America.

Meanwhile, back to early 1960. I left Harrods Record Department before their January sales, complaining of tired feet and got a job at Shepperton Studios. Nobody said a sad goodbye. I'd never fitted into their cosy group where they gave awards for sales figures. One Jimmy Yancey blues L.P sale was worth a million Anthony Newleys, to me. They never realized my parting gift till after I'd left: while the department Xmas party was in full swing I had held the fort out front and given away cartons of records to customers as Father Christmas presents.

Out of school and at sea and feeling half made-up, I clutched onto high seriousness in art. I started reading cineaste movie magazines and going to avant-garde art exhibitions, trying to quickly make up for the wasted years at school. I cultivated Oxbridge students. I stayed home on sunny Saturday afternoons and studied the blues.

First I read a lot of sleeve notes. *Blues From The Gutter*, the Champion Jack Dupree LP, had some terrific details: Jack's parents had been burned up in a fire so he'd been sent to an orphanage; a kind lady later took him in and he was brought up in the poverty and violence of 'Back o' Town' New Orleans with its pimps and chippies, its cuttings and shootings. 'Glitter and big-spending and utter degradation alternated in a dizzy, drunken whirl'. Then 'Drive 'Em Down' taught him the blues piano, but that skill wasn't enough to get him through the Depression. He became a boxer. After World War Two he made records for blues labels, singing of non-Tin Pan Alley subjects like tuberculosis, cocaine and bad blood. He'd experienced everything he sang about. He was performing his autobiography! This made Rodgers & Hammerstein seem very artificial. Now, what troubles had I had to get bluesy about? I had flat feet, was slightly overweight, and stammered when I got excited. Was this enough to make blues art? Not blues words perhaps. I turned to the piano to see what could be done instrumentally.

I copied blues piano records till I had tranced myself into a groove, pushing and chasing the main beat – anywhere but *on* the regular beat – and crushing clutches of notes, or else swiping them into anguished cries, and then victoriously raking down the piano in the Jerry Lee flourish, to a hot lick finish that left the performance quivering on the cliff edge of a dominant 7th. Then the neighbours upstairs would politely bang on the floor. So I read some more sleeve notes – maybe about how Pinetop Smith, creator of the original boogie-woogie record, got shot to death in some late-twenties bar brawl.

I spent summer at the seaside again. Alison was developing amply and looked good in shorts. I spent long afternoons on the beach gazing into her green eyes, which compared well with the North Sea, neglecting my copy of *The Country Blues* by Sam Charters, cocking half an ear to her transister radio. The inanities of 'Itsy Witsy Teeny Weeny Yellow Polka Dot Bikini' were offset by the mini-operas of Roy Orbison. When she had a tennis or ping pong match I used to sit and pretend to watch but actually I was leafing through her pop papers. I no longer bought them myself. I was disgusted by the new decade. 'Be A Rebel' said a Billy Fury article, but then: 'Mind you, when I say "rebel" I'm not talking about slovenly dressed beatniks who think that long beards, exhibitionism, walking barefoot and just plain defiance and vulgarity, is all that's needed to be "different".' Art was all about being Different. Here was Pat Boone again doling out advice: 'I'm not prudish, but I would never do anything in front of teenagers which their parents couldn't watch'. As to rock 'n' roll, Bobby Rydell had this to say: 'No one can deny the lure of the swinging type of music. But if you ask me my ambition, careerwise, that's easy – I want to grow up to be an all-round entertainer . . . like Sinatra'. Ugh! Spotted around these articles were ads for 'French girdlettes', anti-itch 'cremes', cuticle removers, glamour wigs, bosom developers . . .

I read, though, with interest about The Alberts and The Temperance Seven. Their music seemed to be infused with humour which left the blues alone. They had fun with the past, destroying any lingering ideas we might have about Britain as an Empire. They wore funny Edwardian clothes. The Alberts had an amplified penny farthing and performed hot solos on revolver. The Temperance Seven included the 'Winner of the Prix D'Honneur at the Bournemouth Centenary Celebrations of 1910 for Original Rendition of Kaiser Rag', plus a member of 'The British Matchbox Label & Booklet Society'. In actuality most of these comic bandsmen came from art schools and were now working by day in such jobs as graphic and ceramic design. I could sympathise with them and their musical fun. Not to be taken seriously of course.

Later that year, to keep my sanity, I too formed a satirical period band called 'The Ragtime Suwanee Six'. Meanwhile the British Film Industry was rapidly getting fed up with my talk about Pudovkin and montage, and my utter incompetence at making tea and coffee. We agreed to part after we'd completed the shooting of a Norman Wisdom comedy. I decided to plunge into education. I knew that I hadn't the credentials for Oxford or Cambridge, so where to study? Luckily I ran across a brochure for Trinity College, Dublin:

'Living in rooms in Trinity College is a unique and complex experience. Round college fires, over supper, world problems, politics, religion and sex are discussed far into the night, while Beethoven or Brubeck tries to make himself heard.'

In October, 1961, I reported to T.C.D. as a Junior Freshman studying History Honors.

I soon located the college syncopation people. Most were professional students, many of them having been at Trinity for years doing a vague course called 'General Studies'. They formed what they called a Jazz Band but really it was a musical unit of variable quantity (sometimes we were augmented by zither and/or celtic lament pipes and variable quality (numbers ranging from 'The Saints' to 'Who Threw The Overalls In Mrs Murphy's Chowder?'). Their pianist having just been called home

to take part in putting down a revolution in his father's central African state, I was welcomed in his place. They agreed to put more blues into their repertoire. My first gig with the band was at the annual 'Carnival of Nations' revue, a show that Trinity was well suited for. We were to follow the West Indies exhibition of Limbo dancing. Our trombonist leader was standing rather near an open mike during the West Indian act and a startled audience heard him explain that 'The limbo originated when a spade spotted a jewboy trying to get under the door of a gent's toilet cubicle without paying, see?' Then just as we were being announced as Great Britain's entry the clarinet player asked the trombone leader, 'What key, dad?' and was told 'Z sharp'. As the curtain rose on this Carnival of Nations act the audience was presented with a fierce and bloody punch-up. But this was all accepted as part of the show.

My college life rapidly developed into a stimulating round which, as far as I was concerned, could go on for the rest of my life. Fear of academics was successfully smashed and high seriousness in art was swamped by a sea of stout, and small talk.

JOURNAL (October 1962)

Back in safe old Ireland after a hectic week in London! Caught the electrifying Alexis Korner R&B band at the Ealing Club. Loudest band I ever heard and completely true to roots. More Muddy Waters than James Brown. Still, why analyse? Sound kicks you right in the guts, which is more than the Shads do with their dainty rock. Glad to say I haven't bought a pop paper for a year, so blissfully unaware of who's in Top Ten.

Wearing U.S. army jacket under college gown today. Got whole wardrobe of military gear at surplus store in vacation. Boring lecture on place of King's signet ring in development of constitutional G.B history. Lecturer's only claim to fame is history of college baths, privately published. Next lecture more interesting as it was conducted up and down Dame St. – Irish history. Dr McBride kept stopping in mid-sentence to examine contents of street litter bins. Shouted 'Eureka!' on fishing up a crisp new copy of today's *Daily Telegraph*. Class ended up in Davy Byrne's bar discussing Irish rising of 1916, with Dr McBride treating.

Dashed round to The Bailey for drinks and discussion with New Theatre Action group. Left-wing Roger Question, senior freshman, wants me to provide 'nasty boogie-woogie' for their projected revue. Over black velvets (champers and Guinness)

he informed me that his revue would 'destroy civilization and the Establishment'. I'm constantly being asked by college activists to play R&B for their ban-the-bomb, ban-South-African-fruit, no-popery marches and wine and cheese parties. Why does R&B have to be linked with Causes? Still, a gig's a gig and we need the practice. First big appearance next month at annual college Jazz Band Ball. I've changed my name to Warren Whitcomb for the occasion: Warren Whitcomb's Bluesmen. Growing a beard too.

In the evening our R&B band gave a demonstration for the college folk society. We're accepted because we're not yet electric. Can't afford it. Singer before us sang about 'Blowin' In The Wind' and his introduction – a talk on the composer Bob Dylan Thomas – took longer than the actual song. Derek, the horn player in our band, made up a parody which went something like: 'How many beans in a full tin of Heinz? The answer, my friend is (fart) blowin' in the wind'. I thought it was quite funny. Small turn-out at Folk meeting. This was due, I'm told, to rock concert in Exam Hall by local Dublin group, The Green Beats. They're electrified. Must get some amps and Fenders, etc. Almost bought copy of *New Musical Express* on way back to digs, but bought Mars bar instead. Goodnight.

Daily Mirror

WED FEB 4 1959

2½ FORWARD WITH THE PEOPLE · No. 17,150

Tragedy of 'Jape' Richardson

THEY CALLED HIM—
BIG BOPPER

TOP 'ROCK' STARS DIE IN CRASH

From BARRIE HARDING, New York, Tuesday

THREE of America's top rock 'n' roll stars were killed in a plane crash today, a few hours after delighting teenagers at a "big beat" concert.

They were BUDDY HOLLY, whose recording of "That'll Be The Day" sold more than a million and a half copies; BIG BOPPER (Jape Richardson), singer of the current hit "Chantilly Lace"; and RITCHIE VALENS, composer of the Tommy Steele favourite "Come On, Let's Go."

All three appeared last night at a winter ball for teenagers at Lake North, Iowa.

Early this morning, they boarded a small charter plane in Mason City to fly to Fargo, North Dakota, where they were billed to appear tonight.

The plane took off in a slight snowstorm — and nothing more was heard of it.

Hours later the pilot of a search plane spotted wreckage on a farm about ten miles from Mason City.

The bodies of the three stars and the pilot, Roger Peterson, lay near by.

Bad weather is blamed for the crash.

On TV Here

BUDDY HOLLY, 22, was married only seven months ago.

He was the star of the trio called "The Crickets" and shot to the top of the hit parade with records like "That'll Be The Day" and "Peggy Sue."

Buddy visited Britain last March and was seen by millions of viewers in a "Sunday Night at the London Palladium" show.

His latest record . . . called "It Doesn't Matter Any More" . . . has just been released.

BIG BOPPER was a disc jockey, and had appeared in minstrel shows where he created the "Big Bopper" character.

And that was the name he adopted for his first record—"Chantilly Lace" —which he also composed.

He was seen singing it on film, on British TV recently.

Last week, "Chantilly Lace" was No. 12 in the Mirror's Pop Twenty.

Richardson, 24, was unmarried.

RITCHIE VALENS gave his age as twenty-one.

But the Hollywood company dealing with his records said tonight that in fact he was only seventeen.

He left school only last year.

Buddy Holly . . . as Britain saw him.

7 days FREE Viewing

D.E.R. 21st ANNIVERSARY OFFER

D.E.R. ...

. . . only 7'6 a week

POST NOW — D·E·R

600,000 JOBLESS ?

By ROLAND HURMAN
Mirror Industrial Editor

TOP trade union leaders are convinced that the total number of unemployed people in Britain is now more than 600,000. Some of them fear that the figure may be as high as 620,000.

Official unemployment figures are due to be published next week by the Ministry of Labour.

The last census of unemployed was taken on January 12 and the job of consolidating the returns from all the employment exchanges has taken longer than usual.

THE NEW FIGURES ARE EXPECTED TO SHOW THE MOST ALARMING INCREASE OF JOBLESS OVER A ONE-MONTH PERIOD FOR MANY YEARS.

In December the total was 532,000.

Mr. Iain Macleod, Minister of Labour, has already revealed in Parliamentary answers steep rises of unemployment in certain areas in Scotland and the North.

If the new total has reached 620,000 it would be roughly 2.8 per cent. of the working population the proportion forecast by Mr. Macleod in the Commons last November as a peak figure for Britain's recession.

SLIM DUSTY HITCHED HIS FUTURE TO A GUITAR

THE name Slim Dusty is known to British fans only through the medium of that plaintive, catching lament "A Pub With No Beer." But if you should go to his native Australia thinking he is just a promising newcomer you would probably be considered as square as a sugar cube!

Down-under, Slim is just about the hottest thing in show business at the moment. He has a fan following there comparable in intensity to that of Elvis Presley! He is Australia's Lonnie Donegan.

The population of Australia is small and scattered about that vast country, making development of the pop music scene difficult, but not impossible, thanks to artists like Slim Dusty, who is somewhat responsible for its progress these days.

Out there, a Gold Disc is awarded when an artist sells a quarter of a million records, quite a feat when you consider the small market. Slim Dusty was the first Australian artist to earn this honour.

The reason for Slim's great achievement is not difficult to see. He thoroughly enjoys singing and his personal pleasure is infectious. In his own words, "You see, I'm one of those fellers who would rather sing than eat.

"Though my friends told me I'd be kind of crazy to hitch my future to a guitar, well, I guess I just had to do it, that's all."

Born in Kempsey, New South Wales, in June, 1927, Slim moved with his family into the country when he was still very young. But even when he was going to school he was too keen on music to pay much attention to lessons.

First song

He got the habit of putting what he had done during the day into rhyme, calypso-style, and on this principle wrote his first song at the ripe old age of eleven.

Slim says: "I guess it was no epic, that first song of mine. But I sure liked singing it." When he left school Slim saved up hard and bought himself a guitar for thirty shillings.

But let Slim tell you himself: "It wasn't much of an instrument, but I soon got the hang of playing it and after a while I began singing and playing at dances and parties.

"Folks thought I was fine, so I got to planning on how to get myself a job in town so I could earn some real money."

Slim eventually talked the broad-

casting company in Kempsey into giving him a chance. His hillbilly style caught on immediately, but after a few months the wanderlust bug began to bite and he became a roaming singer, also doing some composing.

At times he was reduced to busking in the streets, but mostly he earned a living with travelling shows in cinemas and at country radio stations.

In 1945 his father's wish, just be-fore he died, was that Slim would keep on singing. Slim promised.

Despite Slim's great prowess as a songwriter, he was not the composer of "A Pub With No Beer"; it was written by his great friend, Gordon Parsons. Nevertheless, Slim has penned "The Answer To A Pub With No Beer," which is due for release here some time next month. It should be just his cup of tea!

DAVID SAMPSON.

NEW "Tuxedo"

american style SLIM ELECTRIC GUITAR
• SOLID BODY
• SPEED ACTION for EASY FINGERING of MODERN CHORDS

as featured by GARR MILLS on A.T.V "Sunday Break"

Tuxedo

High sensitivity pickup. Tone an volume controls. New-style pre sure bar tailpiece. Black pick guar Short 23¼ in. scale for easy fingeri of modern chords.

17½ Gns.   H.P. TERM AVAILAB

The original solid body with t speedster action. Insist "Tuxedo" the ONLY guitar wi the features for the new style. G in the spotlight with the dazz white finish against your bla "tuxedo."

"TUXEDO" on a P.C. brings you the ge

Dallas

DALLAS BLDG., CLIFTON ST., LONDON, E.C

The newest releases from the Film Star label

and top America

Capitol

The one show you cannot miss!

Included in next Tuesday's Show, March 24th

GENE VINCENT

with a new record you musn't miss

'OVER THE RAINBOW'

45-CL15000

BY SPECIAL REQUEST!   A new voice with a great new version

Not R&R but I liked it – a tune reminiscent of 'Beautiful Dreamer' – by the way, 'Dreamer' lent a key bar or two to Pat Boone's 'I'll Be Home.'

Vincent goes the Broadway/Hollywood route – and is angry when old fans barrack him as he tries to sing smooth on stage.

EDDIE COCHRAN ROCKS INTO TOP 20!

VERY few people in this country outside the record-buying fraternity have ever heard of Eddie Cochran. Yet in the disc industry he has created a tremendous impact on both sides of the Atlantic. He is undoubtedly one of the names who should be noted for future international success on a large scale.

It has long been claimed, not without reason, that America is more rock-conscious than Britain. Yet, so far as young Mr. Cochran is concerned, he not only did almost as well in Britain as in the States with his first major hit. "Summertime Blues," but is now forging ahead with his follow-up release in Britain to an extent far in excess of that in America.

Last week, Eddie's recording of "C'mon Everybody" entered the NME list entries list in 20th position (this week it is in 15th place), an outstanding achievement by a young man who is virtually unknown here.

Eddie's only important showcase in Britain was in the Jayne Mansfield film, "The Girl Can't Help It", in which he performed a number called "Twenty Flight Rock" to good effect. The only trouble was that there were so many guest appearances in this movie that Eddie's solitary song tended to "get lost!"

He has subsequently appeared in a film called "Untamed Youths", which starred Mamie Van Doren, and has now just completed a picture which gives him his biggest part to date. It's called "Bop Grill" and is expected to open here shortly.

Will Eddie Cochran · last? Well, first and foremost, it is this writer's opinion that, based upon the standard and appeal of his waxings to date, Eddie is no overnight sensation.

I think he's here to stay. He's already proved that he's no one-disc wonder.

His recording career began purely out of his own initiative. Out in

California he met up with up-and-coming artist by the name of Jerry Capehart, who was sufficiently impressed with the youngster to recommend that he should try for a disc contract.

Jerry had been recording for the Liberty company, and he suggested that Eddie should go along and see his bosses, Si Waronker and Jack Ames. Being an ambitious artist, Eddie took the advice, and presented himself at the Liberty offices.

Hit potential

Liberty is a go-ahead concern, and they are always prepared to listen to prospective talent; they made no exception in Eddie's case. Within a matter of minutes of the audition commencing, the two executives were quick to realise that here was hit potential indeed. They signed Eddie

to the dotted line as a Liberty recording artist.

He was rushed into the recording studio to cut his first sides for commercial release. Before long his waxing of "Sittin' In The Balcony" was on sale. It proved no world-shatterer by any means, although it was a moderate hit in America.

However the follow-up release boosted Eddie to world-wide acclaim. Eddie's version of "Summertime Blues" rose to No. 13 slot in the "Billboard" charts in America, while over here he climbed to 18th position.

Now, with his latest "C'mon Everybody" issue, we in this country have taken the lead and pushed Eddie into the top twenty before his own fans at home.

Eddie is only twenty years old and hails from the State of Oklahoma. He is one of a family of five children and, rather surprisingly, is the only member of the family to show any leaning towards the world of entertainment.

In demand

He began by performing at local functions around Oklahoma City and then, much to the benefit of Eddie's career, the family moved to California. He soon found himself in demand at dances and social functions, and it was at one such event that he met Jerry Capehart—and the chain of circumstances leading up to Eddie's recording contract was launched.

He has subsequently appeared at some of the nation's most important cabaret spots, and is currently engaged upon a lengthy personal appearance tour.

A thoroughly competent singer and guitarist, Eddie has more than proved his entitlement to recording success.

If he maintains the consistency which he has shown from the outset, it is more than likely that some enterprising impresario will bring him across the Atlantic to Britain in the near future.   DEREK JOHNSON.

HENTOFF'S COLUMN FROM AMERICA

WHAT'S HAPPENING IN THE BATTLE FOR THE BEAT?

TAKE A LOOK AT THE TOP TEN.

Done it? Notice anything odd? No? Aa-haaa! Neither does anyone else. And that is the whole trouble.

There is scarcely the smell of a rock number there, and it has been like that for weeks. Now, I would not mind that so much, but what gives me the willies is that nobody cares. The only rock these pages ever contain nowadays is of the eel variety together with six of chips.

Apathy has crept in, folks. A few months ago, a startling absence of the old rock 'n' roll would have been greeted by an uproar of yells and jeers from the grey-haired, wrinkled, embittered old rectangles in their gloomy Fleet Street offices. But to-day —never a word.

Maybe they have cried "Wolf" so often that they dare not risk declaring yet again that rock is dead.

But I fear that worse conclusions are to be drawn.

Can it be that rock is now actually —ACCEPTED?

The thought sends a burning dart quivering through my heart. The moment there is no longer a fight about the big beat, then we can expect a steady decline in its power. If rock is now accepted, then it has lost its news value, and very soon it will lose its interest and excitement.

Why, things have come to such a pretty pass these days, that my Mum knows more about the top ten than I do. What with "Side Saddle," "Petite Fleur," "Little Drummer Boy," and that pre-war Boy Scout ditty about chewing gum, it is clear that the record industry must be severely reprimanded for catering exclusively to one age group.

It is all very well cashing in on the immature fads and fancies of the middle-aged, but doesn't the industry realise that there is a large potential buyers market among the teenagers?

Come on, kids, keep the battle for the beat going strongly. Do not be content just to leave it up to Teddy Johnson and Pearl Carr to keep the flag flying!

● *The week before last, we managed to keep the screaming on "Oh Boy!" down to an absolute minimum. I am not sure whether it was better that way, or whether the screams—however irritating in themselves—create the atmosphere. What do you think?*

Cliff has a new one

DO you remember that when Cliff's last record, "Livin' Lovin' Doll" was released, that I thought it was a pity that the best side that he had made since "Move It." had been shelved—a number by Ian Samwell called "Mean Streak."

Well, it is to be released in a couple of weeks time, together with a brand new rocker called "Chopping And Changing."

I have not yet heard the recording of this last one, but I have heard Cliff and The Drifters perf——

Top value from Presley

I HAVE just heard the other side of the new Presley, to be released around mid-April. "I Need Your Love Tonight" is the up-tempo side—taken at "I Got Stung" speed, but with a better tune.

It has the same bass voice gimmick as "I Got Stung" and, in general, the same sound. In fact, I should not be at all surprised to hear that this record and "One Night/I Got Stung" were made at the same session.

Presley is really fantastically consistent with his records. They are always top value, and this one is no exception.

Both sides are beautifully performed and both sides have a melody worthy of the performance.

I expect the sales will follow the same pattern as the last one. The faster side will make the more immediate impact, but the slower number will pull up alongside slowly but surely, and eventually overtake.

'Men don't make passes...'—oh yeah!

DO *you think of the majority of "Oh Boy!" viewers as teenage girls? Most people seem to. Well, if you do, you are sadly mistaken. A recent survey reported that the show's viewers were predominantly male—and well over the teenage.*

This could explain why the girl with the glasses, Margaret Stredder, gets more fan mail than anyone else in the team. Many of the letters are addressed: "The Blonde with Glasses."

I'll tell you now that Margaret's hair is blue-grey. Barbara, who stands on the left of the trio is blonde, and Jean on the right is auburn.

The Vernons Girls are the hardest worked of all the "Oh Boy!" team. You see, they have two TV series to rehearse and perform—"Oh Boy!" and Brian Tesler's "New Look." Both programmes involve memorising dance routines and harmonies—although the styles of each show are totally unlike. This seems to present no problem to the girls, who move from one to the other with complete ease.

Large credit for this must be attributed to the brilliant work of Leslie Cooper, the dance director, who took over the group when they were completely untrained and effected a transformation comparable with turning a pumpkin into a golden coach.

On the vocal side, it was Peter Knight who made a choir out of a group of girls who, for the most part, had no training as singers. And now his work is being ......

out of
...vation
... "But
...d he's

...oltrane
...Europe
...because
... for a
...d that
...m."

...o-Ameri-
...al Hall
...previous
...ening to
...eport on
...ISC.

Vince
...e Woody
...with him
...migrant,
Victor

...bum last
... Koenig
...atin jazz
... Conte
... and a
... Walter
...cotty La
...re were
...mmers.
...get over

...stay of
...intet for

Carmen
...ugh her
...t of her
...go Club

...s in her
...that she
...r feeling

Her stage
y relaxed
ISC Pic)

...ldliness than
...who has yet
...rtainly more
...d less coyly

...ballads with
...rred her at

Buddy Holly died three months ago. Is he . . .

THE NEW JAMES DEAN?

by Bill Halden

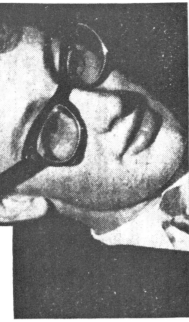
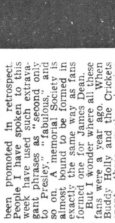

THREE months ago, disc star Buddy Holly was killed when his hired plane crashed in a fog near Mason City, Iowa.

Now, Britain's mourning disc fans look like building up the 22-year-old Texas singer in exactly the same way as they did Hollywood film star James Dean, nearly four years ago.

This week. Holly's last recording, ironically titled "It Doesn't Matter Any More," is dominating the MM's Top Twenty.

than a normal issue of this kind. And the same goes for the 'Buddy Holly Story.''

Melody

Says Tony Hall, Coral label manager: "Holly was the first artist to bring back melody to rock-n'-roll. He was an extremely good performer and was a prolific songwriter—he didn't just write 12-bars all the time."

Already Buddy Holly has

been promoted in retrospect. People I have spoken to this week have used such extravagant phrases as "second only to Presley," "fabulous," and so on. A memorial Society is almost bound to be formed in exactly the same way as fans formed one for James Dean.

But I wonder where all these fans were a year ago. When Buddy Holly and the Crickets spent three weeks touring Britain, most box-offices were a long way from breaking any records.

Fan mail

Far more startling is the fac. . .at an LP of his hit recor. . . "The Buddy Holly
St. . .s No. 5 in the MM's
Top . . LPs. And the record
was . . .eased only two days be-
for. . .e returns were made.
M. . .arriving at Decca's
of. . . office which markets
Hi. . . record in Britain, has
tro. . . since he was killed.
Fa. . .ave written wanting to
kn. . . very conceivable detail
ab. . . him.
B. . . Decca are naturally re-
tic. . . about any suggestion of
ca. . .g in on his death.

New sound

Sa. . .Michael Littman, public. . .as spokesman for Decca:
"T. . .as to be remembered that
'It . . .esn't Matter Any More'
is . . .very good record, that it
ha. . .something of a new sound
—. . .s a first-class orchestral
ba. . .ng and that Buddy
Hol. . .was always a firm favour-
te. . . Britain.
. . . e record has not re-
ce. . . any more exploitation
thrown. . .

The lesson of Esson

THE E. . .
held. . .
al. . .
had al. . .
merits—o. . .
faults—o. . .
nental s. . .
Both. . .
long—fo. . .
too muc. . .
studded. . .
And th. . .
way of c. . .
example, . . .
there we. . .
piano th. . .
Oscar P. . .
Levy Tri. . .
Trio.
The S. . .
two gues. . .
can tr. . .
Williams. . .
Dutch S. . .
Buck Cla. . .
band.
On the. . .
a feast. . .
thrown. . .

The legend starts. Did the fatal plane crash aid it? Of course. The winning combo of Rock and Death begins.

The Coasters were one of the groups that formed part of the Leiber and Stoller theatre group. They acted out the song stories concocted by these super-sharp neo-Alleymen from New York's song factory, the Brill Building. Really, the first conscious R&R song writers. Later they got under the influence of Brecht and Weill; and Art smothered them. That's progress – the ogress.

n—now off—has boosted ...

THE COASTERS' 'CHARLIE BROWN'

By DEREK JOHNSON

THE BBC banned "Charlie Brown" and, two weeks later, bemused by their own red-tape restrictions, they removed it from the banned list.

This remarkable about-face by the people who control your radio listening has probably done more to whip up interest in the record than any amount of playings on the air.

You'll know "Charlie Brown" in two different guises, of course. Initially, he is the much-misunderstood, round-headed hero of the "Peanuts" strip cartoon which appears on the back page of the "Daily Sketch," and is syndicated throughout America in hundreds of newspapers.

Popular

Because he is so popular with cartoon enthusiasts everywhere, a novelty song was written about this amusing character, who is always wondering "why is everybody always picking on me?". With this background, it was not really surprising that the song should jump into prominence — especially as recorded by such a hit-making vocal group as The Coasters.

Unfortunately, the powers-that-be at the BBC decided that it was unfit for human ears, because the lyric contained a disgustingly delinquent word in "spitball" (which is American slang for "peashooter," though

we can't really blame anyone for not knowing that).

Ray Ellington's recording similarly suffered, but Bernard Bresslaw was very wise in that he substituted a slightly different lyric, thereby enabling him to overcome the ban.

But evidently publicity due to the widespread publicity the ban received, including our readers' letters—the BBC had second thoughts.

For they have now relented, and now listeners can pick on "Charlie Brown" to their hearts' content!

It was particularly appropriate that The Coasters should have been asked to record this number, for America is currently enjoying a tremendous boom in vocal groups—and these four boys seem to specialise in novelty renditions.

"Charlie Brown" certainly comes into this category, as does their smash international hit before it—"Yakety Yak," for which they won a Gold Disc.

The Coasters are currently one of the most popular acts in the States —they've recently been playing some of the largest theatres in New York, Chicago, Philadelphia and Washington; have undertaken an extensive tour on the major night-club circuit; and are in great demand for guest appearances on important TV shows.

The reason why the promoters are continually seeking their services, quite apart from the popularity of their material, is that they have built up a really slick, polished act. They indulge in all manner of amusing antics in their comedy routines, whilst on the more fiery beat numbers, their rhythmic movements are much akin to Presley in quadruplicate!

Indeed, one American journalist recently described them as "specialists in hip choreography."

No wonder, then, that they reached the top in America—land of singing contortionists. And The Coasters themselves must be specially pleased that they have achieved such widespread recognition in this country, where the fans have only their recordings as evidence of their worth.

Zoomed up

The boys originally zoomed into the limelight through the medium of their big Stateside hit, "Searchin'," on the Atco label—which has its British outlet under the London banner. The four young men in question are Carl Gardner, Billy Guy, Bobby Nunn and Leon Hughes, though there is a fifth member of

the entourage in the person of Adolph Jacobs, their regular guitar accompanist.

There are two other names who must be mentioned, for they are closely associated with The Coasters, and have played a large part in their success story. They are, one of America's strongest rhythm-and-blues songwriting teams, Jerry Leiber and Mike Stoller.

You will doubtless remember them for such titles as "Hound Dog", and "Young Blood".

Compliment

They are now devoting by far the greater part of their efforts to The Coasters, and have been responsible for much of the boys' material, including the infectious "Yakety Yak" and their smash-of-the-day, "Charlie Brown."

It looks as though beat music is going to be around just as long as there's a Tin Pan Alley, and there's certainly never any lack of demand for novelty numbers. So when a talented team can combine the two as effectively as The Coasters, they can't go wrong.

Seems to me these boys have found the ideal formula for giving the youngsters what they want. With "Charlie Brown" at No. 8 this week, they're sitting pretty. But after hearing so much about their visual attributes, let's hope we get an opportunity of seeing them at work in this country before long.

CHRIS BARBER

E SOU.RAB..
..5, Melody
..mboree 3.15
..quest Shows
..h World Of
..how.

.05 Outpost
..Jamboree
.6.05 Music
.8.30 City
.11.05 Late

1.45 Guest
In Music:
..sic Views
..sic In The
..Night; 8.05
.9.05 Band
..ng On Two

8.30 Meet
..o Time; 9
Melachrino:
liff Richard:
.o The Bible:
.n.

Thursday's
.8.30 Ray
.This Week's
.es Old and
.10.45 Italy
..val Hour.

HE IS AMERICA'S TOP TV DISC JOCKEY

Dick Clark—a fortune being shy!

DICK CLARK is one of the busiest young men in America today. It's all because he has a clean-cut, youthful, almost shy way about him that comes across the TV screens of America like a load of dynamite.

In approximately 18 months, Clark has risen from the relative obscurity of a local radio show in Philadelphia to the status of a by-word in most American homes where teenagers live.

There have been and there are other successful TV disc jockeys catering to the teenage, pop-music audience. In fact, there are more and more of them cropping up on a local basis all over America.

Many have a way of patterning themselves after Clark. A number of them essay the deliberately casual air that has become a Clark trademark.

But despite the number of competitors, Clark's number one rating goes unchallenged. And despite recognition by record companies that other disc jockeys are important in getting records exposed to the public, the Dick Clark "American Bandstand" show —every afternoon, five days a week, on ABC-TV — is the number one exposure medium for artists with a new record.

FORMULA

What's the formula of success? Perhaps in a day when popular music is largely associated with rock-'n'-roll, which in turn has been maligned as evil and incendiary by many adult observers, Clark's unusually clean-cut appearance—just like the boy next door—has resulted in an acceptance of the music by adults as "not so bad, after all."

For despite the often tough and unschooled appearance of some of the artists who appear on the show, Clark's winning appeal is the saving grace.

REN GREVATT
reports from New York

Another facet of the winning formula is Clark's belief that pop music today hinges on a danceable beat.

"If a record isn't danceable it has a tough time," Clark told me recently. "The new dances are tied in closely with hit records. We've started the chalypso, the circle dance and the walk on our show. The kids love the dancing."

Clark's show actually takes the form of an on-the-air record hop. With each record played, the camera focuses on the dancing teenagers, roving throughout the room.

Guest acts merely mouth or mime the lyrics to their hit discs as the records themselves are played. No live musicians are employed.

Last year, as a result of the success of his daily afternoon show, Clark undertook a weekly Saturday night show. This, too, has been a tremendous winner.

Here again, guest stars are featured with their hit records. The only variance is the lack of the dancing couples.

• Dick Clark and the dancers in his show.

Instead, there is a seated studio audience and the camera frequently roves among the faces of the guests in the studio.

These disc jockey shows have led to even bigger things. Clark is now in the process of building a production dynasty, covering live and filmed TV and motion pictures.

With his outspoken stand in favour of teenagers, his continued activity in record hops, where he talks to hundreds of teenagers about their likes and dislikes, and his approach of "giving them what they want" on his record shows, the likeable, 29-year-old Philadelphian figures to stay number one in the hearts of the American teenage public for quite a spell.

• Julie—she even made the tea!

Mistake gives Julie big TV break!

EVEN in these tough times, romantic rises to television fame do occur. Take, for example, Julie Stevens, the pretty 22-year-old who introduces ABC's "Sunday Break."

Her own "break" came as the result of a mistake. Julie was a hospital nurse when she called at the Manchester musical instrument store operated by NDO saxist Johnny Roadhouse, to make a private recording of her voice.

Johnny was impressed and persuaded her to take singing lessons. He was also impressed by her natural personality and showmanship, and again persuaded her to apply for a spot in ABC-TV's "Bid for Fame."

Then by chance he bumped

By JERRY

Dallas ... RECORD LOW PRICE

They tried to get Dick Clark on a payola charge – but all he'd done was to reflect the teen mood and put a spotlight on talent. Of course, you had to get to Philadelphia first. No good being a mute, inglorious, Milton – ending up in a country graveyard, without even an elegy.

STEELE
REAL NAME: Tommy Hicks

WILDE
Reginald Smith

DENE
Terence Williams

EAGER
Roy Taylor

POWER
Ray Howard

The man behind Britain's Big Beat

HOW many artists do you handle?

Apart from Tommy Steele and Marty Wilde, I have Terry Dene, Vince Eager, Billy Fury, Johnny Gentle, Dickie Pride, Duffy Power and Sally Kelly.

WHERE do you find these teenage stars?

I like to go out and look for them. I find them, usually by sheer luck, in coffee bars, pubs, amateur contests or just in the streets.

WHAT do you look for?

Firstly personality and secondly what I call "inner talent."

WHAT is "inner talent"?

If I see a boy bubbling with vigour and vitality. I turn him down. I prefer an inner talent that I can bring out in stages.

Grooming

HOW do you turn such raw material into a working act?

They go through a very extensive grooming. It is sometimes five months before they appear on a stage or three months before I let them do any recording.

To start with, they have

Larry Parnes is the man who has combined Big Business with the Big Beat. With John Kennedy he was the discoverer and publicist of Tommy Steele and today he runs a stable of teenage rock stars. Looking rather like one of his own entertainers in a vividly striped shirt, the Beat Svengali this week took time off to answer the following questions:

physical grooming. I have their hair cut—that is very important. Sometimes they may have bad skin which has to be attended to. Then I get them suitable clothes and provide them with comfort.

COMFORT?

I like them to have a touch of luxury from the start so that if they make the big time they don't lose their heads. I like them to live in a good home, get three good meals a day, get to bed early and have plenty of fresh air.

DO you still have your artists living at your home?

No. I feel rather lonely at the moment as none of them are with me.

Marty has always lived at home and Vince Eager now has a place of his own. Billy is living at Dickie's house, where there is a nice garden—he likes to keep pets. Duffy lives with

his parents and Johnny is staying with a friend who originally came down from Liverpool with him.

I like them all to know they have their freedom and responsibilities.

Radio

HAVE you had any failures?

All the boys I have selected are still with me. Whether they will all have success in the future, I don't know.

IS it possible to build a new star without a hit record?

Yes, definitely. Vince Eager is a good example.

HOW important is TV to a new artist?

TV is very important, but one can't rely on it. Radio is really more important now. If one took a census, you would find that teenagers listen to the radio far more than they watch TV.

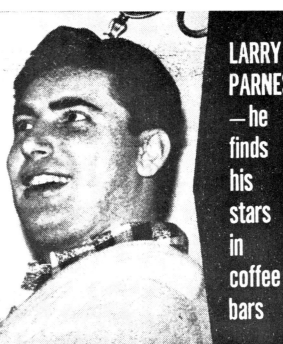

LARRY PARNES —he finds his stars in coffee bars

Mathis is top star

HOLLYWOOD, Wednesday

Jack Scott

TOP RANK RECORDS

NEW RELEASES

CRAIG with a new odds-on favourite for the Number One Spot

CRAIG DOUGLAS
Wish it Were Me
coupled with
The Riddle of Love
45 - JAR 204

A new hit from the American group that hit the jackpot with "Come Softly to Me"

THE FLEETWOODS
Mr. Blue
coupled with
You Mean Everything to Me
45 - JAR 202

A new name—but a great beat disc. Grab it, it's a Top Rank TIP!

DEE CLARK
Hey Little Girl

HAS POP MUSIC GONE ALL RESPECTABLE?

Just over a year ago the top tunes were all wild and frantic, with **◄ LITTLE RICHARD** throwing himself into every number. Today all is quiet, with story-telling lyrics and the piano-playing of **RUSS CONWAY ➤** leading the field

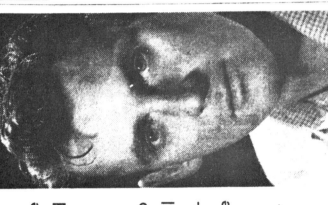

DOUG GEDDES investigates and finds that sanity prevails again

A GLANCE at the Top Twenty charts these days and I ask myself, "Has pop music turned respectable?"

Just over a year ago the hit parade music was wild and frantic, the lyrics virtually unrecognisable. But today's crop of tunes have a nice "old fashioned" air about them.

Melody seems all important and the accent is on story-telling lyrics.

However much the loyal fans might shout, the days of the early-type Bill Haley recordings have gone.

I was never an enthusiast of the Bill Haley rock treatment, where beat and

tic sales of his records are anything to go by. However, you must admit that the music and style of Russ Conway is quite different from that of the recent rock and roll period.

"Side Saddle," the item which really put Russ on the pop record map, is a most attractive melody, reminiscent of days past when only the spinet and harpsichord were vying for a place in the Top Twenty. It has an air of "olde worlde" charm such as one would never have expected would have caught the fancy of the young record buyers.

His "Roulette" and "China Tea" have that same touch about them, yet

Russ is not the only contender, for even our ballads have become "refined" and of high order.

Some of Marty Wilde's plaintive offerings would have had difficulty in surviving a year ago, and the gentler approach of "Only Sixteen" by Craig Douglas, plus the haunting "Here Comes Summer" by Jerry Keller, are a good indication of the softer, more melodic approach, to one's pop songs today.

Even the tempo of Cliff Richard's "Living Doll" was brought down to suit today's requirements.

Better quality

When I see in the charts such delightful songs as "Broken Hearted Melody" and "High Hopes", by such great artists as Sarah. Vaughan and Frank Sinatra, who certainly do not have to be poppish about them, then

TRAD JAZZ

...onopoly

...killing

...od jazz

...split between the pro-...ted clubs and the ... clubs from by a band ...s) widens every week. ...are at most six organi-...running clubs in the ... London area. Yet ...re literally hundreds ...

...ght that a virtual

...ke a look at the Top
...enty and ask yourself

If it Wasn't for Love

45 - JAR 196

A Timely — and fabulous —
release from the singer
with a big new T.V. series

DAVID HUGHES
Teach Me
(How to Love Him)

coupled with
You Would Have Done the Same

45 - JAR 205

Sound off with a new
organ instrumental

TONY LOVELLO
Amore Mio

coupled with
... Serenade

TEENS FREED ON VICE CHARGES

From REN GREVATT

NEW YORK, Wednesday.
—Two members of the
Royal Teens rock-'n'-roll
vocal group were freed of
moral charges levelled
earlier this week by an
18-year-old girl in North
Vernon, Indiana.

The road manager of the
touring package show,
Harold Grossman, also
known as Hal Charm, how-
ever, was still being held by
authorities there, on statu-
tory charges.

Activities leading to the
charge were believed to have
taken place in the theatre
manager's office. Originally,
the girl had claimed that
attempts were made to force
her to commit unnatural sex
acts.

girl had refused to leave the
theatre manager's office after
seeking autographed photos of
the group. When the manager
threatened to call police to have
her ejected, she is believed to
have made her own charges to
the police.

Upon their release, one of the
Teens said, "We are not
monsters. We are just four guys
trying to make a living and
advance in show business. We've
never had any trouble of any
kind until this. We quit college
to take up the profession we
wanted to make our life's work.
I think this has killed us pro-
fessionally."

IVO ROBIC

Another story held that the

Only PRESLEY seems to have weathered all the storms

more obvious.

Pick where you like in the charts
and the answer is invariably the
same. The tempo has certainly de-
creased, the melody has improved and,
most of all, I think the quality of
artistry has increased tremendously.

The rock was certainly ousted a
while ago, and most people said that
beat would take its place and remain.
If it has, then that beat has become
considerably steadier than
most people expected. Is it
also on the way out? Will
the ballad, which always
seems to find its way
back, come completely
to the fore?

Look again at the
charts. Sanity seems to
prevail again.

melody as our first requirement,
making the subdued beat that Russ
certainly provides of secondary importance?

Pile-drivers

From his early success with "Rock
Around The Clock," Haley kept up
a stream of similar pile-drivers until
virtually, it seemed, our poor old
frames could stand it no more. We
just had to "sit the next one out" and,
in doing so, many forgot to get up
again to dance to his music.

Looking back over that era, we certainly put up with a load of so-called
musical items which added material to
the battle, but did not contribute much
for the music world as a whole.

Alongside Haley we had such artists
as Jerry Lee Lewis, Fats Domino,
Little Richard and Johnny Otis, all
whipping up the tempo of our daily
musical lives.

But listen to them now how subdued they are!

He is unique

During the out and out rock and
roll phase, Elvis Presley weathered
all the storms. But Presley is unique.
He has a consistent following never
known before by a pop star. His
original followers are still there and,
as each month passes, so he adds to
his record admirers.

But as trends have changed so, too,
has Presley. There is no doubt that as
the swing has gone towards ballads
with a beat, Presley has learned more
and more about his business. Nowadays the Presley we hear is more
polished and refined.

One of the most surprising trends
in recent times has, to my mind, been
the swing towards piano discs such as
Russ Conway produces. I like all
that Russ does. And presum-
ably so do many of you, if the fantas-

fantastically popular—and much
copied. He met the demand for music
which could be jived to with abandon.

Fabian – one of the last of the 'rough trade' rockers raised by management who realized that their taste in males was probably the same as that of several million girls (a dream of a hulk who carries you off for just one animal night).

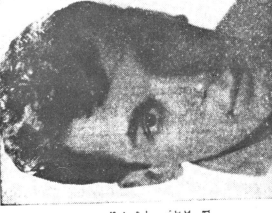

R. November 14, 1959

YOU HAVE TO CATER FOR ADULTS TOO

says FREDDIE CANNON

AMERICAN singing star, Freddie Cannon, who arrived in Britain this week for TV's "Boy Meets Girls" appearance tomorrow (Saturday) and November 21, is 19, has a swinging little band of his own, loves genuine rhythm-and-blues and hopes to be around a long time—certainly long enough to break into films.

The Lynn, Massachusetts, youngster, who has clicked with three records, told me just before departure. "I'd love to get into films. A lot of the other pop singers have done it and I've been acting in school plays for as far back as I can remember. Why shouldn't I take a crack?

"I know I've been lucky with some record hits. But I want to stay around for awhile.

"Films can do that for you. It also helps if you make different kinds of records.

"As soon as I come back from Britain, I'll be starting an album. You know what I'll be doing? Not rock. The songs will all be great ballads.

"I hope grown-ups will go for this kind of singing. I think the adults like 'Way Down Yonder In New Orleans,' my latest record.

"You have to think of the adults, not just the teenagers if you want to stay on top."

REN GREVATT
reports from New York

Freddie Cannon is a product of the well-known song-writing, record producing team of Frank Slay and Bob Crewe.

The pair were in Boston plugging one of the many records they make for different labels when they were told to catch the hot little guitar combo of Freddie Cannon.

This they did, and met Freddie, who promptly showed them a tune he had written, called "Tallahassee Lassie."

"They changed it around quite a bit, but what difference does that make?" Cannon said. "It was a hit, that's the main thing. Then we sort of worked out the same kind of an idea with 'Okeefenokee.'"

The kid who will meet his British friends on "Boy Meets Girls" is no newcomer to the performance scene.

Guitar band

"I've been working around Boston a lot with my guitar band. When I was in school we'd play for a lot of the dances.

"Then we got to doing record hops with a lot of the Boston disc jockeys, Bob Clayton. Norm Prescott, Sherm

Feller and guys like that. It was a lot of good experience for a bunch of young kids like us.

"Freddie is a deep admirer, like many others, of such great rhythm-and-blues artists as Ray Charles, Fats Domino and Lloyd Price.

"I like Sinatra too, and, of course, I'd say that Elvis is, well, just the greatest. What more can you say about a fellow than that? He's terrific."

Despite his admiration for all these artists, Cannon, with his gentle Boston dialect, has a style all of his own, which people here are predicting that British TV viewers will like most.

By BOB DAWBARN

at all. I am very limited, both technically and musically, but I can feel something coming.

"Sometimes I get so depressed with my playing that I don't even practise. At other times I

Sixteen-year-old rock 'n' roller, Fabian, is making his first film, "Hound Dog Man." Unusual, but not extraordinary. BUT . . . Fabian is wearing the clothes that Elvis Presley wore in his film debut (also for 20th Century Fox). The similarity does not end there. Fabian plays a younger brother—so did Elvis; Fabian is called "Clint"—so was Elvis.

In the picture (below) Fabian is wearing the jeans and shoes provided for Presley in "Love Me Tender."

I have always been a firm Cannon fan – he has such a hoarse shout; he never sings, he shouts till he croaks, like the funfair barker calling you to his stall. In fact, like Connie Francis, his records sound best bull-horning out of a tinny Tannoy speaker. And because of his vocal limitation he has never gotten out of R&R. So he has never betrayed the cause. Nor does he publicly utter much (like the equally taciturn Del Shannon) so he never breaks the bubble. No doubt about it. The real McCoy! And those punchy, foghorn band backings by Frank Slay and his Ork! *Slay* – just the right description. Frank Slays with slabs of smouldering sax . . .

R&R is stripped of everything except its essential: The Big Beat.

MEET 'TEEN BEAT' *Sandy Nelson*

NEW TO THE HIT LISTS

MAKE way for a drummer! Not since Cozy Cole made the Charts with "Topsy" last year has a drummer come near to breaking into the Top Thirty.

Instruments which have broken the magic sound barrier and got themselves into the sellers have been guitars, in the hands of Duane Eddy and Bert Weedon, and pianos, played by Russ Conway, Winifred Atwell and Joe Henderson.

Now Sandy Nelson comes along with his throbbing drum beats and follows up his success in the American Charts by entering the British ones with his "Teen Beat." In the U.S. he won favour towards the end of September and has since shot up the list.

Over here, Sandy entered the NME frame last week at No. 28 and appears in the No. 18 spot this week.

Born in Southern California 19 years ago, Sandy received his early training with local bands, always in the drum department. Hollywood wasn't far away from his home town and it was natural that he should want to try his luck in the film capital.

He found work and graduated to playing on sessions as a studio musican, learning quite a bit about recording technique, and what it takes to make a hit at first hand.

The most important factor, he discovered, was the beat. On this assumption, he concluded quite logically that a platter packed with beat—and very little else to distract from it—must sell like hot cakes.

The sessions he did were for the Original Sound Record company of Hollywood, and he asked if he could wax a little drum epic called "Teen Beat." He was given the okay, and the master was made. At the time the second-r man had no idea it would be a hit.

But it clicked in no uncertain fashion. Elaborating on his success, Sandy Nelson said: "I created my own sound, which I call 'Rhythm Drums,' for lack of a better name, and this means that I change rhythms, or beats, throughout a musical number.

"I strive to give my drums 'personality,' making the beat the thing that matters."

How right he's been. Hearing of the success the disc had in the States, Top Rank, who have access to Original's tracks, soon had it released here.

However, this will be the last Sandy Nelson disc they'll be issuing. The energetic drummer was offered a contract with the major Imperial label, whose waxings are issued in this country by London.

Follow-up

Already Sandy has recorded his follow-up to "Teen Beat." This is "Drum Party," backed with an "oldie" from the Glenn Miller days, "Big Noise From Winnetka." Both sides are winning favour in the States, and this week, Sandy's pal, Freddie Cannon, said: "It is a great platter, specially 'Drum Party.'"

Freddie, visiting Britain this week for "Boy Meets Grls" (see article on page 10), has been touring in a package show with Sandy and says: "His act is a wow. He's got lots of comedy about him, but all the time he's drumming it up good. He's very funny, and a terrific showman. Offstage, he's a real nice guy to know."

Freddie also said that Sandy is always dreaming up something new in percussion excitement, so it seems we'll have Sandy Nelson round for quite some time now.

IFOR GRIFFITHS

Here's a great disc from

CLIFF RICHARD
is at the
GAUMONT STATE, Kilburn
for One Week only commencing
MONDAY, 16th NOVEMBER

Advice from Brook

Advice from Brook

From NA

AMERI
AIR

Tony

ON the for...
tacular.
Cyd Charisse...
will dance a...
that one of th...
draws in the...
one of the mo...
of records—...
Trio. They...
$10,000 as th...
nighter in Ma...

● **Zola Tay**...
is in real estat...
buying a secon...
in Los Angeles...

● **Guy Mitch**...
world heavy...
Ingemar Joha...
riding.

● **Pat Boone**...
Fernando Val...
near Steve All...

● **Frank Sin**...
filming the lif...
NBE executiv...
whom he and...
ness personalit...
close.

A newcomer to the Top-of-the-Charts

ADAM FAITH IS CERTAIN

WHAT HE WANTS

says BRUCE CHARLTON

WITH Adam Faith seeking the self-same information practically every time I switch on the radio, I decided to turn the tables—by asking him the question that he is perpetually propounding on his current hit.

"What do **you** want?" I enquired—but without the benefit of that dynamic John Barry backing with which Adam is blessed.

"I want to make another hit record." he replied, without a moment's hesitation. "If there's something I'm terrified of it's being an overnight sensation. I certainly don't want to be a flash-in-the-pan—that's why I'm developing my acting."

All of which is very commendable thinking on the part of this young man who, as he puts it, still can't believe that his latest Parlophone waxing is selling in such vast quantities.

"It's one of those things that every newcomer dreams about—only, in my case, the dream has come true," he told me in an interview this week.

Now, it so happens that one of The Raindrops, Johnny Worth, besides being a solo singer in his own right, is also a composer. One day during the summer, Johnny took along a few of his songs to Freddy Poser at Mills Music, who tried them over without displaying very much excitement.

"Got anything else?" asked Freddy.

"Well, there's another one here in my pocket I've been carrying around for two years," said Johnny.

"But it's not very good—hardly worth your time."

However, he was persuaded to fish it out, only to be stunned by Freddy's comment that it was by far the most commercial song of the batch.

Johnny went back to his "Drumbeat" rehearsals and during a break asked Adam Faith if he would care to listen to a song he had written. In turn, Adam was extremely impressed, and called John Barry over

disc in preparation. It involves the same team of Johnny Worth composition, John Barry scoring and backing—plus, of course, Adam's individual vocal style.

You can expect it in the New Year, once the demand for the current hit begins to subside to some extent.

I asked Adam about the acting he has been doing recently. "It all started purely by chance." he told me. "A film producer saw me to go along for a screen test for 'Beat Girl,' which I passed."

Shortly afterwards, the director of AR-TV's "No Hiding Place" series saw some photographs of Adam, invited him to Television House to read some lines—on the strength of which, the young star was given a lead role in one of the programmes.

Adam is now taking his acting seriously. He's about to start dramatic training at the Royal Court Theatre, and in the meantime a 13-hour television play, for production early in the New Year, is being written specially for him.

Which does he prefer, acting or singing? "They're completely different," he says. "They're like two foods, both of which I enjoy separately, but which don't mix."

He maintains, however, that his acting has helped his singing— made the record while I was rehearsing for the play, and I was able to put a great deal more into it. Before hand, I'd always felt that there was something lacking on my records.

to listen to a song he had written.

Yes, you've guessed it—the name was "What Do You Want?"

Agreed

When Adam came to see me, I was surprised at his genuinely humble demeanour and unexpectedly small stature (" 2¾ teaspoonsful of sugar, please—I'm trying to build myself up")—and most impressed by his sincere gratitude to everyone who has been of the slightest assistance in boosting his disc into the top table.

In fact, he was still in the process of sitting down when he started enthusing about John Barry's sensational arrangement and backing.— and he went on to remark that, due to this, he doesn't think he would ever want to make a record without having John Barry behind him.

And to think that, after a degree of success last year, Adam quit the business because he wasn't making sufficient progress!

He had actually returned to his old job as assistant editor in a film cutting room when one day John Barry, whom Adam knew well from their tour together with the "6.5 Special" stage show, phoned to suggest that he should go along for an audition for BBC-TV's forthcoming "Drumbeat" series.

Resident

Adam duly clinched a resident spot on the show, renewed his acquaintance with John Barry, and struck up a close friendship with the members of The Raindrops vocal group.

Adam asked his recording manager, Norman Newell, if he could cut the title and by the way, discussed the disc (and, by the way, unanimously voted it a hit), the panel was particularly struck by the startling, pouting manner in which Adam pronounces the word " baby " several times in the lyric. So I asked him about it.

" When you make a record these days, you've got to pull something out of the bag," he explained.

" I learned that from my earlier records. This 'baby' business wasn't pre planned—it just seemed to develop when we were in the studio. As everyone agreed it sounded effective, we kept it in."

But Adam confessed to me that because both song and treatment are rather unusual he was very worried in case the teenagers didn't go for it. Fortunately, they liked it.

While "What Do You Want?" resides proudly at the top of the hit parade, there's a new Adam Faith

Demand

Adam is in considerable demand for concerts at the moment, and TV dates are being frantically lined up for him. Yet he continues to live quietly at home with his parents in Acton, as though nothing had happened.

Two sisters and a brother also live with the family (and there's another brother who has married). But everything is quite normal at home," says Adam. "It's only when I come up to town that things are different!

Possessing a very wide musical taste, Adam spends most of his spare time listening to records. Current favourites — anything by Sinatra, Henry Mancini's " Peter Gunn " album, and Sibelius' First Symphony. He also plays golf extensively.

Girl friends? Two or three he takes out occasionally, but no steady date. Maybe he daren't run the financial risk of continually asking her "What Do You Want?"...

EW DUANE EDDY on London

Adam Faith was something new: a cool look, a minimum of the soothing smiles, lean and hungry as Cassius. No danger of him stepping into the Music Hall tradition. He later became R&R's first intellectual, putting up a good show against the hard-hitting questions of BBC TV's ace prober John Freeman

TOP TWENTY

MAX SAILS IN WITH 'JINGLE BELL ROCK'

Compiled from dealers' returns from all over Britain

WEEK ENDING DECEMBER 12

Last Week	This Week	Title	Artist	Label
2	1	What Do You Want?	Adam Faith	Parlophone
1	2	What Do You Want To Make Those Eyes At Me For	Emile Ford and The Checkmates	Pye
4	3	Oh Carol	Neil Sedaka	R.C.A.
3	4	'Travellin' Light/Dynamite	Cliff Richard	Columbia
5	5	Seven Little Girls	The Avons	Columbia
6	6	Red River Rock	Johnny and The Hurricanes	London
13	7	Little Donkey	The Beverley Sisters	Decca
11	8	Snow Coach	Russ Conway	Columbia
10	9	Teen Beat	Sandy Nelson	Top Rank
8	10	Mack The Knife	Bobby Darin	London
7	11	Mr. Blue	Mike Preston	Decca
12	12	Put Your Head On My Shoulder	Paul Anka	Columbia
20	13	Little White Bull	Tommy Steele	Decca
—	14	Jingle Bell Rock	Max Bygraves	Decca
—	15	More And More Party Pops	Russ Conway	Columbia
17	16	Rawhide	Frankie Laine	Philips
14	17	'Til I Kissed You	Everly Brothers	London
19	18	Among My Souvenirs	Connie Francis	M.G.M.
18	19	Piano Party	Winifred Atwell	Decca
15	20	Deck Of Cards	Wink Martindale	London

ONE TO WATCH

Some Kinda Earthquake   Duane Eddy

TEENAGERS CHAMP! —THAT'S ADAM FAITH NOW

By DEREK JOHNSON

THE teenagers' champion — that's what they're calling Adam Faith these days. Whenever any controversial topic involving the younger generation is brought to light, you can bet that Adam will be there to speak his mind in their support. Only a fortnight ago, he was quoted widely by the daily Press and interviewed on TV, in connection with the latest report on teenage morals.

I asked Adam how he reacted to this new rôle which he has adopted in recent months, and in which he now seems to be fully accepted. Does he mind being regarded as the official spokesman of the teenagers' cause?

"I haven't deliberately set out to secure this position," he told me. "It's just that radio, TV and the Press have apparently elected me to speak on the youngsters' behalf. I suppose it all stems from those two discussions I had on television with John Freeman and the Archbishop of York, in which I defended the young people of today to the best of my ability."

Adam hoped youngsters didn't mind him championing their cause. He didn't want them to think he was speaking out of turn. But he felt that, when he was approached by a reporter to comment on some thorny topic, it was up to him to defend the younger generation.

"I don't know why so many people—usually those in high positions, I might add—go out of their way to discredit the youth of today. They certainly don't deserve it," Adam insisted. "They're no worse than any other generation, and in many respects they're a darned sight better.

"**I'm not long out of the teenage category myself, so I still feel I'm one of them. That's why I always speak for them whenever the opportunity arises.**

"As I say, I didn't ask to be made their spokesman. But if the Press, the Church or Parliamentary commissions want to seek my opinions, they are welcome to do so. I certainly shan't say anything against today's youth."

Maybe the reason why such bodies have been approaching Adam so frequently is that, from his various TV discourses, it has become apparent that he is an extremely deep thinker on subjects of social significance. More than that, he is able to express himself eloquently on these topics. There are very few artists capable of discussing matters of import outside of show business, and it's obviously to the teenagers' benefit that Adam is rooting for them.

Of course, there's always the risk that he'll be taken to task for delving into matters which aren't strictly his province—as happened to Cliff when, on returning from South Africa, he dared to venture a comment on the colour problem there. "But that's a risk I must take," says Adam. "If they think I'm unqualified to speak, they shouldn't question me in the first place."

To his credit, I found that Adam was far more reticent when it came to discussing his own career in general, and his present chart success in particular. He admitted to being delighted at the chart entry of "If He Tells You," but apportioned its success more to the efforts of the Roulettes and composer Chris Andrews, than to his own singing!

"Chris is a great writer in the modern idiom," he assured me. "I have the utmost faith in him—no pun intended! And as for the Roulettes—what a tremendous group they are! I feel sure they must succeed in their own right in the near future, and I'm keeping my fingers crossed for them."

Next month, Adam embarks upon a lengthy one-nighter tour, his first for 18 months. He tells me that he's eagerly looking forward to the experience, and that he and the Roulettes have already been rehearsing for it for weeks.

"It's not that we're planning any major surprises in the content of the act," he explained. "For the most part, it will consist of much of my record material. But after such a long absence from the one-nighter circuit, we want to make sure the act is as polished as possible.

"I expect I shall be doing some r-and-b items and, by way of contrast, I may slip in a ballad when nobody's looking!"

ADAM FAITH ... "I won't say anything against today's teenagers," he says. And plenty of people ask him.

BOYS, BE A HIT!

ARTISTS PROMOTIONS LTD.,
... ngham Street, London W.1 ...

Published by Charles Buchan's Publications Ltd., 161 Fleet Street, London, E.C.4.

2'6 *

JACK GOOD

I SHOULD like to take up the topic of Beat Shows. They are certainly NOT finished. No one present at the Marty Wilde—Gene Vincent package at Tooting could possibly deny that the beat makes sweet music on the cash register.

The Granada was packed, packed as I have never seen it packed before.

Larry Parnes has discovered the formula of success. You need at least two big star names. Until now the attendance at beat shows has been getting progressively worse. And understandably so.

The public have been offered, time and again, the same bunch of beat singers.

Once bitten, twice shy, the teenagers now demand the big names and the

GENE SPURRED MARTY TO NEW HEIGHTS

new faces. I hope that Parnes persists in the double-top billing idea.

That way the public will begin to regain confidence in the beat shows and bring new life into a sagging business.

The Tooting show (second house) was an experience I am glad I did not miss. Gene Vincent, the shy, modest boy who addresses even the screaming kids as "Sir" or "Ma'am," limped on to the stage to a deafening roar of applause.

TWITCHING MONTH

He looked scared, and his mouth twitched nervously when he discovered that his mike was not working.

He found another that was. There was a slight embarrassed pause, then quite unexpectedly he swung his iron- cased left leg right over the mike, spun round a complete 360 degrees, and tore into "Be-Bop-a-Lula."

The effect was electrifying. A

Jekyll and Hyde story come true.

The nervous, silent, bewildered Texan was suddenly transformed into a crouching wildcat. Gene is no sexbomb. He neither uses nor needs any of the suggestive movements that are usually associated with the stage performances of star rockers.

Vincent is a man's man, a toughguy. He is rock 'n' roll's James Cagney and it is for this reason that an unusually large proportion of his fan club consists of boys.

When I say that Gene uses no sexy movements, do not think that he does not move on the stage. He moves all right. And, visually, it is the most unusual rock presentation I have ever witnessed.

For a start, Gene carries his mike like a gun. He is, by repute, the third fastest draw in Hollywood: Jerry Lewis is number one. He crouches with the mike almost throughout the act. He has to, since he keeps it at a height of two feet six inches.

CROUCHING TIGER

He never faces the audience, not even while talking to them, but keeps his head bent over the mike or turned towards the wings.

He spins, throws and catches the mike, and swings his leg over it in a single short burst of movement. Then, like a crouching tiger awaiting its prey, he will be stock-still for minutes on end.

It has been suggested, because of the noticeable use of repeating echo on his discs that Gene's voice is a figment of the electronic imagination.

This is false. The very characteristic sound belongs to Gene, not to the echo chamber, and it comes across very clearly over the not-very-good sound systems used at these concert dates.

At this particular concert, on the second house, the audience was by no means satisfied with hearing only five numbers from Gene. They roared "We Want Gene" continuously so that the compere, Billy Raymond, could not get a word in edgeways.

Marty had the unenviable task of following the Texan. The battle cry "We Want Gene" smothered the first words of "Mack The Knife"—Marty's opener—and persisted for short bursts for fully half his act.

I felt sorry for Marty, of course, but I cannot help admitting that I was glad that this had happened.

At last we were getting a battle of top talents. Marty's position of billtopper was being strongly challenged.

GENE VINCENT—he keeps his head bent over the mike or turned towards the wings. (DISC Pic)

And what a power of good it did Marty! He and his band appeared on the stage in aggressive mood. They determined to give the show of their lives, and by George, they did. Marty has never given such a strong performance and in the end the shouts of "We Want Gene" were transformed into a universal acclaim for Marty.

This is the sort of thing our boys need. Competition. Let us have more of it. Larry Parnes.

Revolting

I SAY that the beat shows have been till now mediocre for the most part, but I must concede that one boy impressed me very much at the Tooting session.

Johnny Gentle's performance is becoming as controlled and polished as he is good looking. The girls dig him and the boys do not object. Not so with Billy Fury. Billy annoys me.

His stagecraft is superb, but he uses it for such horrible effects. I have seldom seen such a revolting sight as Fury rolling in a frenzy on the floor with his microphone. He has a good voice, and writes very good songs. He looks good on stage. Off stage he is charming.

He should change his act.

NEIL SEDAKA will not be with us until later in the series, "Boy Meets Girls," unfortunately, but it now looks as though Conway Twitty will be returning in January.

Two versions

DON GIBSON (R.C.A.), and Ray Charles (London), have each recorded "I'm Movin On." Both versions are excellent and completely different. Those artists doing cover jobs, please note. What suits one artist does not necessarily suit another.

● Interesting to note that Fats Domino's latest platter has a new lineup, a trumpet being featured and there being a notable absence of the typical Domino sax solo.

DANE MARLOWE, NME HOLLYWOOD CORRESPONDENT, INTERVIEWS A FIRST-TIME-HERE VISITOR TO BRITAIN—

Eddie Cochran

THE first sound that poured out of Liberty Records' modern recording studios was that of a guitar. Then came the smooth, rhythmic tinkle of a jazzy piano. The low wail of a blue clarinet was followed by the rapid-fire staccato of percussion.

And then the thump-thump of a follow-the-beat bass rolled out into the noisy Hollywood street and seemed to keep tempo with the cacaphony of automobile sounds.

"What's the name of the group warming up?" someone asked.

"Don't know. What say we take a look-see?"

Complete surprise greeted the two individuals. For no group was in evidence. Only one young, handsome youth.

As a warm-up for his recording session and before the actual group arrived, Eddie Cochran, one of the hottest singers on wax today, was just enjoying himself doing the things he does so naturally.

Although known around the world as a singer, Eddie is quietly biding his time before he makes public the complete repertoire of entertainment he commands.

An expert on the guitar—naturally —Eddie is also a swinger on the piano, is a good clarinettist, will give Shelly Manne a run for his money on the drums and can pluck a bass to fit most any combo.

He has yet to demonstrate these varied talents before audiences.

But as soon as he completes his current recording commitments with the American Liberty label (London here) he's going to put together a night-club act that should have the applauding "hurrahs" from coast-to-coast.

Close-up on Eddie

IT'S strange, but true. If Eddie Cochran hadn't been shot in the leg when he was a boy, he might never have become a singer! How come? He and his brother often used to go hunting in the Minnesota woodlands near their home.

One day, a gun fired accidentally, and Eddie was wounded in the leg. He spent months in hospital, and during the long hours began to think about the future.

It was during this spell that he made the decision to try his luck at singing.

The disc break-through came when Eddie was introduced to Jerry Capehart of Liberty Records.

Eddie came out of the meeting with a record contract in his pocket, and was soon in the studios cutting his first title, "Sittin' In The Balcony."

Film executives were the next to assess the potential of the personable young Cochran, claiming that in looks he was a younger edition of Marlon Brando.

20th-Century Fox gave him a role in Jayne Mansfield's "The Girl Can't Help It," in which he sang "Twenty Flight Rock."

Then along came Warner Brothers with an attractive offer, and Eddie found himself alongside Mamie Van Doren in "Untamed Youth," a movie in which he sang three songs.

Now Eddie has just completed his role in the Hal Roach production, "Johnny Melody."

During this venture into pictures, Eddie's recording activities were in full swing. His two most successful waxings so far as this country was concerned were "Summertime Blues" and "C'mon Everybody," both of which achieved top table status here.

Now Eddie is coming to Britain. He arrives this weekend for two "Boy Meets Girls" appearances, followed by a one-nighter tour in the Gene Vincent package.

Eddie's new recording of the oldie "Hallelujah, I Love Her So!" has just been released in Britain, and his arrival here could well nudge it into the Charts.

---

followers of popular music are flipping over Eddie's latest release, "Hallelujah, I Love Her So". The record has caught on like wild-fire in the United States, and Liberty's pressing plants are working overtime to keep up with the demand.

"It's probably one of the best songs I've done since I began singing," Eddie said as he played a few bars from the song on the piano.

"It has a heart-beat rhythm and a pulsating touch — like the beat of your own pulse," he added, this time whopping the percussions.

"I'll probably hit the road in a couple of weeks to meet the deejays and do some one-nighters before the teenagers," he continued, doing a riff on the clarinet.

"Then it's back to Hollywoodland and a few television shows and maybe a feature-length motion picture," he opined, beating out the bass.

"What next? My night club act," he finalised with a zing, zing, zing on the guitar.

Big 'romance'

Meanwhile Eddie has become the talk of Hollywood with his "romance" with beautiful young actress Connie Stevens. Eddie disclaims that it's a romance. He says they're "just good friends".

It all started when Eddie was invited to a chi-chi Hollywood party where several syndicated photographers were to be present. A friend suggested that he call up Connie Stevens for a date.

They had only met briefly, but she accepted.

As soon as the youthful twosome arrived at the party, the shutterbugs swarmed about posing them time and time again. A few Hollywood columnists picked up the couple and played it big in the papers.

Then several weeks later a fan magazine came out with pictures of Eddie and Connie together and the ball began to roll.

"I think the newspapers and the magazines are the greatest marriage bureau ever invented," Eddie said. "They can make you in love and get you out of love so fast it'll make your head swim.

"But the truth of the matter is that Connie and I are just good friends.

"We like to go out to the movies, have quiet dinners and listen to records. Sometimes we get together with friends and have a beach party."

Regarding his latest release, "Hallelujah, I Love Her So," Eddie's pals jokingly explain that he really means what he's singing. Could be that the object of the song is pretty, perky Connie Stevens.

Welcome to London **EDDIE COCHRAN** Record of

Early in the 1960s Jack Good, fed up with pop's twinkly violins and wet rock, packed up and went to America where he soon revitalized rock TV with 'Shindig,' a development of 'Oh Boy!' Meanwhile, I was selling records in Harrods and getting into Trad Jazz and the Old Blues. Pause.

✱ Reviews by the P

JOHNNY blows up a STORM!

Johnny—of Hurricane fame—has dressed up an oldie for his latest release. The Pop Panel tips it a hit.

GALE warning! Here's that whirlwind group, Johnny and the Hurricanes, all set to blow up another Top Twenty storm.

They've taken that old traditional " Gimme Crack Corn," knocked it around a bit, and out comes " Beatnik Fly " (London HL19072).

Their rockin' organ and sax trade mark, plus some heavy amplified guitar, makes this the brightest and best pop of the week —by a long way.

★ Big Doll

SWINGIN' PREACHER/ Fascinating Rhythm (HMV POP718). Big Doll hides the identity of one of our most talented pianists —Ralph Dollimore. With its heavy off-beat rhythm and vocal rifling from the Michael Sammes Singers, Preacher—a Dollimore original—is a likely contender for best-seller status. Less successful is the somewhat Brubeck styled waltz-beat backing. But Dollimore reveals his pianistic mettle.

★ Fats Domino

COUNTRY BOY / If You Need Me (London HLP 9073). Fats Domino is in calmer mood with this attractive Country Boy side. But the disc still packs enough beat and excitement to take it ahead of the field. Grade A potential.

POP SINGLES

★ Lonnie Donegan

MY OLD MAN'S A DUSTMAN/ The Golden Vanity (Pye 7N15256). My Old Man's a Dustman, the Cockney favourite of the old-time music halls, is dusted off in typical Donegan style by Lonnie who has added new words and music. And for good measure, he throws in a few jokes.

Donegan's humorous delivery, plus the salty sentiments of the song, make this a strong contender for the Hit Parade.

★ Renato Rascel Teddy Reno

ROMANTICA/LIBERO (RCA 1177). These are two of the Italian Eurovision contenders. Romantica came first and Libero second. If these are a sample of the opposition, Britain need not worry about bottom place. This disc could put the Italian tourist industry back 10 years.

★ Clyde MacPhatter

THINK ME A KISS When The Right Time Comes Along (MGM1061). Clyde MacPhatter could have a hit waiting for him when he arrives for his in-person tour next week. With a little plugging. Think Me A Kiss could make its mark in the charts.

ASTONISHING NEW BRITISH INVENTION!

BIG BOPPER'S SONG GIVES PAL FAME

MEET the 21-year-old Texan, Johnny Preston, who this week shoulders his way into the British best-sellers, after spending four weeks at the top of the American hit parade with his recording of "Running Bear".

It is particularly appropriate that the record should make its initial impact here at this time—one year after that fateful air crash which took from us Buddy Holly, Big Bopper and Ritchie Valens.

For "Running Bear" was composed by J. P. Richardson, better known to his millions of fans as " The Big Bopper ". And it constitutes an admirable tribute to his memory.

JOHNNY PRESTON

It was The Big Bopper, in fact, who encouraged Johnny to make his first recording, and as a token of gratitude for this help he decided to wax the song written by his late friend.

But it's ironic to reflect that, had he lived, The Big Bopper would probably have recorded the song himself. In which case Johnny might not be nearly so popular as he is today.

It also underlines the very essence of the show business tradition—that, in the very teeth of calamity, there can always be found someone capable of taking over the reins.

The Big Bopper would have been proud of young Johnny Preston's triumph. Certainly the American public have taken his recording to their hearts and, now that the disc is making itself felt so effectively here, Johnny looks an odds-on favourite to win a Golden Disc.

Johnny, who has green eyes and is of medium height, hails from the small town of Port Arthur, in Texas. He started singing with the school choir and later, when he began work as a grocery clerk, he formed a small combination called The Shades, with which he performed at local weekend dances.

His fame soon began to spread, he won a coveted AFM Certificate of Achievement, and secured his biggest break when he was signed to a Mercury recording contract.

Johnny's been doing quite a bit of travelling lately, having just completed a tour of U.S. cities and appearances on top TV and disc-jockey shows, including the highly rated Dick Clark Show.

Another recent honour was being voted one of the most promising new pop artists in the recent disc-jockey poll conducted by "Cash Box".

Now Johnny Preston is an internationally accepted recording star—thanks to "Running Bear," and to a fellow-artist who died a year ago.

emanating from the West Coast.

Some months ago, Wayne Shanklin was about to launch a new record label, Signet, and he was looking for a girl singer with a big voice to sign for his new venture. A music publisher played him a demonstration record which Toni had made, and Wayne immediately decided that this was the girl he wanted.

Now she is even more in demand in America, where her television appearances are no longer limited to local shows—she frequently guests on the major coast-to-coast shows.

It is unusual for a girl singer to achieve international stardom for the first time when she is nearly 30 years old. But that's precisely what Toni has done.

For the record, by the way, she is something of a winter sports specialist, and is particularly fond of skiing and hunting. And since our picture of Toni doesn't give you the full story, let us tell you that she has red hair and blue eyes.

The Skiffle King turns music-hall; after trad jazz and skiffle, Donegan became a family entertainer with songs like this and 'Does Your Chewing Gum Lose Its Flavour On The Bedpost Overnight?'

BAN THOSE BOMBHEADS!

A LIVID, white-faced Bobby Darin stormed off the stage after his British debut at Lewisham on Friday, shaken after his duelling with a small group of barrackers.

It should have been a night to remember—the first show in Britain of the "Mack The Knife" star. Instead, a small bunch of youngsters almost wrecked the show for the 4,000 packed house. It all started when Darin went into his slow version of the standard, "My Funny Valentine."

After an evening of beat music, and after 20 minutes of the twangy guitar sound of Duane Eddy, a handful of hooligans in the circle took advantage of the lull to make themselves heard.

If someone in authority had moved in quickly it would have been all over before it had started.

Instead, the wreckers were allowed to carry on.

Had it been any other artist than the talented Darin, the consequences might have been more serious.

As it was, Darin's quips won the day—to the cheers of the other 99 per cent. of the audience.

At the second house, the running order was moved so that Duane Eddy closed the first half and a number from the Bob Miller Band preceded Darin's entrance.

✱ Barrackers

Even so, a few barrackers once again chipped in on "Funny Valentine." But Darin soon brushed them off—to the applause of the packed house —with: "I thought you people lived on the other side of Town."

This was just an isolated instance at Lewisham. The next night at Edmonton, Darin really wowed the packed houses.

And you could have heard a pin drop during "Funny Valentine." And the same went for Leicester on Sunday.

But Lewisham was one case too many. Surely, the time has come when cinema managers have got to get tough with these bombheads — youngsters who only go to pop con-certs to entertain themselves, and not to be entertained. They spoil it for the thousands who have travelled miles to see their disc favourites.

This is the best pop package show that has hit Britain. Altogether, there are four disc stars on the bill.

Opening the show is Clyde McPhatter, the star who came to the front after forming his own group, the Drifters.

He is now solo, and the best number in his act is his current release, "Think Me A Kiss."

✱ Promising

From Britain there is Emile Ford—surely one of the most promising disc stars of today. Then came twangy guitar star Duane Eddy. And Eddy is the surprise of the show.

He achieves something that hardly any other U.S. disc star has managed to do—sound even better than his records.

This is due to the fact that he has been allowed to bring over the whole of his group— Larry Knechtel (pno.), Jimmy Troxel (drs.), Truman Campbell (bass) and his co-star saxist Jim Horn.

But if Eddy is the hit of the show as regards the beat music, Darin must surely be the most impressive for pure talent. He dominates all the time.

✱ 'Hambone'

He is a natural-born performer although, as he admitted back-stage, he has not

says BILL HALDEN

It isn't fair to thousands who want to hear their disc favourites

New Darin disc out

THAT folky old gal "Clementine" is taken for a rollercoaster ride by teenage darling Bobby Darin on his latest single release (London HLK9086).

This swinger is right out of the "Mack the Knife" stable, and Darin urges himself and his powerhouse band backing along with the "hups" and "whoops" which are now part of his trademark. And he even does a Basie "one more time" coda for good measure.

It clicks all the way.

had much training. "I guess it's just that natural hambone in me," he said.

All this makes the unfortunate incident at Lewisham even worse. Said Bobby Darin's school friend and accompanist Dick Behrke after that first house:

"This show really hurt Bobby. If this had happened in the States, Bobby would have shrugged it off. But this was going to be something special and the audience really shocked him."

✱ Bob Miller

But both Darin and Dick Behrke heaped praises on the Bob Miller Band which managed to recreate the spectacular Darin arrangements perfectly.

Said Behrke: "This band is much better than the bands we usually get when we go on tour."

Like Paul Anka, Darin was really a spurious rocker. He quickly gravitated to high-class show ballads like Weill's 'Mack The Knife', and 'A' movies. On stage he was a slick and snappy finger-clicker, sure-fire Vegas material. His R&R records were always well-produced, with a nervy, edgy New York feel. Atco, his label, were heavily into R&R. And Darin himself was like his itchy backing tracks – always on the go, upwards. A typical mobile American, responding to that Green Light that the Great Gatsby saw across the bay. Before his first hit he broke out in a fierce rash. Once on the charts and climbing fast the rash vanished.

Melody Maker

April 23, 1960 — FIRST AND FOREMOST — Every Friday 6d.

Bu qu Co Pages

GENE VINCENT: SHOW MUST GO ON

CHRIS IN—&

"THE Show must go on." That timeless show business slogan was endorsed by Gene Vincent on Tuesday when he told the **MELODY MAKER** that he was determined to "carry on" in the Larry Parnes big-beat package despite the tragic death of his co-star buddy, Eddie Cochran.

MIDNIGHT CRASH

Cochran was killed when he and his fiancee, American songwriter Sharon Sheeley, and Gene Vincent were travelling to London Airport from Bristol on Sunday night after the first lap of their nationwide tour.

Their hire car crashed at midnight on the Bath Road outside Chippenham

Gene Vincent spoke to the

Page 10, Col. 4

Eddie Cochran (l.) and Gene Vincent caught by the camera during rehearsals in Manchester for a February date on Jack Good's "Boy Meets Girls" ABC-TV show. The two stars were together again in the Larry Parnes big-beat package show.

Fans star J

ONE week to go! It's just seven days to the start of the North's biggest jazz event of the year—the **MELODY MAKER's "Jazz Week-end"** in Manchester.

And the rush for tickets is on. Already the All Night Jazz Session at the Free

EW TRAD BAND ON THE WAY?

TRUMPETER Ken Sims is leaving the Acker Bilk nd at the end of its 18-day r of the Continces, which ted on Wednesday.

aking his place will be Colin from

Trad Frida to S mark Pro stop M A

PERRY COMO—LONDON STYLE

Brenda Lee has a big, big voice for a little girl

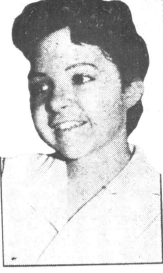

MEET the little girl with the big, big voice—15-year-old Brenda Lee. Talent abounds in this pint-sized American show business sensation! After winning a place in the U.S. Top Ten, she makes her British hit parade debut this week at No. 24 with a story about "Sweet Nuthin's."

Already, Brenda—who televised in Britain last year on the ABC-TV "Oh. Boy" series—is being hailed as a second Judy Garland. Two major film companies are at present out-bidding each other for her Hollywood screen debut, while top TV networks are after her signature, too!

Where did it all begin? Little Brenda (she was born in Atlanta's Emory University Hospital on December 11, 1944) was discovered at the age of 12 by country-and-western star Red Foley, who happens to be Pat Boone's father-in-law.

He heard her at an amateur talent show in Augusta, Georgia, and signed her for a TV appearance on the "junior" edition of the famous "Ozark Jubilee" show.

After seeing the programme, back in April, 1956, critic Jack O'Brien wrote in his popular New York Journal—American column: "Didn't catch the name of the young singer on last night's Ozark Jubilee, but she belts out a song like a star!"

The show led to a five-year TV contract and a Decca disc deal. Her first release, "Jambalaya," was a sure-fire hit and put Brenda on the road to stardom. Then came another big break—a guest appearance on the famed "Perry Como Show."

Again, Brenda hit the highspots—and drew this admiring tribute from Perry himself: "The quickest learner of a song or a script I've ever encountered in show business."

Word soon got around that a bright new talent was at hand and dates on the "Steve Allen Show" and other major network productions prefaced her success in Britain in 1959.

Although she's currently scoring with rock 'n' roll, Brenda's first love is the country-and-western style. She can't read music or play any instruments, but dreams up all her own arrangements and learns most of her songs by listening to records.

Described by her mother as "just about the biggest tomboy you ever saw," Brenda has a fantastically big, powerful voice for her age.

British composer Ian "Sammy" Samwell, who wrote Cliff Richard current hit "Fall In Love With You," is one of her most ardent fans here.

His opinion? "She's just great," he told me. "She has a voice twice as loud as any other girl singer I've ever heard. It's just unbelievable. Yes, she's certainly one of the most exciting girl singers around today."

Everybody, it seems, is impressed by the way little Brenda belts out her songs in an almost Sophie Tucker-ish voice. This is most evident in her current LP—"Grandma, What Great Songs You Sang."

'Fabulous'-ugh!

● Gene Krupa—see 'Disgust'

WHY do so many people in show business use the word FABULOUS? The dictionary definition is "feigned, invented, forged, false." So, in many cases, fans who use this word are probably more correct than they think.— *Anne Christine, Ripon, Yorks.*
● LP WINNER.

Stupid

LAST week's letter stating American artists can't hold a candle to ours is the most stupid ever written. Not one British artist even bears comparison with any American.—*Russell Young, High Wycombe, Bucks.*

Fairer

A FAIRER approach would have been to compare Marty, Cliff and Co. with

Sammy Davis, Nat Cole and Bobby Darin.—*E. R. Brewer, Welling, Kent.*

More!

AT last I've seen it. A jazz programme at peak viewing time—"Jazz à la Carte," with Humphrey Lyttelton and Sylvie St. Clair on BBC-TV last Saturday at 10.10 p.m.

It was the best presented jazz I've yet seen on TV. More please.—*Allen Elliott, Dagenham, Essex.*

Correction

A FEW weeks ago I wrote saying how little I thought of Sammy Davis. After his TV show I must take back my remarks. He is a great performer.—*Joan J. Armstrong, Sidcup.*

What?

CAN someone tell me what is so great about Sammy Davis?—*John A. Shirley, London, W.7.*

Woody

THANKS for the Woody Guthrie article. It's one of the best you've had for a long time.—*J. S. Asquith, Wakefield, Yorks.*

Mail

ANYONE who cares to brighten Woody Guthrie's days in hospital should write to him at Clinic Building, 16, New Jersey State Hospital, Greystone Park, New Jersey, U.S.A.—*Jim Marshall, Brighton 7, Sussex.*

Attacks

YES, please—Vic Dickenson and Ed Hall with Muggsy Spanier MUST happen. What a blessed relief to Dixieland and Mainstream fans who have recently suffered severe attacks of Granz, Acker and Barber!—*P. G. Hewitt, Birmingham 12.*

Disgust

I WENT to see the film "Drum Crazy" (the Gene Krupa story). I was disgusted at such a poor tribute to a great drummer. He deserves better than that.—*Len Howe, Barking, Essex.*
● LP WINNER.

Moans

IT strikes me jazz enthusiasts enjoy moaning. Hardly a week goes by without someone grumbling about the lack of jazz on radio or TV. Surely there are enough jazz clubs for them to go to.—*Kenneth Hall, Denton, near Manchester.*

Important

IT'S time some enterprising film company made the life story of a really important jazzman like Louis, Duke or Count Basie.—*Mike Dunn, Bath, Somerset.*

By popular demand—the return of our fact-a-line feature *Life-Lines*

starting off with

DUANE EDDY

At the persistent request of many readers, it's welcome back to one of the most popular features ever introduced into the NME . . . "Life Lines."

It was first began in January, 1958, with Michael Holliday as subject, his recording of "The Story Of My Life" gave us the idea, and we continued to publish these fact-a-line features regular until the Spring of last year. And now, by readers' request for a second run—at your request. And here, under our detailed cross-examination is top guitarist—

Real name: Duane Eddy.

Date of birth: April 26, 1938.

Place of birth: Corning, New York.

Subsequent Home: Arizona

Education: Graduated from Cool-idge High School, Arizona.

Age at which started playing guitar: Five.

Early influence: A deep interest in American Frontier History and folk music of that period.

Age at which decision to enter show business taken: Sixteen, immediately on leaving school.

First professional engagements: Local dances and charity functions in Arizona.

Stand for records: At age of 17, by James R.

First major award success: Dick Clark Band and Poll

"Outstanding Instrumentalist," two consecutive years. New Musical Express, "World's Outstanding Musical Personality" runner-up, 1959.

Visited Britain: March-April, 1960. Played one-nighter and variety tour with Bobby Darin, Clyde McPhatter, Emile Ford. Subsequently played variety as top-of-the-bill.

Television in Britain: ATV "Saturday Spectacular," April 23, 1960.

Biggest achievement: Only instrumentalist with six successive discs in American hit parade.

Film: Appears in Dick Clark movie, "Because They're Young"—latest disc, "Shazam," featured in this film.

Cars: Recently purchased a Cadillac for his father. Owns a Japanese jeep.

Hobbies: Hunting, swimming, fishing, reading, collecting records.

Tastes in music: Wide in the extreme. Likes anything, as long as it is good of its kind. Favourite musical styles are gospel and country-and-western.

Present home: Lives with parents at Phoenix, Arizona.

Number of guitars owned: Four, all Gretsch guitars.

Recording managers: Lee Hazelwood and Lester Sill.

Origin of disc material: Mainly written by Duane himself, in conjunction with Lee Hazelwood.

Favourite clothes: Sweater and jeans, or Italian-styled suits.

Favourite food: Steak, or Mexican food.

Marital status: Unmarried.

Height: Six feet

Characteristic of style: Predominant use of single bass string.

Latest venture: Formation of own 50,000-dollar TV company, Greg-mark Productions. Has just filmed pilot show of new half-hour series.

Favourite singers: Elvis Presley, Ella Fitzgerald, Pat Boone, Tommy Edwards.

Favourite guitarists: Segovia, Chet Atkins, Barney Kessel, John Smith —also Jimmy Wyhele, who tutored him.

Forthcoming disc projects: Two albums — a folk-song album, featuring Duane on guitar and banjo; and an LP showcasing Duane with big band backing.

How principally occupied: One-nighter tours, TV appearances.

Ambitions: To make more films, to make a success of his own TV company, to return for another tour of Britain.

Next single release: "Because They're Young"—to be issued as and when "Shazam" sales start to slacken

MIKI AND GRIFF
"LONG TIME TO FORGET"
PYE 7N 15266 (45)

JAMES DARREN
"P.S. I LOVE YOU"

NEIL SEDAKA JOINS INTERNATIONAL SET

LATEST disc artist to join the ranks of the truly international stars is RCA's Neil Sedaka, who is currently climbing up his "Stairway To Heaven" towards universal recognition.

For, while it's a common-place occurrence these days for singers to make their presence known on both sides of the Atlantic, the number of artists who achieve world-wide acclaim (including countries where English is not spoken) is obviously much more restricted.

In recent months, Neil Sedaka's stock has been steadily climbing—not only in his own territory, but also throughout the British Commonwealth. To expedite this process, he has been playing an exceptionally successful Australian tour, which has boosted him high in the estimation of the fans . Down Under.

On the Continent, too, Neil's records have displayed a peculiar

Neil's formula for big-selling records revolves around the fact that he is scarcely out of his teens—and he is therefore able to cater for the

8

PATCH-EYED JOHNNY KIDD KEEPS ROCK ROLLING

I USED to think that out-and-out beat titles like "Shake Rattle And Roll" and "Whole Lotta Shakin' Going On" went out with the heyday of Bill Haley and Jerry Lee Lewis. But not on your life! For in these more enlightened days, when rock has reputedly become more subdued and sophisticated, along comes Johnny Kidd with a number called "Shakin' All Over".

Admittedly, it's not a frantic, tear-up beat opus as were the two others I've mentioned. I think a fair description of this new title would be "a slow rocker". But certainly this disc reverts to the original, basic conception of rock 'n' roll even if only in title.

Johnny Kidd, you'll recall, is the young man who took the recording industry by storm last year, when he burst into the best sellers with his first release, "Please Don't Touch". And he climbed into this select position without so much as a single live radio or TV appearance to help exploit his disc.

The initial success of the record, in fact, was based upon a few plays on Radio Luxembourg, and a couple of airings on BBC's "Saturday Club"—a remarkable tribute to the pulling power of both media.

There have been a few releases between-times which haven't quite made the high spots for Johnny. Although he did manage a brief Chart entry with his version of "You Got What It Takes".

But now comes "Shakin' All Over" an immediate success for this young British singer, though on this occasion he has had the opportunity of "plugging" it on television, in ABC-TV's "Wham!" programme.

This new number, written by Johnny himself, is on the same pattern as his earlier "Please Don't Touch" hit, but without the vocal backing which was used on the latter.

In fact there has been a considerable change in Johnny's accompanying group, The Pirates, since his recording debut. In those days the

of the staying-power of beat music. "No doubt about it, rock is here to stay", he assured me.

"Mind you, there are two or three distinct types of rock today, as opposed to the one blatant kind when Haley was king", said Johnny. "We consider ourselves rockers nowadays, but we're very different from Bill Haley".

Which led on to the logical follow-up question: "If you're not in the Haley mould, who would you say has influenced you?" I asked.

Johnny pondered for a moment, then replied: "You know, I'm not really influenced by anyone. I just open my mouth and sing! After all, there are so many people in the business these days, you've just got to have originality".

But ask Johnny who has influenced him most, from the point of view of production and projection and he won't hesitate for one moment in telling you—Jack Good.

Jack has been a tower of strength in helping to polish and develop the boy's personality and individuality.

He recently persuaded them to adopt a trade-mark — and now, wherever they appear, Johnny Kidd (as leader of The Pirates) wears a black patch over his eye!

Johnny's great ambition is to become a successful entertainer of widespread appeal. His great idol in life is Sammy Davis, Jnr., though he freely admits that "there'll never be another". Still, you never know, if all goes well we may one day all be singing the praises of Sammy Kidd, Jnr.!

JIM RICH

unit consisted of six, but now The Pirates have been reorganised and reduced in number to three.

Johnny tells me that this is partly for economic reasons, and additionally because he has now adopted a new approach to his music.

The present members of The Pirates are Brian Gregg on bass, and Clem Cattini on drums (both played for various singers from the Larry Parnes rock stable before joining Johnny), while on guitar there's Art Caddy, who has been with Johnny from the very beginning, and about whom Johnny vehemently declares, "I wouldn't swap him for all the tea in China!"

I asked Johnny for his opinion

JOHNNY KIDD
AND THE PIRATES
Wish to thank all their friends and fans for their help in making the charts with
SHAKIN' ALL OVER

NAT HENTOFF'S
U.S. AIRMAIL

One of rock's early casualties – the wreck of Eddie Cochrane's car.

Girls who gave lads 'quivers down the membranes' inspired my hit

confesses JOHNNY KIDD

MAYBE you think it's strange that I should ever have written a piece called "Shakin' All Over." Several people have intimated to me that they consider it an unexpected choice of title, if only because it seems rather dated. Titles like this, they say, went out in the very early days of rock 'n' roll.

Perhaps they're right and I agree that it was taking something of a gamble to come up with a tune of this name. But the way things have turned out, the title hasn't had any adverse effect whatever — in fact, quite the contrary.

After all, I think the secret of the record's success is to be found primarily in the lyric. You see, it's very simply constructed and easily memorised. From this point of view it has a sort of nursery rhyme appeal about it.

You know, there's quite an amusing story behind the number, and how I came to write it. When I was going around with a bunch of the lads and we happened to see a girl who was a real sizzler, we used to say that she gave us "quivers down the membranes." It was a standard saying with us, referring to any attractive girl.

Well, that phrase stuck with me, because I saw in it a new angle on the old familiar shakes routine.

I can honestly say that it was this, more than anything, that inspired me to write "Shakin' All Over."

But now that the record has become so successful I have to admit that I am extremely surprised at what has happened. It never occurred to me that it would catch on to this extent. I've just arrived back from a seven-day Scottish tour and I find that the disc is still in the Top Five. How about that? Fantastic, isn't it?

You see, if I am to be honest, I must tell you that in my opinion there's nothing worth-while musically in the number — no chords even!

Not a song!

In fact, I don't really consider it is a song — I regard it as a piece of material. But it's certainly been very lucky for me, and I only hope that I can produce more like it.

I shall be rehearsing next week for my new record. I can't give you any indication of what it will be like, because I haven't even written it yet! I'm thinking like mad, trying to work up an original idea—the most important thing, in my estimation, is that

this new disc will have to have an unusual sound.

This I can promise you—it will be quite different from "Shakin' All Over," although it will still have a pronounced beat.

Of course, at our disc sessions we are largely dependent upon the ideas and suggestions of our recording man...

'I'm not a rock singer' says MARK WYNTER

WHEN underwriter Ray Mackender broke into the entertainment business with his singing discovery Mark Wynter, he decided on a welcome change from what he crisply calls "the sweaty check-shirt-and-jeans rig-out."

Elevating his perky protégé from a menial occupation in a self-service store, and ditching his family name of Terry Lewis, he completed the transformation of the Cockney kid by giving him "a fresh, well-scrubbed appearance."

Contracts

Steering his protégé and his disc "Image Of A Girl" to a place in the charts has not been easy for college-boy Mackender, tied eight hours a day to an office desk at Lloyd's.

But the result has been a satisfying bundle of contracts for Mark, who is being fostered by Decca and impresario Harold Fielding.

Mark was singing for a bandleader friend, Hank Fryer, at Peckham Co-Op Hall, just over a year ago. Ray spotted him and offered

to pay for a twelve-month course in singing and production.

Mark agreed and was sent along to the well-known

vocal coach Mabel Corram, whose successful pupils have included Dickie Valentine, Valerie Masters and Craig Douglas. Presentation was

entrusted to Mary Phillips, of the Royal Academy of Dramatic Art.

To acquire audience experience, Mark was tried out with 10-minute spots at suburban dance-halls in London. Wisely, Mackender took his time, planning with conscientious care.

Two weeks after Mark's initial disc, "Image Of A Girl" and "The Glory Of Love," reached the shops, it crept into the Hit Parade, favourably reviewed by critics and eagerly played by disc-jockeys.

Says Mark of his record hit:

"Both my current titles are sung in a dreamy fashion, but it's not a pattern I propose to follow. I shall specialise in beat ballads. But I'm not a rock-'n'-roll singer.

"But choosing a song is an art," he confesses. "So we have now asked Lionel Bart to act as my adviser. And he is writing a special song for me, something happy and joyful, just the sort of number I like."

CHRIS HAYES.

Melody Maker

November 5, 1960   FOR THE BEST IN JAZZ   Every Friday 6d.

BAN THIS BOOK CRY U.S ELVIS FANS

TWO days after the release in Britain of the book "Operation Elvis," a big storm blew up on Wednesday over its alleged "poor taste" and "disrespect to Presley." Show business had its own version of the "Lady Chatterley's Lover" dispute. And already hundreds of Presley's U.S fans have boycotted the book.

They wrote to the 4,500-strong England and Commonwealth Fan Club in London, recommending fans here not to buy it.

Letters from angry Presley fans in the States poured into the London offices of British fan club presidents Dug Surtees and Jan Soward.

One "recommended" people not to buy the book "as it ridicules Elvis and his fans ruthlessly."

JAZZ GALA AIDS

Life-lines of the SHADOWS

	HANK	TONY	BRUCE	JET
			Bruce Welch.	Terence Harris.
Real name :	Hank Brian Marvin	Daniel Joseph Anthony Meehan		
Birth date :	October 28. 1941	March 2. 1942.	November 2. 1941,	July 7. 1939.
Birthplace :	Newcastle-on-Tyne	London.	Bognor Regis.	Kingsbury.
Height :	5 ft. 11 ins.	5 ft. 6½ ins	6 ft.	5 ft. 6 ins.
Weight :	142 lb.	126 lb.	192 lb.	126 lb.
Colour of eyes :	Blue	Blue.	Brown.	Blue.
Colour of hair :	Dark brown.	Light brown.	Dark brown.	Blond.
Parents' names :	Margaret and Joe	J. & M. Meehan.	Mrs. S. Welch	Frances and Bill.
Family :	One brother	Three brothers, one sister.		
Present home :	Finchley	London.	Westminster.	Lancaster Gate.
Instruments played :	Guitar, banjo, piano	Guitar. drums, percussion.	Guitar.	Bass.
Education :	Rutherford College. Newcastle-on-Tyne	Regent's Park Central School.	Rutherford College. Newcastle-on-Tyne.	Willesden Technical College.
Musical education :	Nil	"Mostly self-taught but lately Max Abrams."	Nil.	"Taught by Sammy Stokes, ex-Ted Heath jazzman."
Age on entering show business :	16 years	15 years.	16 years.	16½ years.
First public appearance :	Kalin Twins tour. October 5, 1958	Barrow-in-Furness, one-night stand with the Vipers.	Kalin Twins tour. October 5, 1958.	Middlesbrough Empire, 1956.
Biggest disappointment in career :	"Saturday Dance" just missing charts.	None.	Not being able to fly home to England when Cliff returned for NME Poll Concert.	Car accident just before last Christmas.
Compositions :	"Saturday Dance." "You And I." "Gee Whiz It's You." " Driftin'," etc.	—	"Please Don't Tease." "Thinking Of Our Love." "You And I." "Tell Me."	"Jet Black." "I Love You So," "I'm Gonna Get You." "She's Gone."
Biggest influence on career :	"So many it is hard to chose any one."	Mother.	Buddy Holly.	None.
Hobbies :	Driving. tinkering with engines.	Studying music. playing snooker.	Driving, listening to records, Western films.	Driving
Favourite colour :	Blue.	Blue.	Turquoise.	Blue.
Favourite singers :	Bobby Darin. Buddy Holly.	Frank Sinatra. Ray Charles. Ella Fitzgerald.	Buddy Holly, Everly Brothers. Jerry Lee Lewis.	Gene Vincent. Jerry Lee Lewis.
Favourite food :	Indian curry.	Steak.	Indian curry.	Anything.
Favourite drink :	Light and lime.	Lager.	Tea.	Light.
Favourite clothes :	Casual, smart suits.	Suits.	Casual.	Anything in leather.
Favourite bands :	Ray Charles.	Count Basie.	The Rebels.	MJQ and the Jazz Messengers.
Favourite instrumentalists :	Chet Atkins, Barney Kessel, Duane Eddy.	Shelley Manne. Joe Morello.	Hank B. Marvin.	Hank Marvin, late Oscar Pettiford.
Favourite composers :	Rodgers and Hammerstein.	Ravel. Gershwin.	Buddy Holly, Norman Petty.	—
Car :	Ford Zodiac.	None.	Rover.	Ford Consul Convertible.
Likes :	Being lazy . . . doing one-night stands . . .	Weird music . . . unusual people . . . eating . . . horse riding . . . snooker.	Money . . . tea.	Cars . . . beer.
Dislikes :	Impoliteness . . . rainy weather . . .	Conceited types . . . aggressive people.	Going to bed . . . getting up.	Stage make-up . . . telephones . . . writing letters.
Tastes in music :	" ny type. providing it's well played."	Jazz. some classics. folk music and Irish music.	Nearly everything.	Anything.
Personal ambition :	To be top guitarist in Europe one day.	To travel more.	Make plenty of money.	Make lots of money.
Professional ambition :	The Shadows to be top British instrumental group.	To arrange musical backings for an orchestra.	To be part of the biggest group in the world.	To make the Shadows England's No. 1 group.

. . . and 'lines' that refer to them all

Biggest break in career : Meeting Cliff Richard.

Most thrilling experience : Hearing "Apache" No. 1.

TV debut : "Oh Boy !", November, 1958.

First important public appearance : The Kalin Twins tour. October. 1958.

Radio debut : "Saturday Club." in 1958.

No. 1 disc hit : "Apache" which was top for six weeks.

Current hit and latest release : "Man Of Mystery" b w "The Stranger."

Albums : All recorded with Cliff: "Cliff." "Cliff Sings" and "Me And My Shadows."

EPs : With Cliff: "Cliff. Nos. 1 and 2," "Expresso Bongo," "Serious Charge" and "Cliff Sings, 1, 2 and 3."

Present label : Columbia.

Recording manager : Norrie Paramor.

Personal manager : Peter Gormley.

Film debut : "Expresso Bongo."

Important engagements abroad : Tour of the States with Cliff. Sweden and Germany.

Origin of group name : "We were originally called the Drifters, until an American group of the same name came on the scene, so we changed it to the Shadows. We don't know who thought of it. but it's a really good name."

JONAH RUDDY, NME's Hollywood correspondent, interviews
JOHNNY BURNETTE

SINATRA. Dino Martin and Perry Como, Mathis. Frankie Avalon and Bobby Darin. Fabian, Ricky Nelson and Elvis Presley—I know them all and I must record that the young singer from Memphis. Johnny Burnette, is among the most pleasant.

He has a breezy manner. a warm smile. a Tennessee drawl. a firm handshake. and talent—lots of talent as a singer and a song writer.

"I guess I was mighty lucky when I was a kid. Mother and daddy gave my brother, Dorsey, and me guitars when I was live and he was seven, and we learned to play and to sing." said Johnny Burnette when we met in the office of Dick Annotico, International Sales Director, at the Liberty Records building on Sunset Boulevard.

"We used to sing hymns and spirituals and folksongs, and we sang at high school.

"I used to know Elvis Presley when he went to Humes High and I attended Catholic High School in Memphis. Elvis used to tote his guitar to school on his back when he rode his motorcycle and he would play during recess. He was mighty keen on singing. I was more keen on football."

Johnny laughed: "But I just wasn't big enough for football. so I turned my hands—literally, I guess—to boxing.

"Brother Dorsey and me. we fought in the Mid-South Golden Gloves Championship in Memphis. Did pretty well, I guess. Professional? Sure I fought in a professional match when I was 18, in Monroe, Louisiana. I made $60—about £22 that would be, huh?—in the first round. I got my nose broken. The quickest $60 I ever did make.

"**Ended my fighting and my football.**

"I worked as a deckhand on the river boats—hard work. heck. but good fun. I used to be on the run from Memphis to New Orleans and New Orleans to Cairo (pronounced Cayro). and every night we used to sing river songs. and songs from the Bayous and Cajun songs.

'Singing up a storm'

"Oh yes. when we were at school. we played in clubs and joints in Memphis. like the Eagle's Nest and the Chatelons and in dancehalls, in a combo with Scotty Moore and Bill Black. What were we paid? Well, we used to pass the hat around!

"**The popular songs were Hank Williams' tunes and 'Beale Street Blues.'** Yes, there was me and Elvis and Johnny Cash and Marty Robbins singing up a storm in places in Memphis.

"Since then I've been across the States several times. I've written songs for Ricky Nelson, Margie Rayburn. Jody Reynolds and lots of others," said Johnny Burnette. quietly.

"But I tell you I was very lucky when I signed with Liberty Records. They're all just wonderful people. They backed me until I got going. until I clicked with what you call 'a bomb.' And then Snuff Garrett. a great a-and-r man. chose 'Dreamin'' for me."

How did he get his break?

"Well. Dorsey and me. we talked it over and we decided to try our luck in New York." said Johnny. "We made it there in our old car and we made the rounds. I'll cut it short and leave out the heartaches. We auditioned for Ted Mack on the Amateur Hour and finally went to Madison Square Garden as a three-time winner.

"**That was way back in 1956. My first professional engagement was on the Steve Allen Show. which led to me making a movie with disc-jockey Alan Freed.**

"I think it was called 'Rock, Rock, Rock' here. and I was with Connie Francis, Chuck Berry, Laverne Baker and a kid actress called Tuesday Weld, who has sure gone places since then.

"While I was in Hollywood at that time, I wrote two songs for Ricky Nelson—'Believe What You Say'

and 'Waitin' In School.' Wasn't easy to get them to him, but I did. I think on one of them. I went to his home. rang the bell and stood on the front lawn and sang for his parents. Ozzie and Harriet Nelson."

I recalled that each of the records Ricky Nelson made with Johnny Burnette's songs sold more than a million each.

"Well. Ricky's a very popular singer," was Johnny's comment.

Sure. but the songs were right. They had the solid beat. How, when and where does he write songs?

"I write on trains. planes and buses. I get an idea and put it down and then the melody comes along to one-nighters. just like the Everlys and Bobby Darin and I'm readin' up on England, and I've got maps so that I know where we're goin'. I've just come back from a tour of one-nighters in Nebraska. Wyoming, Idaho and Colorado. Pretty rough at times on the road. Snow and ice and cold." he smiled.

"But you meet the people who like you in the teenage ballrooms. Rock 'n' roll is still popular. They like songs with a beat and ballads."

Johnny's very enthusiastic about Roy Orbison. He sounded like his manager-press agent combined.

"I've been knowing Roy for a long time. He's one of the nicest guys I've travelled with all over the Eastern states." he said warmly.

"He's the same as Elvis. is Roy Orbison, and to my knowings. one of the best singers we have today. Roy's from Texas—he's a top entertainer, a handsome guy with great talent."

Looks like Johnny and Roy are going to have a good time with you. singing and playing. And a secret included in their repertoire is a medley of Elvis Presley's hit songs.

JOHNNY BURNETTE signs his contract to tour Britain. watched by SI WARONKER, chairman of Liberty Records. and FARI McDANIELS, Johnny's personal manager

Johnny Burnette made some pure R&R small group records which buffs treasure, but his lasting hit, and something of an anthem, is 'You're Sixteen', written by the Sherman Bros; who went on to being Walt Disney film songwriters on 'Mary Poppins', etc.

also had a film role in the new movie "Kanga," and is strongly featured in

What's more, Oriole have now persuaded A.f to launch into song—

too, for their recent essays on to wax for Fontana have proven a

The Drifters shed tears now

FOR all the ardent pleading and heartfelt imploring that The Drifters have been doing during the last few weeks, when they have been soulfully urging an anonymous young lady to "Save The Last Dance For Me," it seems very much as though their urgent entreaty went unheeded.

You see, the lads have now made a follow-up record to their current NME Chart success called "I Count The Tears." One imagines that they must have an extremely sound explanation for this outburst of weeping—presumably the fickle young lady didn't save them the last dance.

It seems that this talented team has another hit on its hands. "I Count The Tears" is already moving appreciably in America, and I'm confident that it will achieve a similar response when London release it in this country. But that won't be until the group's present hit starts sliding down the lists.

There's no sign of a decline at the moment. The boys have been sitting comfortably in second position for four consecutive weeks—and, despite the congratulations which are obviously due to them for such a great achievement, we should also add our commiserations.

If their record hadn't coincided with Elvis Presley's "It's Now Or Never"—which is easily one of the strongest discs of the year—The Drifters would undoubtedly have reached the coveted No. 1 position.

The forthcoming issue, "I Count The Tears," is another number stemming from the prolific pens of Lieber and Stoller, enhanced by a brilliant Stan Applebaum arrangement, who was also responsible for scoring the present disc.

The group has, of course, slightly changed its personnel in recent months. Former lead singer Ben King is now recording solo for Atco (we should be getting his first release over here on London shortly), and the present line-up of the Drifters consists of Charles Thomas, Ellsbury Hobbs, Doc Green (not the one Jack Warner patrols!) and Rudy Lewis.

As yet we haven't had the opportunity of seeing this versatile group in person.

In the meantime, NME News Editor Don Wedge says this about the boys' performance. When he visited New York recently, Don popped into Harlem's celebrated Apollo Theatre. He writes :

"The audience was stamping and clapping in time to the rocking group on stage. There was much of the atmosphere of a revivalist meeting.

"The Drifters were dressed in fawn, casual suits. None was tall, as so many Negroes are, but each seemed to pack the dynamic energy Sammy Davis has led us to expect of midget coloured entertainers.

"The Drifters paid little regard to the microphone in the centre of the stage. They moved about with firm, deliberate steps—helping to set a terrific visual, as well as musical, beat to their numbers."

Four Drifters   and pianist

CAMPBELL CONNELLY GROUP

★ MALAGUENA Connie Francis (M.G.M.)	★ JUST AS Nat 'King
★ LITTLE GIRL Marty Wilde (Philips)	★ I WISH I KNEW Nat 'Kin
★ HERE COMES SANTA CLAUS Ray Conniff (Philips)	★ THE WHO Beverley
★ ANGRY YOUNG MAN Rikky Baron (Parlophone)	★ GEORG Ray C
★ EVERYTHING BUT LOVE Brook Brothers (Pye)	★ JIN Bob
★ I BELIEVE David Whitfield (Decca)	★ ANNA Gene
★ SWEET SUE Jan and Keld (Qualiton)	★ LITTLE Roy
★ WE'RE GONNA DANCE Lorne Lesley (Polydor)	

CAMPBELL CONNELLY, 10 DENMARK STRE

The Big Beat is dissipating. We are reaching a long watershed, a 'state of the Art' season where R&R is becoming more sleek and poppy. The Shadows, with their polite guitar sounds and lever-induced vibrato, do nifty leg-kicks in perfect unison. They are the group others emulate. Bert Weedon, Britain's Chet Atkins, is another guitar master and a homey figure but nobody to get excited about.

Notice the chart appearance of the highly original 'Big O' – Roy Orbison.

SHAKIN GOING ON

DUFFY POWER

H279

fontana

Fontana Records Stanhope House
Stanhope Place London W.2.

NME MUSIC CHARTS

BEST SELLING POP RECORDS IN BRITAIN

(Wednesday, November 16, 1960)

Last This
Week

Last	This		
1	1	IT'S NOW OR NEVER	Elvis Presley (RCA)
2	2	AS LONG AS HE NEEDS ME	Shirley Bassey (Columbia)
4	3	DREAMIN'	Johnny Burnette (London)
3	4	ONLY THE LONELY	Roy Orbison (London)
6	5	MY HEART HAS A MIND OF ITS OWN	Connie Francis (MGM)
5	6	ROCKING GOOSE	Johnny and the Hurricanes (London)
9	7	SAVE THE LAST DANCE FOR ME	Drifters (London)
11	8	GOODNESS GRACIOUS ME	Peter Sellers & Sophia Loren (Parlophone)
16	9	MAN OF MYSTERY	Shadows (Columbia)
13	10	MY LOVE FOR YOU	Johnny Mathis (Fontana)
—	11	THE STRANGER	Shadows (Columbia)
7	12	LET'S THINK ABOUT LIVING	Bob Luman (Warner Bros.)
18	13	KOMMOTION	Duane Eddy (London)
8	14	MACDONALD'S CAVE	Piltdown Men (Capitol)
10	15	MR. CUSTER	Charlie Drake (Parlophone)
20	16	MILORD	Edith Piaf (Columbia)
—	17	LITTLE DONKEY	Nina & Frederik (Columbia)
15	18	HOW ABOUT THAT!	Adam Faith (Parlophone)
14	19	CHAIN GANG	Sam Cooke (RCA)
27	20	JUST AS MUCH AS EVER	Nat Cole (Capitol)
17	21	NINE TIMES OUT OF TEN	Cliff Richard (Columbia)
19	22	SO SAD	Everly Brothers (Warner Bros.)
21	22	BLUE ANGEL	Roy Orbison (London)
25	24	SORRY ROBBIE	Bert Weedon (Top Rank)
25	25	THEM THERE EYES	Emile Ford (Pye)
—	26	MILORD	Frankie Vaughan (Philips)
12	26	WALK DON'T RUN	John Barry Seven (Columbia)
—	28	ROCKIN' ALONE	Miki and Griff (Pye)
—	29	NEVER ON SUNDAY	Manuel (Columbia)
—	30	DON'T BE CRUEL	Bill Black's Combo (London)

BEST SELLING SHEET MUSIC IN BRITAIN

(Tuesday, November 15, 1960)

Last This
Week

Last	This		
2	1	IT'S NOW OR NEVER	(Ricordi)
1	2	AS LONG AS HE NEEDS ME	(Lakeview)
3	3	IN MY LITTLE CORNER OF THE WORLD	(Kassner)
6	4	NEVER ON SUNDAY	(United Artists)
4	5	PASSING BREEZE	(Clover-Conway)
7	6	LOVE IS LIKE A VIOLIN	(Keith Prowse)
16	7	MILORD	(Aberbach)
9	8	ONLY THE LONELY	(Acuff-Rose)
8	9	PAPER ROSES	(Leeds)
10	10	WALK DON'T RUN	(Planetary-Kahl)
29	11	MY HEART HAS A MIND OF ITS OWN	(Nevins-Kirshner)
14	12	NINE TIMES OUT OF TEN	(Aberbach)
17	13	FOUR LITTLE HEELS	(Tin Pan Alley)
5	14	TELL LAURA I LOVE HER	(Lawrence Wright)
13	15	APACHE	(F.D. & H.)
18	16	LET'S THINK ABOUT LIVING	(Acuff-Rose)
12	17	EVERYBODY'S SOMEBODY'S FOOL	(Nevins-Kirshner)
11	18	PLEASE HELP ME I'M FALLING	(Aberbach)
26	19	DREAMIN'	(Edwin Morris)
15	20	HOW ABOUT THAT!	(Mills)
24	21	MY LOVE FOR YOU	(Johnny Mathis)
22	22	THEM THERE EYES	(Sun)
—	23	ROCKING GOOSE	(Vicki)
—	24	LITTLE DONKEY	(Chappells)
30	25	NICE 'N' EASY	(Barton)
21	25	SUMMER PLACE	(Blossom)
19	27	GIRL OF MY BEST FRIEND	(Hill & Range)
20	28	I'D DO ANYTHING	(Lakeview)
—	29	MAN OF MYSTERY	(Feldman)
—	29	NICOLETTE	(Macmelodies)

BEST SELLING POP RECORDS IN U.S.

(Tuesday, November 15, 1960)

Last This
Week

Last	This		
4	1	GEORGIA ON MY MIND	Ray Charles
3	2	POETRY IN MOTION	Johnny Tillotson
5	3	YOU TALK TOO MUCH	Joe Jones
2	4	I WANT TO BE WANTED	Brenda Lee
1	5	SAVE THE LAST DANCE FOR ME	Drifters
7	6	STAY	Maurice Williams & the Zodiacs
8	7	LET'S GO, LET'S GO, LET'S GO	Hank Ballard & the Midnighters
16	8	LAST DATE	Floyd Cramer
—	9	A THOUSAND STARS	Kathy Young & the Innocents
9	10	BLUE ANGEL	Roy Orbison
17	11	NEW ORLEANS	U.S. Bonds
18	12	NORTH TO ALASKA	Johnny Horton
14	13	SLEEP	Little Willie John
11	14	DON'T BE CRUEL	Bill Black's Combo
19	15	ALONE AT LAST	Jackie Wilson
13	16	LET'S THINK ABOUT LIVING	Bob Luman
10	17	DEVIL OR ANGEL	Bobby Vee
—	18	HUCKLEBUCK	Chubby Checker
6	19	MY HEART HAS A MIND OF ITS OWN	Connie Francis
12	20	CHAIN GANG	Sam Cooke

The American chart is published by courtesy of "Billboard"

NAT KING COLE 'The Magic of Christmas'

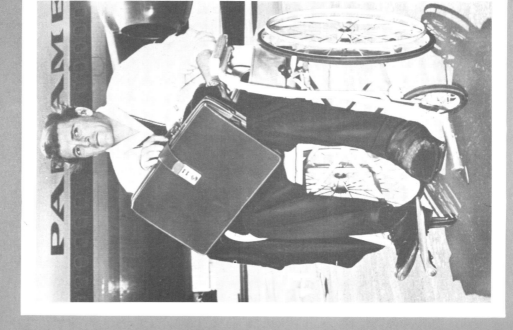

Helen Shapiro is something of a standout in this 'marking time' period, just pre-Beatle. A real home-grown artiste, with British-built songs like 'Walking Back to Happiness', and a real foghorn of a voice. I mean – good! She got an accolade in the *New Statesman* of all places – that dour, leftish weekly – in an article by Jonathan Miller, the super-brain.

Vincent arrives at Idlewild, injured in the car-crash that killed Eddie Cochrane. Note the briefcase – most un-rock 'n' roll!

HELP!

● *Reader Jean Fielder, of London, writes:*

LAST weekend I took part in Jazz-shows' Floating Festival of Jazz, from Tower Bridge to Margate. It was my first excursion into live jazz and I thoroughly enjoyed it—the weather was perfect, the company congenial, and the music excellent.

Only one thing puzzles me. Why on earth were so many of the fans dressed in such outlandish clothes? Admittedly, a floating jazz festival is not the place to stand on formality, but, really, is it necessary to go to such self-conscious lengths?

I cannot help but feel these gentlemen in funny hats are doing jazz a disservice. For that matter, are they really jazz fans at all?

DIZ answers

— Bisley —

"Nobody appreciates that we're simply rebelling against conformity. And anyway, if all your friends dress like this you've just got to do the same . . . ."

Some of the 'gentlemen in funny hats'

I had, unwittingly, always had a hankering for older sounds. Oh, I was a devoted R&R fan—I knew what it wasn't, and I understood it was as much a pair of US blue jeans as a gramophone record—but I was equally devoted, in other moods, to the Original Dixieland Jazz Band, Al Jolson, 'Whispering' Jack Smith and Jelly Roll Morton. Man cannot live by Big Beat alone. I liked traditional jazz because, via such primitives as George Lewis and Bunk Johnson, it was easy to play and you got a cultural bonus because there was plenty of literature to tell you that what you were imitating was real 'truth', and left-wing at that. You were plumbing the nitty-gritty of life when you played a blues in B flat. Ignorance was righteous bliss. Traditional Jazz was played on Ban the Bomb Marches, too—therefore it must be OK. Lots of 'hooray' types began to flock to this jazz. Gradually a British sound emerged—blues without pain, ragtime à la Harry Champion. Jazz without tears. Music hall jazz: Trad! Nothing to do with blackman and suffering and America. So out came all the old clothes, the toppers, the 1930s sweaters and shags climbed into them and raved. Poor old Lord Montagu had his stately home churned up by these brutes.

And Acker Bilk, one of the Traddie heroes, didn't know what was happening. He survived and went on to 'Stranger on the Shore', while the Traddies turned their attentions elsewhere, or got into jobs in the City. As for me, I eventually retreated into Rhythm and Blues, hoping no-one would find my lair.

REN GREVATT, in New York, reports on—
The most vulgar dance invented

Jo Ann Campbell stars in the Paramount film, "Hey, Let's Twist."

SOME have called it the most vulgar dance ever invented. Yet the Twist came into its greatest prominence thanks to the influence of high society, a set regarded as proper in most circles.

It was well over a year ago when Hank Ballard and the Midnighters first recorded "The Twist" on King Records. At almost the same time, the tune was covered by a young unknown artist on the Parkway label, one Chubby Checker.

Checker's record made him a big-time record artist. Following "The Twist," Checker stayed with a good thing and recorded "Let's Twist Again," which became just about as big a hit.

Over a year later, in the early fall of 1961, when the teenagers had long since finished their fling with the Twist, a series of Twist parties was staged at an obscure night club on Manhattan's West 44th Street, known as the Peppermint Lounge.

With an able assist from persons well connected with the café and high society element, the Peppermint boite and its bandleader, Joey Dee, became the rage of New York.

The publicist for the Peppermint arranged with Earl Blackwell, who is associated with a firm known as Celebrity Services, to bring some of his highly placed society friends into the spot.

The idea behind this gambit was to gain mentions for the club in the society columns. This, in fact, is not an uncommon device where publicity is required. Often the idea drops dead. In the case at hand, it took fire fast.

CHAIN REACTION

The well-known Igor Cassini, better known to his society column readers in the "New York Journal American" as Cholly Knickerbocker, is credited with the first plug for the Twist and the Peppermint in his column.

Within a couple of days, Eugenia Shepherd, fashion columnist in the "New York Herald Tribune," also got hip and mentioned the Twist.

These mentions had the effect of a chain reaction, and within a couple of weeks the publicity steamroller was well under way.

The record industry was not far behind. In one week in late October record reviewers in the leading trade journals received eight different new recordings of "The Twist."

Soon, albums too were being rushed out to cash in on the new bonanza. To date, there have already been several dozen albums, including one each by the most renowned "society" dance bands of all, Lester Lanin and Meyer Davis.

CHUBBY CHECKER

The only new single record of the dance song to go over in a big way is that recorded by Joey Dee, the maestro at the Peppermint, with his combo.

Meanwhile, Chubby Checker has come into his own. His original record of "The Twist" sold close to a million copies during its initial reign. Now it has sold an additional half-million copies since its re-release a few weeks back, and his "Let's Twist Again" is not far behind.

Many night clubs have fallen in with a straight Twist policy. The well-known Roundtable in New York, famed as a jazz spot, has adopted this approach and features Bill Black's combo from Memphis.

Meanwhile, Paramount Pictures produced a full-length feature picture in

FULL-LENGTH AND
TWiST-ERRIFIC!

THE FIRST fabulous film about the TWIST
...the country's hottest, hippest
hip-shaking sensation!

COLUMBIA PICTURES presents

HEAR TODAY'S TOP TWIST SONGS!
"TWIST AROUND THE CLOCK"
"DANCIN' TWIST"
"DON'T TWIST WITH ANYONE ELSE BUT ME"
"THE WANDERER"
"TWISTIN' U.S.A."
and many more great hits!

TWiST AROUND THE CLOCK

WITH

CHUBBY CHECKER — **DION** — **VICKI SPENCER**

The top TWISTER in the land gives out with the greatest!

THE MARCELS — introducing **CLAY COLE**

and

John CRONIN · Mary MITCHELL · Maura McGIVENEY · Jeff PARKER

Written by JAMES B. GORDON · Produced by SAM KATZMAN · Directed by OSCAR RUDOLPH · A FOUR LEAF PRODUCTION

ITS TWIST AND SWAY-ALL THE WAY!

NEW MUSICAL

TWIST !

CLIFF RICHARD says: "It knocks me out"

IS Chubby Checker's "Twist" the biggest sensation to hit Tin Pan Alley since Bill Haley and "Rock Around The Clock" or is it merely another one-month wonder like The Madison and Kwela proved to be?

Is this hip-swinging beat really in demand from you, the record-buying public, or is it another case of a commercial craze being artificially engineered by smart profiteers?

Here are some first-hand opinions to shed a little starlight on the twist's destiny.

CLIFF

"Sure I dig the twist! It knocks me out. Haven't quite mastered the thing I must admit, even though I

... and other stars speak out

did get some first-hand instruction from Chubby while he was over here.

"Only thing that bugs me is the constant reports I keep hearing from the medics.

"You know, all this about causing

muscular contortions and spine injuries. Not that I take this too much to heart but I feel pretty achey and stiff myself after trying some twist numbers and let's face it, if you're going to end up all worn out and weary after a few numbers it's not much fun.

"However, could be I'm trying to do it all wrong."

ACKER

"I don't think the public is going to swallow this one whole! The twist's success looks like being short but sweet. As you know we've got the dance in the film I just completed. The girls look great in action! But the fellers—plain daft!

"In America they needed a new craze—something to revive the flagging interest in solid rock 'n' roll. The twist filled the bill, but over here you should remember we've already got one new fad — IT'S TRAD DAD!"

PAUL McDOWELL
of the Temperance Seven

"Somebody once said 'There's nothing new under the sun.' It could be applied to the twist. I was down in St. Tropez about two years ago, looking after a car park, and the current dance rage was something very much like the twist.

"Following that up, you know there is a line on a disc called 'Black Bottom.' I cut a few weeks back which runs: 'Black Bottom a new twister'—and that little epic as everyone knows came out in the 1920s.

"Question is—should we have called the disc 'Black Bottom Twist'?

"In conclusion, I should feel reasonably safe to say on behalf of The Temperance Seven that we are all ardent twisters!"

JERRY LORDAN

"As a composer I hate to see melody and rhythm sacrificed for a raw beat and nothing else. I'm not saying that all twist numbers are like this but too many certainly are. However, it's quite obvious that the dance is the important thing and not the sound.

"For this very reason I can't agree with anyone who describes it as another rock 'n' roll rage. Haley and his Comets had an exciting new sound to offer.

"Chubby Checker himself admits you can twist to almost any beat number—so here is a new dance not a new sound.

"I give the whole thing three months as a peak attraction then a slow fade out. As for myself—the dance is great fun. The music . . .

JOHN LEYTON

"This looks to me as if it will go down big. Maybe it won't reach the proportions that the cha-cha and

---

I'm afraid that the Twist was not a spontaneous explosion but an industry generated fad, like the Monkees. Thus, ammunition was given to those pop haters (of which there are precious few nowadays because they're all scared of being called fuddy-duddies, a Beatle legacy) who believed that the kids will go for whatever is marketed at them; that if you have enough money you can buy your way into the charts by brain-washing via beat.

The Twist can be seen as an unconscious conspiracy by media, industry and public to create some excitement within a dying R&R. The media certainly loved to write about the vulgarity of this new dance. 'The Twist shocked me . . . Wholly frightening . . .', wrote Beverly Nichols in 1962. 'The essence of the Twist, the curious perverted heart of it, is that you dance it alone'. He was *right on* there: it was certainly a masturbatory dance – in theory. In practice it was just ludicrous – especially when the old folk did it, as they did, in millions. This was the first manifestation of adult activity inside R&R.

I'M A ☐ - admits MIKE SARNE!

to DEREK JOHNSON

"YOU know, I'm really a terrible square!" This self-assessment was Mike Sarne's opening gambit when I met him for the first time this week —but I soon discovered that Britain's latest Top Ten sensation was being more than a little unjust to himself.

For although Mike's interests are not confined to pop music (indeed, his favourite composer is Mozart!), he certainly knows what it's all about. In fact, five years ago—when rock 'n' roll was at its peak—Mike specialised in this type of music.

"I used to go round the pubs, wearing a red sweater with a beret perched on my head, playing a guitar," he recalls, with a chuckle. "But this wasn't my first experience as a singer —previously I'd played cabaret in Germany, and sung with a jazz band in Manchester!"

Mike has clearly defined likes and dislikes in pop music. Unlike John Leyton, who is under the same management as Mike, he doesn't think Sinatra is a square—and he also enjoys the singing of other old un's, such as Como, Crosby and Dean Martin.

"So far as the younger set is concerned, naturally I admire Elvis tremendously, and I like Bobby Rydell's work," he told me. "I have to admit that I'm not very keen on Cliff Richard or Helen Shapiro, but I do like Adam Faith and Eden Kane." Well, that's controversial enough, if you like!

As a result of his lengthy travels on the Continent, Mike speaks five languages besides English — he's probably most proficient in German, which was the very first language he learned before he could even speak English.

And it was his fluency in German that was directly responsible for Mike becoming a recording star. For when John Leyton was due to cut "Son This Is She" in German, Mike made a demonstration disc of the number to help John with the pronunciation. Incidentally, he also performed the same service for Adam Faith, when he waxed a couple of titles for the German market.

Robert Stigwood, Leyton's manager, immediately signed Mike to a long-term contract . . . and hustled him along to the office, when he started searching for songs which would make suitable recording material for Mike.

Bob produced a Geoffrey Goddard composition titled "Fountain Of Love," about which he was most enthusiastic—though Mike admits he thought it was terrible when he first heard it!

Nevertheless, Bob was adamant in choosing this song for Mike's disc debut—all that remained was to find a suitable coupling.

'Savage glee'

Just then, quite by chance, musical director Charles Blackwell arrived at the office, armed with a song he had just written called "Come Outside" — and, to use Mike's own expression, "I seized upon it with savage glee!"

So it was decided, there and then, to switch the original plan. "Come Outside" would be waxed as the

"A" side, with "Fountain Of Love" as the coupling.

Bob Stigwood suggested adapting it from a straightforward beat number into a novelty song, complete with throwaway comments by the girl—and, hey presto, the disc was "in the can" within 24 hours.

Last weekend, Mike made his television debut as a singer in ABC-TV's "Thank Your Lucky Stars"— and no doubt many viewers immediately realised that his was no new face on their screens.

They may well have remembered seeing him in an episode of "The Avengers," or in that powerful Rudolph Cartier production "Cross Of Iron."

But, more likely, they would have associated him with various TV commercials—for Mike has made a host of them. You see, his manager Bob Stigwood is also responsible for casting many of the commercials which you see on your TV screens, and this is how Mike first came to his attention.

You've probably seen Mike in several of the Cadbury commercials—and it was also he who took over from Jess Conrad in the advertisement for Bristol cigarettes.

Now that Mike Sarne has made such a sudden and dramatic impact upon the pop world, I asked him how he sees his future. Does he intend to pursue parallel careers— being an actor and singer simultaneously?

"The last thing I want is to be described as a "hyphenated actor-singer," he declared. "I honestly don't think you can choose beforehand in which direction your career is going to take you. I want to wait and see how things develop before I make up my mind.

"I do promise you this, though— I'd like to stay on the music scene. At any rate, for as long as I'm wanted. Obviously I can't expect to stay in pop music all my life and you know, when I do turn seriously to acting, I'd rather do Shakespeare than films."

An intelligent, thoughtful fellow is this Mike Sarne. In fact, I wondered just how he was reacting to this new-found fame.

Was he, perhaps, suffering the hero-worship and plaudits, purely as a lucrative form of income, without really enjoying it?

'A lot of kicks'

"Don't you believe it," he said. "I love every minute of it. I love the teenagers who come crowding around, and I adore signing autographs.

"You know, it's the first time it's happened to me on a big scale — and I get a lot of kicks out of it. The only trouble is that I always blush furiously—I'll have to see if I can rectify that!

"Frankly, I can't stand those artists who tell confidentially that all this fan worship and autograph signing is a bit of a bore. I reckon they're a load of hypocrites."

Now that Mike has made his mark in the hit parade, his supporters are asking when they can expect to see him on the stage in concert and one-night stands. His manager is currently in the process of organising a few dates for him, but Mike himself is being a little wary on the subject.

"I don't want to go jumping into one-night stands until I feel that I've got a really strong act — and I'm working on that right now," he explained.

"Another thing — I want to be sure that I've got a really good group behind me. I think it's so important to give the customers full entertainment value."

Mike, whose "Come Outside" waxing features him with a strong Cockney brogue, has re-recorded the song for the American market adopting a Brooklyn-type accent, and substituting Stateside expressions for the Cockney ones.

But he's now doubtful as to whether this version will, in fact, be released in the States.

"I've had a lot of letters on this point, and most people seem to think that the Cockney version would meet with greater appeal in the States," he commented.

"On reflection, I'm inclined to think they're right. So we shall probably stick to the original recording for America. Oh, and by the way, I've just re-recorded the song in German!"

Mike, who is unmarried and lives in a Soho flat, has plenty to occupy his spare time. He is a keen sports enthusiast — especially tennis and swimming—and he's busy studying Russian at London University.

But there are other, more important, things to be done in the meantime. Not only does he have the task of consolidating his position as a disc star (his next two records are already planned, the first being another Charles Blackwell composition), but there's also talk of him appearing in a revue and two Continental films later this year.

'Ginny Come

Rather a bright lad, with all those foreign languages spoken. He certainly had a sharp manager in Robert Stigwood (later to guide the Bee Gees). Same later directed 'Myra Breckinridge'.

Pop films up until the later '60s, had plots like feature films, and this was good because romantic other-worldliness is an essential of good pop. Falseness is very important, especially with pop singers as in reality they are mostly extremely dull plodders (excepting Jerry Lee Lewis and a few others, but not many).

Then came the cinema verité 'documentary' films – 'Don't Look Back', 'Gimme Shelter' – and we saw the acts 'Off the record' in all their awfulness, as the money-grubbing yobs many of them are. I'm glad to see that recently there's a return to the old story-line exploitation pop films, with 'The Buddy Holly Story' and 'American Hot Wax'. Having said all that, or spat it, I have to admit that 'Play It Cool!' wasn't very good, in fact it was duff. Note the director.

10

ROY ORBISON THANKS PAT BOONE FOR HIS DISC FAME!

ASK Roy Orbison, currently on the brink of the Top Ten with his latest waxing, "Dream Baby," the person who was mainly responsible for his own career as a singer and songwriter, and it's more than likely that he'll point to another chart occupant, **Pat Boone!**

Where's the connection? Well, a few years ago, Roy was studying geology at North Texas State College, when a fellow student named Pat Boone had his first record success with "Two Hearts."

Thrilled and not just a little intrigued at his friend's good fortune, Roy decided there and then that he really wanted to search for gold discs, instead of black gold—oil!

His father, an oil rigger, had spent most of his life searching for the valuable liquid and until that moment it was pretty certain that Roy would follow in his footsteps.

Now the folk in the Texas town of Wink call Roy the oil-driller's son who struck gold with a guitar pick!

The term is a very apt one, you may agree, particularly in view of Roy's string of disc strikes.

Yet it's true to say that 26-year-old Orbison could have done well, financially, by sticking to any one of three careers. He found fame and fortune as a singer, as a songwriter, and, if it hadn't been for Boone's inspiration, Roy might be a Texan oil millionaire by now!

The dual career of Orbison the singer and tunesmith has prospered greatly. He has written most of his own disc successes—among them "Only The Lonely" (a transatlantic No. 1), "Blue Angel," "Today's Teardrops," "Runnin' Scared," "Ooby Dooby," "Uptown" and "I'm Hurtin'"—the latter three being Stateside hits.

Strangely enough, he did not pen his latest chart entry, which this week stands at No. 12, after making its first appearance last week at No. 18. He has a songwriting interest

in the disc, though, for he wrote the flip, "The Actress."

Roy's parents played a big part in his career, too, for his father, a keen guitarist, has a stock of country-and-western songs that he began to teach his son at the tender age of six.

By the time young Roy had barely entered his teens, he was **leading a group called the Wink Westerners.**

He also conducted a radio show from Vernon, Texas, that amassed a huge listening figure, and when he was 16, Roy was honoured in an unusual way by being asked to represent all the great talent from the State at the International Lions Convention in Chicago.

The story of Roy's early life has been told before, but it is interesting enough to be repeated, I feel. After being caught up in the whirl of Pat's first big record achievement, Roy was signed by Sun Records president Sam Phillips, the man who discovered Elvis Presley and Johnny Cash.

His first hit was "Ooby Dooby," on Sun. In 1958 he wrote a song called "Claudette," which is his wife's name, and the result was another hit disc for the Everly Brothers—and a songwriter's contract for Roy with the famous Nashville music publishing firm of Acuff-Rose.

A little while later, Roy switched to Monument Records, for whom he still records. His songwriting activities have earned him a great many dollars over the years, too, for among artists recording his compositions have been Buddy Knox, Jerry Lee Lewis and Buddy Holly.

Reports continually reach us of the kind of person Roy is when he steps into the public eye.

He is said to be a terrific performer and stylist, capable of turning an audience from one mood to another. Wherever he goes, of course, he plays the country music that he loves, and I'm told that some of the greatest c-and-w names borrow from the repertoire his father taught him.

The other side of Roy Orbison? Off-duty he lives near Nashville in a spacious, split-level home on Old Hickory Lake, where his leisure time is spent with Claudette and their son. He loves to fish and pilot his high-powered speedboat. Oh! and I nearly forgot—he likes to spend the evenings teaching his son his repertoire! **MIKE HELLICAR**

An informal shot of ROY, showing his love of comfort and liking for big V-ed sweaters.

WELCOME back to the FRESHMA[...]

Roy Orbison is an outsider here, and also a standout. He's not a rocker, or a rockabilly, or a looker. He is a total original. He may have sprung from the Sun records stable but he sounds not a bit like any of the Sun stars. He sounds unearthly but he sings about earthly bring-downs like 'Crying' and 'Falling' and he addresses 'Only The Lonely'. I write in the present tense because he is for all time, he is not of a period. He is eternal. Quite simply, he is my favourite singer and songwriter.

A seaside girlfriend turned me on to his work in 1960. Only a measly little 45 but that dramatic voice came piping out and

lit up that lonely pebble beach with another brand of loneliness. On later songs he developed pop concertos of anguish that moved from rock to rock, getting higher as he kept changing those keys, while martial drums rolled to his lament. He never turned back to repeat a catch phrase as most songs do, he just kept scaling those notes, sometimes leaping down a huge interval until, summoning up that extraordinary sound that seemed to have been gurgle-cooked around his Adam's apple until it was shot up and out like a Roman Candle, there was a rain of yodel notes – as at the end of 'In Dreams' – and you breathed a sigh of relief for 'Orbie'

was intact and still standing on top of his mountain, with the Gods.

I'm glad to say that when I saw him live and in concert in Dublin he was no let down to my rock dream. He added more details, all just right: the frozen spray of jet black hair, like a heavenly helmet, the black matador's costume, the dark glasses – all added up to a man of mystery. He didn't wriggle or sway or get with the beat. He just took off on his song climbs with a '1-2-3'.

AT LAST: QUIET DEL SHANNON TALKS!

DEL SHANNON has always been an enigmatic sort of character, due primarily to the fact that very little publicity about him has seeped across the Atlantic. We know that he shot into the spotlight last year and has subsequently enjoyed an unbroken string of hits. But apart from a fleeting appearance in "It's Trad, Dad!" we've had no other contact with him.

Imagine my surprise, then, when he readily agreed to a lunch date—and I found him one of the most personable, easy going and inoffensive of the visiting American stars I have yet met.

As a result of my questions, it wasn't long before I was able to draw a very accurate pen portrait of our latest American visitor.

? ? ?

Q. Can you tell me something about your latest release in this country, "Cry Myself To Sleep"?

A. You may be surprised to know that I conceived the idea for it while I was driving my car. I should tell you, though, that this is nothing new—most of my song-writing inspirations come to me when I'm driving around in my Cadillac.

In fact, if ever I'm short of new recording material, I take a spin in the car—and you bet that by the time I arrive back home, I've formulated a new song in my mind.

This new disc is rather different from the others, because it was recorded in Nashville, whereas all my previous numbers had been cut in New York.

? ? ?

Q. How about future recording plans, Del? Do you have any follow-up ready?

A. Yes, my next release is already complete with yodelling, but it also has a pretty strong beat.

It's called "The Swiss Maid," and I cut it in Nashville at the same session as "Cry Myself To Sleep." By chance, it isn't one of my own numbers; it was written by Roger Miller, who has composed a lot of material for Andy Williams.

Say, they certainly know how to inject soul and feel into their recording sessions in Nashville, don't they?

So far as future albums are concerned, I already have a dozen or more sides in the can, including several tracks which are distinctly on the jazz side. It shouldn't be long before I have another LP on the market.

? ? ?

Q. You were an overnight sensation with "Runaway." Have you found that it's been difficult to live up to this first tremendous impact?

A. I must admit that when "Runaway" was so successful, my excitement was tempered with concern for the future. So many critics suggested that I was just a one-shot recording artist and I was very worried in case they should prove to be right.

But what could I do, apart from trying to find another song which would have a similar effect?

Fortunately, I came up with "Hats Off To Larry," which was another No. 1 in the States—and which gave me my second Gold Disc.

You know a lot of us believe that the second hit is always more difficult to achieve than any other—and once I overcame this problem, it's been pretty straightforward ever since.

? ? ?

Q. We are all familiar with your trade-mark of introducing falsetto passages into your discs. Is it a gimmick, or does it come naturally?

A. I certainly didn't deliberately develop it as a gimmick. Fals-

QUESTION TIME by BRUCE CHARLTON

etto comes to me very simply. When I wrote "Runaway," I inserted this passage purely and simply because I felt that it enhanced the song. But it wasn't intended as its main feature. I just thought it belonged there.

Since then, I've stuck to the falsetto—partly to establish a distinctive sound and partly because the fans have expected it.

But I plan to get away from it in the future—and then, I guess, I'll come back to it again. You've got to keep ringing the changes in this business.

? ? ?

Q. How do you envisage the development of your career? Would you like to become an all-round entertainer?

A. I sure would. I'd like to be able to prove my worth as a supper club performer.

I honestly believe that I have the ability to do so, although I realise it will take time.

Otherwise, I guess I shall continue trying to appeal to the teenage following—and at the same time, broadening my scope so as to win the approval of the more adult set. With this in view, I'd like to make some out-and-out jazz recordings.

? ? ?

Q. Who would you say are your own favourite recording artists?

A. I'm a very great admirer of Roy Orbison—I think he's just terrific. Of course, I can always listen to Frank Sinatra. And needless to say Elvis is also tops with me.

So far as the girl singers are concerned, I rate Sarah Vaughan as the tops, but I also like Brenda Lee immensely—she is just sensational.

My favourite tune, by the way, is "High Noon" — I don't know why, but it always knocks me out.

? ? ?

Q. Are you familiar with any of our top British artists?

A. Sure, I try to keep in touch with developments over here as much as possible.

I think Frank Ifield has an absolutely wonderful disc with his "I Remember You." It's a recording which Nashville could have been proud of producing.

I also like Cliff Richard immensely—his records are issued on the same label as mine in the States, Big Top.

Helen Shapiro is another name known to me—and, of course, the Springfields are very hot in the States right now. And I reckon they well deserve to be!

? ? ?

Q. I don't suppose you get very much spare time these days, Del, but when you do get a few hours to yourself, how do you fill them?

A. I'm a golfing addict. There's nothing like it for relaxation—in fact, I hope to sample some of your British courses while I'm over here. I love all sports—I also play a little baseball and American football when I can.

I'd like to see some of your football while I am here. I wanted to see Arsenal play Real Madrid but all the tickets were sold. Still, I understand Arsenal lost!

Like Freddy Cannon, pug-built, tug-boat-voiced Del Shannon had no chance in the wider world of entertainment. Therefore, fortunately, he remains unadulterated rock-pop. A working stiff minus his hard hat, he growled out his sawdust saloon operas in a minor key verse until the storm broke and the skies opened in a major key. But that 'Runaway' girl never came back and she let him down yet again – 'A Little Town Flirt' but he'd 'Keep Searchin'.

I can't praise Shannon enough as a true authentic dyed-in-the-wool rocker. Because he wasn't that articulate in grey real life, and because he let you find out about him in his self-written songs, he was perfect dive-off for a swim around in the ocean of rock'n'roll dreaming.

Terrific steaming fairground organ on 'Runaway'!

MIKE HELLICAR invites you to meet—
JOE MEEK, the man behind 'Telstar' and other hits

THE most unusual Gold Disc winner of all time—that's my nomination for "Telstar," which has topped the million sales figure after a few weeks at No. 1 here, hitting the U.S. Top Twenty, and charts all over the world.

For this disc was made by five young men crammed into a tiny room over a leather goods shop in North London, playing into recording equipment built on a shoestring !

Not for the Tornados, the luxury of a super-modern studio built and equipped by a major record company Not for them every scientific device built into consoles worth many thousands of pounds.

For the entire set-up in Meek's second-floor studio high above Holloway Road costs less than £4,000 —and that's a very generous estimate, taking into account every minor item.

It costs at least five times that figure to equip the average recording unit !

"We make records on a shoe-string—but now there is firm proof that you don't have to record in a plush ultra-modern studio to get the biggest hits," said a jubilant Meek this week. At 28, he is a brilliant and accomplished young engineer, with a fascinating background.

A prolific songwriter, too, one of his first major successes was Tommy Steele's "Put A Ring On Her Finger." He thought up "Telstar" while watching TV in his bed-sitter beneath the studio one night.

"I was impressed by the tremendous scientific achievement the Americans had made—and translated my thoughts into terms of the tune" explained Meek The next day he telephoned the Tornados at Great Yarmouth, where they were appearing with Billy Fury, and arranged for them to record it a few days later.

Few people credit Meek with actually having brought the Tornados together, but he did. The story began earlier this year when Meek brought bass guitarist Heinz Burt to London from his job in Southampton to join up with the Outlaws. Something went wrong—and Heinz was still in need of a job. So Joe advertised in the NME for musicians to form a group with Heinz.

JOE MEEK

From over 100 replies, Meek began auditioning the most likely applicants. They formed the nucleus of the Tornados and became Billy Fury's backing group.

The studio set-up in Meek's home is quite straightforward. You walk up a flight of steps from the street and you are in a passage leading to his bed-sitter (crammed with record players, records and congratulatory telegrams), and his office. Up another flight and you find Meek's control room and the studio.

Complicated

The control room has complicated equipment all round the walls—and yards and yards of edited tape on the floor.

The studio is draped and sound-proofed, but you can still hear heavy traffic moving along the main road.

This sometimes halts recordings. A piano, with several chairs, music stands and microphones, with a screen for the vocalist in one corner, almost fill the room. I wondered how the group got in there, too.

Supremely confident, Meek recorded "Telstar" blowing into a microphone and using a tape-delay

effect to give you the in-orbit sound, and told the Tornados : "This will get to No. 4 in the British charts, and No. 1 in America." They, of course, didn't believe him.

Why was he so sure ? Joe is a shy, retiring person who can count modesty as a quality. Yet he openly forecast success for the record.

"I just had a funny feeling about it. I can't explain how I knew — but I did," he told me. In fact, the number reached the top here, making Joe's estimate rather conservative. Whether his forecast for the U.S. chart is accurate, remains to be seen.

A vocal version of "Telstar," written by Meek before the instrumental was recorded, has been waxed by 15-year-old Kenny Hollywood. "He is a boy with a tremendous future, and will do well " said Meek, no doubt acting on another of his unexplainable hunches.

Decca has postponed release of the Tornados follow-up, "Globetrotter" until early next year—a situation which does not please Meek, but nevertheless exists.

He penned this number too, and, he tells me, already has a vocal version down on paper !

An EP, "Sounds Of The Tornados," is released this weekend, and there are all sorts of plans for further EPs, LPs for Britain and America, and, of course, still more singles. All will be produced in his tiny studio.

Many other hit recordings, among them three John Leyton hits— "Johnny Remember Me," " Wild Wind " and " Son This Is She " — have been put on tape in Meek's front room in the past—and with his current success in mind, it's a pretty safe bet that his neighbours in Holloway Road are going to get previews of a few more big selling numbers, too !

Joe Meek was one of those pop boffins who put together records in the studio that were impossible to re-create live. A sort of Phil Spector (of the Cavernous sound) in space. He seems to have been a complex person with his personal devils, and he came to a tragic end. An original.

Lloyds Bank Chambers, 2, Henrietta Street, London, W.C.2.
TEMple Bar 3611

J.D.S. ENT'S AGENCY
BRITAIN'S BIGGEST BALLROOM BOOKERS
104 HIGH ST., LONDON, N.W.10   ELG 6344

MALCOLM NIXON AGENCY
All enquiries for CONCERTS, DANCES, SOCIALS
46 Maddox St.,   1 Commercial St.,
London, W.1   MAY 1735   Dundee

JOAN REGAN
Direction :
Keith Devon
Bernard Delfont Ltd
Joan Regan Supporters Club,
Longlands Road, Sidcup, Kent.

DAVID WHITFIELD
c/o GRADE ORGANISATION
Tel.: REG 5521

ALMA COGAN
c/o SIDNEY GRACE
235, Regent St., W.1.   REG 5821

DOROTHY SQUIRES
Joe Collins, Chandos House,
Chandos Place, London, W.C.2

HELEN SHAPIRO
Sole Booking Agents :
GENERAL ARTISTES LTD.

THE BEATLES
"Love Me Do" (Parlophone)
Direction: Nems Enterprises Ltd., 12-14, Whitechapel, Liverpool 1.   ROYal 7895

"YOU'VE SEEN THE REST ! NOW SEE THE BEST !"
THE ORIGINAL CHECKMATES
WES SANDS, THE LE-ROYS, BOBBY PATRICK BIG SIX
All communications to :
DON WHITE AGENCY, 72 WARDOUR STREET, LONDON, W.1
GERrard 7080/7089
Sole Agency for Germany's oldest and best beat club—TOP TEN CLUB, HAMBURG

PHOTOGRAPHS 1/- per word   JULIE GRANT

NME TOP THIRTY

(Wednesday, October 24, 1962)

Last This Week

Last	This		
1	1	TELSTAR	Tornados (Decca)
2	2	THE LOCO-MOTION	Little Eva (London)
4	3	SHEILA	Tommy Roe (HMV)
5	4	RAMBLIN' ROSE	Nat Cole (Capitol)
3	5	RAIN UNTIL SEPTEMBER	Carole King (London)
8	6	VENUS IN BLUE JEANS	Mark Wynter (Pye)
11	7	LET'S DANCE	Chris Montez (London)
—	8	LOVESICK BLUES	Frank Ifield (Columbia)
6	9	YOU DON'T KNOW ME	Ray Charles (HMV)
10	10	WHAT NOW MY LOVE	Shirley Bassey (Columbia)
16	11	SWISS MAID	Del Shannon (London)
12	12	SHERRY	Four Seasons (Stateside)
7	13	SHE'S NOT YOU	Elvis Presley (RCA)
19	14	DEVIL WOMAN	Marty Robbins (CBS)
9	15	IT'LL BE ME	Cliff Richard (Columbia)
—	16	SHE TAUGHT ME HOW TO YODEL	Frank Ifield (Columbia)
13	17	I REMEMBER YOU	Frank Ifield (Columbia)
15	18	LONELY	Acker Bilk (Columbia)
—	19	NO ONE CAN MAKE MY SUNSHINE SMILE	Everly Bros. (Warner Bros.)
14	20	DON'T THAT BEAT ALL	Adam Faith (Parlophone)
17	21	IT STARTED ALL OVER AGAIN	Brenda Lee (Brunswick)
23	22	SEND ME THE PILLOW YOU DREAM ON	Johnny Tillotson (London)
25	23	THE PAY-OFF	Kenny Ball (Pye)
21	24	IF A MAN ANSWERS	Bobby Darin (Capitol)
28	25	BOBBY'S GIRL	Susan Maughan (Philips)
—	26	BECAUSE OF LOVE	Billy Fury (Decca)
—	27	LOVE ME DO	Beatles (Parlophone)
26	28	REMINISCING	Buddy Holly (Coral)
18	29	ROSES ARE RED	Ronnie Carroll (Philips)
—	30	THE JAMES BOND THEME	John Barry (Columbia)

BEST SELLING POP RECORDS IN U.S.

(Tuesday, October 23, 1962)

Last This Week (Courtesy of "Billboard")

Last	This		
1	1	MONSTER MASH	Bobby (Boris) Pickett and the Crypt Kickers
4	2	HE'S A REBEL	Crystals
3	3	DO YOU LOVE ME	Contours
8	4	ONLY LOVE CAN BREAK A HEART	Gene Pitney
2	5	SHERRY	Four Seasons
13	6	ALL ALONE AM I	Brenda Lee
6	7	PATCHES	Dickey Lee
7	8	RAMBLIN' ROSE	Nat Cole
20	9	GINA	Johnny Mathis
5	10	I REMEMBER YOU	Frank Ifield
16	11	POPEYE	Chubby Checker
9	12	GREEN ONIONS	Booker T & the MG's
10	13	LET'S DANCE	Chris Montez
—	14	CLOSE TO CATHY	Mike Clifford
—	15	NEXT DOOR TO AN ANGEL	Neil Sedaka
12	16	VENUS IN BLUE JEANS	Jimmy Clanton
—	17	BIG GIRLS DON'T CRY	Four Seasons
—	18	LIMBO ROCK	Chubby Checker
13	19	ALLEY CAT	Bent Fabric
—	20	RETURN TO SENDER	Elvis Presley

BEST SELLING SHEET MUSIC IN BRITAIN

(Tuesday, October 23, 1962)

Last This Week

Last	This		
1	1	TELSTAR	(Ivy)
3	2	ROSES ARE RED	(Leeds)
2	3	RAIN UNTIL SEPTEMBER	(Aldon)
4	4	RAMBLIN' ROSE	(Comet)
6	5	WHAT NOW MY LOVE	(Blossom)
5	6	SHE'S NOT YOU	(Ronnie)
14	7	THE LOCO-MOTION	(Aldon)
11	8	SPANISH HARLEM	(Progressive)
7	9	I REMEMBER YOU	(Chappell)
7	10	SHEILA	(Mellin)
10	11	LONELY	(Filmusic)
9	12	THINGS	(Burton)
21	13	VENUS IN BLUE JEANS	(Parnes)
12	14	SEALED WITH A KISS	(Commodore-Imperial)
17	15	STRANGER ON THE SHORE	(Sherwin)
13	16	IT'LL BE ME	(Aberbach)
15	17	SO DO I	(World-Wide)
15	18	YOU DON'T KNOW ME	(Aberbach)
19	19	DON'T THAT BEAT ALL	(Downbeat)
21	20	GUITAR TANGO	(Mills)
20	21	SPEEDY GONZALES	(Budd-Macmelodies)
23	22	ENGLISH COUNTRY GARDEN	(Novello)
—	23	SEND ME THE PILLOW	(Grosvenor)
18	24	SOME PEOPLE	(Essex)
21	25	BOBBY'S GIRL	(Kassner)
26	26	IT STARTED ALL OVER AGAIN	(United Artists)
29	27	BALLAD OF PALADIN	(Greenwich)
28	28	WILL I WHAT	(Meridian)
—	28	ROCKET MAN	(Merit)
25	30	STEPTOE AND SON	(Essex)

list
enda
Little
Erroll
—plus
Bobby

nnon-
and
aniels-
fulfil
r and
e dis-
were
Bruce
trifle

t was
others
rn to
ll be
verly,
e first

rolific
be
But I
raised
e for
kages

side,
come
ionel
high-
orthy
' or
from
urray
two

men-
aling

3!
T

British recording pre…
And although we have already mentioned Acker Bilk, we cannot omit …

recordings are still being perpetrated by British studios. There is no crime …

Go …
These are counterbalanced by the … top disappointments of the Equity-ITV butter to us!

THE STARS LOOK TOWARDS 1963

TRYING to penetrate the veil of uncertainty which covers the forthcoming year, each one of us cherishes his own ambitions for the months which lie ahead. A new year is always a challenge—and this is particularly true in the field of show business.

I've been talking to some of the names who are news at the moment in pop music, to ascertain their attitude towards the coming year (writes Derek Johnson). These are the hopes which they revealed for 1963:

FRANK   BOBBY   HELEN   CLIFF   DEL

CLIFF RICHARD

I'm crossing my fingers, more than any other reason, in the hope that "Summer Holiday" will be as well received as was "The Young Ones." A great deal of effort has gone into this new picture, and everyone concerned with it is quite optimistic about its chances.

But, as always, the fans are the final judges, and we can only hope that they will receive it kindly. Especially as, if it is successful, I expect it will lead to more filming, which I thoroughly enjoy.

Another aim which I had for 1963 is to establish closer in-person contact with the fans.

But my engagement book shows me that I shall be doing a lot of British stage work next year, so that wish is already fulfilled.

JOE LOSS

How can I possibly hope for better things in 1963, when this year has been so very kind to me? All I can say is that I want to continue to keep people happy and in the mood—and I simply can't improve on that ambition.

If I may be very personal, I would say that my greatest wish of all is to sustain good health. For only by so doing can I maintain my work —which frankly is my life's blood to me.

HELEN SHAPIRO

My main ambition — and the thought that rarely leaves my mind all through the year—is to maintain my place as top British girl singer in the NME Poll. It isn't until you are actually voted into a leading position like this, that you realise how demanding are the fans —I know I've got to work twice as hard in 1963 to do as well!

I also hope to achieve a No. 1 record within the first few months of the new year.

I want, too, to visit as many countries as possible—already I am booked for Israel, South Africa, France and America—but I must be careful not to stay away from Britain too long.

KENNY BALL

When trad started bursting through in Britain two or three years back, it became known as the "trad fad." Well, I'd like to see my kind of music spread beyond this country, and be fully accepted throughout the world. Then it would no longer be a "fad" — it would be recognised in its proper position as a genuine music.

I'd like the boys in my band to be acknowledged, not as a group of jazzers, but for the really fine musicians they are. In other words, I want to see the status of jazz elevated.

MARK WYNTER

In a nutshell, I hope to be able to justify the faith which so many people have placed in me. I feel that I can best do this by learning and absorbing as much as possible about the business. I believe that it's important for an artist to gain as much experience as he possibly can—it's never too late to learn!

I don't have any specific ambitions—like wanting to play the Palladium or appear in a Hollywood film. My theory is that, if I continue trying to improve the standard of my work, the breaks will follow as a matter of course.

THE SPRINGFIELDS

Oh yes, we have plenty of hopes for 1963! We'd like to develop our work to a greater extent on an international basis, and maybe our "Silver Threads" success has paved the way for this.

To further this aim, we should like to record more in foreign languages, and to tour abroad extensively—already we have 1963 offers for Australasia, Sweden, France, Portugal and America, all of which looks very promising.

But our biggest hopes are reserved for here at home. More than anything else, we want to re-establish ourselves in the British charts.

And we'd like to complete a hat-trick of NME Poll successes.

THE SHADOWS

Our one big hope for the new year is that we are able to retain our success and popularity. During 1963, we shall be doing a considerable amount of stage work in Britain—far more than in the year just ending. Now, a stage act can be all-important to one's career.

For, if audiences go away impressed and fully entertained, they will make a point of buying your records.

We're very happy about the way in which our records have fared in 1962, but we're conscious of the fact that there's not been enough of them; so we hope to make a more concentrated attack on the disc market in 1963.

SUSAN MAUGHAN

My outstanding wish is that I should never wake up from this wonderful dream I am experiencing! I can't believe that so much has happened to me in such a short space of time, and I hope with all my heart that I am able to cling on to the progress I have made this year.

To be more practical, though, I'm anxious to gain much more experience as a solo artist.

It was only very recently that I left Ray Ellington to go out on my own and, despite the success of I still feel rather raw. I'm looking forward to the package tour in which I'm appearing in the new year—I'm sure this will help me tremendously. And I just hope I am as happy this time next year, as I am at the moment.

FRANK IFIELD

At the end of 1961, my main ambition was to secure a hit record during 1962—and my resolution at the start of the year was to strive for it. Wow! it was virtually a case of an ambition going berserk!

And I'm almost afraid to state any wishes for 1963, in case it has the opposite effect this time.

I can only say that I'm thrilled, and more than a little stunned, by what has happened during the past six months—and if I am to repeat just some of that success during the coming year, I shall be very happy. One other thing—I should like to continue my attempts to make headway as an all-round entertainer.

BOBBY DARIN

I want to go on making more pictures, because I consider the cinema to be a very rewarding medium. I'm looking forward to expanding my recording activities now I'm with Capitol—I'd like to make a few more albums, though I have no intention of forgetting the teenage market. And perhaps more than anything, I hope nothing comes along to interfere with my return visit to Britain.

DEL SHANNON

I'd like to try my hand at films if the right opportunity arises. I want to show the public that I can do more than make pop records. I hope to get the chance of visiting Britain again. And lastly, I hope my luck holds out!

IT'S HAPPENING

THE SOUND — THE SOUND — THE SOUND
ALEXIS KORNER'S BLUES INCORPORATED
AT THE FLAMINGO (33-37 WARDOUR STREET)
THURS. 8-11.30/FRI. 12-5 a.m./SUN. 8-11.30
FLAMINGO ALLNIGHTERS FROM JAN. 3

1963-4
THE BEATLES BREEZE IN
TRAILING 'MERSEY BEAT'

1963 was the year of the Northern invasion. Hitherto the North had been associated with Gracie Fields, George Formby and numerous drunk acts, the best being Frank Randle's. The North was supposed to produce gormless drolls who could grin and bear it daftly amidst all the squalor and poverty of life up there. We laughed and felt pity down here in the comfy home counties.

1963 changed all that. LIVERPOOL GROUP TAKES BRITAIN BY STORM, roared *Disc*. Inside the paper, Brian Matthew heralded the Beatles as the 'most original musical and visual sensation since the Shadows'. To journalists they were cheeky and charming and right to the point: 'We've been rearranging old pop songs while you down South have been looking for new sounds', said one Beatle, while another one chuckled, 'Yeagh, but our whole act is ad-libbing, we just "make show" as the krauts said, and we've only ever rehearsed four numbers!' 'Look', said the one in the National Health specs, 'We're four creepy crawly things who took a beat and created a storm.' What are your ambitions? 'To record in English'. 'To sing an instrumental'. The journalists scribbled fast, noting this 'whacky sense of humour'. Then they stood back while the boys changed from their maroon suits with waistcoats into Edwardian striped bathing suits, plus bowler hats and umbrellas, for a 'larky photograph' for the musical press. *The Fab Four From Scouseville.*

Journalists trekked up to Liverpool, storm centre of the beat boom. The Cavern, the club where the Beatles had been discovered, was to be found in a maze of narrow alleys right in the centre of the fruit warehouse district. A grotty cellar full of little caverns with flagstone floor and walls that ran with sweat when the beat was going on. Serious sociologically-minded journalists discovered that Liverpool was a dying city and that the groups were fighting for a new life outside of this crumbling relic of another age.

And still more North went the writers and the talent scouts. From Manchester appeared Freddie and The Dreamers, The Dakotas, and The Hollies. From Sheffield – The Debonaires. From Preston – The Puppets. But the South joined battle with Brian Poole and the Tremeloes. By the end of the year The Mersey Beat was being strongly challenged by The Tottenham Sound of the Dave Clark Five.

Would any of these British beat merchants be able to successfully invade America? Big question.

Away in the celtic twilight of Dublin I was blissfully unaware of the Northern Sound. Lost in the mist of Scotch and Irish and malt stout, my friends and I crawled from snug bar to snug bar discussing, arguing, boasting about what we were going to do tomorrow or next week. We were going to amaze the welkin with fantastic sounds. Meanwhile, let's have another jar.

One plan that did come true was a trip to America. The Union of Students of Ireland was advertising a charter flight for that summer of '63 and I signed on. I had had recurring dreams for years and years about being in America. The very word was deliciously shivery, especially when said by an American. Those sloping *Rrrs*! Americans were sexier, it seemed. OK, France was for sexy girls but the men were midgets. America bred Tarzanic types with bullet heads and frames cut to a regular pattern. Also, of course and most importantly, America was where the music originated.

Summer of '63 was a very hopeful time. And America was Scout Patrol Leader. She was full of good sayings about a marvellous future when the world would lay at peace. The night before I left for America I was standing on a corner near Trinity when who should cream past me but President Kennedy and his wife, in an open touring car. They smiled at me and spontaneously I dropped my books and clapped and cheered. I felt very, very happy.

NEW YORK (July)

I took the Greyhound bus out of Nashville and here I am in New York again. Went to Nashville in the hope of finding some real mountain music in hills of Tennessee. Instead I got invited to my first record session, at RCA studios. A very slick country singer called Jerry Wallace was recording. He sat on a stool, chain-drinking cokes and crooning take after take of a pleasant pop song, accompanied by violinists, cellists, a female chorus, and, I'm glad to say, some guitars and drums. The conductor, a merry bald man in a Hawaiian shirt, turned out to be one of my rock 'n' roll idols – Bill Justis of 'Raunchy' fame. He told me I'd find precious little folk-style country music in Nashville and I needed to go to New York for that, to Greenwich Village.

So here I am. And I've just returned from my first venture into that Other America. If you want to be different here you have to go and live where the other 'different' people live. They have enclaves or communes for you. The Village boasts more coffee houses per square foot than any other community in America. 'That's a helluva lotta weirdo punks', a cop told me as he gave me directions. 'Still,' he added, 'at least we got 'em in one place here'. I wandered around the Village streets, noticing that many of the denizens wore dirty clothes and caps and walked scrunched up or slouchy. They were very thin, too. But their girls were real country humdingers! Long, flaxen hair and doe eyes and free-falling bosoms beneath floppy sweaters and long legs encased in fully-fashioned blue jeans. Scrumptious! What were they doing with these ill-nourished arabic specimens? I went into a coffee house and ordered a wholemeal patty melt and carrot juice and watched a spotty youth in a railway worker's outfit strum a guitar and curse the world cryptically. He sang like a crusty old man. He was copying Bob Dylan. The girl who followed him, long straight dark hair and eyes closed and voice plain and virginal, was copying Joan Baez. I struck up a conversation with a tall fellow in owlish spectacles and a battered cowboy hat. He said the acts stank tonight because the singers of any importance were down in West Virginia helping the coal miners in their strike. 'You from Britain? Hey, we had one of your guys down here at the Village Gate a few years back. Lonnie Donegan. Can you believe this guy? He came on stage in dinner suit, gold buckle patent leather boots and all that shit'. I asked what he'd sung. The cowboy couldn't remember because the clothes had 'turned me off'. I suggested he might have sung, 'My Old Man's A Dustman'. The cowboy said that sounded *real* working man's stuff.

By the way, this phrase 'turn on' is one I keep hearing. Already two girls have told me that my accent turns them on. It's good, it's graphic.

SEATTLE, WASHINGTON STATE (August)

Refreshing to be out here in the great outdoors in the heart of God's country! What a change from dirty, dour, nihilistic New York and that Village! The Greyhound bus drew in to the Seattle terminal, the airbrakes sighed and I sighed, and through the steam I saw my fresh-faced cousin Anna waiting for me. She's studying at Seattle University. Everybody I've met is studying for something or else they've already got a degree. Even policemen and bus drivers have degrees. Anna took me to a student-run coffee house in downtown Pioneer Square and I played a few numbers on their piano. The student owners hired me! So now I'm performing a mixed fruit trifle of blues, ragtime and music hall numbers to an enthusiastic audience. Many of the authentic American blues numbers are quite new to them. This is because the other acts here and at the surrounding coffee houses consist of crew-cutted clean collegiate folk groups singing songs they've heard on a popular network TV show called 'Hootenanny'. Songs like 'Three Jolly Coachmen' and 'Michael, Row the Boat Ashore'. On my day off I went to a local school gymn to see a James Brown concert. I must have been the only white person there. Caught in a heavy, inky sea of fans I felt terrific and daring. Can't wait to tell my college chums. I expect all the others on the charter trip have merely seen Washington DC, Disneyland, and The National Parks.

When I returned to Britain, flushed with American success I got severe cultural shock. 'Beatles' was on everybody's lips and I didn't know what they were talking about. Mums and dads, milkmen and taxi drivers drove me mad with this mystifying word. I retired to bed and read about the Beatles – and Brian Poole. What a wet kipper to be slapped on one's face after the rich burger of America!

So it was with relief that I returned to the comparative calm of Trinity College Dublin. This term we were to start studying Karl Marx and Working Class Movements. Such a leap into the nineteenth century got me thinking again about electrification. The problem was eventually solved by a member of my old R&B band who announced that he'd joined a local showband and that if we let them join our group we would then have electric guitars, amplifiers and mikes. I dreamed up a suitable name, Bluesville Manufacturing Inc., and we were soon hard at work learning up numbers like 'I'm Your Hoochie Coochie Man' and 'I'm Built For Comfort'.

I quickly discovered that if I threw myself around onstage I could get the girls screaming. What was happening was that Bluesville, or 'The Bluesvilles' as the Dublin punters soon called us, was catching some of the beat group mania that had infected Britain. The Rolling Stones were becoming popular and as I bore a passing resemblance to Mick Jagger I caught some reflected glory. TCD students became interested in the phenomenon of Bluesville and they attended our shows and dances. Bluestocking girls who hitherto had abhorred pop music now studied us as part of the Beatle craze. A whole load of our history class motored out to see us at a concert at Mount Merrion Seminary. I rushed on singing 'Boney Moronie' and part of the stage collapsed taking me with it. Next the power failed. A senior bluestocking, who now is an editor on the *Observer*, told me later that the experience was 'incredibly therapeutic and definitely a "happening".'

Bluesville's reputation was spreading. We added a saxophone, and I built up my piano playing power by doing weight training with dumbells. This fitted in well with my dieting course. I also started growing my hair much longer. Trouble was it wouldn't reach my shoulders but insisted on curling up after a few inches so that the effect was like a Dutch tulip.

1964 arrived and I was full of ambition. I was determined to make Bluesville into a hit group. In Ireland we only had one rival and that was a group from Belfast called 'Them'. For the first time in my life I felt part of an organization. I was in a group. I started buying the pop papers again and even buying trade papers like *Billboard* when I could get my hands on them. Pop music had never sounded better, there were some terrific sounds on the charts! I started writing a pop column for the TCD weekly magazine:

'"Twenty Four Hours From Tulsa" (Pye). Composer Bacharach dresses his hitparader with sauce of

Mexican relish. Two-note trumpet chord, blown by what I imagine to be two tortilla-eating fox-hunters, opens song. Pitney acts out drama with Conway Twitty croak.'

I began to examine Beatle songs and found that they were well-structured and could take any kind of beating. I tried to add these and other rock songs to our repertoire but the group founder, our bass player, objected. He intended to stay true to American black R&B and that was that. What about recording? OK, so long as it's authentic R&B.

Roger Question's New Theatre group had at last finished their revue and wanted me to provide them with

The King meets the Beatles. Elvis is in the doorway saying goodbye to somebody, Lennon walking away, Harrison far right. It was described as 'a summit meeting'. Were people beginning to take rock'n'roll seriously?

a theme song. So one afternoon I got our founder and bass player to fish out his harmonica and join me in recording this theme. We went to a dingy basement studio in Merrion Square and banged out a blues. The sound lacked punch. We needed *ooomph*. We called in the bass drum player of the Paragon Jazz Band. The result was a sour bounce to the old Bo Diddley beat. Roger Question adored: 'So wickedly abandoned and urban!' The revue was a success and there were enquiries about where the theme music could be bought. Aha!

That summer the Seattle coffee house called me for a return engagement. I took the revue tape and re-named the instrumental 'Soho'. When I arrived I found a huge banner outside the coffee house saying: IAN WHITCOMB – DIRECT FROM LONDON VIA LIVERPOOL!! The Beatles had taken America completely. The whole country had changed. The old 'gung ho' college regular guy stuff had gone and so, alas, had President Kennedy. There was a new air of abandon and a warm welcome to foreign decadence. So far the decadence was only in the early cutesy-pie stage. I went along with the new atmosphere willingly. Being a British beat singer I was a bundle of sexiness for the American girls. Late one night on a couch in Seattle a girl told me my accent was really turning her on. *Turn on*. That phrase again!

To be a rock star you had to have a record deal. I looked up 'Recording Companies' in the Yellow Pages of the phone book. No good – they were all distributors or vanity recorders. Then somebody put me in touch with the local record whizz kid, the rock king of the Northwest, the man responsible for 'Louie Louie', that all-time gonzo smash by The Kingsmen – Jerry Dennon.

I took him my tape, crinkled and torn by much bus travelling. I told him I was going to be the next Mick Jagger. He consulted his trade papers. He played the tape. Finally he said he'd take a chance and give me a contract.

And before I left to go back to Trinity for the first part of the history finals he presented me with a box of 45s. I lay awake for hours just gazing at the tiny plastic thing with its blue label and the magic words:

'Soho'
(Ian Whitcomb)
IAN WHITCOMB
Recorded in Dublin.

How was I to explain the absence of anybody else's name on the label? Jerry Dennon said it was simpler to say just 'IAN WHITCOMB'. Who were this group Bluesville anyway and did they all need separate contracts? I needn't have worried, nobody was very impressed with the 45, we all had a few jars and got down to some more rehearsal. Oh, and I took the exam and scraped through.

As a single piece of plastic 'Soho' was of little interest. Had it become a hit things might have been different. I was to find out later HOW different they might become and the experience was not always pleasant.

But now, in late 1964, I had become bitten by the recording bug. I bought a mass of current hits and took them to pieces on the piano and put them together again.

I tried shouting for days on end so that I could get the right rough texture. I pounded out of the piano upbeat, backbeat, low down rockaboogies, tempered with triple-feel ballads or full hand chord clusters in the gospel shuffle groove. The righteous, upright yet gutsy, tempestuous then soothing, always dramatic blues-gospel funky groove! That was it! I dug up an old folk song I remembered from the skiffle era – 'The Sportin' Life Is Killin' Me' – and fitted some 6/4 blues gospel chords so that it sounded similar to the Animals' whopping summer hit 'House Of The Rising Sun'. Then I roped up the group to rehearse this potential smash. They weren't that excited. Was this R&B? I was in too much of a fever to argue. For a few pounds I hired a studio near the General Post Office (where the rebels had holed up in 1916 and declared the republic) and we made our recording of 'This Sporting Life'. Afterwards we had a few jars and a laugh.

But that winter I flew off to Seattle again – to see a girl friend and also the man about the new record. Jerry Dennon nodded and tapped his foot but we both knew the recording needed something else. That gospel sound wasn't quite there we felt. What was missing? Of course! A blanket of electric organ to wrap around our sound. All good gospel records mixed organ with piano, so could we please get one, and a studio? Jerry did a bit of quick calculation and then nodded. From one of his many Northwest groups an organist was summoned and in the little studio round the corner the kid and his Hammond tossed a great throaty fog over our recording. As a final commercial touch, like the olive spiked to the top of a triple decker sandwich, I rattled a pair of maraccas. Our engineer, who worked a salmon farm as well as this little studio, was impressed by such an elaborate construction. 'See, I done polka bands, cocktail jazz combos, Louie Louie local groups – but Liverpool beat groups from Ireland? Never!'

Jerry nodded to the engineer and looked at his watch. Spellbound I listened to the completed 'This Sporting Life'. I called up my Seattle girl friend to come over and hear a hit. She looked up at me and snuggled close as we listened to the bashing off-beat, chugging bass, chopping guitars, arpeggiated piano, swirly organ and me just out on top, whining in my best cockney accent with plenty of hunger and anguish, I who had suffered little in this life. 'That accent really turns me on', she said when the tape had faded away. I looked at Jerry. He nodded and formed an 'O' with his forefinger and thumb. I couldn't wait for pressings, couldn't wait for fame. Freedom through a little bit of plastic!

'A double wedding would have been real dandy', said my girl friend's father with a sly wink. We were sipping champagne after his son's second wedding. My mind was on other matters. I slipped away to call Jerden Records. Yes, said Jerry, the pressing plant has shipped us some product. Yes, label reads 'Ian Whitcomb *and* Bluesville'. At Jerden Records there were no Greek portals, no gold-braided commissionaires, no furry stars coming and going with the red carpet treatment. These days anybody could make a record and seemed to be doing so. Jerden was full of Jerden Recording Artists that ice-cold morning. I got my box of 45s and hugged it. I told Jerry I was flying back to college next day. 'Whatever's right', he said. And, 'We'll keep you informed'. I was going to say that, though everyone and his daughter was making records throughout the Western World, we in Seattle and Dublin would make our mark with 'This Sporting Life'. I *was* going to say that, but Jerry was a busy man.

As my girl friend drove me through slushy roads to the airport I kept thinking: I can always go into teaching.

U.S. Vee-Jay signs up the Beatles

THE Beatles, yet to have a major British hit, have been snapped up for America by Vee-Jay, the label responsible for the U.S. success of Frank Ifield's "I Remember You" and "Lovesick Blues."

The deal was completed on Monday by Barbara Gardner, Vee-Jay's international chief, who was visiting London. First release will be the group's current Parlophone issue, "Please Please Me."

Miss Gardner was in London to record an LP with Chris Barber and the Alex Bradford gospel group, which was featured in the London stage and TV productions of "Black Nativity."

On Wednesday, she went to Birmingham Alexandra to meet Ifield, who is appearing in the "Mother Goose" pantomime.

She also arranged for Norrie Paramor to visit the Vee-Jay headquarters in Chicago to plan future Ifield discs suited to the American market when he goes to Nashville to record Helen Shapiro.

Personal manager: Emlyn Griffiths.
Musical director: Ivor Raymonde.

You've pleased—pleased us!— SAY THE BEATLES

THINGS are beginning to move for the Beatles, the r-and-b styled British group which crashed back into the NME Chart this week at No. 17. The disc—"Please Please Me"—follows closely on the heels of their first hit "Love Me Do," written by group members John Lennon and Paul McCartney.

Says Paul: "We also wrote 'Please Please Me,' but that hasn't exhausted our supply of compositions. We've got nearly a hundred up our sleeves, and we're writing all the time!

"I suppose 'writing' is the wrong word, really. John and I just hammer out a number on our instruments. If we want anyone to hear it we record it, then send them a tape.

"We've had disappointments, but coming in at No. 17 has pleased-pleased us!" he quipped.

The boys were rehearsing their act for the forthcoming Helen Shapiro tour when I met them in their hometown of Liverpool on Sunday.

And at Norrie Paramor's request, they were composing a song for Helen to record when she goes to Nashville shortly.

Said Paul: "We've called it 'Misery,' but it isn't as slow as it sounds. It moves along at quite a steady pace and we think Helen will make a pretty good job of it. We've also done a number for Duffy Power which he's going to record."

This isn't the Beatles' first taste of

Top to bottom: PAUL McCARTNEY (20), JOHN LENNON (22), GEORGE HARRISON (19) and RINGO STARR (22).

success. The clipped Negro sound they achieve has brought them a fantastic following in Germany, where they had a Polydor single in the charts more than a year ago. They spent Christmas performing in Hamburg—their fifth visit.

In the north of England, too, they've built up a reputation that takes some beating. In the past I've seen them billed with equal prominence alongside such names as Little Richard and Joe Brown!

Talking of Little Richard, the rock 'n' roll star became on the Beatles' biggest fans during his recent visit. He told me: "I've never heard that sound from English musicians before. Honestly, if I hadn't seen them with my own eyes I'd have thought they were a coloured group from back home."

So far it seems that only Northern fans and visiting American stars have appreciated their talents (the Crickets went overboard when they heard them), but "Please Please Me" will change everything.

Already Southerners have been flocking to buy the disc since it was released two weeks ago.

Comments John: "We tried to make it as simple as possible. Some of the stuff we've written in the past has been a bit way-out, but we aimed this one straight at the hit parade.

At the sessions at which "Please Please Me" was recorded, shortly before Christmas, the boys' recording manager, George Martin, told me: "The thing I like about the Beatles is their great sense of humour as well as their talent."

It looks like a bright future for the Beatles, but knowing them I don't think they'll let it go to their heads. It'll be a long time for instance, before they forget the time they provided the music for Janice the Stripper in a Liverpool nightclub."

ALAN SMITH

---

men's last appearance together will be on March 3, at Redcar Coatham.

when she will be joined by Duffy Power.

ance, to enable scenery to be transferred to the West End.

BEATLES HEAD PACKAGE SHOW

THE Beatles will head a nation-wide package tour for the first time in May. A U.S. artist is being sought to share top billing with them.

They are currently touring with Helen Shapiro and next month are set to join Chris Montez and Tommy Roe. In these packages, however, they are the featured supporting act.

The later project is due to start on May 18 and last three weeks. Rank and Granada theatres are among venues being negotiated.

The Beatles, now No. 5 in the NME Chart with "Please Please Me," have decided to accept a seaside resort's Sunday concerts during the summer.

New dates include a return to "Parade Of The Pops" on Wednesday, February 20, and bookings for "Thank Your Lucky Stars"

(February 23), and "Here We Go" (Light, March 12).

Parlophone a-and-r manager George Martin will record their first LP—which may be called "Off The Beatle Track"—in London shortly.

A live album is being considered for some time in the future. The first LP will consist mainly of numbers penned by group members John Lennon and Paul McCartney.

The group is only one of a string of Merseyside recording artists being lined up by its manager, Liverpool record store executive Brian Epstein. He also handles another vocal-instrumental group, the Big Three —due for its debut release on Decca shortly.

Titles selected by Decca a-and-r man Noel Walker are "Some Other Guy" coupled with "When True Love Begins."

Another Merseyside disc signing managed by Epstein is Gerry and the Pacemakers. Their first release, "How Do You Do," coupled with "Away From You," will be on March 1 on the Columbia label.

MONTEZ STAYS LONGER

Chris Montez will now stay in Britain two weeks longer than originally planned. Following his 21-day tour with Tommy Roe, he will spend the first half of April playing ball-

The First Reco 'Miss Talen CHRIS MITC WINNER OF T Quaker Puff TALENT COMPET

I Fall In With

BEATLEMANIA: by the end of 1962 I had lost all interest in pop music. It seemed to have gone all wet with twinkly violins and rather drippy model youth singers. I turned back into old jazz and city blues (particularly James Brown). I had grown up and out of R&R. Besides, it seemed to have died: Holly, Cochran, Big Bopper – dead; Haley had shot his bolt; Elvis had gone Hollywood. So in 1963, as a Trinity College Dublin student, I went off to America to see Nashville, hear some real, Ozark mountain music, and catch James Brown in action. I achieved all these goals and came back to England full of ethnic music and bursting with pride. To my horror nobody was interested – they were all a-buzz over the Beatles and other Mersey groups. I couldn't believe it – must be a pre-planned Press operation. Those bouncy bundles of cheek had to be joking. The North was where knockabout comedy came from. Like George Formby and Gracie Fields. Where everybody was sexless, with false teeth and braces, and thrived on tripe. Or lived by the rule 'where there's muck there's brass' as in films like 'Room At the Top'. How could such an area produce any R&R? Any sex and glamour? How could Liverpool, as commonplace as cold fish and chips, lift us up and away like the Big 'O' could, or Elvis could?

Well, the answer was that the Beatles, though they came suited and tied and governed by a well-spoken manager, were something else. They were a turning point and R&R was never to be the same. After I'd put aside all the mop-top stuff I found that their music really was very good, especially their imaginative use of harmony. It was as if they were inventing music from scratch. The words were ultra simple: 'You' and 'Me' stuff. Dummy lyrics. Of course, I couldn't look up to them as father figures or crazy uncles or creatures from another planet. They were too down-to-earth, plain-speaking. Very bright, very street-sharp. But it was the wrong street for me. Too close to home. Everybody got some charge from them – you could pick a Beatle and follow him – and yet they always remained a totally self-contained unit. And then, after the world adopted them they came astral. Untouchable. Even John, George, Paul and Ringo didn't really know the Beatles. The world had claimed them. A little later came the intellectuals, the quality journalists who hitherto had dismissed R&R as mindless pop. They were pronounced 'poets' and this affected the words of the songs. 'Sgt. Pepper', an aural Music Hall show, was interpreted as something akin to the mad mazes of James Joyce. And Modern Art with all its obscuranticism slithered in like the creature from the black lagoon. First the Beatles looked for refuge in the East, then they eventually found peace in our world. But the mania remains. And the music is still GREAT.

NEW MUSICAL

The BEATLES surround CHRIS MONTEZ (light jacket) and TOMMY ROE on Saturday.

SCREAMS ACCLAIM BEATLES, MONTEZ, ROE

LATEST visitors from America—eel-wriggling Chris Montez and sedate twister Tommy Roe —were given scream-filled receptions for rocking acts when they opened their British tour on Saturday at East Ham Granada. But the Beatles stole top honours for entertainment and audience reaction.

This all-action quartet from Liverpool has everything exciting new sound, terrific instrumental attack, exhilarating solo and group vocal effects, and a fresh energy that leaves them (they told me later) limp at the end of each act.

Admitted they still need better production, and a good choreographer, tailor and barber, but this apart, they are the most exciting newcomers in Britain today.

They crash into their act with a fast rocker, then drift to a harmonica-accented " Love Me Do," " Misery " (led into with some good comedy), and change to soft folk singing in " A Taste Of Honey." George Harrison is tops in " Do You Want To Know A Secret," and " Please Please Me " brought screams throughout as the Beatles brewed up a torrid storm.

A fast, rocking gospel song, with Paul McCartney soloing, brought this breathtaking act to a tremendous (and too early) close.

Tommy Roe was first American to appear, smart and slim in grey jacket, black trousers. He started his lively act with " Whole Lotta Shakin'," then " Count On Me," " The Folk Singer " (his latest single), and " Maybellene."

" Good Good Lovin' " added pace and " Sheila " brought terrific response, the turn ending on a high note with " There's A Great Day Coming," a hand-clapping spiritual. A little shy (he stopped twisting when he heard the screams it brought), but very popular.

Chris Montez kept everything moving (body as well as vocal chords) throughout, doing a strip tease—taking off jacket, tie and unbuttoning his shirt during the act, which puts the accent on fast rockers, such as "Bony Moronie," " Let's Dance " (during which he hip-notises with a weird twist dance), " Some Kinda Fun," and a rocker in Spanish. His one slow number — " You're The One " — got big response, too, and the girls loved him.

In support, the Viscounts do a standard vocal act, which includes their latest disc. " Don't Let Me Cross Over " and ends with so-so impressions ; Terry Young Six (only five due to illness) were solid instrumental backers; Tony Marsh is a pleasant singing compere; and Debbie Lee does her best in the first spot.

ANDY GRAY.

Shirley Bassey : fabulous plus !

THE posters still call Shirley Bassey " fabulous." True—but on her current 20-day British tour, she's so much more. She's sunnier, keener even—a tremendous treat for any fan, old or new. This new Shirley is magnificent—her performance is the experience of a lifetime.

The Bassey ballistics were seen — and cheered like mad—to great effect on the second night of the tour at Bournemouth Winter Gardens on Saturday. She exploded through about a dozen hits, mixed with some surprising extras.

Swathed in a long sheath dress of blue silk, topped with the inimitable sequined Bassey bodice, a stunning new hair-style (all on top like a whipped ice-cream) and her arms free—of course !—Shirley stood there and sang with all her great heart.

Kicking off with " I Will Love You," she had the audience in the palms of her ever-flaying hands.

Following, in a wide-ranging selection, were Jerome Kern's " All The Things You Are," Alma Cogan's " In Other Words," Newley's vastly applauded " Fool," a twisting " If I Were A Bell," a finger-snapping " Such A Lot Of Living To Do," and another of her great successes, " Kiss Me Honey, Honey, Kiss Me."

" I Could Have Danced All Night " led her sheer knock-out of an act ending with the Riddle arrangement of " What Now My Love."

Earlier Shirley had included "Love Is So Much Better The Second Time Around "—did this have a personal, hopeful meaning !

Although billed as guest star, Matt Monro managed 14 numbers in his superb first-half spot. Apart from hits like " My Kind Of Girl " (" I owe everything to this one "), " My Love And Devotion," " Portrait Of My Love," he also included a tribute to Judy Garland.

Matt closed with his latest release, " One Day "—which seems worthy of a chart placing. TONY CRAWLEY.

BIG NEWS FOR RECORD LOVERS!

From YOU to US inspired From ME to YOU

according to THE BEATLES who told Alan Smith

THOSE fabulous Beatles have paid a chart-sized tribute to the NME with their latest hit, "From Me To You"—because the title is based on our popular readers' letters column, "From You To Us"!

Says John Lennon: "As I explained recently, Paul McCartney and I wrote the number on a coach journey between York and Shrewsbury. We were on the Helen Shapiro tour at the time.

"What puzzled us was why we'd thought of a name like 'From Me To You.'

"In fact, it had me thinking until only recently, when I picked up the NME to see how we were doing in the charts. Then I realised—we'd got the inspiration from reading a copy on the coach!

"Paul and I had been talking about one of the letters in the 'From You To Us' column."

Notice that all the Beatles' hit compositions so far have contained the words "Me" or "You"—"Love Me Do," "Please Please Me," "From Me To You," and "Do You Want To Know A Secret," which they wrote for Billy J. Kramer.

Says Paul: "We didn't plan it that way. It just happened. Still, I suppose putting 'me' or 'you' in to a song helps its chances of success a lot. People can identify themselves with it."

"We have such a fairly easy job thinking up tunes, we used to worry whether we were copying from someone else. Then we realised it was probably because they had such a simple melody.

"These days, if we think up a tune very quickly we know we've got a hit!"

Beatles' compositions and recordings are becoming so hot these days that there are even rumours—in their native Liverpool—of "black market" Beatles' discs!

One NME reader wrote to me mentioning that 400 copies had been circulated of them singing "Some Other Guy." I've made some enquiries about this and I can say with all certainty that it did not come from Parlophone or their past label, Polydor.

The story seems to have arisen following a visit to Liverpool's Cavern beat club by a Granada TV unit. As you may know, the Cavern is almost a "holy of holies" on the Liverpool pop scene. In the past few years such artists as Gerry and the Pacemakers, the Big Three and Billy J. Kramer have gained a lot of their stage experience there.

During Granada's visit to the club, the technicians made a demonstration disc of the Beatles singing "Some Other Guy." However, only two or three copies were made—not 400!

There is no doubt that the group's few recordings for the German Polydor label have certainly become collectors' pieces. These include a single with Tony Sheridan, "My Bonny," and an EP issued in France—and I've heard stories of fans fervently searching the continent to get a copy!

I'm happy to report that success still hasn't changed the Beatles. I knew them a year ago and they've remained the same happy-go-lucky crowd, as modest as ever.

"There's only one big difference," Paul told me. "It's the fact that

nowadays we're recognised wherever we go. Mind you, it does get a bit comic at times.

"For instance, I might be in a café and a girl will come up and say: 'You're one of the Beatles, aren't you?' 'Yes,' I say. 'No you're not,' she says. 'You just look like him.'

"But I am one of the Beatles,' I answer — wounded dignity and all that.

"After that she might say 'Come off it, big-'ead'! and there I am frantically looking through my

pockets trying to establish my identity!' It's happened to the others."

None of the Beatles has celebrated by buying very much. "We got a record-player for our van," said Paul, "but I can't think of anything else. We've been established a little while, so we've been able to buy a few things as we've gone along.

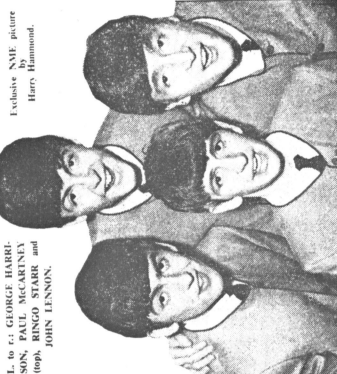

Exclusive NME picture by Harry Hammond.

L. to r.: GEORGE HARRISON, PAUL McCARTNEY (top), RINGO STARR and JOHN LENNON.

STAR QUOTE

QUOTES from Lionel Bart: "I try to find humour in life which on the surface doesn't seem very funny. In true drama (as in life) comedy and tragedy, the beautiful and the ugly, go hand in hand. So I look at the other side. The big part of my ambition used to be success and money. The ambition now is to get on to the next show."

"Apart from that, the royalties haven't come in yet. When that happens ... who knows?

● P.S.: Just received a card from the Beatles, now holidaying in Santa Cruz, Tenerife (Canary Islands, which reads: 'Dear everybody. We have never felt so healthy — now swimming and canoeing and breathing all day.

"'It's a great place with palms, natives, and bananas, and Columba is also very fine.

"We hope 'From Me To You' is still (er ... pardon) in your chart. All the best from ...

The Beatles (a band)."

PETER WALSH & KENNEDY STREET ENTERPRISES
In association with TITO BURNS present

THE ONLY LONDON APPEARANCE OF THE SENSATIONAL AMERICAN VOCAL GROUP

THE FOUR SEASONS

NMExclusive PIC-SCOOP
Dan meets Elvis

... AND ELVIS MEETS TWO NEW LEADING LADIES

DISTRICT BANK FOREIGN DEPARTMENT

You're great—then don't light it."

...happy about!"

Roy Orbison takes audience by storm

FEW stars—British or American—could induce an audience to shout for more immediately before the Beatles were due on stage. But this is just how highly Roy Orbison is scoring on his present tour with Liverpool's two big groups.

Roy succeeds in one of the stiffest tasks any entertainer in Britain just now could face, for the Beatles prove again on this tour that they are currently the most exciting entertainers in the country.

Without a single movement Roy captured the audience from the first notes of "Only The Lonely," which gave us initial hearing of that fantastic Orbison sound.

Roy, who also proves himself a talented guitarist, played his own harmonica introduction to "Candy Man." That preceded what I considered the big hit of his act — "Runnin' Scared," for which he had to encore the final chorus.

Then came the swinging version of "What'd I Say," followed by "Crying," "Dream Baby," and his latest record, "Falling," which is issued this week.

He rounded off a terrific act with "In Dreams,"—and was called back three times by the sustained applause and cheers.

As was expected, the Beatles virtually raised the roof, although little could be heard of them above the screams. They included "Some

Other Guy," "Do You Want To Know A Secret," and "Please Please Me," before a tremendous rendering of their current chart topper," "From Me To You."

Gerry and the Pacemakers also scored, as did newcomers Ian Crawford, Louise Cordet, and Erky Grant, taken on his comedy ment.
CHRIS HUTCHINS.

NEW RECORD-BREAKING COMBO

AT THE

LOCARNO WAKEFIELD

GRAHAM   BILL
WARNER · MEDLAND

Bandleader   *Manager*

CURRENT RELEASE:

CAPACITY CROWDS

BACKED BY

RECORD TAKINGS

Lifelines of the BEATLES

	JOHN	PAUL	GEORGE	RINGO (STARR)
Real name :	John Lennon	Paul McCartney	George Harrison	Richard Starkey
Birth date :	October 9, 1940.	June 18, 1942.	February 25, 1943.	July 7, 1940.
Birthplace :	Liverpool.	Liverpool.	Liverpool.	Liverpool.
Height :	5 ft. 11 in.	5 ft. 11 in.	5 ft. 11 in.	5 ft. 8 in.
Weight :	11 st. 5 lb.	11 st. 4 lb.	10 st. 2 lb.	9 st. 8 lb.
Colour of eyes :	Brown.	Hazel.	Dark brown.	Blue.
Colour of hair :	Brown.	Black.	Brown.	Dark brown.
Brothers, sisters :	None.	Mike.	Louise, Peter and Harry.	None.
Instruments played :	Rhythm guitar, harmonica, piano, percussion.	Bass guitar, drums, piano, banjo.	Guitar, piano, drums.	Drums, guitar.
Educated :	Quarry Bank Grammar and Liverpool College of Art.	Liverpool Institute High School.	Liverpool Institute High School.	Liverpool Secondary Modern. Riversdale Technical College.
Age entered show business	20.	18.	17.	18.
Former occupation :	Art student.	Student.	Student.	Engineer.
Hobbies :	Writing songs, poems and plays; girls, painting, TV, meeting people.	Girls, songwriting, sleeping.	Driving, records, girls.	Night-driving, sleeping, Westerns.
Favourite singers :	Shirelles, Miracles, Chuck Jackson, Ben E. King, Robert Mitchum.	Ben E. King, Little Richard, Chuck Jackson, Larry Williams, Marlon Brando, Tony Perkins.	Little Richard, Eartha Kitt.	Brook Benton, Sam "Lightning" Hopkins.
Favourite actors :	Peter Sellers.	Brigitte Bardot, Juliette Greco.	Vic Morrow.	Paul Newman, Jack Palance.
Favourite actresses:	Juliette Greco, Sophia Loren.	Chicken Maryland, Milk.	Brigitte Bardot.	Brigitte Bardot.
Favourite foods :	Curry and jelly.	Good suits, suede.	Lamb chops, chips, tea.	Steak, Whisky.
Favourite drinks :	Whisky and tea.	Billy Cotton.	Anything.	Suits.
Favourite clothes :	Sombre.		Duane Eddy group.	Arthur Lyman.
Favourite band :	Quincy Jones.	None special.	Chet Atkins.	None special.
Favourite instrumentalist :	Sonny Terry, Luther Dixon.	Goffin-King.	None special.	Bert Bacharach, McCartney and Lennon.
Favourite composers :				Fast cars.
Likes :	Blondes, leather.	Music, TV, Shaving.	Driving, Haircuts.	Onions and Donald Duck.
Dislikes :	Stupid people.			(r-and-w, r-and-b.
Tastes in music :	R-and-b, gospel.	R-and-b, modern jazz.	Spanish guitar, c-and-w.	c-and-w.
Personal ambitions :	To write musical.	To have my picture in the "Dandy."	To design a guitar.	To be happy.
Professional ambition :	To be rich and famous.	To popularise our sound.	To fulfil all group's hopes.	To get to the top.

New series—the PEOPLE behind the BEATLES—1

BRIAN EPSTEIN

By CHRIS HUTCHINS

BRIAN EPSTEIN

A YEAR ago this week the Beatles' "Please Please Me" blasted to No. 1 in the NME Chart. It was their first chart-topper and manager Brian Epstein took the foursome to an Italian restaurant in Soho to celebrate the achievement.

No one recognised the four rather strange looking boys with their Stone Age hairstyles and Chelsea boots, for Beatlemania had still to make its marked impression on the world.

Last week red-headed Cilla Black soared to the top spot with "Anyone Who Had A Heart" and Brian launched his twelfth "No. 1 celebration party" in a year — no less than eleven discs by his artists ("She Loves You" did it twice) have bounded into the chart in twelve months.

A further four discs by stars from his stable have been smash hits.

At 29 this rather shy young manager with the boyish looking face has climbed to the very top of the music business ladder with a trail of major successes that would take a column to list.

Actor

Brian Epstein wanted to be an actor but his father was keen to see him enter the family furnishing business. So when Brian left Wrekin College in Shropshire at the early age of 16, he began a five-year furniture salesman apprenticeship at £5 a week.

But at 21 his love of the theatre diverted him to the Royal Academy of Dramatic Art, where he pursued his first love, the theatre, for eighteen months before returning to the family's Liverpool store.

The story of how he found the Beatles virtually on his own doorstep in Liverpool is now history. From their initial, though modest, success with "Love Me Do," Epstein has never looked back.

He launched Gerry and the Pacemakers, Billy J. Kramer and the Dakotas, the Fourmost and Cilla Black, all of whom were to repeat the "particularly happy moment" which he experiences every time one of them breaks into the chart with a new hit or sends box office bookings soaring with the news that they're coming to town."

But not all of Brian's experiences in the past year have been those "particularly happy" ones.

His amiable nature, tempered with a slight inferiority complex, lends itself easily to embarrassment and the blushes reporters love to write about.

One such experience happened as the Beatles were half-way through one of their earliest recording sessions. Brian criticised a track they had just taped.

"Listen, we'll make the records—you just count the percentage," retorted John Lennon angrily in front of recording manager and engineers.

"Believe it or not, that was one of the most embarrassing moments in my career," Brian told me, quivering slightly at the memory of it.

But Brian need not have worried. This youthful and dedicated manager with the golden touch has the respect of all his artists, and by making such an open retort at the session John Lennon was emphasising the close and frank relationship that exists between Epstein and all his stars.

The well-spoken ex-RADA student who also once had a yen to take up dress-designing—is very different to many of his contemporaries, such as Elvis Presley's manager, Colonel Tom Parker.

Until pop music became his life, Brian was more at home with classical music, though at about the time he entered RADA he "seems to remember liking 'Baby Face' by Little Richard."

With the Beatles' major American success, appearances by most of his artists on the Palladium TV show, and Cilla Black's booking for a London Palladium season already achieved, Brian's ambitions now veer back towards a personal theatrical career.

He is anxious to present, produce and direct a play in the West End —and possibly to act in one.

Jury

Tomorrow evening Epstein makes his second appearance on "Juke Box Jury." He could have made several more in recent months but always needs persuasion to enter the limelight.

He even refuses to answer personally the fan mail which pours in for him daily. "I believe the fans should be for my artists—not for me," he says firmly.

Pressmen track his movements at all times and the telephone in his Knightsbridge flat rarely stops ringing, even late at night, for he believes in taking every decision of any importance in connection with NEMS Enterprises, personally.

Though now one of the most sought after men in the London social world, the young bachelor dislikes parties and social functions. Despite his solid business dealings he is often stumped for words at such occasions.

The company he likes best is that of his artists. With all of them he enjoys the friendly relationship that goes from building a career alongside them.

Gene Pitney puzzles everybo

NEW MUSICAL EXPRESS

The three attractions that will pack theatres everywhere they appear on their current tour—the BEATLES (in shirts), GERRY and the PACEMAKERS (in jackets) and America's ROY ORBISON (in glasses).

The tragic figure of Beatlemania. The New Age's first victim. When the inmates took over the asylum he had no place to go, so he went. It was anarchy time. A sensitive soul and a very nice man.

HOW TO WRITE A HIT!

IF they never sang another note in public, John Lennon and Paul McCartney would still collect five-figure salaries every year. Running parallel with their world-beating success with THE group, is an equally powerful talent for great pop songwriting. Great? They are not the Rodgers and Hart, the Lerner and Loewe of 1964; but they have captured in their bouncing songs the easy effervescence of the young generation — in other, plaintive writing, the simple voice of spurned young love without the maudlin embellishments of yesterday's weepies.

Did the Beatles make the songs, or did the songs make them? Easily answered. The songs ARE the Beatles, with a style so recognisable as to be flattered continually by imitation.

In an interview with CHRIS ROBERTS

Lennon and McCartney maintain they do not know how to write hit songs, a sensible point when you hear their argument.

"We don't know how to write a hit," said Paul. "If we knew, we wouldn't tell you, and if we told you, Britain would have a great new industry, kind of hit factories all over the place."

For the talented two of the fabulous four, it is a dizzy look down from their pop peak to the Valley of the Shadow of Liverpool in the scratching days.

Even now, the story of their early attempts to "do something" with their songs has a pathetic tone, and it doesn't take much imagination to hear them talk over a hundred crazy ideas to launch their efforts on the pop world.

FROM ME TO YOU + SHE

As a publicity stunt, they once intended to swim the Mersey. They decided to write to a national newspaper with a plea for the use of a big recording studio for a day, incorporating a challenge to the stars of the moment. Neither plan came off.

"And there we were with a big exercise book full of songs, wondering what the hell to do with them." John said.

How did John and Paul come to write over 100 songs between them before they knew what the inside of a recording studio looked like? And how do they set about creating the structure of a composition which might, the following month, be sung in factory, shop, school and office all over Britain?

Before they left for their triumphant Paris visit, they spoke to the MM about their songwriting life—the first time it has been fully spotlighted.

JOHN: It started in school holidays. I was about 15, I suppose. We knew each other, yes. I would've looked funny sitting in Paul's house without being introduced. At that time we did "Like dreamers do", followed by "Hello little girl", and "Love of the loved" and "Please please me".

The first song I ever wrote was called "I lost my little girl", then "That's my woman" and we used to do one "In spite of all the danger". The bulk of the numbers was written between 1956 and 1961, when we were at the Cavern doing a lot of the songs. We'd do two together, then I'd do "Please please me" and Paul would do "I saw her standing there" and "PS I love you" all in a normal hour's programme.

PAUL: We were influenced by Buddy Holly, and the Everly Brothers, and a lot of the numbers are Holly-ish. But when we came to do them at the club —we had hitherto only heard them with guitar or piano—the sound changed with the addition of bass and drums, and they came out differently.

We both wrote words or music as we felt like, although we'd suggest changes to each other in different numbers.

We don't think we write very hip words. We try to write words that we would like and not laugh at. Not moon and June stuff.

JOHN: What do you mean, moon and June? We had moonlight and Junelight in "I'll be on my way"

PAUL: That's different. You know what I mean. Not corny.

JOHN: On the music side, as far as I was concerned, if I found a new chord, I'd write a song round it. I thought if there were a million chords I'd never run out. Sometimes the chords got to be an obsession and we started to put all unnecessary ones in.

LOVES YOU + PLEASE PLEA

PAUL: They started to get too complicated, and "chordy". No, not like modern jazz, but just dripping with chords that weren't supposed to be there anyway.

JOHN: We decided to keep them simple, and it's the best way. It might have sounded okay for us, but the extra chords wouldn't make other people like them any better. That's the way we've kept it all along.

We never consciously write 'B' sides to records. We don't just sit down and say "right, let's whip off a 'B' side," just like that. Quite a few of our 'B' sides could have been 'A' sides, I suppose, but something has to go on the back, so we just choose.

PAUL: The best time to write, I find, is sitting down. Seriously, sitting down on our own with a guitar or piano. Smoking helps too. Why guitar all the time? Not always. Sometimes your ideas get blocked on guitar. One night I was trying to write one, with a guitar, and I couldn't get it on the thing. I tried it with piano, and it worked.

JOHN. We don't sort of think of a catch phrase and write around it. It could be quite nice if a catch phrase comes to you, but it doesn't happen often.

E ME + ALL MY LOVING +

PAUL: I don't think we write for this idiom of the moment or anything. All our numbers could be adapted, you know, to meet each style. Our arrangements are in this idiom, yes. But, for instance "I saw her standing there" could be a country-and-western thing, with a big country sound. We don't write for any particular idiom.

None of us read music, still. As far as I am concerned, music is to be enjoyed and if we started studying, it wouldn't be.

JOHN: We have always done our songs and written them down in a weird sort of notation, using chord names like A flat, C, and Dm, and writing the notes separately. It would be much easier if I knew music, yes. After writing the words down and the chords in a night, you can generally remember the tune the next morning. There's more fun in that.

PAUL: Musically again, I don't think the stuff you do chordwise is quite as important as the tune and the words and the feel of the song. I heard two fellers in a club last night, doing one of our numbers and in one place they did the wrong chord —but it didn't matter. The song was there.

JOHN: We though "From me to you" was too way out, although we have always had a fair bit of confidence in our own stuff, always thought it would make it somewhere.

PAUL: I played it on the piano and thought "No, no one's going to like this", so I played it to my dad and he thought it was a lovely tune, and that's how it was. You value other people's opinions.

AD TO ME + LOVE ME DO +

You know, we have always written for ourselves. We don't—we can't write down. If we don't like the songs ourselves, how could we put up with them? People underestimate the intelligence of a lot of the record buyers. They're not so thick.

Our lyrics aren't more intelligent than others have been, but we always try to say something different in the way a song should say it, you know.

Very sensible stuff from McCartney and Lennon. Few songwriters have put it so well and so simply. Pop must be simple – not simple-minded – but easy and instant. It isn't classical music and it isn't jazz. It's pop. And easily grasped, always at hand.

ROY ORBISON says 'THE BEATLES COULD BE TOPS IN AMERICA'

ROY ORBISON—a film fanatic. "It freshens the mind," he says.

By CHRIS HUTCHINS

THE Beatles could be America's Number One group—that's the considered view of Roy Orbison, who is currently touring Britain with Merseyside's two ace groups. He told me as we chatted backstage at Sheffield on Saturday:

"These boys have enough originality to storm our charts in the U.S. with the same effect as they have already done here, but it will need careful handling."

The Beatles themselves were changing into their futuristic suits just a few yards away as bespectacled Roy quietly made his big prediction.

"You see they have something that's entirely new even to us Americans and although we have an influx of hit groups at home at the present time I really do believe your own boys could top our charts as frequently as they seem to be doing here.

"But it would be important to bill them as 'The Beatles of England' to get over their big appeal. In America everybody knew that the Tornados and the Springfields and one-time chart-topper Laurie London were from England and that helped their records as much as it does when the fans here know the artist is an American star."

ac in their sensational, if comparatively short, career. As he walked by Paul McCartney threw a hefty bag of jelly babies into Roy's lap.

"That's the ninth bag we've had given us tonight and it's only '8.30,' called Paul. And he dashed on stage to be promptly hit by another barrage of the sweets, which have found new fame since it became known that the group was partial to them.

I stood at Roy's side and watched as the Beatles thundered into "Some Other Guy," although it must have been difficult, through the screams to make out just what they were singing from the fourth row back.

"It's a chance to see new stars who are not just watered down versions of Elvis Presley," said Roy. "This seems to be a sound they have made famous all on their own, and I really think it is the greatest. Though you know it as Merseyside music, I am sure this will be hailed as the new British sound in America."

It seems the Beatles' good impression on hit-making Orbison is not only professional. Socially they've become great friends and are usually to be found eating together after the show.

Although separate transport arrangements were made for him, Roy insisted in riding on the coach that carries the groups on their present tour.

He leaned back and took a cigarette from the packet offered him by Gerry 'Pacemaker' Marsden: "Now here's another boy whom our kids would really rate. I think that monster smile would sell him before even I heard his voice," chuckled Roy and the famous Marsden grin grew wider.

The Beatles passed us on their way to the stage and what subsequently proved to be yet another roof-raising

Orbison record at its first availability.

Presley is among the numerous friends he has in American show business, but it took his current trip to Britain to bring him into the company of Del Shannon. Though they have both been admirers of each others' work for a long time Del and Roy had never met.

On stage the Beatles were bringing their act to a close with "From Me To You," and as they yelled the final notes Roy told me "Yes sir, even in the States these Beatles would take some beating!"

But one habit they have not been able to follow him in is Roy's ever-keen appetite for films. "I often go to three different cinemas in a day and have seen more than a dozen movies since I came to England. I think '55 Days To Peking' impressed me most.

"When I am recording in Nashville the session never begins before midnight because I like to see at least six hours of films before I begin! It freshens my mind."

"If there is nothing good on at the local cinemas then I watch them on television; we have full length colour films on TV on Fridays, Saturdays and Sundays—so I always try not to get booked on those nights!"

Our attention was focused on the Beatles as they literally swung into "Please Please Me."

"For America I think they would have to do a couple of slow numbers. Even for recording purposes in the U.S. it would be advisable for them to slow down just a little."

Roy should know, for his professional career began at the tender age of eight when once a week he rode a bicycle to his local radio stations and sang in a show of which he proved to be the making.

Though his modesty prevents him from talking about it, it is a well known fact that he is placed high on the list of Elvis Presley's favourite singers and El has seen his henchman as far as ninety miles to pick up an

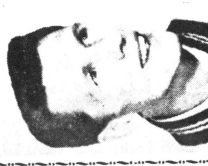

JAMES GILREATH is hit singer of "Little Band Of Gold."

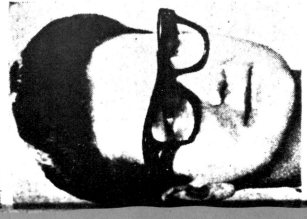

SMILE' WOULD SELL HIM ANYWHERE!

AND GERRY'S 'MONSTER'

WINTER GARDENS, MARGATE
SATURDAY, 1st JUNE, & SUNDAY, 2nd JUNE, 1963

JET TONY
HARRIS & MEEHAN

TOMMY BRUCE & THE BRUISERS
AND FULL SUPPORTING PROGRAMME

FUTURIST THEATRE, SCARBOROUGH
SUNDAY, 2nd JUNE, 1963

DEL SHANNON

JAN & KELLY
AND FULL SUPPORTING PROGRAMME

NORTH PIER, BLACKPOOL
SUNDAY, 2nd JUNE, 1963

JOAN DOUG
REGAN SHELDON

AND FULL SUPPORTING PROGRAMME

THERE IS
The Cavern
IN THE TOWN

YES, there is indeed the CAVERN in the town. And just about the most exciting place any pop fan could hope to visit. I have never seen a more atmosphere-laden cellar in all my career of travels to clubs of all shapes and sizes.

The actual location is the basement of a warehouse. In appearance is resembles a trio of railway tunnels side by side. The centre "tunnel" is used for those who wish to sit and enjoy the music. The outer wings are strictly for dancing, giving and, in particular, the attractive CAVERN STOMP. This dance originated when the fans found space too restricted for normal jiving. Properly promoted, it could become a national, if not international, success.

Once the home of a jazz club, the Cavern has followed public taste and adopted a strictly beat music policy. I was told by owner RAY McFALL. Ray also told me he was not too favourably disposed towards all-nighters (the pride of London jazz clubs) and he therefore adopted a policy of marathon shows. These run from early or mid-afternoon, usually on public holidays or week-ends, and last until sound about midnight.

MARATHON

The next marathon is scheduled for Friday of this week (April 12) and is headlined by the BEATLES. In support will be no less than eight other groups. Full details appeared in last week's NRM, although we erroneously listed GERRY and the PACEMAKERS as headlining.

During our visit to the Cavern, I asked one young lady what she considered the main reasons for the current beat boom in Liverpool. Without hesitation she replied: "Without BOB WOOLER there would be no boom. He is the man most responsible for encouraging local talents to develop . . ."

I had already chatted to Bob on arrival at the Cavern. He is a disc-jockey, master of ceremonies, adviser, you name it, to all the musicians and customers. Whether the music is live or canned, it is Bob's voice you hear introducing each item on the programme. He slips in requests. He chats amiably to the customers —and, between announcements, listens to myriad questions, complaints, suggestions and what have you from all who pack into the tiny dressing room at the side of the stage.

Yes, Bob Wooler is just one of the many attractions which make the Cavern unique as an entertainment medium.

One thing strikes you when you first enter this hub of beat music. It is downright dingy. The walls haven't seen paint

THIS board above a dingy doorway in an archway off a narrow street, in a maze of other narrow streets, is the only outward sign of one of the most exciting music cellars in existence. (NRM PICTURE.)

WELCOME
TO
THE CAVERN CLUB

EVENING SESSIONS 7:30 TO 11
ON TUESDAYS, WEDNESDAYS,
FRIDAYS, SATURDAYS & SUNDAYS

FIVE LUNCHTIME SESSIONS
12 NOON TO 2:15 p.m.
MONDAYS TO FRIDAYS

NEW MEMBERS WELCOME—JOIN NOW
READMISSIONS BY PASS OUT AFTER 9:30

NOTE: NO ADMISSIONS BY PASS OUT AFTER 9:30

BILLY J. KRAMER and the DAKOTAS are another fine group popular on the Liverpool scene though they in fact hail from Manchester. It looks like they are soon destined to join the Beatles and Gerry and the Pacemakers at the top as they have been signed by PARLOPHONE A&R Manager GEORGE MARTIN. First disc is scheduled for release within a matter of weeks. A most exciting group with an especially outstanding drummer. (NRM PICTURE.)

for years. The floor is concrete cracked and chipped. BUT the customers won't have it any other way. Should Ray McFall or Bob Wooler suggest titivating the place there would be immediate howls of protest from all sides.

Apart from the fact that the present "decorations" help create the tremendous atmosphere of the Cavern, another point could be mentioned: in this way the fans can really let themselves go without fear of damaging some exotic décor. At present, the décor comprises scribbled slogans on the wall ringing the praises of the various star attractions.

If any pop fan happens to be in Liverpool at any time I strongly recommend a visit to this fascinating home of the BIG BEAT. No true pop fan curriculum can be complete without such a memory.

Music Trade people thought that there must be endless gold in Liverpool, forgetting that the Beatles were unique. The Music men pounced off trains at Liverpool station and signed everyone up, including each other.

The Liverpool Big Beat Scene concluded

"MY ROCKING CITY"

By BILL HARRY, Editor of 'MERSEY BEAT'

EXCITING, unusual, thriving—that is the state of the Merseyside Big Beat Scene. Although the success of The Beatles has turned the spotlight on Liverpool, it was a recognition that was inevitable. So many groups and artists have been involved in such fantastic competition that there would eventually be an explosion of some sort . . . and Merseyside groups have certainly exploded on to the National scene.

All the groups who have so far succeeded nationally have come from the management of Brian Epstein of Nems Enterprises. Soon other managers and other groups must also appear in the limelight.

Colonel Joe, for instance, "Colonel Joe" is the nickname of Joe Flannery, personal manager of Lee Curtis and the All Stars and leading light of the Carlton Brook Agency.

RIVAL

Joe has already achieved results with his artists and the first recording by Lee Curtis was released by Decca on April 5. There is an opinion on Merseyside that with his voice and looks, Lee could well be a major rival to Elvis Presley—and anyone listening to "Just One More Dance", the flipside of "Little Girl", will understand what they mean.

Lee Curtis and the All Stars were voted Merseyside's No. 2 group only four months after their formation—and the group who came 1st. The Beatles, had a record in the charts at the time.

It is interesting to note that Pete Best, drummer with The All Stars, was a member of The Beatles for three years.

Beryl Marsden, also under the management of Joe Flannery, is only 15 years of age but she is recognised as Liverpool's leading female beat vocalist and I have no hesitation in predicting that she will also become a major star.

Recently Beryl has received vocal backing from The Chants, five coloured boys who are unique on Merseyside, and, indeed in Britain. The Chants have been

backed by the Beatles the Big Three Lee Curtis and The All Stars and received backing from Eric Delaney when they appeared at the Odeon, Liverpool on Good Friday in the "Meet Your Lucky Stars" show.

They recently signed with Ted Ross of Manchester's Ross Enterprises.

Another major figure on the Merseyside scene is Les Ackerley, the man behind the Iron Door Club, the Black Cat Club and Northern Variety Agencies. Mr. Ackerley has a dozen Liverpool groups on his books including Sonny Webb and the Cascades, The Searchers (who recently recorded an L.P. in Germany), The Four Clefs, The Coasters (Billy J. Kramer's original backing group) and The Mersey Beats.

Several other clubowners and promoters on Merseyside have also taken groups under their management, the most notable being Ralph Webster of the Orrell Park Ballroom who handles The Undertakers, Ian and The Zodiacs, and Mark Peters and the Cyclones.

UNIQUE

Ralph, I am sure, will benefit from his faith in the Undertakers who have developed a unique, driving sound of their own. The group made quite a visual spectacle on TV recently when they appeared dressed in their outfits of frock coats and stetsons.

The most recent agent to appear on the scene is Doug Martin of Ivormar Promotions who has formed "Stuart Enterprises", which is concerned with the development of new talent.

Johnnie Sandon and the Remo 4, The 4 Mosts, Faron's Flamingos are three more groups who could well make an impact nationally. In fact, the potential in "The Rocking City" is tremendous. Although there is a definite, recognisable "Liverpool sound", there are still many groups who have their own individual sound, and new groups are appearing almost every week.

What puzzles me is the fact that no one seems to realise that Liverpool is

also the centre of country and western music, and The Blue Mountain Boys, Hank Walters and his Dusty Road Ramblers, The Boot Hill Billies, The Country 4 and The Centremen may one day explode into national fame and so add to the legend of Liverpool The Rocking City on Merseyside.

A BEATLES' eye view of the audience at the CAVERN.

JOHN, PAUL, RINGO and GEORGE backstage at the LIVERPOOL EMPIRE, admire a gift from some fans. (NRM Picture.)

FOOTNOTE: Pye A&R manager Tony Hatch last week signed Johnny Sandon and the Remo 4. He plans to record the team immediately.

On his trip to Merseyside Tony also put the Chants under contract but is not rushing to record them in order to allow time for gathering the right material and polishing up their performance.

Rumour has it that another leading Liverpool team was also signed last week but no confirmation had been received at press time.

BERYL MARSDEN is destined for major stardom, they say on MERSEYSIDE.

R&R is a life-style as well as a music – here are some of the clothes required.

'MOD' SHIRTS AND HATS

37/6	32/6	32/6	29/11

LONG JOHN
White or Blue

KILDARE
Collarless shirt.
White only

PAISLEY
Blue-Green-Wine

PLAIN TAB
White or Blue

'BEAT' CAPS
Imitation leather.
Black only.

19/11

'MOD' HATS
Narrow ½" Brim
Navy or Grey

32/6

When ordering please state style, size
—small, medium or large, and second
colour choice. Add 2/- for P.P.
Send crossed postal order to:

GARTH Modern Mens Wear
2 CHURCH STREET,
DUNSTABLE, BEDS.
MONEY BACK GUARANTEE

IAN DOVE

GO! GO! GO! RINGO! RINGO!

The new BEAT BOOT 'RINGO'

Telephone : SYDenham 9001

Be the envy of the crowd in your RINGOS.
The latest rave—2¾" heels, 7¼" uppers, elastic
gusset sides, centre seams, rounded toes. Made
from finest quality black leather. sizes 6 to 11.
Get with it before they GO! GO! GO!
Move now—we've had a terrific response
to these fab boots!

REGIS SHOES LTD.
(Dept. NME2), 134E Kingsland Rd., London, E.2

SPECIAL RINGO STARR LICENCE !
Full guarantee.

79/9

Plus 3/- P. & P.
Cash or C.O.D.

LOOK GOOD & FEEL GOOD in Lewis Leathers

Just look at these great new styles in
leather casuals ! Slimline-tailored from
Black Chrome leather, luxuriously lined
with smart contrasting satins. Go along with the
modern trend and wear
one of these fashion-
setting styles !

CLASSIC
Cat. No. 980
Superbly crafted. Three
welded pockets. Two-
button breast
pocket. Slim-
tailored for the
lean look.
£9.12.6 or 40/- dep.
and 6 mly. pyts. of
29/5. P. and P. 3/-

REGENT
Cat. No. 982
Three - button styled
Super scarlet lining and
two patch pockets and
inside breast pocket.
£9.12.6 or 40/- dep.
and 6 mly. pyts. of
29/5. P. and P. 3/-

Alpine
Cat. No. 453
Navy blue quilted
nylon jacket.
Windproof,
showerproof.
Front zip and
three zip-up
pockets. Scarlet
lining, detachable
hood.
£6.19.6 or 20/- dep.
of 22/10. P. and P. 2/6.

Elite
Fashionable
black jacket in
real black
leather. Latest
collarless style
Centre vented
back. jetted
side pocket.
with flaps
Lined blue and
silk.
£9.12.6 or 40/-
dep. and 6 mly
pyts or 29/5
P. and P. 3/-.

All these great "Lewis Leathers"
styles are in sizes 34" to 44" chest.
Post orders or call to

D Lewis (Dept. NME/27),
124 Gt. Portland St.,
LONDON, W.1

BOYS, BE A HIT !

in this latest
BEETLE STYLE
JACKET
in popular
BLACK CAVALRY
TWILL
with fancy lining

SEND ONLY 5/-
dep. 3/-
Plus Post/Pkg.

Beautifully made in this ever-popular
material with 2 outside pockets, dummy
breast pocket and inside pocket. Lined
throughout. Metal buttons with "Caesar"
design.

● WONDERFUL BARGAIN
AT ONLY £5.10.0. CASH

or sent on approval for 5/- deposit, then
balance by 5 equal monthly payments;
or return garment immediately in perfect
condition for deposit refund.
ADD 3/- for post/pkg.

SEND NOW
AND GET WITH IT !

SUITABLE FOR
14 -20 AGE GROUP
Chest sizes 34 inch
36 inch, 38 inch

ABURTRIM LTD. (Dept. ME), 43 GREAT PORTLAND STREET, LONDON, W.I

"WELL STRIPE ME PINK—OR GREY—OR BLUE"
say the "APPLEJACKS"
(shown here AS AL JACKSON)

THE APPLEJACKS SHIRT

EXCLUSIVE TO US from the makers of
their stage shirts.
Fluorescent White Tab Collar and Cuffs,
with Fine Chalk Weave Stripe Body, in
Pop Pink, Charcoal Grey and Beat Blue.
Sizes 13½ — 16

Post your order now to :

CHANDLEYS (Dept. NM)
36 James Street, Oxford Street, London, W.1

40/-
POST
FREE

ANDY GRAY.

10

WE'RE NO GLAMOUR BOYS
says Freddie of the Dreamers

DARK brown eyes twinkled behind Freddie Garratty's glasses, "The Dreamers and I have always been daft. I mean, you couldn't call me a sex-idol, could you ? Collectively, we're no glamour boys.

"That's why it's so great about 'I'm Telling You Now' jumping up the chart like that. Isn't it fantastic—No. 7. It's wonderful to know our act is paying off, because we've put a lot into our sound and presentation."

He kept talking in his homely, Manchester accent, telling me of his early days as an entertainer and his hopes for the future. "I've been in the business seven years now," he said. "I've been with the Dreamers for four years, but I used to be with a skiffle group before that.

from the top:
ROY CREWDSON
PETE BIRRELL
DEREK QUINN
BERNIE DWYER
FREDDIE

"I formed it in the big days of Lonnie Donegan, and we called ourselves the Red Sox. We were doing quite well for a time, then I packed it all in for a young lady. She got fed up with being traipsed around to all the different venues, cinema halls and Labour clubs, and places like that.

"Anyway I sold all my gear to Roy, who's now with the Dreamers. He was with a group called the Kingfishers at the time.

"A couple of months later I was with this young lady and I met him on the street. 'How's things?' he said. 'Great,' he said. 'Why don't you come and join up with me ?'

"Honestly, this girl gave a look that could kill. 'Just you do,' she said. I could tell she was flaming mad, but I didn't care any more. I liked music so much, I decided to go along and play. In the end I was made the leader.

"One of the neighbours in our street had the idea of calling us the Dreamers, although in between I did a bit of singing with a little outfit called the John Norman Jour.

By ALAN SMITH

"What made us go in for comedy? Well, as I say, we've always been potty. I little accidents might happen while we were on-stage, and they got such a big laugh we'd put them into the act the following night !

"I think pantomime is going to be the big thing for us. We'll be able to develop all that clowning about. Doing comedy is a good thing really, because if we ever go abroad I think it would make us more acceptable to the foreign audiences. I haven't been abroad before, except to the Isle of Man and the Isle of Widged. That's the Isle of Wight to anyone else !

"I'll tell you one thing I'm grateful for—I don't suffer from nerves. Not when we're on the stage anyway. I suppose if anything ever went wrong we could always say it was intentional !

"The only time I get a bit scared is when I'm being interviewed, on radio or television, and I have to speak about myself. I sometimes get a bit worried in case I get lost for words.

"Songs ? I suppose I've written about a dozen since I started. 'Feel So Blue ' was one of them, and it went on the back of ' If You Gotta Make A Fool Of Somebody.'

"'I'm Telling You Now' was composed by me. At least, I got the tune in the first place, then Mitch Murray got hold of it and added a bit of the tune and a few more words.

"It's funny the way I make up a tune. I get a tape recorder, then I sing the first thing that comes into my head ! Any old rubbish I sing, just till I get the tune. I usually try and work on a catch phrase.

"We still can't get over the way things have happened for us. It was tremendous the way the first record did so well. I knew it would get into the charts—I mean, it's such a great tune, it had to do well.

"To be honest, I think the original James Rae version was far better than ours, but I'm not complaining that we got the hit and he didn't !

Dumpers

"I suppose you could say entertaining is in my blood. I love to get out there and start performing. I served my time as a mechanical engineer in Manchester, but I wasn't that happy with it. The firm made dumpers and loaders — what about that !?

"Anyway, I left in the end, then I did a spell of selling brushes from door to door.

"I don't think many people knew about that. It was quite a good job, but I gave it up after a while to work in a shoe shop. That didn't last, so I got a job doing a milk round.

"That job suited me fine, because I had the afternoons off and I could spend by time songwriting. If there's one drawback it was the time I had to get up in the morning. It wasn't too much fun getting up at 5 a.m. when I'd been working late with the group the night before.

Freddie may be modest about his appeal as an "idol," but the fact remains that many girls regard him as their favourite pin-up. He's already built up a small army of massive following.

FROM YOU TO US

JOHN WILLIS (Liverpool 25) writes: Surely it's about time that Columbia released an EP of the Shadows' first hits — tracks like "Feelin'" Fine," "Driftin'," "Jet Black " and " Saturday Dance."

All of them were minor hits and since they have been deleted, the black market prices for second-hand copies are very high. "Feelin' Fine" regularly appears in adverts in the NME for "Records Wanted."

They cannot be as bad as Bruce Welch says they are. So come on EMI, make the Shadows' fans happy by allowing them to complete their collection.

"FARHAM" (Castle Bromwich, near Birmingham) writes: How cruel can record buyers be ? The Dakotas get into the NME chart with "The Cruel Sea", whereas just as good—and in some cases far superior—instrumentals from the Fentones, Cougars, Outlaws, Zephyrs, Hunters, Volcanoes, the Boys, and the Ventures either never looked like gaining chart success . . . or were poorly treated as "potential."

"I've got one here," he told me with a wide grin. "It's come from some place in Scotland, and I've never been there in my life.

"Dearest Freddie," it says. 'You are the kindest person I have ever seen. You probably have lots of girl friends in Manchester, but if not, would you consider me ?.' Then she goes on to ask me to marry her.

"Don't get me wrong, I'm not laughing at her. It's very, very flattering to get a letter like that, but you can see it's a tricky problem."

THE NEWEST SOUND FROM MERSEYSIDE

THE MASTER SOUNDS

wish to thank all their many friends and new fans they made at the RICHMOND NATIONAL JAZZ FESTIVAL last Saturday. Also for the tumultuous reception they received.

Sole Representation:
CUMMINS & BROWN, 11 BALMORAL RD., LIVERPOOL 6
'Phone : ANFIELD 6833 between 10 a.m. and 5.30 p.m.

Also numerous other Top Liverpool Groups available, including :
MERSEYSIDE'S OWN EVERLY BROTHERS — THE MERCHANTS

GERRY AND THE PACEMAKERS reveal their success secret 'WE LET GO!'

"UND JETZT," said Gerry (of the Pacemakers), "ein wünsche für . . ."

The rest of his announcement was drowned by a burst of good-natured jeering from the crowd in a Liverpool ballroom. He recalls: "It took me a few seconds to catch on. Then I realised what it was all about. We'd spent five weeks in Hamburg, and I was still introducing the numbers in German! It took a lot of living down."

Though they've only recently become a chart sensation topping the list this week with "How Do You Do It" — Gerry and the Pacemakers have overcome such dangers like this to become firm favourites in the north in the past years.

By ALAN SMITH

Formal

Album

The follow-up to "How Do You Do It" is still undecided.

Andy Williams revives the 'lasting' ballad trend in Top 30!

I HAD hoped that, with the chart upsurge of artists like Matt Monro, Danny Williams and Shirley Bassey, ballads of a standard and durable nature were beginning to make their presence felt in the hit parade.

Gerry and Freddie were lively lads, full of pep. They were always leaping and grinning, and they put on shows that would have done well on piers and in pavilions. And that's where they eventually settled, becoming part of a great British tradition. The British blues is bright and always has been. What have we got to worry about? It's a decent, safe country.

GERRY and the PACEMAKERS (left to right): FREDDIE MARSDEN (drums), GERRY, LES McGUIRE (piano) and LES CHADWICK (bass guitar).

STAR QUOTE

SAID guitarist Jørgen Ingmann (co-winner of the Eurovision Song Contest): "I think my . . .

DEREK JOHNSON.

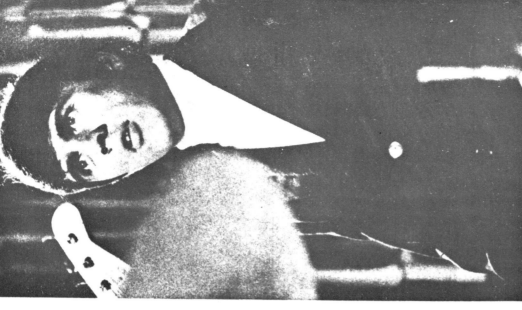

Of course I'm no Krupa

says Dave Clark to Keith Matthews

"IS your image slipping," I enquired of Dave Clark during our chat prior to his colossal American tour. There is an impression around that Dave and the Five are on the decline over here . . . while at present in the States they are indisputably on the incline.' A sort of "carrying coal to Newcastle" sort of thing . . .

"It's very hard to say", said Dave. "The worst thing about us being so popular, is the attitude that all our records have to make No. 1. When you don't do it, then you're slipping. We don't hold with the view that making No. 1 every time is great. We would much prefer consistent hits a little lower down the list.

SLIPPING

"Also remember we have actually only been professional for six months. I'm not the one to say if we are slipping — it is the public who decides, whether you are top or not. You can't get a No. 1 every time. I believe in the crowd pulling power an artiste or group has — to "pack 'em in" is my criterion of complete success. When we played at Blackpool, there was a full capacity audience all the time."

One of the most envied things about Dave from his fellow recording artistes is the royalties percentage he accrues, on sales of his discs. No one collects as much as he does, due to astute shrewdness on his behalf when he negotiated the initial contract.

Dave said in retrospect. "At first, we were playing for kicks, just like any other group, and didn't really want to go professional. Any-

way, after having two big hits we had no option but to take it up full time — there was too much money to lose otherwise. I know the sound I want — the stomp more or less came by accident at one of our performances. I took it from there and it seems to have payed off handsomely."

You always get a successful person getting a few unnecessary criticisms when they hit the big time, and the Dave Clark Five is no exception. We had a laugh over one of these niggles: that the Five should be renamed the Mike Smith Five. A bad reflection on Dave's leadership and musicianship?

"I haven't really heard it at all." said Dave. "But it could stem from a particular liking for certain personalities in the group. And Mike's seems more in favour, ha! Comments on that from the boys were as follows: Mike, "Having all that worry on me, oh no!"

Rick Huxley: "I'd prefer it to be the Rick Huxley Five actually. Seriously though, Dave is a good boss man to work for, and we have no intention of changing it." Dennis Payton said: "He started the group . . . and he made it. The others don't take any notice, and just laugh about it." And Lenny Davidson acquiesced to all that!

CRITICISM

Dave's ability as a drummer, from the technical aspect . . . is much debatable. How does he accept this criticism? "I'm no Krupa, or no drummer in the accepted sense — and have never said so," he replied. "I'm not talented enough yet, and it takes years to improve on technique. We find by playing simple things effectively, the stomp sound was growing by experience. The perpetual smile on Dave's face while he is playing, gives

offence to some of his critics. Does this worry him, and is it a gimmick or completely natural? Certainly no gimmick, for the group has got to be natural. I enjoy my work, and am happy when I am playing . . . so it is obviously reflected in my face. In fact, the neighbours used to call me "Smiler," so you see . . ."

About their present disc's success, the boys were really chuffed. They weren't too worried about the fact that they shall be in America and Canada for around two months— doing 47 one nighters! Thereby not being available to exploit their disc to its fullest. "We don't believe in getting overexposed," was their verdict.

GREAT DISCS

The D. Clark Five dispense more of a sound than any lyrical impact — but then, what group does otherwise nowadays. Any special preference for other sounds outside their own? "Yes, the Phil Spector sound is a knockout in my opinion," said Dave. "And that group, the Ronettes, that he has with him . . . have a terrific performing act, besides making great discs."

As artistes who have "made the grade," have they any personal nomination or preference for anyone in particular, to do likewise? "Mark Wynter, if he isn't already there," they unanimously replied. "He has a lovely voice, and a good stage act. Also Cliff Bennett and the Rebel Rousers." But we all now know how successful they are becoming.

If all this fabulous success had would they then like to do or be? taken away from them, what Dave said: "Buy a business to

direct films or go on the production side." His expensive acquisitions are a red "E" Type, and a recent £17,000 house for his parents. Mike Smith would not: "like to go back to an ordinary 9-5 job. I'd also like to go into films, but lack the experience for the present. Also I would like to work my way around the world."

Rick, Lenny and Dennis, are great camera fiends — and get "snapping" as frequently as time permits. On the sartorial side, the group have had new stage outfits specially made to their requirements. Resplendent on stage at all times, wait till their fans get a look at their new outfits! Consisting of white silk mohair jackets, pale blue shirts with paisley cuffs and collars, and trousers made of blue silk mohair. These can be switched around with their other outfit, and provide four combinations. The boys gave me a preview — and to coin a well worn phrase, "it was real gear!"

With the fantastic pending States and Canadian tour uppermost in their minds . . . and though they were looking forward to it—they all prefer working in and around London as frequently as it's possible. But being musical flagwavers —they realise the importance attached to their visit. Dave said: "We made lots of friends, met numerous people, and visited many places. But there's no place like home." Last time over there, he piloted a plane over the Niagara Falls.

The box office takings and attendance fixtures, are reported to be astronomical at the theatres and other venues they shall be playing. Fan fever is at maximum pitch and America is already theirs for the taking. Yet all they have to say in respect of all this simple and sincere proclamation: "We would rather be playing for the crowd back home . . ."

DAVE CLARK — some startling answers from Dave to some frank questions, posed by Keith Matthews

THE TOUR WITH THE FACES

HELLO! Just wanted to let you know that this tour with the Hollies and the Dixie Cups is going very well indeed. Even though things are more than usually chaotic as we whistle-stop from place to place. Like when our Tornado band-wagon got held up in traffic and we had to borrow equipment from the other groups to put on a show first-house . . .

Maybe Jess Conrad is having the toughest time. He's hitting now in the day-times—with Kim Novak in "Moll Flanders". In view of the fact that we Tornados are having ACTING parts in pantomime this year as a band of robbers, we've become mad keen on the histrionic bit. Specially that histrionic bit called Kim Novak. But it's a tremendous rush for Jess to get from the studios back to wherever we are on tour.

Those Dixie Cups are marvellous. Wonderful senses of humour, all of them. Barbara, the lead singer,

---

THE GREAT
VOCALION
LABEL
gives you fab discs and fab stars

LET'S SURF AGAIN!

A L T H O U G H we haven't latched on to the surfing craze here it seems that we are certainly beginning to latch on to the music. "Wipe Out" by the Surfaris is the second surfing disc that looks like being a big, big hit.

The first one was the subtle "Pipeline" by the Chantays, which made the twenty some weeks ago. The brasher "Wipe Out" (which means falling off the surfboard into the sea) has a rather bizarre voice laughing insanely and yelling the title at us before the pounding surf-beat instrumental gets underway.

"Pipeline" on the other hand was just a straight-forward instrumental without any gimmicks. It also happened to be extremely well played and well-timed. And when that one was a hit, no-one even knew it was a Surfin' record!

Successes

Both of these discs were made on the Dot label in the States, the same label which handles pop stars like Pat Boone and Lawrence Welk, and the R & B phenomenon Arthur Alexander. Recently Dot have been having a huge amount of success with these teen instrumentals, a field in which they haven't recorded very much before.

"Boss" by the Rumblers, and "Hot Pastrami" by the Dartells were just two of these. All have been issued here due to the excellent representation of Dot material by London.

They manage to play dance-hall dates in and around their home town of Glendora, California, but have no chance of turning fully professional until all of them leave school. Which won't be for another four years!

But whether or not you know how to stand up on a surf board whilst in a tight spot wave wise is of no importance when it comes to listening to the Surfaris. In fact in the States many hundreds of Surf fans who live in the States that aren't near the west coasts go around dressed in all the surfing rig-out without ever having seen the sea in their lives. So don't let the fact that you can't stand on a surf board put you off the excellent surfing records . . . .

NORMAN JOPLING.

Vocal

Flip of the number is an off-beat vocal performance called "Surfer Joe", one of the more interesting of recent flip-sides. The boys have already cut an L.P. in the States which is selling pretty well. It's called "Wipe Out" believe it or not, and these are the tracks it contains: "Wiggle Wobble"/ "Green Onions"/"Torquay"/"You Can't Sit Down"/"Teen Beat"/ "Memphis"/"Wipe Out"/"Yep"/ "Wild Weekend"/"Surfer Joe"/ "Walk Don't Run".

And an L.P. after one single can't be bad for any artist — especially young 'uns like the Surfaris.

The youthful SURFARIS have really bounded up the charts with "WIPEOUT". They have already cut an LP in America. Average age of the team is 16!

The Surfaris themselves are a very young group — oldest is 18-year-old Ron Wilson, the group's drummer. Guitarists Jim Fuller, Bob Berryhill and Pat Connelly are 16, while sax player Jim Pass is all of 14.

All the boys still attend school, and are very thrilled at the success of their disc which is at No. 5 in the States this week. They haven't been playing together for very long, and were surprised that Dot saw fit to audition them, as they were such a young group. But it paid off!

B-DAY Is August 31

The South's answer to the Northern invasion: Dave Clark and his pounding kitchen percussion. 'Glad all over' is a classic. By this time managers and A & R men were mining other Northern cities, like Birmingham and Newcastle, searching for the regional sounds.

Back to the American Dream – golden lads from golden beaches in the land of the endless summer. Big Wednesday was every day of the week in surf city where it was two girls to every boy. California was the Promised Land – and still is, though the styles have changed.

Beach Boys brought their own vegetables

SO AUDIENCES BEWARE!

MEETING the Beach Boys is like meeting those people that kick sand in your face in the "I-trade-new-bodies-for-old" advertisements.

They are tough, cynical and very self-assured. British groups are concerned with paying tribute to "influences" and "authenticity".

The Beach Boys talk about money, women and competition.

Mike Love, lead vocalist, sat in a dressing room at the BBC television centre, shortly after a rehearsal for BBC-2's "Beat Room", displayed his bare torso and talked casually about the group's aims.

"Our main aim is to be more socially acceptable. We want to appeal to a wider audience. I don't mean adults. We don't care too much about them. I mean more teenagers. We are here to sound out the British scene and for record promotion. But we want very much to do live performances here too. Maybe we can do this next year."

The Beach Boys are now in Europe and they told me last week that if the French audiences at the Paris Olympia start throwing vegetables at them as they do so often to visiting artists . . . "We will throw them right back. We are taking vegetables with us!" said Mike.

What do the Beach Boys think of British groups in America? "There is no animosity at all," said Mike. "We don't mind them. In fact our sales rose while the Beatles were in America. We don't play rhythm and blues and I think we are a kind of relief from that.

We are a change of sound. I like rhythm and blues but as a group, we don't. There are enough groups doing that kind of stuff so we don't need to."

What about the much vaunted "Surfin" sound that the Beach Boys claim to have pioneered?

Mike said that basically it was a falsetto lead voice and Chuck Berry guitar sound with a lot of reverberation. Seemingly the lyrics, dealing with surfing subjects, were the most important.

The Beach Boys followed up surfing with cars and motor cycles. Dancing is next on the agenda. Their record, "Dance, Dance Dance" is trend setting at this very moment in the good old USA.

"We want to take credit for the surfing sound, but we don't want to live in the past or rest on our laurels." said Mike. But he was a bit vague about what would happen next.

only thing wrong with the music scene that was printable were the awful records being released in America.

"There are some terrible records coming out," he said, naming no names. "Some of the singers are really horrible."

EXPERIMENT

"We started with our own style and keep to it on live appearances. On record however we can experiment with different sounds and beats."

Friendly Carl Wilson, aged 17, the lead guitar player, stretched out on a bed and said he thought the

UNPATRIOTIC

He listened to some unpatriotic remarks about the Beatles by an English publicist with an expression of disbelief, then said he loved the Beatles sound.

"The bass sound is so good and John's vocals — what a voice, it's great!" he said. CHRIS WELCH

THE BEACH BOYS — CYNICAL, TOUGH, AND A HIT SOUND WHICH STARTED THE SURFING CRAZE IN THE STATES

'Surfin' up the charts

JAN & DEAN
SURF CITY
LIBERTY LIB 55580

THE BEACH BOYS
SURFIN' U.S.A.
CAPITOL CL 15305

MARIANNE

THE ROLLING STONES —GENUINE R & B!

EXCHANGE TRAVEL LTD.

AS the trad. scene gradually subsides, promoters of all kinds of teen-beat entertainments heave a long sigh of relief that they have found something to take its place. It's Rhythm and Blues, of course—the number of R & B clubs that have suddenly sprung up is nothing short of fantastic.

One of the best-known — and one of the most successful to date—is at the Station Hotel, Kew Road, in Richmond, just on the outskirts of London. There, on Sunday evenings, the hip kids throw themselves about to the new "jungle music" like they never did in the more stinted days of trad.

And the combo they writhe and twist to is called the **Rollin' Stones**. Maybe you've never heard of them —if you live very far away from London the odds are you haven't.

But by gad you will ! The **Rollin' Stones** are probably destined to be the biggest group in the R & B scene if it continues to flourish. And by the looks of the Station Hotel, Richmond, flourish is merely an understatement considering that three months ago only fifty people turned up to see the group. Now club promoter bearded **Giorgio Gomelsky** has to close the doors at an early hour—over four hundred R & B fans crowd the hall.

by NORMAN JOPLING

GENUINE

And the fans who do come quickly lose all their inhibitions and proceed to contort themselves to the truly exciting music of the boys who put heart and soul into their performances.

The fact is that, unlike all the other R & B groups worthy of the name, the Rollin' Stones have a definite visual appeal. They aren't Jazzmen who were doing trad. eighteen months back and who have converted their act to keep up with the times. They are genuine R & B fanatics themselves, and they sing and play in a way that one would have expected more from a coloured U.S. R & B team than a bunch of wild, exciting white boys who have the fans screaming—and listening—to them.

Lineup of the group is Mick Jagger, lead vocal and harmonica and student at the London School of Economics. The fierce backing is supplied by Brian Jones, guitar and harmonica, and also spokesman and leader of the group. He's an architect, while Keith Richards, guitar is an art student. The other three members of the group are Bill Wyman, bass guitar, Ian Stuart, piano and maraccas, and drummer **Charles Watts**.

Record-wise, everything is in the air, but a disc will be forthcoming. It will probably be the group's own adaptation of the **Chuck Berry** number, **"Come On"** (featured on Chuck's new Pye L.P.). The number goes down extremely well in the club's session on Sundays — other Chuck Berry numbers that are in the group's repertoire are **"Down the Road Apiece"** and **"Bye, Bye, Johnny"**—which is one of the highlights of the act.

DISC/FILM

Even though the boys haven't dead-certain plans for a disc, they do have dead-certain plans for a film. For club promoter Giorgio is best known as a film producer, and he has made several imaginative films dealing with the music scene. But for the Rollin' Stones film, there are some truly great shots of the team in action, singing and performing **"Pretty Thing"**, the Bo Diddley number. The film itself lasts for twenty minutes, and will be distributed with a main feature film.

The group are actually mad about Bo Diddley, although pianist Ian is the odd man out. Diddley numbers they perform are **"Crawdad"**, **"Nursery Rhyme"**, **"Road Runner"**, **"Moaner"** and, of course, **"Bo Diddley"**.

They can also get the sound that Bo gets too — no mean achievement. The group themselves are all red-hot when it comes to U.S. beat discs. They know their R & B numbers inside out and have a repertoire of about eighty songs, most of them are the numbers which every R & B fan in the country knows and near enough loves.

The boys are confident that, if they make a disc, it should do well. They are also confident about their own playing, although on Sundays at the end of the session at Richmond they are dead-beat. That's because on Sunday afternoons they also play the R & B session at the Ken Colyer Club.

SUPERFICIAL

But despite the fact that their R & B has a superficial resemblance to rock 'n' roll, fans of the hit parade music would not find any familiar material performed by the Rollin' Stones. And the boys do not use original material—only the American stuff. "After all," they say, "can you imagine a British composed R & B number—it just wouldn't make it."

One group that thinks a lot of the Rollin' Stones are The Beatles. When they came down to London the other week, they were knocked out by the group's singing. They stayed all the evening at the Station Hotel, listening to the group pound away. And now they spread the word around so much in Liverpool that bookings for the group have been flooding in — including several at the famed Cavern.

All this can't be bad for the R & B group who have achieved the American sound better than any other group over here. And the group that in all likelihood will soon be the leading R & B performers in the country. . . .

The ROLLING STONES in action at the Station Hotel, Richmond, Surrey. They are "packing them in" with their R&B material. (NRM Picture by BILL WILLIAMS.)

MARTIN YALE AGENCY
30a St. Peter's Ave.,
Cleethorpes

Representing:—
CARTER-LEWIS
KEITH KELLY
HOUSTON WELLS
and the MARKSMEN
THE SOUND OF
THE ECHOES
with PAUL KEENE
JAMIE LEE and the
ATLANTICS
RiCKY WILSON and
the YOUNG ONES
ERIC LEE and the
4 ACES
The SHELL CARSON
COMBO
and many other attractions
for stage and ballroom

The Rolling Stones (i.e: Mick Jagger) didn't give a damn. To hell with band uniforms, to hell with press reverence – all we want is to play our music. Was this for real or was it a pose? Andrew Oldham certainly encouraged this Bolshie attitude. In the end it boiled down to the group providing a trampoline for Jagger to bounce on, to perform his proud struts, to show off his sexy, hipless body. No doubt about it that Jagger appealed to all sexes. He was the first uni-sex act. He appealed to your basest instincts, and he, in turn, loved basic things like – lots of money, model birds, cars and planes and faraway places. He got 'em all and he showed no regrets. There was no pretension in the Stones' world. The 'B side' to all this jet-setting rock life is best forgotten, though Altamont remains a monument to rampant irresponsibility.

What a pity that the Headmasters of R&R resigned in the middle 1960s!

Are We CLAIRVOYANT?

The NRM has gained a reputation for picking Pop winners. Our latest successful prediction...? The Rolling Stones

WE'VE come to the conclusion that here at the New Record Mirror offices work a bunch of clairvoyant blokes.

Why?

Well, folks, just look at the number of stars who were given their FIRST write-up in our publication: The Beatles, The Searchers, Gerry and the Pacemakers, Billy Fury, Marty Wilde, ad infinitum.

But this time we've REALLY excelled ourselvies. Not only did we give this group their first write-up—but we paved the way for their recording contract and subsequent hit disc.

Yes, we DO mean The Rolling Stones, of "Come On" fame. After the first NRM feature, the major record companies phoned up the NRM to find out whether or not they were still in time to get the Stones on wax.

They were, and the result was shortly issued on Decca.

Now let's look at the progress of the group. In a bare three months they have made the charts with a disc that had been rush-released by Decca.

And they are now regarded as one of London's top beat groups, as can been seen by their overflowing list of engagements, including the Everly Bros/Bo Diddley tour in September. There's a mistake there by the way. **The Rolling Stones** don't particularly

by NORMAN JOPLING

like being referred to as a 'rock' or 'beat' group. They are, they stress, a Rhythm and Blues group, always have been and always will be.

"We don't intend to change our sound now," said lead vocalist Mick Jagger. "And although a lot of people have accused us of 'going commercial' by employing a group vocal we certainly had no thoughts of that when we deviated from our original style. We changed because we found we could embrace a lot more R & B material into our act by having a group vocal as well as a lead supported by the group."

On stage the boys are just about completely uninhibited. They don't bother about what they wear, and they certainly don't have a tightly planned stage act. Their act is wild and loud and carries the new message to the audience of the big R & B sound. And the Stones reckon they have just about managed to cover all fields of R & B now, after practising for years. They feel competent to play any number in the R & B vein.

And future recordings? Well, titles are still being kept secret but fans will like to know the top side is 'Catchy, and very much in the R & B vein—but unlike "Come On"

The latest picture of the (fast) ROLLING STONES—an NRM Pic by DEZO HOFFMANN.)

They also have an L.P. scheduled for some time in the future on which they intend to record some way-out blues stuff which they all rave over.

What do the Stones think of all the Liverpool-London controversy.

"It's all a load of rubbish," said Brian Jones. "It's all a big thing invented by the newspapers. We are on very friendly terms with the Northern beat groups, and there's a mutual admiration between us. We like the Northern groups and think they've added a lot to the pop music scene. Obviously we prefer the Americans, but there hasn't been anything beatier in Britain for a long, long time."

All I know is there is one thing a lot beatier.

The Rolling Stones . . . .

Elsdon Changes

ALAN ELSDON'S banjoist, Johnny Barton, has left the band to freelance.

Mick Emery, already featured with the band on guitar and vocals, will take over the vacant position, doubling on banjo. Alan rates Mick as one of his most versatile musicians.

This is the first personnel change since drummer, Keith Webb, joined the group at Christmas, 1961, which points to the Elsdon band being one of the most stable jazz outfits on the scene today.

Current engagements for the band include: Osterley Rugby Club (August 2), Dancing Slipper, Nottingham (3), Fishmongers Arms, Wood Green (4), Jazzshows Jazz Club, Oxford Street (5), B.B.C. Band recording (afternoon) Assembly Hall, Barnet (evening) (6), B.B.C. Easy Beat recording (7), Smiths Aviation, Basingstoke (8).

"ACCIDENTS WILL HAPPEN"

IT was no accident that Patsy Ann Noble was chosen for a guest star appearance in the Three Kings film "Live It Up".

Patsy, who is already a household name because of her co-starring television series with Dave King, keeps company with Kenny Ball, Gene Vincent, Heinz, Jennifer Moss, Sounds Incorporated, The Outlaws and Andy Cavell and the Saints in the new British musical which is scheduled for release in early autumn.

Patsy features a new song "Accidents Will Happen" composed by Norrie Paramor and Bob Barratt in the film. A recording of this song will be issued on August 9 on Columbia.

IT'S RHYTHM-AND-BLUES THAT'S BOOMING NOW

Say The Rolling Stones

RHYTHM 'n' blues is as popular in Britain today as trad was in its boom period, say the Rolling Stones, who are currently enjoying their second hit parade success.

The group, which began like so many others playing weekly in an out-of-town club and which shot to fame almost overnight, had much to say about r-and-b in this country when I spoke to them this week.

"In the trad boom a couple of years ago, only British bands made any real impression, but look what is happening to r-and-b today," said Mike Jagger. "British and American acts are getting into the charts, and everywhere you go groups are playing it.

"Even with the trad boom, none of the bands did all that well as far as the hit parade went."

Since the Rolling Stones have achieved national status—via songs by Chuck Berry and Lennon and McCartney—it has been said that they have deserted their r-and-b style and gone over to more commercial numbers.

"That's untrue," exclaimed Mike. "We play the same now as we have always done. So many people have suggested that we have changed our style that we are a bit tired of hearing it.

"When we played at the Craw Daddy and Eel Pie Island we did

By RICHARD GREEN

exactly the same type of stuff, and the scenes were really raving."

He went on to explain: "It is like this: if we play two numbers and one goes down a bomb and the other falls flat, we drop the unsuccessful one. Obviously we are not going to play a tune if audiences are not going to like it, but that is as far as it goes.

"**All I can say, and this goes for the rest of the boys, is that we have not changed our style and do not intend to.**"

While the r-and-b influence has been around for a good many years, with artists like Chuck Berry, Jerry Lee Lewis and Ray Charles having big hits, it is only lately that the

British public has gone for that music in a big way.

With the advent of so many groups trying to hitch a ride on the r-and-b bandwagon, an outfit that is going to stay on long after others have fallen off must have something different and extra about it.

The Rolling Stones can claim a collection of differences.

Ask anyone to name something about the Stones and it is a fair bet that the group's hair styles will be in the answer. Their shoulder-length hair, which dances wildly as they fling themselves about the stage in reckless abandon, is really unusual.

Then there is Mike's own individual shake routine, which he lapses into during a number. It has caught on in such a big way that teenagers all over the country are emulating it on the dance floors.

Above all this, is the sound which the Rolling Stones create. A sound so exciting and gripping that few other groups can come within shouting distance of it. When they really get worked up during a performance, an electric current seems to surge through the listener's body.

"We are going on tour with the Ronettes soon," said Brian Jones, "and after that there is talk of a Continental tour, and a television series."

Talking about the Continent, **Brian added: "We don't want to play at the Star Club, though. This is because British groups are only booked there to fill in.**

"The club features American names and any British outfits that have appeared there have not starred.

"I know the Beatles, the Searchers and Gerry and the Pacemakers have all played the Star Club, but that was a long time ago, before they became famous. It is all right for experience, but that is all."

If the Rolling Stones have the courage to admit that they do not want to play at a scene that is

---

Stone us! Liverpool NODS to London!

THE Iron Curtain has been breached, friendly relations have at last been established and representatives from London have succeeded in creating goodwill in the opposition's capital! Don't worry, this isn't a political commentary—and I'm not even discussing the Anglo-Russian situation.

I am referring to the invisible barrier, which has for so long divided London and Liverpool and which the Rolling Stones (left) have finally penetrated.

Not only have the Londoners won the hearts of all Northern fans following their two visits to the hub of the Liverpool entertainment scene, the Cavern Club, but they have also entered into a coalition with the Beatles, because the Rolling Stones' new chart entry was written by John Lennon and Paul McCartney!

The boys' first visit to the renowned Cavern was a few weeks ago, when the Big Three were recording there.

The Stones, who had been playing a date in Manchester, dashed to Liverpool to watch the session as members of the audience—and found themselves hailed as celebrities!

"We were really chuffed," said lead singer, Mick Jagger. "We only went there to relax, not to perform. But as soon as the word got around that we were there, we were swamped with requests for autographs.

"You know, you hear some talk about the animosity which some Liverpool musicians and fans feel towards London groups, but it just isn't true. Everyone was really friendly!"

The Cavern crowd also besieged the boys with requests for a live demonstration of the Nod, that rather bizarre "dance" which the Stones pioneered and which can be seen weekly on AR-TV's "Ready, Steady, Go."

"Some of the girls in the Cavern already knew it," continued Mick. "So we were all very much in demand to partner them on the dance floor."

It wasn't surprising that, as a result of this initial visit, the boys were booked to perform at the Cavern last week. They thus became one of the first top London groups to play there—and I understand that they were a resounding success.

And to their delight, the Stones' found the Nod in full swing at the Cavern when they arrived there!

The explanation for the Rolling Stones' widespread popularity in the North undoubtedly lies in their style —which is raw, exciting, down-to-earth, and strongly r-and-b flavoured.

By DEREK JOHNSON

This is the music Liverpool loves. It's closer to their own Mersey beat than anything else, as the Meteorological Office might say, south of a line from the Humber to the Bristol Channel.

The two-city link is further enhanced by the Stones' latest hit, "I Wanna Be Your Man," which was written by the invincible Lennon-McCartney team. Not written specially for the group—but offered to them, when the two Beatles learned that the Stones were looking for material.

It seems that the Stones' publicist, Andrew Oldham, was chatting with the Beatles just after they had received their Variety Club awards in London. He happened to mention the difficulty in finding suitable r-and-b material, whereupon John and Paul told him they had just written a song which might appeal to the London group.

More than that—they offered to go with Andrew there and then, to sing it over to the Stones who happened to be rehearsing in a club a few blocks away.

The Stones heard it, liked it, learned it—and recorded it the following week!

The other side of the group's disc is a bluesy instrumental titled "Stoned," which is perfect material for Nod dancers! It is also interesting in that it features the Stones' road manager, Ian Stewart, on piano.

Travelling sometimes presents unpredictable hazards. Such as the time when, on their way back from Abergavenny, they ran out of petrol in a quiet lane, miles from anywhere, at two o'clock in the morning.

"There we were, wandering around trying to think of a way of getting some juice, when along came a policeman on a bike," said Brian Jones.

"I don't think he was too sure what we were up to at first — but after searching the van for mail bags, he ended up by helping us shove it to a farm. I reckon they should call it the strong arm, not the long arm, of the law!"

Rolling Stones defend their 'Juke-Jury' stint and discuss new disc

with RICHARD GREEN

"**SOME** people take these programmes too seriously. They could always switch off!"

That was Bill Wyman's answer to the many self-styled critics of the Stones' "Juke Box Jury" appearance, who liberally panned it.

Since the Rolling Stones gave their frank opinions on TV, letters attacking them have poured into the NME. They have been described as "very off," "rude," "disgusting," and a lot more not so polite things.

When Bill telephoned me, I asked him what he thought of the programme. And the criticisms.

"Producer Barry Langford was happy," he began. "He said it was marvellous. And the audience were okay, too. People knew what to expect when they invited us to be on the show.

"They didn't want a sophisticated panel and they didn't get one. They got what they wanted. If some of the viewers didn't like it, they should have switched off. I don't care what they thought of us."

At the end of the show, Bill told me, half the audience wouldn't leave. They stayed behind in the studio, hoping to "capture" the Stones. But the boys were waiting in a private room for the moment they could escape.

"We were there for over an hour before we could get out," said Bill. "We were besieged!"

With that bit of controversy over, I turned to another matter which has been a major teenage talking point for the last few weeks — "It's All Over Now."

Was the record, I asked Bill, intended to turn out with a Cand-w flavour or did it happen by accident? I told him that a lot of people thought the record sounded like the Beverley Hillbillies.

"Oh, knockout!" he laughed. "We just like the sound of it. We didn't think it sounded country-and-western until we read it somewhere. I think it's the 12-string guitar and harmonising that do it."

Bill didn't think the style was a sudden change for the Stones, either. "Everyone of our records has been different," he explained. "We don't want to do the same old thing every time or people would get fed up with it."

Soon, the Rolling Stones begin yet another nation-wide tour.

That will mean plenty of work and, for Bill at least, some sleep at nights. "If that sounds a little Irish," this is what Bill told me: "For the last three nights, I haven't been able to sleep much. It's not working what does it.

"We're used to dashing about and going mad. Now we've got a holiday, I'm just not used to doing nothing! I want to get up at three in the morning. Yesterday, I got up at 5.40 a.m. and walked round the streets for ages!

The ROLLING STONES take it easy on the grass in a London park. Left to right : MICK JAGGER, CHARLIE WATTS, BILL WYMAN (way at back), KEITH RICHARD and BRIAN JONES. (NME-exclusive picture).

"My wife can't understand it. She's used to me laying in until noon. Soon as we get back to work, though, I'll be okay !"

Now over to another Stone whom I met by accident in a West End pub a few days ago. I was standing at the bar having a drink when Brian Jones walked in and joined me.

Chess

We sat at a corner table and Brian talked about "It's All Over Now," and the recording scene in America.

"I'm not all that keen on the record," he confessed, somewhat surprisingly. "It's all right, but, I don't know, there's just something

He swallowed some lager, shifted in his chair and went on: "The Chess place where we did the recording was marvellous. There was everything there you could wish for. All the apparatus was so different to the stuff here.

"I'd like to go back to Chicago to-morrow just to do some straight session work !

"I wouldn't even let people know who I was or anything. The scene is so fantastic, you can't believe it until you've seen it."

Brian may not be raving about the record itself, but its success must have meant a lot to him and the rest of the Stones.

The last word comes from Bill, who wasn't talking about records, or America, or touring or anything like that.

He simply stated: "You can say we're definitely not going on stage in topless dresses !"

STAR QUOTE

EXPLAINING why he finished his work for a journalism degree at Florida University, Johnny Tillotson observes: "A young person would be foolish to pin all his hopes on one dream that might not come true. Today, if I had to, I could go into the radio and TV field as a news writer and really enjoy the work."

'Who, us cause trouble? Never! We're just doing our thing'. The three ringleaders pose coyly for Cecil Beaton.

Life-lines of the Rolling Stones

	MICK JAGGER	BRIAN JONES	KEITH RICHARD	BILL WYMAN	CHARLIE WATTS
Real name:	Michael Philip Jagger	Brian Jones	Keith Richards	Bill Wyman	Charles Robert Watts
Birth date:	July 26, 1944	February 26, 1944	December 18, 1943	October 24, 1941	June 2, 1941
Birthplace:	Dartford, Kent	Cheltenham	Dartford, Kent	Lewisham, London	London
Personal points:	5ft. 10ins.; 10st. 6lb.; blue eyes; mousy hair	5ft. 8ins.; 10st. 1lb.; greeny-blue eyes; blond hair	5ft. 10ins.; 10st.; brown eyes; black hair	5ft. 10ins.; 10st.; green-brown eyes; black hair	5ft. 8ins.; 10st. 3lb.; blue eyes; brown hair
Parents' names:	Joe and Eva Jagger	Lewis, Louisa	Doris and Bert	William, Kathleen	Mr. and Mrs. Watts
Brothers and sisters:	Christopher	Barbara	None	John, Paul, Judy, Anne	Linda
Present home:	Hampstead	London	Hampstead	Beckenham, Kent	Wembley, Middlesex
Instruments played:	Harmonica	Guitar, harmonica	Guitar	Bass guitar	Drums
Where educated:	Dartford Grammar School; London School of Economics	Cheltenham Grammar School	Dartford Tech. School; Sidcup Art School	Beckenham Grammar School	Tylers Croft; Harrow Art College
Musical education:	None	Self taught	Self taught	Piano lessons	
Age entered show business:	18	18	18	21	18
Biggest break in career:	Meeting rest of Stones	Meeting other Stones	Meeting rest of Stones	Meeting Beatles	Joining Rolling Stones
Radio debut:	"Saturday Club"	"Saturday Club"	"Saturday Club"	"Saturday Club"	"Jazz Club" with Alexis Korner
Biggest influence in career:	It varies	All r-and-b greats	Chuck Berry	Chuck Berry	Different people in different circles
Former occupation:	Student	Various	Layabout!	Engineering	Graphic designer
Hobbies:	Boats, records	Women	Sleeping, records	Science fiction, records	Women
Favourite singers:	Chuck Berry, Jimmy Reed, Bo Diddley	Johnny Cash, Bo Diddley, Jimmy Reed	Chuck Berry, Shirelles, Crystals, Muddy Waters	Chuck Berry, Jimmy Reed, Jerry Lee Lewis, Les Paul	Bo Diddley, Muddy Waters, Mick Jagger, Buddy Greco
Favourite actors and actresses:	Sophia Loren, Steve McQueen	Tony Perkins	Paul Newman, Sophia Loren, Jinx	Kirk Douglas, Burt Lancaster, Gina Lollobrigida	All of them
Favourite colour:	Blue, pink	Black	Black	Blue	Red, black
Favourite food:	Continental	Steaks	Chicken	Escalops, scampi, pork chops	Good
Favourite drink:	Orange juice	Milk whisky	Orange juice, bloody Mary	Orange squash	Tea
Favourite clothes:	Casual	"Gear," "Annello" boots	Leather, dark & casual	Modern, casual	My taste is too good to answer this one!
Favourite band:		Muddy Waters Band	Flintstones	Chuck Berry Combo	So many
Favourite composers:	J. Lieber and Mike Stoller, John and Paul, Chuck Berry	Willy Dixon, Bach, Lennon-McCartney	Goffin-King, Chuck Berry	Cole Porter	George Russell, Gil Evans
Miscellaneous likes:	Driving at night by myself; girls	Having a shower	Girls; boats; guitars; high-heel boots	Cashew nuts; astronomy; poetry; girls	Girls; clothes; myself
Miscellaneous dislikes:	Motorway cafés, intolerant people	Public transport	Policemen, two-faced people	Arguments; marmalade; travelling	None
Taste in music:		Very catholic, but hate trad. brass bands	R-and-b, country music	R-and-b, popular classics, jazz	Good

Common to all

First public appearance: Marquee Club, Oxford Street, London
TV debut: "Thank Your Lucky Stars"
First important public appearance: Eric Easton

Managers: Eric Easton and Andrew Loog Oldham
Agent: Eric Easton
Origin of stage name: From the Muddy Waters' number "Rolling Stones Blues"
Recording manager: Andrew Loog Oldham
Present disc label: Decca

Discs in NME Chart and highest position reached: 1963 "Come On" (20), "I Wanna Be Your Man" (9). 1964 "Rolling Stones" LP (15), "Not Fade Away" (3), "Rolling Stones" EP (23), "It's All Over Now" (2).

No. 1 hit and current best seller: "Little Red Rooster."
LPs: "Rolling Stones."

Here are the ROLLING STONES as seen by caricaturist B. R. Cunningham, who seems to have caught the mood and motif of CHARLIE WATTS (sitting down, and l to r) BILL WYMAN, KEITH RICHARD, MICK JAGGER and BRIAN JONES. The big question next week is—can the Stones hold on to their No. 1 position with "Little Red Rooster" or will the Beatles depose them with "I Feel Fine"?

BRIC NATIONAL PICTURES PRESENT

The Top Musical of the Year!

JOHN LEYTON · MIKE SARNE

Friday. May 22. 1964

1964 STONE AGE

Mick Jagger always speaks his mind !

by Richard Green

IF you reckon the Stones are rebels—with or without a cause — then you must also hold Mick Jagger up to be the biggest of the rebels.

It's Mick that people go to when they want to hear something sensational. They know they can expect him to speak his mind. If he likes something, he'll say so. If he doesn't, watch out !

You get lots of groups going around saying that they flog themselves to death to earn a living but that it's really very funny.

Mick says : "It's not all a big laugh, but I can't take it seriously either. What happens is, we go along to play somewhere and when it's time to go on, we go on and that's that.

"We know a lot of people don't like us 'cause they say we're scruffy and don't wash. So what ? They don't have to come and look at us, do they ? If they don't like us, they can keep away !"

That seems fair enough. But there are bound to be some parents who will read this and then moan about Mick's attitude.

"A load of the fans treat us like ordinary blokes and we like it that way," Mick commented. "We don't go for all this big star bit. We're doing a job the same as anyone else."

Clothes

When Mick's not working, he often shoots down to the West End in the Carnaby Street area and spends a lot of money on clothes. If something takes his fancy, he is quite liable to go into the shop and buy it.

"He spends money like water and has no idea of its value," the Stones' co-manager, Andrew Loog Oldham, told me once.

Which is strange when you come to consider that Mick once studied economy. If things hadn't got to the stage they reached about the time of "Come On," he might still be stuck in an office.

"When I was at Dartford Grammar School," Mick began, "I wanted to go to university and study economics. I didn't go to university as it happened, I went to the London School of Economics.

"With economics, you don't become an economist, you go into the business. While I was in my second year at the LSE, we began playing and I was still there when the first record came out."

The Rolling Stones were formed as a result of general appreciation of r-and-b. Keith, Brian and Mick used to meet at various clubs and get together.

"I was just interested in music and playing generally," said Mick. "I knew Keith from primary school and we used to go to clubs and things where we met Brian.

"I was doing a bit of singing with Alexis Korner. I had loads of r-and-b LPs and singles, and I'd play them all the time. I still do, when I get the chance. Thing was, we all used to talk about r-and-b, so one day we decided to do something about it."

That was the beginning of the Rolling Stones. Mick gave up his odd singing spots with Korner and concentrated instead on his own group.

"We used to mess around for hours playing things, but it wasn't until we went down to Richmond that we got going at all," he pointed out. "After that, we all got busier and busier until we made the record. Then when that got in the charts, things got to such a state that I left the LSE."

Pullover

More often that not, I have seen Mick wearing a pullover that he appeared to have just laid his hands on and donned. We all know what his hair looks like.

"We dress this way because we want to," he maintains. "It's a load of nonsense to say we do it for an image. When we started out, people began to identify us by our style, now we're stuck with this image whether we want it or not. I don't really care whether parents like us or not."

I don't know how many reasons are given for the Stones' phenomenal success, but it must be a lot to do with the fact that, given the chance, half the kids in the country would like to be like Mick, Keith, Charlie, Brian and Bill.

The way they have rushed out and bought the LP must support that view to a certain extent because Mick regards the album as a true representation of the Stones as they are.

"It was a thing we wanted to do for a long time, make an LP," he said. "We did the numbers on it 'cause they're the ones we picked out from the rest as being most like us. I mean, you take 'Tell Me,' it's completely different from the next one 'Can I Get A Witness,' but they're both songs that appeal to us."

ORBISON'S FAREWELL

IF Brian Epstein's Sunday night concerts at the Prince of Wales, London, do nothing but draw attention to supporting acts like Cliff Bennett, the Chants and Lorne Gibson, they will have served a useful purpose.

Sunday's bill was headlined by Roy Orbison making the last British appearance of his current tour. He was his usual quiet, melodic, dramatic self, ably backed by the Federals and his own drummer. The audience gave him a great send-off.

Eden Kane fared less well — his backing group was over-loud. Despite this, Eden went through his well-drilled routine including " Boys Cry," that was a mixture of old and new Kane.

Cliff Bennett opened the show with a torrent of rhythm 'n' blues-type noise, Lorne Gibson provided high-quality country music, the Vernons Girls belted out beat of average or high quality (depending on which girl was the lead singer) and Alan Freeman, the compère, did his best to whip up excitement in a heat-dazed Sunday evening audience.

But my vote goes to the Chants, a Liverpool Negro vocal group who have all the weird sounds of the Four Seasons and the Marcels in one. They move about the stage relaxed and confident, changing lead singers at the drop of a falsetto vowel.

IAN DOVE.

YOU to US

hard always on the move with little

Had it not been for the NME I would

ANOTHER HIT FOR

Newcastle's pride – with the accent of oppressed US negroes, and not a trace of the Blaydon Races.

The typical early 60s position – in mid leap. A period of great hope and joy and effervescence. At least, at the start, before the chemicals, the dope and the Crap crept in.

The feeling's there

"**A** WHITE person can sing the blues with just as much conviction as a Negro. All these coloured singers singing about 'Walking Down The Railroad Track' . . . they've never walked down a railroad track in their lives. Nor have I. You've got more to sing the blues about in the Archway Road, near my home, than on any railroad track I know! The speaker: **Rod Stewart**, resident of the Archway Road, London—and maker of "Good Morning Little Schoolgirl" on Decca. Talented soccer player, highly-skilled blues singer. Has worked with **Jimmy Powell** and the **Five Dimensions**, then **Long John Baldry** (as second singer)). Has played and worked with **Memphis Slim**. Has lived in a beatnik community on a derelict houseboat at Shoreham. Says, outspokenly: "Most of the third and fourth rate R and B bands are giving the music a bad name. I think most of them would be better off at home listening to **Bill Broonzy**." Plays guitar and has busked around France and Spain with folk singer **Wiz Jones**. Was arrested there for vagrancy and sent home. A colourful six-footer, Rod's ambition is to sing with the **Count Basie Band**.

THE ROCKIN' BERRIES—A curious state of chart affairs for the group.

The original naughty schoolboy, who was later to hand the Heathrow Immigration man a cold fried egg in lieu of his passport. High jinks with a strep throat = £, $, $, $.

'SURE I'VE GOT A SEXY ACT'

P. J. Proby, the most controversial figure on the pop scene talks to David Griffiths

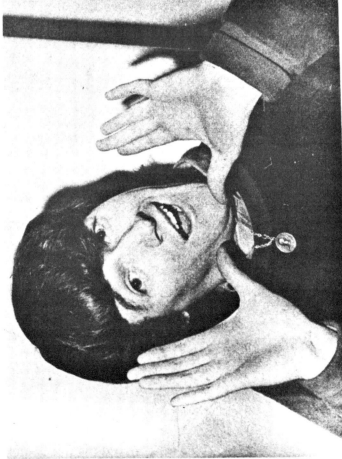

P. J. PROBY—a star used to causing sensations—had a shock himself recently. And, much to his surprise, it was a pleasant shock!

"For once," he told me, "I didn't get a bad press, though I fully expected I would.

"Here's what happened: I was appearing at the Town Ballroom, New Brighton, and had to wear a new pair of trousers. But they didn't fit—had a 28-inch waist and my waist is 34. I guess this guy must have thought he was supplying Steve Reeves or somebody. On top of this, the pants had no zipper and in order to wear them I had to pin the pants on me with safety pins.

"Unfortunately, this didn't work very efficiently and four or five times during my act the pins kept coming undone and I had to hitch my pants up. By the time I was through I had to hold my pants up. I know the whole show must have looked embarrassing from the audience and next morning I was all set to read about what a disgusting show I'd put on. But nobody said anything."

★ ★ ★ ★ ★

★ ★ ★ ★ ★

★ ★ ★ ★ ★

never far enough to offend. Believe me, I know the difference."

With all the troubles — most of them financial — that have dogged his career in Britain, P. J. Proby has always done his raving best to bring thrills" to the public. He's a pop-music perfectionist who pays top money to surround himself with a lot of highly competent musicians.

"I can tell you one thing — I'll make sure all my tailoring is in good shape before we start."

For P. J. has learned, the hard way, that it's risky (never mind risqué) to be too trusting with trouser-makers. He'll make darned sure he's not caught with his pants down again.

COMPLAINTS

Nevertheless, I told P.J., the Record Mirror did hear a few complaints from those who were there.

Do you—I asked P.J.— sometimes get a bit carried away with your efforts at crowd-pleasing?

"No, never," he assured me. "I'm in control at all times. No matter how wild the show may be I'm always aware of exactly what I'm doing and conscious of my responsibility to decent fans.

"Sure, mine is a sexy act but my aim is to go just far enough to please but

P. J. PROBY describes an interesting incident on stage, which caused considerable embarrassment to him!

CLIFF BENNETT—HE HATES LONG HAIR!

"Off the Cuff"

...managers, Ken Howard and Alan Blakeley.

Proby on Beatles' 'Shindig' TV show

P. J. PROBY, Karl Denver, Tommy Quickly, the Carefrees and Sandie Shaw join the Beatles and Sounds Incorporated in tomorrow's ampexing of Jack Good's U.S. TV show "Shindig." Good is telerecording the Honeycombs as well as Cilla Black for his series.

Good flies back to Hollywood on Sunday with the film of the Beatles' show which American viewers will see next Wednesday evening. It may subsequently be shown here as a result of negotiations between America's ABC-TV and an unnamed British company.

Good will use his telerecorded shots of Cilla Black and the Honeycombs on later editions in the series.

Next week Adam Faith films his "Shindig" appearance in Hollywood. As reported in last week's NME, the Rolling Stones, Gerry and the Pacemakers and Billy J. Kramer will all guest in the show during their forthcoming visits to the U.S.

THE KINKS KONQUER!

THE Kinks come as somewhat of an anti-climax. They are quiet, clean and, apart from Kink Dave Davies, have relatively short hair. Aside from that, they talk a lot about "Long Tall Shorty," birds, and blues singer **Big Bill Broonzy, which is normal talk for any group. Not quite so normal are long digressions about growing onions on the top of Mount Snowdon.**

It's completely unintelligible to the uninitiated, and after a time everyone gets the idea that you can't fill a feature with the merits of mountain-top onion growing. Then they start to talk of how they first got into the beat business.

Pete Quaife started. "It all began," says Pete, "when I was playing on a corporation rubbish dump at the age of 11. There was this chute, see, and we used to shoot down it. Anyway, we were all doing this when suddenly I reached the bottom of the chute and put my hand on something horribly sharp. It was a spike, and it went right through my hand. Dead gory it was—don't forget to put that bit in.

"Well, after it began to heal, the doctor said that what I needed to do was to exercise the hand. So I got a guitar.

"Before we got going with the group, I did some time at Hornsey Art School. Actually, it was only three weeks. There was an argument between them and me. They said I was a 'Ted', and I said I wasn't. Well, after a couple of weeks of arguing, they said, very nicely, 'I wonder, Mr. Quaife, if you would care to leave this school?'. So I did.

"Then I did some time as a commercial artist. Great? You must be joking. I sat down at a desk at nine in the morning, and I didn't get up again until five in the evening. Anyway, after a few years of this, I looked at myself one day, and said: 'Pete, you've got to get out of this. You're getting bottom heavy,' I was sitting all day at this desk, see?

"Anyway, the group scene got better and better, and here we are."

Stones

Mick Avory, serious looking and 20, continued. He has the distinction of once playing with the Rolling Stones. "I did it for only two weeks, though, because they were playing in London, and it was too far to travel every time. There were only Mick Jagger and Brian Jones in the group then. But they were a wild couple, even in those times.

By CORDELL MARKS

"The worst problem when I first started playing was transport. I did two grocery rounds and a paper round to raise the money to get a drum kit, and when I finally bought it it suddenly occurred to me that I had no way of carting it around.

"I solved it in the end, though. Every time I went to play on a date, I used to strap the bass drum on my back and go pedalling off on a bicycle."

Ending

Talking of their hit disc for a moment, Dave Davies, the long-haired and the youngest Kink, said, "We've changed the ending on 'You Really Got Me.' It used to have a very abrupt ending. So abrupt, in fact, that when we'd finished playing it, the audience just sat there silently. We had to yell at them, 'Come on, you lot, clap.'

"We've got a dead wild act. Once, though, I made a real idiot of myself. We'd just got to the end of a number (this was when we were on the Dave Clark tour) and I went jumping up and down like we always do, when it suddenly occurred to me that the floor was an awfully long way away.

"I'd jumped right into the orchestra pit. The audience loved it. They all thought it was part of the act.

"There was blood dripping down my face, and yet the audience never did realise that it wasn't supposed to happen," laughed Dave.

Ray Davies, Dave's brother, laughed about it, and said: "I never thought we'd get this far. Course, our parents are pleased at what's happened. They can't quite believe it. They keep going around mumbling, 'Strewth, that mob have actually got themselves a job.' They can't quite believe it," laughed Ray.

The four KINKS—their parents are pleased!

From You to Us

PAT GEORGE (Dudley, Worcs.): On my favourite disc Elvis's "Such A Night." I find I have more for my money, because at the end of the last chorus of "Such A Night," the sound dies off but seconds later a voice rather surprisingly says "Phew!". I would very much like to know am I the lucky one? Or has every copy got this little voice that sounds so relieved that the recording is all over with?

SUSY MARLAND (Leamington Spa, Warwickshire): Why isn't Ian Stewart's name mentioned on the cover of the Rolling Stones latest EP—"Five By Five"? Stewart is featured almost throughout on piano or electric organ, and on one track—"2120 Michigan Avenue," the electric organ is highlighted. By the way, congratulations Stones on another smash hit, as Chuck Berry said—"the sound's a-coming" and I reckon they're almost there.

MICHAEL WALDEN (Letty Green near Hertford): Audrey Nell may be interested in the reason why Elvis fans have a lot to say. Basically it's because Elvis has a vocal capacity far superior to any other singer yet he is addicted to more petty, ridiculous criticism by people who don't know...

S. SCULLY (Cheadle, Cheshire): When asked by Derek Johnson last week how the Blackpool show was going, Dave Clark answered, "Wonderfully." As far as I can see, Dave Clark must be totally unaware that members of the audience get up and walk out during each performance. When I saw them at Blackpool recently, during their performance of "Shout," all that could be heard was the incessant pounding of Clark's drums, and the volume of the amplifiers was so great that the group's perfect backing was utterly distorted.

HERMAN HAT TRICK

"I'M keeping my fingers crossed for a hat trick," admitted independent disc producer Mickie Most. And now he can start uncrossing them for his third chart bid has paid off—in the...

And the group who sing it, Herman's Hermits, join Mickie's other chart names, the Animals and the Nashville Teens by charging in at No. 25.

Herman's Hermits first came to the attention of Mr. Most when he...

MOODY BLUES ARE REALLY QUITE HAPPY

I DON'T know why they are called the Moody Blues. They aren't moody or blue.

Chart success with "Go Now" has made them more confident and assured than before, but even before this they were quite happy. "We came together earlier this year, and after that it was work all the time," says Graham Edge, drummer. "Nobody had any time to be moody.

"All of us at one time or another had led our own group so we knew the scene. In fact, this leader-business almost led to about a fortnight of punch-ups when we first organised ourselves. We had to learn to listen to each other at first.

"Now it's working out fine."

There are outward signs of success. For instance, the Moody Blues have moved from their centre-of-London flat into a large house, with patio and garden, in the rather exclusive south London area of Roehampton.

To fit in with this image, they have bought themselves unbelievable, old Hollywood-film type dressing growns in all kinds of patterns—except sombre . . . or moody!

Confesses Graham: "Ray Thomas, who does vocals and plays harmonica, has a fantastic one in gold and red. He has also bought a smoking jacket which makes him look very distinguished. In dark green! The rest of us think it makes him look very funny!"

by IAN DOVE

Clint Warwick, bass guitarist with the group, put forward another reason for moving from London's centre. "Fresh air. We generally work in smoky clubs and theatres, get confined to dressing rooms and so on. It's essential to get out in the open air. Maybe that's why fishing is one of my hobbies."

Success came quietly to the Moody Blues. "Go Now" crept into the bottom of the NME Chart one week and they were quietly delighted, although Graham Edge complained, while their taxi stopped at a traffic light, that very night: "My God, nobody recognises us!" (He was, of course, only joking).

If they celebrated their chart status at all, it was to disappear into a joke and novelty shop in the West End and buy up items like itching powder, false fingers, fake house flies on a lump of sugar . . . and soap that makes your hands black!

"That night," says Graham, "we took this haul back to the flat where we were all living then. The flat below us was occupied by a group of girls, which was pleasant, and they used to borrow cups of sugar and eggs from us. We used to borrow things from them, too, of course.

"Amazingly, one of the girls came up this night and wanted to borrow some soap so we gave her some of that joke stuff to turn her hands black. We never saw them again!"

Putting on the moody—although it's only for the benefit of the camera—are the five MOODY BLUES. Actually they are highly delighted with the success of "Go Now" in the NME Chart . . . and with the reception they are getting on the Chuck Berry tour.

Mobbed

The Moody Blues are at present on the Chuck Berry package tour and on Friday had their very first experience of being mobbed on stage, when two girls climbed up. They flung their arms around two of the Moody Blues before being hauled off by attendants.

Commented Ray Thomas: "That was strange. We've played for a long time in clubs in the West End, with no protection against the audience, such as an orchestra pit. And we've never been dragged off the stand by fans. In fact, we find the audience for club work much quieter—they really listen.

"Still we were mobbed at the 'Ready, Steady, Go!' Christmas Day party. We closed the show and just as the cameras switched off us, Graham disappeared in a sea of girls with the rest of us following seconds later . . . ."

The Moody Blues like their hit, "Go Now" and not only because it's a hit. Mike Pinder is the Moody Blue who takes great interest in the sound of the group—his ambition is to go deeper into the a-and-r world.

"Essentially we want to get the same sound we get on stage and I think we manage it," he says. "Certainly 'Go Now' is better technically than our first disc, 'Lose Your Money' because we ourselves are more used to recording techniques. I think it's the kind of music we play as well.

"'Lose Your Money' was strictly rhythm-and-blues, with the harmonica and maraccas and so on, which is only one side of the music we play."

Denny Laine, who plays guitar, piano, harmonica, bass and banjo, sums up the musical approach of the group simply: "We want to play soul music."

★ NEWCOMERS TO THE CHARTS ★

Family support saved Betty

"IF my family hadn't followed me from Greenwood, Mississippi, to Chicago, I don't think I'd be making discs today," the quiet-spoken, silken-haired, free-smiling young lady told me over lunch last week.

BETTY

She is 23 year old Betty Everett, the latest entrant into the NME Chart at No. 26 with "Getting Mighty Crowded." That summed up her schedule in Britain these last few days . . . TV, radio and personal appearances to promote her disc. She flew back with rotund manager Al Smith on Saturday to do a coast-to-coast [illegible] of the States but Al did say: "If Britain likes her record enough, we'll cancel engagements and come back in the spring."

Betty, known in the States as the "Shoop Shoop" girl, due to her hit [illegible] sang lead in the Greenwood [illegible] at the age of 13, for three years. Then she left the South for Chicago where coloured people get a better deal. But she was so lonely she nearly gave up and went home.

"Getting Mighty Crowded," she will have been issued on five labels. She started with Cobra, went to C.J., then Renee, before recording manager Calvin Carter, of Vee Jay, heard her.

She became a big American seller with her third disc, "You're No Good"—a hit here for the Swinging Blue Jeans—and followed it with "Shoop Shoop ... Hot 100

from the NME 5 YEARS AGO

TOP TEN 1960—Week ending Jan. 15

Last Week	This Week	
1	1	WHAT DO YOU WANT TO MAKE THOSE EYES AT ME FOR Emile Ford (Pye)
2	2	WHAT DO YOU WANT Adam Faith (Parlophone)
3	3	OH! CAROL Neil Sedaka (RCA)

When Gene Pitney was Billy Brian!

"I FIRST met Gene Pitney when I was peddling me songs around New York publishing companies," singer Jimmy Radcliffe told me in Britain this week.

America, but girl groups seem to be happening now."

Jimmy, quite a musician himself, plays, guitar, vibes, piano, bass, organ and drums. His chief

FROM Y... TO US

D. MINIFIE (Paignton, D... any other NME readers ... rotten fade-out finishes ... lately? Quite a few ... have been spoiled by t... outs—Sandie Shaw's "... Better Off Without Yo... Mann's "Come Tomorr... Righteous Brother... Lost That Lovin' Feelin... the same way. Come... men, make it a New Y... to fade out fade-outs.

NICHOLAS C. CLARKE ... Cumberland): After ... Black on "Ready, St... one assumes her LP is ... Black Covers Tamla-M...

"ELVIS FAN" (Huck... How many more songs ... be made about ton-up... killed? With songs ... and "Leader Of The ... is the pop world comin... mean to be nasty, but ... take a delight in pulli... pieces. How do you ... feel when they hear so... just after their son or ... gone out on their bi... assure you that the b... do not like these song... a Rocker made a song ... getting killed, it would ... But when it's the othe... it goes straight to the ... only morbid it's unfa...

KAY NICHOLS (Dallas, ... the past several mon... received the NME from ... in Yorkshire. I thor... every page of it, and ... had things of this type ... States. All you... English stars in our mag... papers are "rumours" ... NME is all truth.

R. J. SMITH (Whitton): ... about time somebody a... American singers for t... which their discs are c... for note, by our Briti... singers. Last year, I m... Americans who were den... hit in our charts by blat... by our warblers.

KEITH R. WATT (King's ... folk): Thanks for the "... Elvis" articles. If any ... Stones fans read them ... realise that their idols ... match Elvis.

J. SUTCLIFFE (South Surrey): Why all this ... Georgie Fame and his ... The record is okay, but ... go wild about, and i... original. I suppose no... getting all the usual ru... Georgie "beating the B... also read with amazement ... to film his life story. Wh... is there to film when th... only 21?

MICK JAGGER of the Rolling Stones asks...

WHY DO PARENTS HATE US?

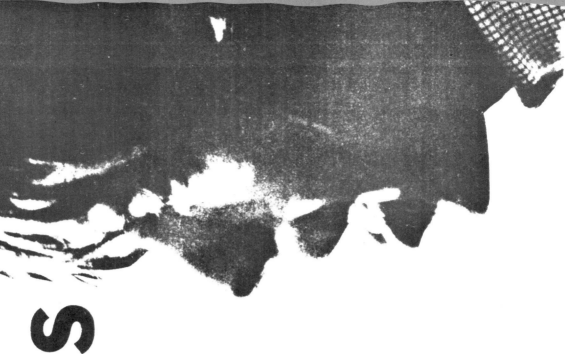

WHAT is your conception of the five far-out figures who make up the Rolling Stones? Nice boys — or ugly cave men? Do you wake in the middle of the night screaming with horror at the faces that stared at you from the TV screen a few hours earlier?

Or are you among the thousands worshipping every rebellious move they make against conformity?

Whatever your feelings about the Rolling Stones—sleep tight. Because the stars themselves couldn't care less.

"I still haven't grasped what all this talk of images and all that is all about," said Mick Jagger, lead singer and harmonica player, after a one-night-stand at York. He was groaning about lack of sleep but managed to spout coherently enough.

"The first I knew about images was when the Melody Maker started asking us questions and there was a big thing in your paper about it," he continued.

"**I don't particularly care either way whether parents hate us or not. They might grow to like us one day—then they'll like us for some reason. It's a thing you can't make out.**

"I reckon some of them think we are ugly cave men, and others think we are cuddly, like teddy bears.

"We don't set out to try to be grizzly. And—well, I can tell you this much. My parents like me!"

Talk of images confuses the Stones, but they are not blind.

"We're getting to understand the things they say

about us a bit better," said Jagger. "But some stupid things have been said. For a start, we're not shy, as some people have said.",

Has the success of this London beat group changed them, or their attitude to music or life, in any way?

"What d'you mean?" pleaded Mick. "I'm not a chameleon!"

He switched to talk about their new hit, "Not fade away."

"I suppose I suggested it," he admitted. "I have the song on an EP by Buddy Holly—he always seemed to go in for these Bo Diddley things.

"**For some reason or other I mentioned it to the rest of them when we started talking about a new single.**

"Well, we all tossed the idea around, and in the end we thought it was a good

'un because it had a vague tune—which does help commercially, and that's more than you can say for a lot of the tunes in that Diddley style, isn't it?"

As Mick spoke, the Rolling Stones were in the middle of a British concert tour. I asked how he felt about leaping around the country.

"**I hate it," said Jagger. "I don't like touring at the best of times, but as tours go this one has been quite good. The audiences are good.**

"We get on well with the Swinging Blue Jeans, but

they are leaving the tour soon. So we'll be on our own then.

"One thing I find about touring the country is that it's hard to find somewhere to eat. Last night, somebody suggested we went to a night club and that was all right, but usually we wind up having Chinese chop suey—not because we like Chinese food but because the English stuff is so bad.

"**STILL," SAID MICK, "I SUPPOSE GOING ROUND THE PROVINCES IS NOT TOO BAD... I SUPPOSE."**

Ray Coleman

I can tell you this much—

MY parents like ME!

JUST WHAT IS R&B?

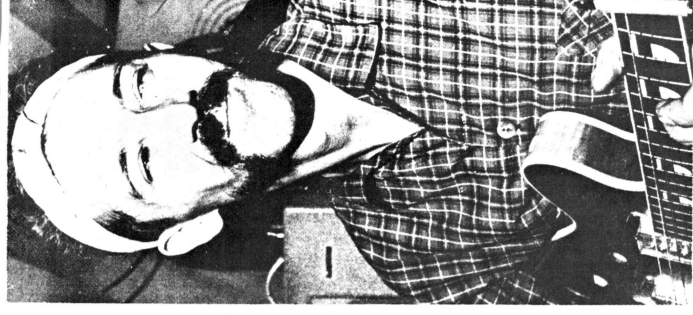

Alexis Korner—'Negro pop music'

For weeks MM readers have been asking this question

THE air is thick with talk of rhythm-and-blues. With groups like the Rolling Stones and Manfred Mann roaring into the chart, it's the topic of the day.

But R&B has also brought arguments—and confusion. For it has arrived in a big way at the same time as the beat boom.

The result is that many people are puzzled. They can't tell the difference.

MM reader Tom Stares, of Lymington, Hampshire, writes: "Will someone please tell me the meaning of R&B? I am told that Chuck Berry, Bo Diddley, and the Rolling Stones are R&B boys but, listening to so many 'examples,' I find dozens of different styles among them."

And V. Smith, of Romford, Essex, declares: "People who created the group boom are mainly responsbile for a lot of misunderstanding.

"Rock is not new, but it should not be confused with rhythm-and-blues."

Rhythm - and - blues has roots in the blues, and rock is just a form of pop, he adds.

Today, with the group sound so predominant on the music scene, R&B is a thorny label.

First, how did it get its title?

Chris Barber, a pioneer of British R&B, explains: "In America, the record business used to categorise various forms of music, so things were easily identifiable.

"Between fifteen and twenty years ago, I believe, they found they were getting too many divisions. So western and country sections became country - and - western generally, and blues and rhythm became rhythm-and-blues.

"That is the story of the title."

Getting down to the music, Barber recalls that when R&B giant Muddy Waters arrived here in 1958 to tour with Chris's band, he brought an amplified guitar.

Many blues purists were horrified, and asked Muddy why he did not bring a simple acoustic guitar.

Last year, Waters arrived here for a tour—with the requested acoustic. But . . . "everyone's playing electric guitar—trying to sound like me," Muddy told Chris.

"So you can see," says Barber, "how the scene has changed.

"The truth is that many of the newer groups using electric guitars and electric basses have the SOUND of real rhythm-and-blues, but they don't have the STYLE.

"It's all back to the old thing—it's not what you play, but how you play it that counts. That applies to blues as well as to jazz.

"What so many people fail to remember is that to play rhythm-and-blues you must play the blues. It is wrong to mix up the blues with so many of the beat groups around.

"And I'd rather hear a good beat singer singing what he calls beat music —well—than someone saying he does R&B and doing it badly!"

How does Chris rate some of today's stars who have the R&B tag?

"The Rolling Stones do a splendid job of country blues in the Bo Diddley style," quite like them," says Barber.

"Manfred Mann is playing a sophisticated form of blues, but it's still an authentic style of R&B.

"But Long John Baldry and his Hoochie Coochie Men come closest to the sound of authentic R&B, like Muddy Waters.

"In my opinion, this is the most genuine rhythm-and-blues group in Britain.

What is rhythm-and-blues? Negro pop music—that's the beginning and end of the whole argument," says Alan Price, organist-leader of the Animals, the Newcastle group now planted in the hit parade.

"That doesn't mean white men can't play it. It's the same as jazz. Would anybody ever suggest that white men can't play jazz?

"Mind you, a lot of blues has Negro humour in it that not only audiences can't understand, but which white artists cannot absorb.

"It's all a matter of feeling —either you know what the blues is all about or you don't.

"But I'll tell you this much. We play R&B. My own influence was Pete Johnson, the boogie pianist.

"We think the best rhythm-and-blues people are Jimmy Reed, Ray Charles—of course —and Sonny Boy Williamson. And Muddy Waters.

"But Mose Allison is white. Would anybody say he wasn't a marvellous R&Ber?"

To get the gospel truth, I asked Alexis Korner.

"Rhythm - and - blues," he said categorically, "covers everything in Negro popular music from Louis Jordan, through the various Buster Bennett groups, including the Muddy Waters field, right up to present - day American artists like Martha and the Vandellas, Marvin Gaye, the Temptations.

"That is the current Negro pop market. It is absolutely the blues. Little Stevie Wonder is definitely R&B. Tommy Tucker certainly is—that hit record of his is very nice.

"Rhythm-and-blues is the popular music of the Negro at any given time.

"If it takes us two or three years to catch up with them, that's our hard luck!" —RAY COLEMAN.

Ahoy There!

ON JACK Dupree

to a club don Dupree

Jack Dupree, most potent er - pianists, Britain last a tour with Climax Jazz

en telerecording 2 show with er's band at arquee on Sun-year-old New orn character now lives in : "If I can get , I'd do it. I'd t would be a ace for a lot of ting, say, '75. I'd Yeah, find me*

is visibly gassed with Dupree, not surprising, rolling style ll cry on Sun-performance.

lowers while I'm touching hen shack"

1965
THE EVE OF
DESTRUCTION

We all have our moment and mine was in 1965. I happened to find myself on pop's moving staircase. I went down as fast as I went up – but while I was going up it was great fun and I was fancy free. Though I'd made plans for this journey, once I was on the staircase everything was outside my control. The Public took over, as they always do.

1965 was an important year, a watershed year, for pop, and though I was a minor figure my adventures were a microcosm of what was happening in the business at large. In my dreams I often travel that year again; on paper alone it makes some kind of sense but the story sometimes melts like albums under the LA sun.

Dublin, February: I had been leading my double life as history student and blues rocker, Karl Marx by day and Howling Wolf by night, when the telegrams started arriving: 'RECORD OUT HERE NATIONALLY VIA TOWER LABEL SUBSIDIARY OF CAPITAL RECORDS FANTASTIC REACTION HERE YOU ARE TOP TEN IN SEATTLE IAN I FEEL THIS CAN BE A LEFT FIELD SMASHEROO REGARDS JERRY EXCLAMATION POINT.' Sinatra was on Capitol, so were the Beach Boys! More cables came flying in. 'Sporting Life' was about to chart in the US Top Hundred. Could go Top Ten so 'Keep Active' urged a cable from Gordon 'Bud' Fraser, President, Tower Records Corp. Bluesville and I were playing the local venues – grotty, sweaty ballrooms and cellars – and I found that falling about on stage could raise shrieks of pleasure from the biddies, so I did that a lot. I had a great thing going for me: I was often mistaken for Mick Jagger by Dubliners ranging from young girls to bus conductors and I didn't bother to correct them. At College my political science lecturer took an interest in my American success and wrote a long article about me in *The Irish Times*.

'PLEASE GET BLUESVILLE IN ACCORD AND I MEAN ACCORD AS I WILL BE OVER TO CUT ALBUM BEFORE YOU CAN SAY PHIL SPECTOR REGARDS JERRY'. The record had become that hot. I had to stop treating the biz as a joke. 'In accord' meant that the band must start turning up to dates on time, must be at the recording session, and must be clear as to who were members and who merely hangers on. We had never decided about a leader. I was the one who got most of the screams, though the sax player had a damned good try and sometimes elbowed me off the stage, and I was the one who'd organized all our recordings. In between cables I had phone consultations with Jerry, explaining the problems of getting the band to show any commercial foresight and to put their birds and booze on the back burner for a while. It was hard.

A few days before Jerry and his wife jetted in there was an upset for me: after 'bubbling under' the Hot Hundred and then making the Number 100 for exactly one week poor little 'Sporting Life' had vanished without trace. I rang *Billboard*'s London office and asked whether there had been a printer's error.

Keeping a brave face and putting my mind on Marx, I welcomed Jerry and his wife and installed them in an Americanized hotel complete with ice water. That evening, as we were tucking into steaks the size and consistency of hob-nail boots, Jerry had a long-distance call from a Beverly Hills agent. The man had had to pull off the freeway, after hearing my fantastic record, to find out if I was signed. A very important agency, GAC, but Jerry acted cool. Or was he just bemused? After dinner we retired to his suite where I signed a pile of contracts pertaining to management, publishing and record production. I would have signed more for I was impressed by the acres of small print and the archaic language. I loved feeling important and being treated like a racehorse.

A few minutes later a deputation from Bluesville arrived unannounced. I retreated into a clothes closet but was able to hear them demand separate contracts. Failing that, they wanted a few pounds in advance.

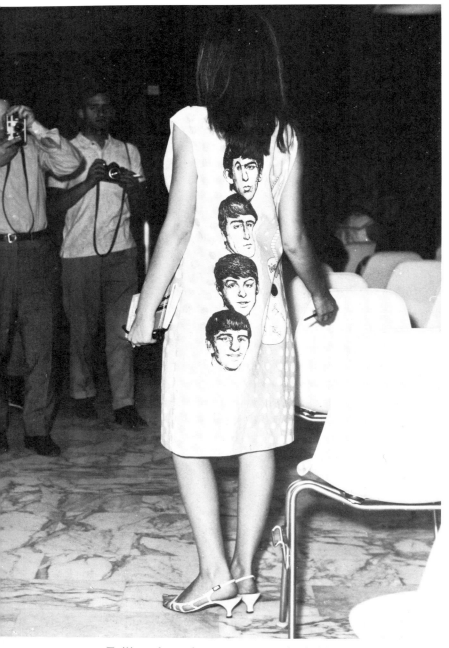

Jeremy). I rushed it to Jerry just before we left for the studio and he said, 'Whatever's right'. He was very fond of that phrase and I realised he was far more eloquent in cables than in conversation.

For the recordings we had booked the same pokey potting shed of a studio where we'd recorded 'Sporting Life'. They were still amazed we'd want to record music when all they ever recorded was speech. The famous Eamonn Andrews owned the place but we never saw him. A Trinity College student was engineer in charge of the two portable EMI tape machines. He was proud to have an extra track on his tapes. We knew nothing about over-dubbing so we played our material live. Most of the songs were ones we'd got screams with at dance dates. One or two were real blues for which we'd got apprecia-tive nods from our male blues fans. After we'd cut the anti-war protest song I felt pretty fulfilled, like a cross between Joan Baez and Bob Dylan. I felt I'd done my duty. Just as I was relaxing the band started mucking about, or 'jamming', as they call this irritating habit in jazz circles. Oh Christ, I thought, what a waste of time, still I'd better let them get it out of their systems. Jerry thought it was a rehearsed number and gave us a thumbs up – and the engineer rolled his tape.

Bluesville had struck up a boogie shuffle to a riff I'd copped from Jerry Lee Lewis who'd probably copped it from Chuck Berry who must have heard it in a million dives and bars and clubs. Everybody's property. Any-way, we'd been performing a number like this in our stage show, adding a lot of heavy panting. Remembering that cute line girls had used on me in America, I kept slipping it into the blues as we shuffled along. You know the way you get a catch phrase on your mind? 'You turn me on.' Saying it brought back all the delights of those cuddly, squashy American girls. During the number the drummer's cymbal dug into my back, an ash tray slid off my piano and thudded to the floor, and I thought of rhymes as we went along. What a shambolic din in that little room! Thank God for the tight rigid form of the blues! You say the same line twice and then round it off with a comment: 'Huh, huh, huh – that's my song!' After the thud of the ash tray I thought the tape was a wash-out so I'd camped it up with an impersonation of the Sup-remes' little girlie voices.

We finished the number cleanly and Jerry had it played back for us. I was terribly embarrassed but the band roared with laughter and we agreed to call it a day. I told Jerry that all in all it had been a good day's work, hadn't it? At least we had our 'Sporting Life' follow-up in the protest song from Hal Shaper. Jerry answered by making an 'O' sign with his thumb and first finger. Hal Shaper saved the day by suddenly sweeping in, immacu-late in blazer and cravat. Swiftly he dismissed the band and then he took us to the Turf Fire Cabaret Club to hear a Frank Sinatra impersonator, accompanied by a local group called 'The Rolling Tones'. We had prawns à la Wolfe Tone which Hal said you could bounce like a rubber ball and Jerry said he wished he'd published

Failing that, they got a round of drinks. Jerry assured them he'd do 'whatever's right'.

Next day we cut our album. Jerry managed to lure the band along with promises of ready cash. Tower Records were anxious for a follow-up to replace the vanished 'Sporting Life'. As this song had had sugges-tions of seriousness – it was borrowed from an old folk song – I was keen to pursue this line, combining my college courses with my pop music. Sex, screams and a bit of substance. A rocking Dylan. As luck would have it there suddenly appeared on campus an extraordinarily vivacious fellow called Hal Shaper who told me he was my publisher for the world, excluding the USA and Canada. I was most grateful and even more so when he presented me with a brand new song, an anti-war protest called 'No Tears For Johnny' (as recorded by Chad &

'Rubber Ball' and Hal said he knew Bobby Vee personally. The talk continued later when we had adjourned to my rooms. My friends, greatly amused, kept us all well supplied with Guinness and mulled wine.

Jerry returned to America with the tapes and I flew back to London for the Easter vac. Hal Shaper had offered to introduce me to the new pop Society as an Anglo-American artist. I was surpised to find that many of the new rock entrepreneurs were public school types. Some of their ways struck me as being morally dubious but on investigation I found that the worst offenders werre from decidedly minor public schools.

At one party, thrown by a Northern group who wore Regency ruffles and velvet pantaloons, I was introduced to the ritual of the shared 'joint' which reminded me of the Red Indian peace pipe routine, except that in this case the effect of the puffing was not peace but pretentiousness. The group said I reminded them of managers in general and 'Eppy' (Brian Epstein) in particular. I must say I found the public school pop Mafia a fearsome bunch, putting me back to some of the worst moments of boarding school bullying.

No sooner had I returned to Trinity for my last term, the summer one, when the cables started again. Within weeks of the release of the 'Sporting Life' follow up I had myself a rocketing hit! The record was 85 'with a bullet' (as they phrased it in *Billboard*). It was certain to be a smash. Enquiries were being made in America about who I was and, indeed, what sex I was. There was only one problem: the track that Tower Records had decided to release, the one that was zooming up the charts, was not 'No Tears For Johnny', the anti-war plea. It was that damned blues shuffle jam. By the middle of May 'You Turn Me On' was heading straight into the American Top Ten. My feelings were mixed: on the one hand I had always dreamed of crashing big into the American pop scene, but on the other hand I wanted to be taken seriously as an artist. I had not yet learned that art and pop do not mix.

I was now to experience stardom, if only for a few days. In New York men with Italian names taught me to lip-synch to my record, escorted me round the trade paper offices, and saw that I faced the right cameras on the teen disc party TV shows. These shows were all the same and seemed very disorganized and were certainly unrehearsed. I remember one, in Buffalo in up-state New York, which featured an endless array of musical stars including Aretha Franklin, Dizzy Gillespie and Sammy Davis, Jnr – all lip-synching to their current record. The kid audience showed little interest in these stars and a lot in me, screaming at every shake of my shaggy head. I was wearing my best Dublin-tailored herring bone suit (by George VI's old tailor) and this went down well, together with a deerstalker hat I happened to find in my luggage when I left Dublin. A little of the Beatles' stardust had fallen like dandruff onto my shoulders and the kids cried at me because of this magical connection. I commiserated with the legendary

Dizzy Gillespie but he shrugged his shoulders and emptied spittle from his trumpet. The biggest scream, though, was for a regularly handsome singer called Bobby Sherman. I'd never heard of him, but I was informed that he was currently hot due to his weekly appearances on the networked rock & roll TV show, *Shindig*. One of the Italianate Tower execs told me I was 'skedded' to appear on this show next week.

Having always been a fan of Jack Good, his pop paper columns and his TV shows, I was delighted to learn that *Shindig* was his creation. A Tower promo man had wangled his way, at a party, to Jack's teen assistant and described me and my record in such colourful language that the boy, David Mallet, ex-Winchester and well-connected, thought I might be good for a yuk. Jack agreed and I was booked.

At Los Angeles airport I was mobbed. Tower had tipped off the local radio stations and word had been broadcast of the imminent arrival of 'Mr Turn On'. My section of the airport was closed down due to the crush, but several girls broke through and handed me furry animals, sweets, and various self-baked cakes. Burly cops escorted me to a getaway car and it was in this car that I met Tower's ace promo man, 'Jumping' George Sherlock, who had actually had a song written about him by Mick Jagger, 'The Under Assistant West Coast Promotion Man'. Jagger had known him when he was pushing surf records and dressing that part, beach blonde and wind-swept. Now he was riding his own British Invasion wave and so was dressed in a Sherlock Holmes cap and cape. He also brandished a Holmesian curly briar pipe. I thought the bedroom slippers were taking things too far. However, he was very friendly, informing me that I was Number One on all LA charts and that people were dying to know what sex I was, what nationality, and was I *for real*.

Finally we reported to ABC TV for the 'Shindig' show. The Beach Boys were the stars, closely followed by the Shangri-Las and Britain's Cilla Black. I soon learned that I was to be a comic relief, dressed as a motor cyclist and playing the Shangri-Las rough trade boy friend in their song, 'Give Him A Great Big Kiss'. As the network censors had vetoed 'Turn On' as too suggestive I had to sing 'This Sporting Life'. The director had me lying on my back on a ramp, and as I was all in black and the shots concentrated around the crotch area the effect was a slightly sinister sexiness. George Sherlock wasn't sure about the image, thinking it might confuse the teens, but being as this was a national plug he went along. I said I'd do 'whatever's right', taking a line from Jerry.

I was terribly taken by the Beach Boys. They seemed to be quintessentially American pop: cool, laid-back and smiley. When they sang they sounded like angels of the ocean, when they relaxed they certainly relaxed, sipping coke and casually cuddling the extremely sexy and squeaky-clean Shindig dancing girls. As for the backing musicians – men like Glen Campbell, James Burton, Delaney Bramlett, and Leon Russell – they were effortlessly professional, producing edgy blue-bright rock & roll from their axes, horns and keyboards, with an ease that bordered on boredom. Rows of gleaming perfect teeth told one that they were still in the land of us mortals.

Just prior to taping time the great Jack Good, dressed in city gent black trousers and braces and with a bowler hat at a jaunty angle, assembled all of the cast backstage and delivered a really inspiring exhortation: 'Now look here Beach Boys, Shangris, Britishers and US rockers, I want you to go out there and pulse, throb and shake so that western civilization is amazed', he shouted.

I was waiting in the wings, trembling in black leather, when an aged stage hand whispered to me that this was the very stage on which Al Jolson was filmed singing 'My Mammy' in the first talkie feature, *The Jazz Singer*, back in 1927. Being a Jolson fan I was thrilled to death and when I strode out to join the Shangri-Las I felt full of the spirit of Al, the world's greatest entertainer.

All went swimmingly, the Beach Boys rounding off the show with their well-oiled routine and the audience screeching as one (under their prowling cheerleader, Jack Good). It was all as it should be, all like the dream, and afterwards George Sherlock and the Tower executives took me to an important record biz club where I was introduced to more disc jockeys and I actually saw the great Phil Spector.

And so the show raced on. I was booked on tours with the Beach Boys and Sam The Sham and The Righteous Brothers and Jan and Dean. There was more velour and deodorant. I was nice to hordes of well-behaved girls, I was charming to teen mag interviewers. Mick Jagger came to meet me backstage at a Seattle show. He wanted to know if I was for real. A high note was reached in Vancouver, Canada, when during my act a squadron of teeny girls rushed towards me and were met halfway by a battalion of Alsatian dogs under the command of the Mounties. I was very impressed and felt something of the power of the Beatles.

This stardom could last just as long as I was in the charts. Tower were now very anxious to get a hot follow-up as 'You Turn Me On' was slipping very quickly down the charts. I was becoming bored with singing this number and the other blues I had in my repertoire, I was also keen to educate my audience in the delights of British Music Hall and American ragtime songs. I also had a spoken word single lined up. However, Tower wanted teen material – and the best I could come up with was a blues thing called 'N-N-Nervous' which I used to sing with Bluesville and which used to get the girls excited. So I was rushed into RCA's big studio together with some of the *Shindig* band and, under David Mallet's supervision, we cut the number and hoped for the best.

But 'You Turn Me On' was a one hit wonder, a novelty that strikes only once. It was to be my albatross, preventing me from ever being taken seriously as an artist. A conflict was arising: I was starting to enjoy life in the seemingly endless summer of California pop, but at the same time a movement towards serious artistry was developing within what had hitherto been enjoyable, if mindless, pop. Thought, current affairs and *meaningful relevance* were creeping into this wonderland, and the result was much finger-pointing at the illness of the world in general and an invitation to journey on an escape route via the locomotive of drugs. Even worse, *music* itself was elevated into a position of grandeur.

In 1965 this new development was called Folk-Rock and Protest. University graduates and drop-outs, thinking people, were intruding into pop, which had once been the preserve of shopgirls and Alley hacks and hillbillies. In 1965 here was I, lucked into the hit world, my head full of history and my heart set on bringing America the good news about ragtime and rediscovered silvery moons. In 1965 came the Byrds and then Dylan and then more thoughtful Beatle songs to put the seal of doom on that safe old pop world that had been synonymous with comic books, cowboys and dripping doughnuts. I suppose we all have to grow up, but I really resented having to do so.

I had met Sonny and Cher on my Hollywood perambulations with George Sherlock. They shook my hand. I saw them as no threat, finding their furs and redskin aura to be most colourful and in the grand tradition of hokum. But then I did a TV show with the Byrds and it was here that I ran across the new bolshie mentality: they made no attempt to 'mak show', to smile and show the teeth, to bounce and jig. They simply stood there and looked mildly rebellious and they sometimes smirked as if at some private joke. And they didn't lip-synch at all. This was scandalous and both George and I were shocked. But they were in the charts and, as George explained, one must never knock success.

From all sides I was told not to knock success. A good song is a hit song, a hit song is a good song. Yes, but would they feel the same way if, say, 'I Love A Nazi' by The Storm Troopers became a hit? Well, this was not the age for that. Tower and my manager Jerry sent me off on a string of cross-country tours and I soon forgot my troubles, settling in to the routine of bus drive, show, eat, sleep, maybe get a cheap trick, bus drive, show, eat, sleep, etc, etc. My fellow acts on one such tour were mostly soul singers who spent their spare time fixing their hair or playing cards so I palled up with the only Britishers there, Peter and Gordon. At first neither would talk to me and I felt I was back at prep school, in Coventry. Eventually they relented and Peter Asher confessed he'd mistaken me for a moron based on his reading of 'You Turn Me On'. Then he'd spotted my work books – the Karl Marx and the history tomes – and thought better. As we bussed across the mid-West Peter told me about the terrific progress pop was making – from crude rock & roll to sophisticated rock – and how Bob Dylan's poetry would revolutionize the business.

Things could only get better. At Omaha we were joined by Brian Hyland of 'Itsy Witsy Teeny Weeny Yellow Polka Dot Bikini' and I was staggered when Brian agreed with Peter's theories of pop progressiveness. However, I was most grateful to Peter for reading the tougher books on my history course and giving me easy-to-grasp summaries. We parted friends.

Back in LA all was pandemonium at Tower. 'The Eve of Destruction' by Barry McGuire had broken loose and protest was the rage. How could Tower and me cash in on this new loot music? 'N-N-Nervous' was falling like mad and anyway we were being sued by the famous blues singer I'd 'borrowed' the number from. I went into the studio with David Mallet and revived a late ragtime vaudeville song called 'Where Did Robinson Crusoe Go With Friday On Saturday Night?' It was fine fun but, asked Tower, where was the relevance and where the protest?

I persuaded Tower that the next trend would be vaudeville – and the very next year we had 'Winchester Cathedral'. Tower were very kind (or dazed) and went along with 'Robinson Crusoe' and even with my spoken word track ('Memoirs of an Old Soldier'), while dropping Pink Floyd and Nillson. The end of the Sixties were for me, and for a few others, a psychedelic swirl which caused coughing and spluttering. My brain seemed to have seized up. But by the end I had found a cell of fellow souls, of ragtime and early Tin Pan Alley fans, and there have I rested ever since.

Rock simply won't die, it just keeps recycling. I'm glad I had my few days in the sun during that last summer of innocence, 1965. In the late 'forties I started my pop journey at a mini-piano at our family home on Putney Heath. Now, as Western Civilization falls about us, I am back in that same room typing at the dining room table with that same piano a few yards away. It is still the best escape, that piano. Who needs electricity and chemicals? And why leave home? Because when you return you're so relieved!

A whole lotta shakin' may well be going on outside, but inside it's hot milk and an early bed.

Good night.

Ian Whitcomb
Wildcroft Manor
Putney Heath
1981

THE SINGULAR Mr MANN

Bob Dawbarn talks to the Manfred menn

Sonny Boy

IF you want a good confusing conversation I can recommend an interview with Manfred Mann.

For twenty-two years, Manfred Mann has been the name of a South African who, a year or two back, started making his name as a jazz, and then a rhythm-and-blues, pianist and organist.

Now Manfred Mann is also the name of an entire R&B group with each member answering to the name Manfred instead of his original handle — Mike Hugg (drs, vibes), Paul Jones (vcls, harmonica), Tom McGuiness (bass), Mike Vickers (gtr, alto, flute) and, of course Manfred Mann (pno, organ).

PROBLEMS

"We don't want to present a personal image," says Manfred Mann (singular). "That's why we call the whole group Manfred Mann (plural)."

I suppose its simple once you get the hang of it. Anyway this particular Manfred I was talking to, went on: "I'm not necessarily the leader, we are a fully co-operative group."

This, I suggested, might produce policy problems.

"There is an authority which rests with Hugg and myself, which is slightly over-ruling," amplified my particular Manfred, making everything as clear as mud.

On simpler matters, the group's third single, "5-4-3-2-1" is doing well, and has now become the new signature tune for AR-TV's "Ready, Steady, Go!" — an enviable plug spot.

"Actually we prefer the 'B' side, which has modern flute and vibes," said Manfred.

"You know, when a record does well you have people ringing up and offering work although they've never heard the group and don't know what it sounds like.

"Our policy is not to base our career on the charts. If a hit comes along, then good, but we won't be pushed around—and our manager, Ken Pitt, agrees.

"Whatever happened, even if we had a number one hit, we would insist on one night a week doing a West End residency in a jazz club.

OWN THINGS

"Our policy is not to make 1964 the year of our stuff, but rather to make a steady living from 1964 to 1984. Everything we are doing is aimed at the long term.

"We hope people will turn our record over and hear the flute and vibes on the other side.

"Every number we have recorded was written by ourselves and we will continue to do our own things.

"Its up to the record company whether they release them of course, but we decide what we are going to do.

"Personally, I think the group is a lot better than it sound on records."

The group has been signed for Larry Parnes' spring pop tour.

"We don't yet know what spot we will do on the show," said Manfred. "We shall certainly include something like 'Hoochie Coochie Man' as one of the numbers.

"We always think that there are a few people in the audience who have some because they want to hear rhythm and blues.

CONJECTURE

"Actually we play a wide range of stuff. We modify it slightly according to where we are playing.

"If a group just plays hit tunes, the audience tends to remember the tunes and not the group."

Manfred agreed that the group had "evolved" since the days when it was the Mann-Hugg Blues Brothers, used tenor and trumpet and featured Charlie Mingus pieces.

And for anyone who believes that R&B musicians are an unschooled bunch, I would point out that Manfred went to the States at the age of nineteen and studied under John Mehegan, the composer and teacher at Juillard which has spawned a number of today's top modern jazzmen.

He also studied with Professor F. H. Hartmann, a pupil of Schoenberg.

Whether the Professor or Mr Mehegan will ever see "Ready, Steady, Go!" must

AMERICAN SONNY SON has been permit for a f will remain February 21 one of the s Davies Benef don's Marque

Other date Sonny Boy i tonight (Thur Hall, Manche Croydon Jazz Jazz Club (2 Club (31), M ary 1), Manc Aylesbury (11

Further app rently being s

ALAN ELSD due for relea tomorrow (Fr nessee Stud "Titanic." Both MICK EMERY

Tonight, the George Hotel, by dates at H tingham (25) Leicester (27), and Oxford (2

The DON R records a coup for Moderns" January 28. Ot include: Londo Goldington Swa (27) and Kloo Hampstead (29

Don is the S Lifeboat, Cleet ary 26.

The MONT Jazzband plays on February Grammar Scho

Run on str lines, the cl senior member The Sunshine attended by fa number of Mi

JOHNNY DA present his Dickens" recor ICA on Janu of the program up by his tl RUSSELL'S p records.

The MM's turns to the C Light Prog Scene" on Feb

Another jaz dezvous, Po switched to opening its February 1 w

MANFRED MANN—we are a fully co-operative group

THE TROUBLE WITH SOME POP MUSIC....

IT'S part of the mystique of showbiz to sigh for "the good old days" of popular music. This invariably turns out to mean jacketed dance bands and solo stars singing lyrics of sickening sentimentality.

Such nostalgic dreamers would get little support from Paul Jones, singer with Manfred Mann, whose recent "Juke Box Jury" comments on the Bachelors caused many raised eyebrows.

"What I object to is the sentimentality of things like the Bachelors' records," Paul told me this week. "And it's not just the lyrics. You get it in the musical side of that type of tune and arrangements. Those awful violins!

"In the lyrics, it's lines like 'No one else before opened heaven's door' that got me. It's got nothing to do with anyone's experience. And then there is the tone in which the man sings it, which I also find objectionable.

SUCCESS

"Surely there has been a massive improvement over the past few years. Those old days were awful. Mind you, 'The Minute You're Gone', is as bad as anything from those days. It's Cliff's worst record for ages.

"I'm afraid sentimentality is a permanently saleable commodity. And it's not only the words. 'Stranger On The Shore' was the most sentimental record I ever heard—and the most successful record I can remember.

"Elvis' biggest was 'Now Or Never' which is sentimental. And then the continued success of Roy Orbison is another example. Terrible! He even brings tears to my eyes when he goes for those high notes."

The Manfred Mann group has always been opposed to the cult of the personality. Paul's name has appeared on their last two singles. Is this a change of policy?

"I think it's awful and I won't let it happen again," declared Paul. "It smacks of the Joe Loss Orchestra featuring

PAUL JONES speaks out

Ross McManus. I have awful memories of myself with a palais band. They had blue blazers with their initials on the pocket and I had a scarlet one.

"Kids do tend to pick out the singer, but that's no reason to encourage it by sticking the name out as a special thing. Anybody who is the slightest bit interested in the group knows who the singer is."

FOLKSY

Paul doesn't think the current Bob Dylan-Donovan cult is at all significant.

"I don't think it means a boom of any kind," he mused. "It's only two people and the folk thing is a rather secondary in their case. There are lots and lots of folk records coming out and not meaning a thing.

"It is possible there will be a bigger folk influence on pop music in general. There was John Lennon writing that very Dylanish sort of thing. I haven't heard it said, but to me the Beatles new single seems rather to have a folksy thing about it—listen to the first line."

Does Manfred Mann find that audiences vary much throughout the country?

"I don't think they change according to area" says Paul. "We do change our approach—like if we play at a University we tend to present things in a more adult way.

BLOOD

"Then, if it is obviously an audience of 15-year-olds I will lie on my back and all the gear. University students tend not to want to see you lying on your back."

I asked how Paul enjoyed his "Juke Box Jury" appearance.

"I'm very disappointed because everybody says 'Oh, I liked your 'Juke Box Jury' bit," replied Paul.

"I feel I deserved a couple of poison pen letters and I didn't get any.

"I thought at least the secretary of the Bachelors Fan Club would do something—like write in blood on our walls. But nothing!"—B.D.

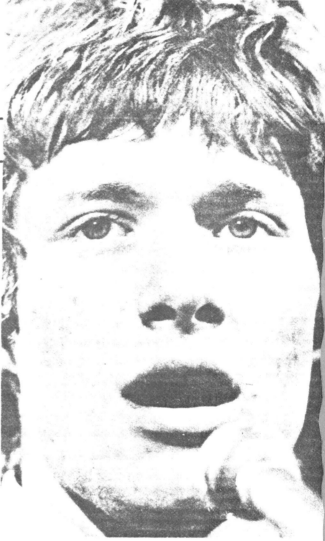

PAUL JONES . . . sentimentality is a permantly saleable commodity!

Just as I was about to enter the wonder-world of pop the scene started changing. Other college people were entering, bringing with them adult ideas. They wanted to improve the music and bring some sense and do away with the tinsel, gold and razzamatazz. But I still saw R&R as Elvis in his gold suit standing by his gold Cadillac. So I was escaping to never-never land only to find that my own kind was already there. Paul Jones typifies this new breed of party-poopers.

NEW MUSICAL EXPRESS

MARIANNE NEVER DOES WHAT A POP STAR SHOULD

Says Keith Altham

SHE has a pert, child-like face which darts out at you from a cascade of fine, fair hair. The face seems to be concentrated into the blonde fringe and the expressive, blue-grey eyes beneath. Around the bridge of her nose is the merest suspicion of freckles to come this summer.

When she is pleased, her whole face dimples into an inhibited smile, and she plays at being sex-kitten and society hostess in turn. Marianne Faithfull is a very interesting girl.

"I'm a journalist's nightmare," she said. "I never do anything a pop star is supposed to do. I don't own a mink coat, or ride around in an E-type Jag. There's a man who keeps ringing up to sell me a horse. I think he fancies me. I'd love a horse, but . . ."

We were lunching at a quite exclusive London club, and my first tete-à-tete with Miss Faithfull was proving an education.

"Sausage and mash," requested Marianne, after perusing the ample menu. She smiled sweetly. A slightly sickly smile spread over the waiter's face.

"We eat, of course, do you some," he said, with just the slightest amount of injured pride. For one desperate minute, I thought Marianne was going to verbally barbecue him, then she countered graciously by changing her order to lamb cutlets.

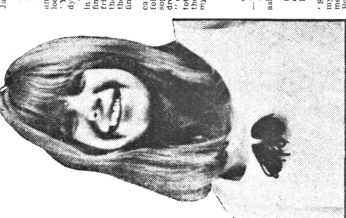

"Well done, and Marianne the cellars, sir," it is, apparently, looked after. She recalled that highly effective.

● Baby Darin has produced — Buddy Darin has produced — and sold the concept of a television series to Screen Gem, one of the leading independent packagers.

● In one week after its release, Elvis Presley's new album of songs from the film, "Girl Happy," sold more than 100,000 copies.

● Shani Wallis has signed with Capitol Records.

● Sandie Shaw, Reprise Records reports, is saving her money so that she can leave England to live overseas. "I want to get away from machines," Sandie adds. "Away

copy of a hotel in Switzerland that she knew where the waiters have that lovely young face. Like Cathy McGowan, Sandie Shaw and Jane Asher, she typifies the "ideal teenager," and finds herself modelling fashions for women's magazines.

"I have been mistaken for Jane Asher," admitted Marianne. "Because my fiancé, John, was a friend of Peter's, I got to know them quite well. There used to be lovely scenes round at the Ashers with Paul McCartney, Peter and Gordon sitting in chairs with

from the coffee percolators and the taxis and the typewriters. The only machines I can stand are cars."

● Johnny Mathis may have his own network television series in U.S. next season. He says he already has two possible sponsors.

● Steve Lawrence is set as host of his own musical variety show on CBS-TV this fall. Lawrence has also signed an exclusive, long-term deal with CBS.

● A determined quote from Eartha Kitt: "When I'm 110 years

Bob Dylan is in the money

IN a single one-nighter in Santa Monica, California, recently, Bob Dylan grossed more than $10,000. With a single now in the charts, the folk singer will certainly have his biggest year in 1965.

Much of Marianne's fortune lies in

---

aprons tied around their necks while Jane got to work on their hair."

Marianne had recently operated on John's hair — somewhat to his annoyance, I gathered.

"He keeps letting it grow longer and longer," smiled Marianne. "He looks at it in the mirror and says, 'Yes, it's getting better now,' and I'm dying to get my scissors to it."

Only just returned from a short tour in Scotland, Marianne was pleased to find she was working with her old friends the Hollies. She claims that the group are the most professional on the scene, and that Allan Clarke is the finest mover on stage.

"I did some cabaret at an R.A.F. camp," said Marianne. "I had to follow Alma Cogan, who is terribly sophisticated and was wearing a low-cut dress with great assurance. I thought, 'Oh, no, I can't do it.' Then I tottered on in my dress buttoned up to the neck, and said I was going to sing my next record. I was terrified."

'Bad mistake'

We talked about that "bad mistake" — "Blowing In The Wind."

"What made you record it?" I asked.

"Andrew Oldham," she replied, simply. "It's funny, now that I don't work for Andrew I really dig him.

"I recorded a number called 'Strange World' for the follow-up to my first disc, and then Andrew wanted me to try 'Blowing In The Wind.' Both discs were presented to Decca, and they made the wrong choice, in my opinion."

Marianne is very much looking forward to the release of her folk LP, and told me the story of her return to the folk club in Reading where she used to play.

"They really hated me," she said. "They said I had done a great disservice to folk music. I had com-

---

mitted the unforgivable sin of becoming a success.

"There is this very silly attitude in this country that once someone gets into the Top Twenty they are no longer any good. Take the Yardbirds, for example. I think they are great, but soon you'll get the people who will turn around and say that they know them before they went commercial. The Beatles and the Stones and all the others are just as good now as when they were unknown."

We talked about "Ready, Steady, Go!", and Marianne mourned its move to Wembley.

"It used to be a social rallying point where you could go down and meet old friends. It was an AD LIB club with lights. I'm sorry it has moved."

We talked about horses. Marianne is a keen rider and took lessons at the Roehampton Stables.

"I ride quite well, but not expertly. My posture leaves something to be desired. I don't want to be instructed."

As we left the restaurant, Marianne donned a pair of round-lensed sun glasses and scampered across the road to peer along the rows of shelves outside a second-hand book shop.

I caught up with her, and she clutched my arm, blinking like a somewhat bemused mole entering the sunlight.

"I must buy you a book," she shrilled. Delighted with the idea, she scuttled off into the shop, and returned with a little yellow volume entitled: "Big Ben," a light opera in two acts, by A. P. Herbert.

Marianne Faithfull is a very interesting girl.

NAT HENTOFF's
U.S. AIRMAIL

MCA. Among Miller's responsibilities will be the search for new talent.

● Trini Lopez has made good use of his new prosperity. In addition to buying his family a new home in Dallas, his father a new Cadillac and sending his brother to college, Lopez intends to headline a concert in his home town and donate the receipts to his church.

● Nashville continues to grow in importance as a recording centre. RCA-Victor has just opened a sizeable new recording studio there.

● Mitch Miller, formerly pop a-and-r head at Columbia Records and then creator of the successful "Sing Along with Mitch" television series, has joined the new creative development division of the gigantic show business packager and producer,

old. I want people to remember Eartha Kitt."

● American papers are giving sustained space to Louis Armstrong's triumphal tour of East Germany and other East European countries.

● Trumpeter Al Hirt, with whom RCA-Victor has had considerable sales success, gets his own summer television series on CBS. Producer of the show will be Sullivan Productions, headed by Ed Sullivan.

● Hank Williams, Jr., son of the late, renowned country singer, will star in an MGM picture, "Cold, Cold Heart,"

PEP by EV

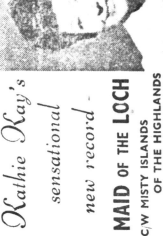

FRANK SINATRA
on Vol. 1 of ... Swing, faithfull and his orchestra. Believe In You, I Want In Other Words, and Lovin'.

KEELY SMITH
Vol. 1 from her own McCartney Songbook. Sings The John McCartney Songbook. Versions of the Love Day's Night Very Day's Night ... and all P.S. I Love You. Love,

ROCKIN' BERRIES
falsetto on I Didn't You and What In The Over You, two medium and so fast for You Home and Flashback mural backing.

MINK MARTINDALE
a disc jockey. With through his hit single back. Deck of Cards more sugary recital organ and exotic sou. Sunset, Stifling W and Trees.

IVY LEAGUE
(Pacer combine current to with a faint folk-ish Get You home by with Walt A Minute, add What More Do You W off with two beat GEORGIE FAME (Co deep-down Negro 'Fame At Last' El for himself and 'grou group behind for Get Track Baby, Point I Love The Life I That Wine.

Kathie Kay's
sensational
new record -

MAID OF THE LOCH
c/w MISTY ISLANDS
OF THE HIGHLANDS

An ARROW *Recordin*

obtainable at the shops and bookstalls of John Menzies and W

THE BEATLES HELPED BOB DYLAN TO FAME HERE

John Lennon tells why

To CHRIS HUTCHINS

INTO Britain this weekend flies the world's No. 1 folk star, Bob Dylan. But for some strange reason it has been only in the last two or three months that Dylan has become recognised on any major scale in this country.

Since that happened he has become a trend in his own right, yet few people seem to know anything about this singing phenomenon. People who do know something about Bob Dylan are the Beatles; by constantly referring to him in answers to questions about their own favourite artists, they helped to launch the folk star here.

It was from the lips of John, George, Paul and Ringo that most of those who are now his fans learned the name.

So it is appropriate in welcoming Dylan to our shores that we should have asked a Beatle to throw some light on this star

NMExclusive

his singing you somehow imagine him as a tall man He is about Ringo's height and very thin.

"I don't know what all the people who have bought tickets for his concerts are expecting but I think they're bound to accept him. His work will be good.

"As you know we've got tickets for his London concert on May 9 and providing nothing crops up in the meantime we'll be there digging Dylan with the rest of 'em."

And that's the first American visitor to be welcomed to the NME by a Beatle.

Take a bow, Bob Dylan.

DYLAN—same sense of humour

from the shadows John Lennon had this to say:

"We began admiring him during our visit to Paris in January of last year when we cadged a Dylan LP off a d-j who came to interview us. Paul had heard of him before but until we played that record his name did not really mean anything to us.

"We went potty over the LP —I think it was 'Freewheelin' —and tried to get more of his records.

"Then when we were in New York during the American tour last summer somebody said 'Do you want to meet Dylan?' and we said 'Sure, if he wants to meet us,' so he came up to the hotel room and we did nothing but laugh all night. He kept answering our phone, saying 'This is Beatlemania here.' It was ridiculous.

"He has got the same sense of humour as we have and our tastes in music, though not the same, cross somewhere . . . you can tell that if you listen to his latest single 'Subterranean Blues.'

"He's a little fellow, that surprises you at first because from

MONEY QUOTES

WORDS of economic wisdom from Colonel Parker, Elvis Presley's manager: "The difference between Elvis getting a million and Elizabeth Taylor getting a million per movie is that Elvis never takes longer than five weeks to shoot. So the good folks at the studios make a nice profit on us."

SAID Ringo Starr to John T. Wasserman of the "San Francisco Chronicle": "The only thing that's really important is my personal life. All this other stuff is a great joke. Money can be a trap. If you're happy it doesn't matter whether you're making it or not."

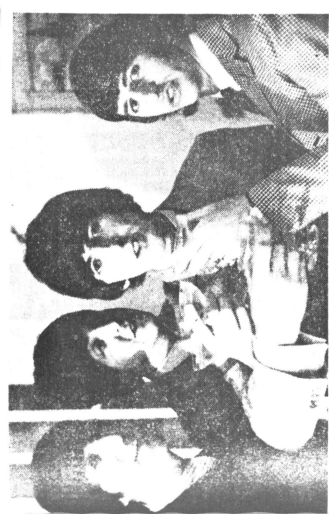

THE BEATLES are making a toast—but it's not to Bob Dylan's arrival in Britain—though we're sure they'd be quick to do that, too. The toast is GEORGE HARRISON (third from left), on his recent birthday.

Billy Fury co-stars with Anselmo

"I'VE GOTTA HORSE," Britain's newest screen pop musical, sets out to present the likeable personality of Billy Fury—and succeeds. He sings all kinds of songs, admits to liking animals better than human beings, and gets on well with an assortment of children.

The film, of course, features Fury's own race horse, Anselmo, and also several of his dogs, and the situations into which he gets himself are the sort you can imagine would give manager Larry Parnes headaches most of the year.

For in the film Billy takes his singing career light-heartedly and devotes far too much time to the horse and does, causing no small annoyance to a frustrated producer, who is doing his best to stage a summer show around Billy.

The Bachelors make a couple of amusing guest appearances—once riding horses across the sands at Great Yarmouth in cowboy outfits.

Billy's backing group the Gamblers is frequently to be seen in the picture.

The cast includes Amanda Barrie, Michael Medwin, Bill Fraser and Jon Pertwee.

Billy has graduated—he has moved up from the era of poor pop films (i.e., "Play It Cool") to the kind of screen musical that Cliff Richard has been scoring success with for three years.

And although "I've Gotta Horse" has nothing of the subtle wit and clever camera antics of the Beatles' "A Hard Day's Night", I found it refreshing — nobody was corny, nobody was trying to be clever, and the result was good entertainment.

CHRIS HUTCHINS.

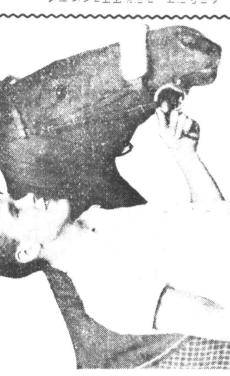

DYLAN FETED, BUT REMAINS UNMOVED!

by JOHN WELLS

DYLAN'S here! The world's most talked about folk singer flew into London Airport on Monday for his sell-out tour. And somebody who looks less like a star than he does I've yet to meet. Hair that would set the teeth of a comb on edge. Crumpled suit. No tie. A loud shirt that would dim the neon lights of Leicester Square.

And our meeting—Cathy McGowan take note—was in London's plush Savoy Hotel.

DYLAN—small, hardly noticed when first he came in, shielding his eyes from photographers' flashlights. Dark glasses go on and off with every flush. And there are some flashes!

DYLAN—evading more questions than he answers, but more diplomatic than President Johnson's Press Secretary.

DYLAN—above all looking bored and strangely out of place against the luxury that surrounds him. Almost the little boy lost.

Until you speak to him.

"I don't give the impression of being a star," he drawls, because I don't think of myself as one." This isn't 'the talk of a naïve person. He believes it. Like when he says: "I've sat back and seen all these crazes come and go, and I don't think I'm more than a craze. In a coupla years time I shall be light back where I started—an unknown."

A lot of today's stars secretly think this . . . none of them would dream of saying it!

I go along with Dylan and ask him if he'll be sorry when it's over.

"Nope!"

Wouldn't he even miss the money?

"Nope! I spend most of what I get now, anyway—and how I spend it is my business. Not on material things, I don't need ten cars, a mansion and a yacht.

"Of course, I'd be a fool to say money means nothing to me, but I don't really care."

A battery of cameras fire. Dylan looks as if he's been hit, replaces his dark glasses. "All I'm really interested in," he says, "is singing to people who want to listen to me. And I don't care how many that is."

Fortunately, if not for Dylan, for somebody, thousands of people want to listen.

Thousands are buying his records. Thousands are paying to see his tour. My shoulders are aching from the crush that surrounds him. I retreat to recap on this phenomenon.

Born in Duluth, Minnesota, May 24, 1941, Dylan lived for the first seventeen years of his life in Hibbing, Minnesota.

Dylan himself wrote: "Hibbing's a good ol' town. I ran away from it when I was 10, 12, 13, 15, 15½, 17 an' 18. I bin caught and brought back all but once."

So much for Hibbing.

By the winter of 1961, Dylan, still only twenty, had sung his way through one half of the American States. From New Mexico to South Dakota, from Kansas to California. He later wrote: "I's driftin' an' learning new lessons. I was making my own depression. I rode freight trains for kicks. An' got beat up for laughs."

Finally though, Dylan reached the Columbia Records studios and cut his first album called simply enough Bob Dylan. That was the start.

A lot of authorities state that Dylan's been greatly influenced by that other folk great, Woody Guthrie.

write finger pointing songs this term for 'message') because I think I can put the world to rights. I don't think I can. And I don't really care if I can or not.

"I just write what I feel. If other people think it has a message it's up to them, but I'm not, deliberately trying to put one across.

As more and more people squeezed into the room at the Savoy to welcome Dylan to Britain, he became more and more surprised at this acknowledgment of his popularity. Not that his face displayed much emotion.

"I seem to be more popular here than I am at home," he muses. "I reckon you could call me a Top Ten name here but in America I'm only Top Forty."

Someone asks him if there was a massive welcome from the fans at London Airport when he flew in a day before.

"Don't remember," he says. But on someone prompting him by saying: "Surely you MUST remember?" he admits: "Yeah, there were some people there."

He's really bored by now.

He brightens when I talk about

BOB DYLAN salutes England? Or is he getting in the mood to write a new Civil War song? Actually he said: "I was trying to attract a passing bird." NME picture by Russell Napier.

---

has brought: is that I must feel I must make my records even better."

"Before I made records to please myself and though I still do this I'm now also conscious that the public deserves the best I can give. This I owe them."

Even before it starts, Dylan's **tour is one of the biggest successes a visiting American artist has had for quite a while.**

But even this apparently leaves him unmoved. He told me the main thing he was looking forward to while here was buying a pair of boots.

But even if he gives the appearance of living in a world of his own, bored with the outside, he can't go wrong. To his fans he represents the rebel, the man who believes in the things they do. And acts the way they'd like to.

And I must admit that I liked him personally—if only because of his courage in remaining completely detached while being so lionised. If he appears on stage and decides to stand on his head and not play a note during his entire tour, he'll still be loved.

His fans will probably read something into it.

his latest record, "Subterranean Homesick Blues," and tell him it's in the NME Chart—giving him two side by side in the list.

But he doesn't greet the news with abandoned enthusiasm! It's just: "Nice to hear that."

I say I found "Subterranean" a little different from his usual records. I wonder, in fact, if it had been cut for some time.

"A bit different?

"I just make them as I feel at the time."

With chart successes and a sell-out tour Dylan means big business and big money. And it's usually at this stage that the pressure to become intentionally commercial is applied. But Dylan assured me it won't happen to him.

"As far as my records are concerned the only difference success

Influence

I shouldered my way back into the throng to ask about it.

"My eyes and ears have been my great influence," he says. "Nothing or nobody else really."

He shrugged his shoulders.

"People who have tried to influence me have been so wrong. I don't know why—they just have been. They aren't with what I'm trying to do.

"And the same goes for me. I'm not trying to influence people. In fact, I don't want to."

A voice, well in the background, asks him if he hasn't been influenced by Donovan! His press officer winces!

But Dylan's expression doesn't change. "Who is this Donovan? I'd never even heard of him until yesterday," he says. And he means it. Hastily I get him back to "influence."

"No," he tells me. "I don't

Rep. KEVIN DONOVAN, 3-3a RIDGWAY CHAMBERS, TOWN ROAD,
HANLEY STOKE-ON-TRENT. Tel: S.o.T. 22901

Released on DECCA today!

CAN'T LET HER GO

Dot RECORDS

One type of music I always hated was folk music, which when it wasn't harping on about tragic rural maids in monotonous tunes was finger pointing at the benefits of modern life. Folkies were full of *complaints* about our conveniences and defense plans. Also, they were grubby and ugly and quite without romance or flash. Also, I never understood a word of 'Blowin' in the Wind' —but I did understand 'Wooly Bully'. And the irony was that Sam the Sham was an expert on British Political Thought, especially John Locke.

THANK GOODNESS WE WON'T

GET THIS SIX-MINUTE BOB

DYLAN SINGLE IN BRITAIN

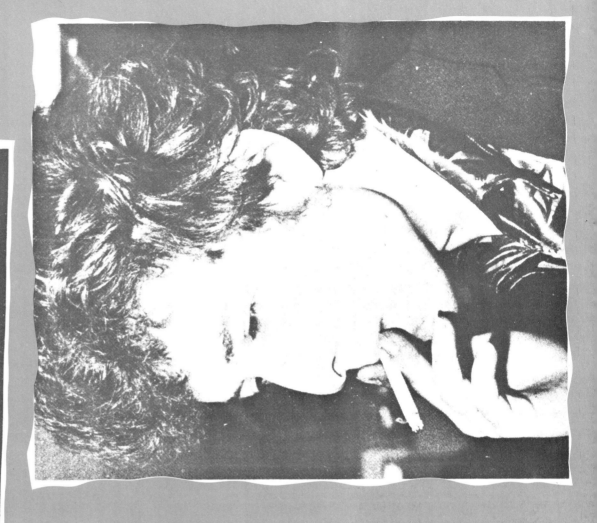

BOB DAWBARN LISTENS TO THE NEW, SIX-MINUTE LONG BOB DYLAN SINGLE, AND COMES TO THE CONCLUSION THAT IT'S JUST AS WELL IT'S NOT SCHEDULED FOR BRITISH RELEASE.

BOB DYLAN's latest American chart entry is the world's longest single — a six-minute epic entitled "Like A Rolling Stone".

In Britain, CBS have no plans to release any Dylan single in the immediate future. And when a single is released, it is by no means certain to be "Like A Rolling Stone".

For once I'm on the side of a record company. Frankly I can't see "Like A Rolling Stone" pleasing either faction of Dylan's British fans — the folk collectors or the pop pickers.

To start with, Dylan is saddled with a quite horrific backing dominated by syrupy strings, amplified guitar and organ. Mick Jagger fans will also be distressed to learn that the song title refers to a rolling stone and not a Rolling Stone.

The lyric has its moments of typical Dylan imagery, but the monotonous melody line and Dylan's expressionless intoning just cannot hold the interest for what seems like the six longest minutes since the invention of time.

There are times when Dylan sounds faintly like Eric Burdon and, in fact, the song would be a much more suitable vehicle for the Animals than for the composer himself.

My copy of the disc bears the legend "Prod. by Tom Wilson." Somebody should have prodded Mr Wilson until he agreed to lock the backing group in the cellar until the session was over.

The paucity of "Like A Rolling Stone" is emphasised by the flip side which also runs for nearly six minutes. This is "Gates Of Eden", familiar to those who attended Dylan's British concerts and a track from his "Bringing It All Back" album.

This is just Dylan with guitar and harmonica. And without the extraneous backing noises one can concentrate on what the man is saying — and some of the writing is magnificent. What other popular writer would sing "The lamp post stands with folded arms"?

DONOVAN — one of the folk song sensations of 65 —

'I'LL QUIT AFTER TWO MORE YEARS'

GIPSY DAVE sat in Donovan's dressing room playing a strange instrument— a leg off a Queen Anne chair strung with one guitar string.

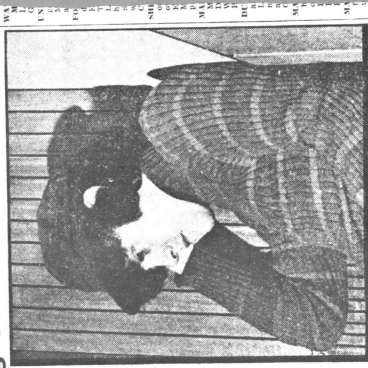

"Hey, listen to this, man," he enthused and wound the string, thumbing it violently and extracting a tortuous, high-pitched whine from the instrument. "Great, man, great!" he grinned happily.

Before he began working for Donovan Gipsy's only claim to fame was that he played kazoo on the track of Don's LP "Keep A-Trucking." He also gave Don his last pair of boots.

I shook hands with the-road-manager-of-the-year and noted the green and red winged serpent which was tattooed on his forearm.

"I saw this guy having one sewn in at a shop," explained Dave. "His whole arm was covered in blood—looked a horrible mess. When they washed his arm, there was this fantastic picture. So I had me done."

Don describes Dave simply as a friend. He is the same age, eighteen, talks the same language and they dig the same music.

"I met Dave during an Aldermaston march," Don told me. "He knows most of the folk songs I know and we struck up a friendship."

Dave describes his arrival in London thus: "Don wrote to me in Manchester. I was living under this bush by a church so I came down."

Behind a chair, seated on the floor, was another addition to the "Crazy Mixed Up World" of Donovan. He said that his name was Derek and he had just walked in to see Don. He then folded his arms and stated stoically at the floor.

● Gimmick

"Seen the latest gimmick?" smiled Don drily, as he took off his cap and handed it to me. A tiny silver badge in the shape of a broken rifle was pinned to the side.

"It's the badge of ' The War Resistance International'," said Don. He must be copying someone, but I couldn't place the name!

Donovan idly strummed his guitar and began singing. Once he gets that guitar in his hands they just keep pouring out like water from a tap.

While tuning the guitar, he snapped a string and shuffled off to see Dave Wendles of the Rebel Rousers for a replacement.

Manager Geoff Stevens and I sat back in our chairs and waited his return.

"You know, one day I'm going to look around and that boy will be gone," said Geoff. "He couldn't care less about the money in this business. He'll stay as long as it

suits him and then just go." He looked pleased and worried alternately.

The loudspeaker on the dressing room wall blared, "Donovan on stage, please," and Geoff looked around. Donovan was gone.

He opened the dressing-room door and met the other half of the management rushing in.

"Seen Donovan?" chorused both Peter Eden and Geoff together.

A frantic search evolved and the star was found nonchalantly posing for a fan outside the studio. She had a box camera and wanted to take his photo.

I decided this interview should be continued the following day. Donovan very suggested lunch and we fixed a time.

At a small restaurant off Charing Cross Road, Donovan, Peter Eden, Gipsy and I dug into a huge plate of scampi and mushrooms. This is Donovan's staple diet.

Among his new projects, books and poems to be published he told me about plans to produce his first film.

"A friend of mine called Paul is going to help me produce our own film. We want to do a very artistic thing. No script and no actors. Just an observation of life. Flies buzzing on a window pane. Sunlight through the trees. A girl's hair blowing in the wind. My father used to be a photographer. I think we'll make a good job of it."

Donovan has just moved into a London apartment that was recently vacated by Rolling Stones' manager,

Andrew Oldham. He lives there with Gipsy, Paul and his wife and their eighteen-month-old baby.

"You know, I'd like to write an article for your paper about my observations on the pop scene," said Don.

He wants to call it, "The Age of Misinterpretation" but I think we can talk him out of that! Should be an interesting article.

As Donovan got up to leave I noticed his jeans were still sitting down.

"Going to get some more clothes now," I asked pointedly.

"Well, I don't feel obliged to keep wearing the old gear," said Don. "But these are my clothes at the moment, so they'll do."

Donovan revealed to me that he only intends to remain in show business for two years.

● Deadline

"I think I could continue for much longer making a living as a singer," said Don. "I've decided on a deadline of two years, then I intend to travel around the world and just write."

As we walked out of the restaurant and into the street I noticed Gipsy was looking very miserable. In fact he had been very quiet all through the meal.

"What's wrong?" I asked. "Did someone rub out your tattoo?"

"Worse," sighed Dave. "I broke the string on my one string guitar. That's showbiz!"

KEITH ALTHAM

FROM THE NME

| 5 YEARS AGO | 10 YEARS AGO |

TOP TEN 1960—Week ending April 29

Last This
Week

6	1	CATHY'S CLOWN
		Everly Brothers (Warner Bros.)
1	2	DO YOU MIND
		Anthony Newley (Decca)
7	3	SOMEONE ELSE'S BABY
		Adam Faith (Parlophone)
5	4	HANDY MAN
		Jimmy Jones (MGM)
4	5	FALL IN LOVE WITH YOU
		Cliff Richard (Columbia)
3	6	MY OLD MAN'S A DUSTMAN
		Lonnie Donegan (Pye)
11	7	STANDING ON THE CORNER
		King Brothers (Parlophone)
2	8	STUCK ON YOU
		Elvis Presley (RCA)
9	9	SWEET NUTHIN'S
		Brenda Lee (Brunswick)
8	10	FINGS AIN'T WOT THEY USED T'BE
		Max Bygraves (Decca)

TOP TEN 1955—Week ending April 29

Last This
Week

2	1	CHERRY PINK
		Perez Prado (HMV)
1	2	GIVE ME YOUR WORD
		Tennessee Ernie (Capitol)
3	3	STRANGER IN PARADISE
		Tony Bennett (Philips)
5	4	CHERRY PINK
		Eddie Calvert (Columbia)
4	5	SOFTLY, SOFTLY
		Ruby Murray (Columbia)
11	6	STRANGER IN PARADISE
		Tony Martin (HMV)
10	7	EARTH ANGEL
		Crew Cuts (Mercury)
7	8	UNDER THE BRIDGES OF PARIS
		Eartha Kitt (HMV)
12	9	READY WILLING AND ABLE
		Doris Day (Philips)
	9	WEDDING BELLS
		Eddie Fisher (HMV)

DONOVAN WROTE SONGS IN PRISON

The beach is out of reach,
of those who teach,
and preach,
and screech,
that play with clay,
in God's hands."

DONOVAN wrote that. I don't know what it means, but then nothing about Donovan is easy to understand when you first meet him. He can be deep; but open. Friendly; but cynical.

This is how I found him in an amazingly frank conversation this week. He told me: "I write songs and poems everywhere. Man, they just come into my head.

"The police in Manchester arrested me before I got known. I was thrown into Strangeways Prison for two weeks. I wrote two songs while I was cooped up there.

"They accused me of breaking into a cinema and stealing some cigarettes. But when the case came up I was acquitted. My trouble was, they relied on evidence they shouldn't have done. I'd been framed, but the Law didn't know that," he alleged.

These were out-of-the-rut days for Donovan. He told me candidly: "I don't see much of my parents. I'm not a row. We just don't speak the same language. There's nothing there for me, man. So I left home.

"Sure, I've slept rough. Lots of times, in old houses, on beaches and derelict sites. You don't like it when you're doing it, I wouldn't recommend it.

"In fact, I wouldn't recommend the life at all. It's not fun. Live like that and you either turn out to be mad or ..."

I asked him how he thought he would turn out himself. He thought deeply. "I don't know, man. I'm working at a few things out with myself. I just don't know yet. There's a lot to do in a lotta time.

"Would I've ever give up those fab clothes and wear a suit?" "I don't think so," he told me, "not for long. I couldn't take care of a change, though. Who knows? I'd swap a right to change his views. I like him for this. He might not be an interviewer's dream come true, but he seems almost utterly honest.

I asked him how he felt about the Dylan-v-Donovan controversy. Was he tired of it all by now? How did he feel about Bob Dylan personally?

He pushed back his blue denim cap. "Some of it's a bit sick," he told me. "I don't like the hecklers. Some of them want to kill me. I mean that.

"They get really worked up about this business, but occasionally they ...

BY ALAN SMITH

... understand what I'm trying to do. That I mean what I'm doing and they come up and apologise.

"I think I've convinced some people I'm not a Dylan fiend Bobby's a good fella and I've met him often on his stays here. Sometimes we've talked he remembers me from last time he came over. He has a fantastic memory.

"What else can I say? We're both in the business, he seems to like what I'm doing, and I like him. We get on good.

"Reporters are funny people sometimes. They ask questions that aren't relevant, that have no connection with the things I'm trying to do," he said, changing the subject.

"I pointed out that people would understand more about what he was trying to do if they felt they knew him better. Newspaper articles could help him to explain himself to the public.

"Sure," he said, " but I can't do ...

... that in interviews. I'll have to find some other medium."

That medium is poetry, but Donovan himself intends to be highly selective about the poems he would like to see in print. "I wrote a lot at school," he told me, "and I carry them about in a book. But I wouldn't want those released. They're not of the right standard."

"No, man, I don't write much of it down these days. It's all going round in my head. That's the way to write.

"You can't turn out poetry like a machine, it just has to happen. I can't remember them for days; the only one I can think of right now is that one about the beach. It goes at the beginning or end of something I did, I can't remember now."

Money doesn't interest Donovan at all. "It doesn't mean a thing," he told me. "If I flopped, I'd only be sorry for the people behind me, the people who've helped me. I might buy a big house and look after my friends, but that's it.

"I look at myself like this; I'm an easy-going guy, and I don't want to do anybody down. I just want to show what I can do."

TOP TEN

JOHN CARTER

BLOWIN' IN THE WIND by Peter, Paul and Mary : This is a really beautiful song. One of Bob Dylan's best compositions. I prefer the Peter, Paul and Mary version to all the others because of the superb harmony arrangement. There's so much feeling and sincerity in the voices.

YOU'VE LOST THAT LOVIN' FEELIN', by the Righteous Brothers : This record just cuts me up. It's so emotional. The combination of voices is just perfect.

WASN'T THAT A PITY AND A SHAME from " Black Nativity ", LP : This is a song that only Negroes could ever sing. " Black Nativity " had some great music, but I thought this was wonderful. It was sung by the chorus, and once again there was so much emotion in the song.

KEN LEWIS

LA BAMBA by Ritchie Valens : This song came out about seven years ago, and I always associate it with the deep feelings of my youth. It's such an inspiring and ...

PERRY ● JOHN ● KEN

... exciting record—half rock, half Latin-American. I still get cold shivers whenever I hear it.

THE HOUSE ON THE HILL by Peggy Lee : Peggy's my favourite " standards " singer. I love to listen to this very late at night. It's so relaxing.

CATCH THE WIND by Donovan : You could say I was biased about this one, as I was Musical Director on the disc — but everything this guy does knocks me out. I'm sure he'll develop into a good singer and guitarist and an even better songwriter.

PERRY FORD

THE NITTY GRITTY by Shirley Ellis : This girl has so much soul, ...

by the IVY LEAGUE

... and this disc really shows her at her best. It's very exciting and by far the best record she's made.

I LEFT MY HEART IN SAN FRANCISCO by Tony Bennett : This one always makes me cry. How wonderful it is that someone could write such an emotional song about a city he loves. And Tony sings it so beautifully.

YES IT IS by the Beatles : John and Paul are such great songwriters that it's very difficult to pick just one. But I think this one is just a little bit cleverer than their others. There's a beautiful harmony and the lyrics are so sincere and understanding.

THE GROUP FAVOURITE

DON'T WORRY BABY by the Beach Boys : This is the " B " side of the Beach Boys' "I Get Around." It has wonderful chord constructions, and shows the Beach Boys at their best. Besides, it's on our LP.

NAT HENTOFF'S American Airmail

ELVIS PRESLEY says he has no intention of changing his musical style. "I'll just continue," he adds, " to do what I think is good to listen to—not specialising in any one thing."

● Sammy Davis has been nominated for a Tony, one of the most prestigious theatrical awards, for his work in " Golden Boy."

● Capitol has just released its first Georgia Brown album, " The Many Shades Of Georgia Brown."

● There will be sixteen songs in "Girl Crazy," the MGM musical with Connie Francis, Paul Anka, Harve Presnell.

● A curious passer-by saw this in Sammy Davis' Rolls-Royce—a TV set, a hi-fi, two telephones, a two-way short-wave radio, and a bar.

● Julie Andrews is now definite in the role of Gertrude Lawrence in a picture to be made in London next year by Robert Wise and 20th Century-Fox ...

... "Girl Happy."   Said the "New York Post": " Elvis is growing more sophisticated in his acting as well as his singing."

● "Sugar City," a musical with score by Duke Ellington, opens on Broadway in the fall with Walter Slezak as star. It's based on "The Blue Angel."

● Murray the K, the friend of the Beatles, will host and produce an hour-long CBS-TV rock 'n' roll programme addressed to nation's unemployed youth.

He will try to convince them that they can get help through the Government's War on Poverty.

This is one of the first times the Government has officially used rock music as part of its educational programme.

● Hillard Elkins, producer of " Golden Boy," is considering boxer-performer Sugar Ray Robinson as a replacement for Sammy Davis when the latter goes on vacation.

● Zero Mostel and Phil Silvers will be in London in August to film "A Funny Thing Happened To Me On The Way To The Forum." Dick Lester, director of both Beatles films, will direct.

● Elvis Presley received generally good reviews for his new picture, ...

America fights back— with groups that look just like ours!

AFTER the avalanche of British groups in America, here comes the retaliation.

Solo stars from the States have been gigantically popular—Elvis Presley, Gene Pitney, Roy Orbison.

But now two groups are being talked about as the spearheads of America's retort: the **Byrds** and the **Sir Douglas Quintet.**

Ironically, both groups look British.

The influence of the Beatles and Rolling Stones among young Americans has been so enormous that the Byrds and the Quintet are featuring long hair and British-style clothes.

A sobering thought.

The Byrds roared in to prominence with "Mr. Tambourine Man", a Bob Dylan composition so haunting that it was a natural hit from the moment an opportunist group put it out as a single.

Given Dylan's blessing—"they're good musicians," he said—the song was born for the hit parade.

It is on its way down from the top position in the American chart.

"But I'm very glad we are getting liked over there in England," said Byrds leader Jim McGuinn over the transatlantic phone from Hollywood this week.

McGuinn, at 22, is the 12-string guitarist and lead singer with a folk music background. The other Byrds are **Chris Hillman** (22), bass guitar, mandolin. **Gene Clark** (23), guitar, harmonica, tambourine, vocals; **Mike Clark** (21), drums;

BYRDS LEADER JIM McGUINN PHONES FROM HOLLYWOOD

harmonica, congas; and **David Crosby** (23), six and 12-string guitar.

McGuinn is the lead singer on "Mr Tambourine Man". He's an ex-folk singer who used to play in coffee houses. He also played with the New Christy Minstrels and was in Bobby Darin's backing group.

He talked of Dylan: "He's a friend of all of us. We like him and his music, and his whole attitude to life, as a matter of fact.

"I've been on the same scene as him, singing in coffee houses in Greenwich Village since 1961.

"But I don't think I'd like the Byrds to be called a folk group, strictly. Folk is what we came

from. We passed through it. I wouldn't put us down as rock and roll, either. We're somewhere in between. We are keen on all contemporary music. We don't care for labels."

The Byrds have written their new A side for their American single release, "I Feel A Whole Lot Better". In Britain, the major side will be "All I Really Want To Do"—another Dylan composition.

"We simply like the sort of music that Bob Dylan writes," Jim continued. "Music that is associated with the jet age. All Dylan's material can have the jet age applied to it."

How did the Byrds explain their

sudden success with "Mr Tambourine Man"?

"I think we were lucky with a combination of circumstances," McGuinn answered. "Perhaps there was a gap between the pop music that was currently going on, and between the folk and rock fields, that needed filling.

"Maybe we filled it. But I don't want to state it categorically.

"It's all so insignificant. It's part of the natural evolution of music."

What about the charge that the Byrds are cashing in on Dylan by performing his songs?

"Bob's a good friend of ours and we like his songs," McGuinn replied.

JIM McQUINN . . . Byrds' leader, with his Pickwick sunglasses

Keith Altham took Sonny and Cher along to see and hear . . .

BYRDS' WEAK STAGE ACT

ALONG with Sonny and Cher I went to see the Byrds on stage at Finsbury Park Astoria last Saturday. Following on their No. 1 hit, "Mr. Tambourine Man," the group arrived in this country with a publicity theme along the lines of "America's answer to the Beatles." On Saturday's performance, it was a pretty pathetic reply!

After tuning up for a full five minutes behind the curtain, they were treated to a traditional slow handclap by the impatient audience. Then their first two numbers were completely drowned by over-amplification.

I have it on good authority from Cher that the first number was "I Feel A Whole Lot Better" but the vocals of that and the next number were inaudible.

The "chiming whining" effect which runs through their numbers may be good for a few, but not for all seven tunes in their repertoire.

Stage presentation is non-existent and so is any communication with the audience, although at one stage Jim McGuinn did say "Hello."

Numbers I could distinguish, from having heard them before, were "The Chimes Of Freedom," "The Bells Of Rhymney," "All I Really Wanna Do," "Mr. Tambourine Man" and "The Times They Are A-Changing." But they need much more stage know-how to make an impact.

Boz opened the first half with a pleasant selection of easy-beat ballads, best of which was "Point Of No Return." Elkie Brooks followed, proving she can sing well "I Gotta Get Out Of This Place" and cannot sing well "There But For Fortune."

Polished Lynch

Most professional artist on the show was Kenny Lynch, who got a great ovation from the audience with his polished performances of "Down At The Club," "Stand By Me," "Can't Help Falling In Love With You," "Broadway" and "Things."

I caught Donovan's act as he was closing the first half and his pleasant, soft voice was well received by the audience. Best numbers were "Josie," "Colours" and "Universal Soldier." He also sang, "Ballad Of A Crystal Man," "Catch The Wind," "Candy Man" and "Last Thing On My Mind."

At the interval, compere Rod Cameron announced Sonny and Cher were in the audience and so ruined any chance they had of seeing the rest of the show! We fled backstage, where a mountainous Irish sergeant did stout work by keeping out the people he was supposed to allow inside! After letting Cher through, he barred the way for Sonny, Cher's sister, their managers and myself!

Finally rescued by two friendly policemen, we got backstage and I tried to communicate with the Byrds. I spoke to Dave Crosby, who looks like Batman Jr. with dimples.

"I thought we were good tonight," he said. "We don't 'alk much to the audience because we like our music to speak for us. I wonder if people realise how tired we are? We had a month's tour of America before coming here and we're knocked out."

With that he wrapped his green cape around himself and turned his back on me to talk to Donovan.

What about the Byrds? Jim McGuinn is a likeable person. He wears his squared glasses permanently on the bridge of his nose and peers at you over the top like an admonishing school teacher. He never raises his voice above a whisper and in his most emotional moments can be heard to say: "But I trust it will turn out all right in the end."

A year ago Jim was hobo-ing his way round Greenwich Village, starving with folk singers like Bob Dylan. He got a few jobs with artists like Bobby Darin, playing banjo on some of their recordings.

"It was a drag," said Jim. "I met Dave in a Los Angeles coffee bar and we got the idea of the group."

On Britain Jim says: "I dig your buses." He carries an air rifle and 35lb. of ammunition around with him "I couldn't ever kill anything," he states. "It's just for target practice."

Gene Clark walks around in a Mountie's hat, saying "Hi all!" Chris Hillman seldom says anything and Mike, the drummer, reads papers through a fringe combed over his nose. He says: "Cool it" and "When do we eat?" occasionally.

The Byrds biggest fault is this "cool, couldn't-care-less" attitude on stage and off. The audience don't like it. Neither do I.

● Should Them, Johnnie B. Great and Charles Dickens be wondering why I did not review their acts in the show I can only say "sorry" but after fighting with officials to get into the theatre (despite complimentary tickets and Press pass) and fighting to go backstage, I gave up ever getting back to my seat.—K.A.

FROM their appearance one would expect the Byrds to be the American version of the long-haired English groups—raving, ebullient extroverts.

In fact, you leave a first meeting with an impression of introverted calm. Only David Crosby seems likely to burst forth and you have to lean forward to catch the words of the remaining soft-voiced four.

Leader of the group is Jim McGuinn who wears those curious, narrow, oblong, dark glasses which have become the rage among the Byrds' American fans.

Black

I asked how they came to record "Tambourine Man" as their first single.

"Our manager, Jim Dickson, is a friend of Bob Dylan's and he gave him the tape before he had recorded it himself," explained Jim. "David was staying with Dylan at the time—he had nowhere to go—and we all sat around his house discussing the song.

"Dylan thought we had the potential to do it and Jim Dickson thought it

Cool, oh so cool . . .

was the right song for us."

Jim looks politely bleak when asked if the Byrds have copied British groups.

"We are going for an international thing," he said. "Ours is a sort of broken-down declaration between human beings.

"We all have strong folk background and our influences are widely varied —Pete Seeger, Hank Williams, Muddy Waters and the blues singers, Dylan and lots of others.

"I see the Walker Brothers say they had a big influence on us to start with. Well, in Hollywood we hung out in the different rock clubs and we

certainly visited the clubs where the Walker Brothers were working a few times. But I wouldn't say we took anything from them.

Hair

"We weren't the first to grow our hair long in the States. There were others who preceded us, like the Beau Brummels. Then we came along, and the Sir Douglas Quintet came after us.

"The name? We just picked Byrds out of the air. It seemed to be a good label to start with, and alphabetically B seems

to be a pretty successful letter."

Jim started singing with the Limelighters when he left High School and, after six weeks, left for a two-year stint with the Chad Mitchell Trio. He worked with Bobby Darin before forming the Byrds.

Gene Clark was with the New Christy Minstrels for over a year.

"I was looking for something to start a little more inclined to pop music," he told me.

"I ran into Jim in a coffee house in Los Angeles exactly a year ago, and we decided we had the same ideas."

Are the Byrds a sign that we will soon have the Hollywood sound, following the Nashville and Liverpool sounds?

"Hollywood has always been a major record place," says Jim McGuinn. "It's a focal point for teenage music. But the scenes that happen in the clubs there are sort of on-and-off. It's not really too exciting, but we have fun.

"Are we trying to get a message across in our music? Not really. If it's a song we dig then we'll play it and act the part."

This is the group's first trip outside the States. Are they nervous about the reactions of British fans?

Stage

"I've heard a good performer is always nervous before every performance," says Jim. "I suppose fear of the unknown is a prominent thing with us right now.

"Apart from that I don't think we really are nervous. I guess everything will work out all right.

"We haven't found out yet how long we will be doing on stage, but it will probably be around 25 minutes or so.

"We like doing concerts —and dances and TV. But you can get tired in clubs when you work in one place too long.

"I prefer to move around." — BOB DAWBARN.

STONES IN IRELAND

ON-THE-SPOT REPORT: CENTRE PAGES

Melody Maker

September 11, 1965   9d weekly

POP PROTEST
SONGS SOAR

POP protest is really with us! Songs with a message are becoming more and more common in the Pop 50 — the latest example is Barry McGuire's "Eve Of Destruction" which jumped in—at 32 this week.

The song — described by Mick Jagger in last week's MM as "phoney" and "awful rubbish" — follows such recent Pop Protest hits as Donovan's "Universal Soldier", Joan Baez's "There But For Fortune", Manfred Mann's "With God On Our Side" and Bob Dylan discs.

And you won't hear "Eve Of Destruction" on BBC pop shows!

A BBC spokesman told the MM: "We don't consider it suitable for light entertainment. But it could be used for documentary purposes in a programme on pop. We don't ban records, but we occasionally restrict them."

Readers have written to the MM asking: "Should politics be mixed with pop?" Many don't seem to think so.

And hit-maker JONATHAN KING violently disagrees with Jagger's summing up of the Barry McGuire song.

"This is going to be a big hit because it's a great sound, whether it's sincere or not," declared King.

"And why should it be sincere? Since when has pop music been a vehicle for sincerity?

"Pop music combines escapism and imagination." Other stars have different views.

DONOVAN: "Universal Soldier" isn't politics to me. I don't know anything about politics or protest. I'm just singing songs that are written."

JOAN BAEZ: "I regard myself principally as a politician. I like being referred to as a pacifist. And I suppose I don't mind being called a folk singer. But music is secondary to me.

"A lot of people, I know, are furious with me for meddling in politics. But it is cheating for me to pretend I'm only a singer."

MANFRED MANN: "Anyone who records a song has a certain responsibility, and we wouldn't record a protest song if every member of the group didn't agree with the message.

"But songs tend to oversimplify things anyway, so you can only broadly agree. But we wouldn't record a protest song if we didn't broadly agree with it."

BOB DYLAN: "All I can hope to do is sing what I'm thinking and maybe remind you of something. Don't put me down as a man with a message.

"My songs are just me talking to myself. I have no responsibility to anybody except myself."

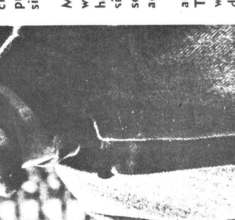

● BARRY McGUIRE

● MANFRED—'group must agree'

● JOAN BAEZ—'I'm a politician'

● DONOVAN—'not political'

HERMAN HITS OUT!

'Destruction' ban doesn't worry me

✱ "I READ this sort of ban is the new way to get a hit in England."

BARRY McGUIRE'S "Eve Of Destruction" is one of the most controversial hits for quite a while.

The BBC considers it unsuitable for its pop shows. And Mick Jagger, reviewing it in the MM's Blind Date, described it as "written because it's commercial", "phoney" and "not sincere in any way."

Record buyers apparently disagreed and the disc is roaring up the Pop 50.

This week Barry McGuire phoned the MM from his Hollywood home to say he was delighted at the record's British success.

"The BBC thing doesn't bother me too much," he admitted. "I read somewhere that this sort of ban is the new way to get a hit in England."

Until "Eve of Destruction", Barry was the lead singer with the Christy Minstrels.

"I have nothing more to do with them now, except on a friendly basis," he told me. "Nothing professional — although I'd like to do a TV show with them some time. I joined them when they first started, 3½ years ago."

Does Barry describe himself as a folk singer?

"I guess so," he answered the question. "I'm really glad the opportunity has come along for the new folk-rock thing. It makes folk singing such a lot of fun.

"It's nice to hear songs with a big beat and the sort of lyrics that have been accepted for so long in the folk field."

How did "Eve Of Destruction" come to be written?

"It was done by a 19-year-old called Phil Sloane," explained Barry. "He used to write rock-'n'-roll music. Then he heard a Bob Dylan album and that changed things.

"He told me he thought: 'Oh, man! I got things I don't care about, too. I think I'll write about some of those.' And he came up with a couple of great songs. This afternoon we are working on the follow-up to 'Eve Of Destruction'."

What difference has his first solo hit made for Barry?

"Well, I'm going to play a lot of clubs and I want to do a

BARRY McGUIRE phones the MM from Hollywood

lot of concerts and TV," he mused.

"But the big thing is that this has given me the opportunity to say a lot of things I feel. Six months ago nobody would have listened to what I had to say.

"Now, they may not agree with me, but at least they will listen and think about it—and that's all that matters."

What were Barry's reactions to Mick Jagger's review? He listened as I read it over. There was a long pause.

"That's OK," he said at last. "That must be the way he thinks and I can't change what he thinks or feels. But I know how I feel about the song — and how I felt when I first heard it."

We changed the subject.

"I want to get over to Britain some time in October, but I'm not too sure how things will work out," said Barry.

"There's a lot of things happening for me right now. I have to play the Lincoln Centre in New York and then there is a new club in Los Angeles opening up. I shall be there the opening week and it sounds quite a place.

"But I really want to get across to Britain and I hope something will definitely be worked out — particularly now the record seems to be going well over there."

Barry also plans to write some of his own material.

"Since I left the Christy Minstrels I've written two songs," he told me. "Both are real winners, and they say what I want to say.

"I'm recording one of them next week and I'll do the other on the album we are working on."

We said our goodbyes. But before the line went dead, Barry called: "And when you see Mick Jagger, tell him to listen to the record again!"

The Shure Unidyne 55S will pick up every shade of sound, without distortion and with virtual suppression of random background noise. Superb performance combined with rugged reliability makes it the choice of the world's leading entertainers. They can't afford to take chances. Why risk your reputation on less than perfection?

THE

Bassey has parted from John Hey-   publisher Bill Phillips....

★ NEWCOMERS TO THE CHARTS ★

Barry McGuire beats the ban

BARRY McGUIRE

NEARLY EVERYONE has said EVERYTHING about "Eve Of Destruction," Barry McGuire's record which gives him his chart debut this week at No. 24.

The BBC, and some U.S. stations, banned it, the record industry questioned the sincerity of the anti-hate lyrics, only Radios London and Caroline went out of their way to say they liked it. They—and now a few thousand disc buyers.

The pirate stations, in fact, can take a big pat on the back for helping make it a hit. And on Tuesday Caroline gave it an extra plug with a quarter-hour lunch-time interview with Barry on the transatlantic phone.

He told d-j Tony Blackburn the message was intended for the young of today, the rulers of tomorrow. He stressed his sincerity and belief in the lyrics.

Barry McGuire visited this country some months ago with America's New Christy Minstrels for TV appearances. He is a founder member of the group and at the time of their trip was lead singer.

Born in Oklahoma, Barry moved to Southern California with his family and after leaving high school—where he admits he was "no great shakes as a student"—he decided he wanted to sing.

The first audition for tall, blond, blue-eyed Barry got him his first job—with the New Christy Minstrels, then being formed.

● The writer of "Eve Of Destruction," which is also high in the U.S. chart, is 19-year-old P. F. Sloan, nicknamed Flip. Inevitably he's ac-cused of just being a Dylan copyist, but he takes this calmly.

"Bob Dylan," he says, "is the greatest writer I've ever heard. I don't mean to copy him — he just started me off into examining my own thoughts, which I had never done before.

"When I used to live in Long Island everybody was verbally annihilating everybody else behind their backs.

"Then they'd all go off to church and say 'Thank God for giving us bread.'"

P. F. Sloan is fighting for honesty. At home in America they call him the Voice of Youth.

JOHN WELLS.

Comes the Dawn
JAMES GALT
Isn't it?

TWO FOR THE TOP!!

NEW MUSICAL EXPRESS ★

cable **NMExclusive** interv

BARRY McGUIRE (l.) with " Destruction " composer P. F. SLOAN.

BARRY McGUIRE

... protests about protests

"**I** LEFT to be myself. I felt there were better things to be said. If I can't have fun then I'm not real, and if I'm not real, I'm no good. The Christies have a definite image. I have no image. I change every day. I want people to realise this," said Barry McGuire.

Until recently the voice of the tall and husky Barry has been somewhat camouflaged by eleven other voices— the sound of the New Christy Minstrels, a top American folk group. Now on his own, with his first single, "Eve Of Destruction," a big hit, he was talking on the set of the first West Coast "Hullabaloo" in Hollywood, explaining to me his reasons for leaving the well-established Christies.

Between calls for him to "run through the song one more time" at rehearsals, he described how he happened to come across the "Eve Of Destruction" composition.

"I was dancing and watching the Byrds at the old Ciro's club in Hollywood, really having a good time. In the middle of all the noise, P. F. Sloan came up to me. He'd heard I was looking for a song. He sang his song and I knew it was the one for me."

On his new album, conveniently titled "Eve Of Destruction", Barry tries his own hand at song writing with "Why Not Stop And Dig It While You Can." The song suggests that people stop worrying about their troubles and start thinking about how to enjoy life.

Controversy has seemed to plague his recordings, despite the fact that they suffer no financial set-backs!

One Los Angeles radio station banned "Destruction" from the air play during Los Angeles' Watts Riots.

About the charges against the song, Barry calmly comments: "I sang the song, that's all. If everyone wants to argue about it, it's up to them. Once I leave the recording studio, it's out of my hands."

But he added : "It's not exactly a protest song. It's merely a song about current events."

ANNE MOSES

'Destruction' was as sincere as 'As Tears Go By': that is – feigned emotion, in the spirit of Tin Pan Alley. If I want serious analysis of a social or political situation I go to a newspaper, or an informed friend. Certainly not to an entertainer!

FROM NEW YORK—THE NEW TOP-POPPERS

Sonny and Cher— the message is love

SONNY and Cher Bono flopped on a couch in their de luxe Hampshire House suite and caught their breath after two frantic days in New York, which included scores of interviews, a wild Atco Records cocktail reception and a picture-taking session.

And through it all, the fondest recent memories were of Britain, and the fondest hope was to get back quickly.

"England is great because you can be a hit overnight there," said Cher. "One day they've never heard of you, and the next day you've got a smash. They hadn't ever heard of us before we got there, really. But everyone's so record conscious there."

"The adults are much more liberal, too," Sonny interjected. "They were beautiful to us on street corners. We took a film director and a colour camera and a little portable tape recorder. We went all over London lip-synching our songs from the tape on street corners and all kinds of interesting places.

"WE sang to a guy on a horse. In another place, we found some guards who weren't allowed to smile and we sang 'I Got You Babe' to them.

"But nobody came along and told us we were a couple of nuts. They just took snapshots of us and a lot of kids followed us all over town. I haven't seen the film yet, but if it turns out, I'd like to make a television deal for it. I think

SONNY AND CHER . . . "the kids have made us what we are."

it was a good idea because it was honest and real. I admire those things.

"I guess what I like most about England is that there are some real people there who have something to say. We both love the Beatles. You can't do better than that."

"And Donovan," Cher broke in. "He's my favourite person there, the sweetest guy in the world. The thing about Donovan is that he believes."

NEXT to the British, whom they hope to visit again in November ("they've asked us already"), Sonny and Cher have an infinite love for young people.

"I think we owe just about everything to the kids," Sonny continued, "and I want to give something back to them. I've been producing records for eight years—now I want to try movies. I want to create something new.

"I think kids want and deserve more in the movies than a bunch of kids with surfboards on the beach or a rock and roll group. They want more

than that terrible unnatural dialogue that a bunch of executives think they want. I feel I owe them whatever creative thing I can give them that's still fun.

"We'll be off to England probably and more tours here. These kids have made us what we are and it's only fair to show ourselves to them. We owe a lot to all of them who say, 'I don't care how you dress but I love you.' And those kids made it possible for us to work without a white shirt and tie.

"I haven't worn a suit in a couple of years. If somebody said I have to wear a tuxedo because that's the rule, I would.

"I'm not rebelling with clothes or my hair. I grew my hair like this three years ago because it was fun. Someday I may get it all cut off."

"NEVER," said Cher, who claims that her hair is very out of fashion right now because it's so long.

"But I don't worry about the styles. I have my own, I've

been wearing the bell bottom pants for several years and long before they came into style here. I must like them. I haven't worn a dress in a year and a half, because I like pants better."

About message songs, Sonny and Cher have their own specific points of view. "There aren't that many that really have something to say. I think the Rolling Stones are great," Sonny continued, "and Newsweek's story about their dirty lyrics last week, well, you can read almost any meaning you want to into the lyrics of a song.

"With us, I think the universal message is really just love. I build everything around that. I don't think anybody really believes in war so I can understand why some of the war protest songs come about. But I don't really know whether it does any good to sing about it, you know."

"Everybody," said Cher, "should really love one another, because nobody's here on earth for that long a time."

Ren Grevatt

Sonny and Cher were two 'protest' singers I could get on with. Probably because they were protesting nothing more than that their new single should be higher on the 'Billboard' chart, because 'Cash Box' had them higher: We toured around a lot together. My brother was one of their drummers. They were salutary because their records and stage actions made a mockery of the pathetic, pompous political stance of so many 'protest' singers of the time. Look, they said, let's have fun with this folk protest thing. It's a fad, like hula hoops.

Smashing time costs WHO fortune!

ANYONE who has ever seen a demolition gang smashing down a building will know what it's like when the Who get up steam. Their music rolls and crashes and throbs like a berserk thunderstorm—and naturally, it doesn't do their instruments any good.

Vocalist Roger Daltrey slumped into a chair at the NME this week and told me: "This isn't a gimmick and I'm telling you no lies, but we have to get new guitars and drums every month or so. They just get smashed up. And it's costing us a fortune!"

Then he sat up and gave it to me straight: "It's so expensive, you could even say we Who are running at a loss at the moment."

There wasn't even the slightest trace of a smile. For Roger Daltrey, helping to produce the group's screaming, soaring brand of music, is the most serious person in the world.

Jumps up

This is the kind of dedication that has sent the Who's "My Generation" absolutely C-C-CRASHING up the NME Chart this week. It stands at No. 3 in the current list, a jump of 13 places.

So many theories have been advanced about the disc and its stuttering gimmick that I asked Roger if one story credited to him—that the number is about someone who was "blocked" (or on drugs)—was true.

He denied he had ever said that. "The song just tells about a young kid who's tryin to express himself, y'know?"

Then he grinned: "Apart from that, it was freezing in the studios when we recorded it. That's why I stutter on the lyrics!"

As usual with the Who, "My Generation" was recorded and released in about two weeks flat. They have always done this and they intend to go on for as long as possible. Even the song itself was written only a few days before the session.

There was also a lot of disagreement about "My Generation" and the treatment they should give it. "Near punch-ups," according to Roger.

He has never disguised the fact that quite often the members of the Who can't stand each other. He claims that this is all to the good.

"Don't believe whatever you've seen before," he says heatedly. "The Who will never split up. We have arguments all the time but this is what gives us that extra spark. The Who thrives on friction."

Like it or not Roger's regarded by many as an avant-garde Mod spokesman in the pop business. I asked him for his views on the current pop scene.

He feels that it is in "a bad state" at the moment, but that discs like Ken Dodd's "Tears" are purely a momentary lapse!

At the same time, according to Roger, he doesn't want to stick his neck out by making a prediction about the next big pop trend. "We don't want to follow anybody else's trend," he told me. "We want to set it.

"The worst thing about starting something new, like we have, is that everybody else jumps on the bandwagon! Then you get dozens of imitations."

He looked thoughtful. "In one way I suppose it's a good thing, because it makes us change to something new. And that's what we want to do—keep changing. We just feel we never want to get in a rut or grow old."

ALAN SMITH

The WHO (l to r) JOHN BROWNE, ROGER DALTREY, PETER TOWNSHEND and KEITH MOON.

Dylan's BAND angers audience

HARTFORD, CONNECTICUT

Heavy, heavy, heavy! Smash, bang, scowl!
They aim their guns at themselves, then at US.
They are angry with the world. Their anger makes them stutter.
It will take a lot of heavy print and an opera to explain this complaint.
But still have my records of Roy and Elvis and Bill and Gene. I still have my memories of the Golden Days of Rock 'n' Roll and how I almost became part of it. And they can't take that away, can they?

Photographs are reproduced with the kind permission of the following:

Camera Press, London, for pages 5, 14, 36, 58, 82, 83, 88, 97, 102, 128, 137, 141, 142, 147, 148, 151, 162, 164, 172, 173, 192

Michael Ochs Archives, Los Angeles, for pages 16, 18, 23, 38, 39, 40, 45, 57, 61, 71, 80, 84, 96, 121, 123, 127

Arrow Books Limited
17–21 Conway Street, London W1P 6JD

An imprint of the Hutchinson Publishing Group

London Melbourne Sydney Auckland
Johannesburg and agencies throughout
the world

First published 1982 in association with EMI Music
Publishing Limited, 138–140 Charing Cross Road, London, WC2H 0LD
© in text and selection Ian Whitcomb 1982

This book is sold subject to the condition that it shall not,
by way of trade or otherwise, be lent, resold, hired out,
or otherwise circulated without the publisher's prior consent
in any form of binding or cover other than that in which it is
published and without a similar condition including this
condition being imposed on the subsequent purchaser.

Photoset by Rowland Phototypesetting Limited
Bury St Edmunds, Suffolk

Made and printed in Great Britain
by The Anchor Press Ltd
Tiptree, Essex

ISBN 0 09 927170 2